M

Art On The Line

Essays by Artists about the Point Where Their Art and Activism Intersect

Edited by Jack Hirschman

CURBSTONE PRESS

Front cover print by Naul Ojeda
Cover design by Stone Graphics
Printed in Canada on acid-free paper by Best Book/
                                    Transcontinental Printing

This book was published with the support of the
Connecticut Commission on the Arts, and
donations received from many individuals.

Library of Congress Cataloging-in-Publication Data

Art on the line : a series of essays, interviews, and manifestoes by
    20th century artists : socially conscious or politacally engaged
    artists speaking from the point where commitment and art
    interact / edited by Jack Hirschman.— 1st ed.
        p. cm.
    ISBN 1-880684-77-1 (alk. paper)
1. Arts and revolutions—History—20th century. I. Hirschman,
Jack, 1933-
    NX180.R45 A783 2002
    700'1.'03—dc21
                                        2002073632

Published by
CURBSTONE PRESS
321 Jackson Street • Willimantic, CT 06226
info@curbstone.org • www.curbstone.org

TABLE OF CONTENTS

INTRODUCTORY NOTE
by Jack Hirschman

This anthology has evolved out of the important pamphlet series of the same name, which was originated and edited by Richard Schaaf, and published by Curbstone Press in the 80s. The six pamphlets published in the series—by Roque Dalton; Vladimir Mayakovsky; two by Cesar Vallejo; a collaboration by George Grosz, John Heartfield, and Wieland Herzfelde; and Jorge Sanjines—form a modern classical foundation in Marxist and Marxist-Leninist cultural ideas and attitudes.

I'm honored to have been asked by Curbstone publishers Sandy Taylor and Judith Doyle to gather articles for what is hoped will be an enlightening continuation of what Scully began.

I begin the anthology with that first series. Five of the six pieces pre-date 1970. I've chosen to continue the discourse with essays and interviews written or transcribed in the 80s and 90s. These represent strands of an emerging multicultural (class, race, and gender) discourse in a time of rapid technological and ideological change.

The Big Question, as I compose this introductory in 2002—after the 9/11 attack and the ensuing planetary war on "terrorism" that is being engineered by the United States—is: Are these essays in fact of any use anymore? Aren't they out-dated, what with the fall of the Soviet Union, the defeat of the Sandinista revolution in Nicaragua (where for a brief time, poetry was intimately linked with revolution), and the overwhelming domination of the "techno-locracy" that governs the lives of people the world over these days?

The Simple Answer, of course, is that they are not out-dated at all. In fact, since we all have seen the savage effects of capitalism most recently manifested in its full military might, with the attendant intimidations that go hand-in-hand with fascist tendencies—if not direct declarations—the need for ideas with respect to revolutionary collectivity, especially along the cultural front, is essential.

Such ideas are, really, our true heritage of the last century. This book is a reminder of them in a time when, culturally speaking, poets, writers, artists, musicians and intellectuals who want to transform the world and not simply express it, find themselves more and more atomized and individuated, without the spine of real collectivity bringing them together with the more material forces of struggle and change, that are themselves sporadic and divided, among the working class and the new class of poor proletarians the world over.

The battles against the IMF and the WTO—the manifestations in Seattle, Prague, and Genoa and the continuing demonstrations of "the movement of movements"—are a shining light in these darkest of times. And cultural activity there has certainly been an important part of the demonstrations against the economic rulers of the earth. But if nothing else has revealed to us that collective struggle on a wider and deeper level of consciousness and commitment is absolutely essential, now that the forces of capitalism have manifested full-scale military policing of the lives of people everywhere, this small contribution to that task hopes to open paths toward that necessary understanding.

Poetry is a major concentration in many of the essays, but mural art and song are also dealt with. The activist-intellectual is significantly represented, as is the novelist-in-exile and the cultural guerrilla for the Liberation Radio movement. A three-way conversation of women writers, as well as essays and an interview by other women, are important contributions to the discourse; as are the accounts of cultural struggle and collectivity as presented in their relationship with liberation movements in Haiti, Nicaragua, and Kenya.

Of the first series of essays, both Jim Scully and I would especially call your attention to the collective essay by George Grosz, John Heartfield, and Wieland Herzfelde—the fifth essay in the series—as we believe that work to be among the most "grounding" of the texts in relation to the tasks of revolutionaries today.

This anthology is therefore dedicated to the young men and women who are emerging as genuine revolutionary poets, writers, artists, musicians, and intellectuals for the struggle ahead. We who have written here hope our ideas throw some light on your future works.

My especial thanks to Sarah Menefee for her thoughtful and ever-revolutionary insights.

San Francisco
March, 2002

ART ON THE LINE

ROQUE DALTON
Poetry & Militancy in Latin America

I

What do I propose to do, working in poetry? In general, to express life: the life I witness and help create: my time, its people, the resources we share, along with all their interdependencies. Such is my purpose, starting from the apparently simple fact of being Salvadoran, that is, part of a Latinamerican people which pursues its happiness struggling against imperialism and the Creole oligarchy, and which, for quite concrete historical reasons, has a truly impoverished cultural tradition. So impoverished, that only to the slightest extent can it be incorporated in that struggle which has a crying need for every sort of weapon.

These basic facts make every kind of concern consequential by providing my work with a national content, making it expressive of the people of El Salvador. But in speaking of the 'Salvadoran people' I speak of the workers and peasants, of the middle class and, in general, every social sector subject to oligarchic/imperialist oppression—all whose fundamental community interests coincide with the larger interest of building a free, sovereign nation teeming with the best incentives for human progress. That's why I try to write for the people, in a democratic way.

In the preceding general outline of my poetic intentions I have distinguished the needs which, in order to develop my work, I have to set forth and try to satisfy in view of the historic panorama manifesting my people, that is to say, the human medium that grants me roots, a reality to hold onto in time and space. It would be appropriate now to attempt a brief, general appraisal of the personal circumstances under which I engage in creative work. Not out of eagerness to offend modesty, but to provide a rationale for the proposals I will have to make later on.

II

My attitude regarding the ideological content and social consequence of poetic work is basically determined, as I understand it, by two extremes: that of my long and deep bourgeois formative period, and that of the communist militancy I've held to for some years now.

Experience in the ranks of the party has informed my ongoing concern with the problems of the people around me—"the people" in the fullest sense—and focused my attention precisely on the fundamental responsibilities one must assume, as well as on the actual ways of carrying out those duties in the course of one's life. But long years in a Jesuit school, my early development in the womb of the mean-spirited Salvadoran bourgeoisie, my attachment to irresponsible lifestyles, my recoil in holy terror from sacrifice or from the core problems of the epoch, have left their marks on me. These scars, even now, are painful.

I've become conscious of this latter fact in keeping with the general self-critical trend we all pursue now, when the people call for our native sons to be spotless and straightforward. What I cannot do, in this respect, is cross out the present effects of the past with a stroke of the pen, so that—at least for the analysis of my literary potential—it's better to accept that past as a given fact: surmountable, if one wants, but a given. From a serious analysis of my own poetic work—that which I consider most representative, which best expresses me—I can say that what gets in the way of the viewpoint I now have, as a communist, is the attitude I had before, as a bourgeois: beyond the intentions of the communist lie the consequences of bourgeois roots. In applying these considerations, and questioning how the work of art ought to function in the actual context of El Salvador (and Central America in general) I think it would be well to ask: has the bourgeois outlook, among us, exhausted all its potential? I personally believe not—and that, furthermore, it is constructive to take advantage of all its creative possibilities, so that we may not only leave its essentially negative aspects behind, but use it as an instrument to create ideal conditions for the new peoples' art that will spring up, no matter what, and reflect the new life that we Salvadorans will know how to win for ourselves. *The possibilities of bourgeois art and culture have not been exhausted* (though the oligarchy and imperialism have imposed it on the artists, and on Salvadorans in general in a manner grossly lacking in subtlety) *and so it's well that we revolutionary writers open the way to future art, to the future revolutionary Salvadoran literature, from within the very bowels of bourgeois culture, hastening its collapse and disintegration by confronting it with its insurmountable internal contradictions, making it face itself and what it springs from—taking it, finally, consciously, with the people's blessed cunning, to the dead end it would come to anyway if we let it develop untroubled in the hands of its logical creators, the bourgeois artists, the artists/ideologues of the bourgeoisie.*

III

Extending this deliberation, and therefore coming nearer what touches on my own individual work, it would be fitting to pose the following questions: to what extent has the *nation* been manifest in the literature produced thus far in El Salvador? The history of Salvadoran literature...is it capable of giving us a vision of the whole of our social development? It would seem not. But if the most significant portion of that literature has been produced in the last fifty or sixty years, during which time our country has become a semifeudal wasteland dominated by North American imperialism, with a great mass of dispossessed peasantry on one side, a rapacious landed oligarchy on the other, and in the middle a weak, embryonic working class, together with an alienated petty bourgeoisie, and the germ of a national bourgeoisie lacking an expansive outlook—can we, in our literature, follow the trail of declarations made by some or each of those classes and ascertain that they are authentic expressions of those classes? Or, owing to the economic, political, social and, therefore, cultural distortions that, in our development, the imperialist domination implies—distortion that hinders the classic step-by-step rise of the various social classes into consciousness of themselves *as* classes—is it necessary to propose that all problems of the artistic superstructure correspond to a single, basic, general contradiction between the people and the nation on one side, and imperialism and its middlemen on the other? Because if this is so, all the previous questions could become irrelevant, being answerable only on the basis of dividing our literature into two parts: that which in general corresponds to, or does not oppose, the interests of the overbearing "two-headed monster"[the Creole oligarchy and U.S. imperialism], and that which in general has claimed to be the expression of the people, of their life, their problems, their struggles and hopes. But I suspect the matter is not so simple.

IV

Given those two considerations—the needs of Salvadoran literature and my own personal situation as regards creative work—I became anxious to direct my cultural labor toward the following general objectives that, certainly, I'm still quite far from fulfilling: 1)To fight to have the work of Salvadoran writers and artists of my generation nourish itself on the national reality, the end being to help transform that reality in a revolutionary way. 2) To elucidate, in definitive form, the problem of the Salvadoran cultural tradition so as to incorporate it in our work, along with a new conception of cultural development. That is to say, to establish its principal constant features, its scope on the universal plane—what is living and what is dead, the useful and the useless—so as to confer on the fragmented Salvadoran culture the essential characteristic of any culture: organic unity, interconnectedness, the grounds of existence at once particularized and general. And, in keeping with my first general objective: 3) To advocate the scientific understanding of our reality (applying the Marxist-Leninist method) and to back up my creative work with militant activity within the ranks of the Revolution—grand objective of all modern literature or art dedicated to the elevation of humankind.

V

Having made, then, some definitive statements, it is necessary to begin drawing some details and distinctions. I've said that I am a poet who, in relation to political militancy, works within the ranks of the Communist Party. But this fact suggests only that I have social concerns, making clear my direct contact with the organization that, as time will tell, most adequately explains social phenomena. All this generates in me a sense of responsibility regarding the human struggle. Further, this responsibility is carried out principally through the specific work of the Party, in concrete acts of the Revolution. My poetry, *besides safeguarding this responsibility with its own particular resources, pursues other ends*, becoming something other than a mere ethical instrument the moment the power of the imagination, among other things, comes into play. Imagination, for instance, heightens reality, and in those circumstances its expression must be, to some extent, valuable to people, inasmuch as it not only

4

grants them a primary understanding of the real—which could be enough for their fight for liberty—but puts them in touch with the truly transcendent, we could say eternal, aspects of that reality. Here it may be suitable to call attention to the function that art and literature have of 'improving man and nature.' But there's no need to forget that in pursuing the political end (achievement, on the part of the people, of becoming conscious of itself and of its needs) poetry and art must do so with their own special means, that is to say, artistic means, which are the most effective means of picking up on the *reality* that needs to be *expressed.*

VI

For this reason I've been saying for a while now that major poets of today, to build a body of work, must have two necessary starting points: profound understanding of life, and their own imaginative liberty. So such poets will have had to live intensely, in the thick of nature and what is human, to have gone down into the dark hollows of their heart of hearts, and risen to the glorious dramas of the people, to have borne witness to the nakedness of insects and the catastrophes of orography. Out of this experience, gained through years of hard, wonderful everyday comings and goings, the imagination, with its expressive instruments (style, artistic genre), will be able to undertake the making of great works of art if the proprietors of that imagination have a clear conception of creative freedom and of their responsibilities regarding beauty. In doing this, many helpful material measures may be taken: the incorporation (critical assimilation), in modern creative work, of the cultural tradition of humanity; the satisfactory treatment of myths and the use of the symbol in the sense appropriate to each epoch.

VII

Basically poets must keep faith with poetry, with beauty. They must take the content that their outlook on life and mankind imposes on them (as the great responsibility that goes with coexistence, with living together) and steep it in the abundance of the beautiful. And here there's no room for subterfuges or the inversion of terms. The poet is such because he makes poetry, that is to say, because he creates a beautiful work. While he does something else he will be whatever he wants to be, except a poet. Which certainly does not imply, with respect to the poet, a privileged position among men, but only a precise placement among them and a rigorous limitation of his activity, the same that would also take effect in specifications of the capacities of doctors, carpenters, soldiers and criminals.

VIII

The poet is communist as well?—I'm asked. In reply, I'll begin by repeating what I've already said: the great obligation of the poet, communist or not, is to the very essence of poetry, to beauty. This assumes—as professors of algebra are wont to say—the poet's own proper responsibility or, if one prefers, his degree of revolutionary consciousness regarding the concrete demands of the time as they suggest to him—as he carries on with his creative work—the correct thematic trends to follow. And since we're speaking of themes or subjects, I have to add that in this area I have an old postulate, one I consider thoroughly honest: all that fits into life fits into poetry. The poet—above all the communist poet—will have to articulate all of life: the proletarian struggle, the beauty of the cathedrals left us by the Spanish Colony, the wonder of the sexual act, the prophecies of the fruitful future that the great signs of the day proclaim to us.

IX

Now then, of what beauty do we speak? To what do we refer when we say 'the beautiful?' Clearly we recognize the danger of working with terms that idealism has tried to reclaim for itself. From Plato to the wistful sighing moderns who cling to what was never more than a piece of stupidity, the concept of 'art for art's sake,' some words have been manipulated with such baffling meaning that now it's quite difficult for a revolutionary to use them without being suspected of holding views that mark the opposite philosophic pole. As I've made clear in statements above, when speaking of beauty and the beautiful we don't have to give up for an instant the grounds of form. So then, form and content make up an inseparable unity, shaping the artwork. It's in that sense we say beauty is a matter of the very essence of poetry. Moreover, we consider the concept of beauty and the beautiful as cultural realities, endowed with historic scope and social roots.

X

And the forms of poetry, of art, that cultivate 'the ugly?'—I'm asked again. This is not a valid argument against the beautiful essence of poetry. It is there in the so-called 'ugly' forms, or else the beauty is more hidden than usual (by virtue of the nontraditional means by which it is transmitted), or else it appears by way of contrast.

XI

The creative work of the communist poet, I think it's evident, has various levels. Depending on the daily demands of the struggle, the poet immersed in the party of the workers and peasants will have to produce fast-moving agitational slogans, satiric verses, poems that call for the raising of rebellion against oppression. To what extent is the result of this labor poetry? There are unusual cases but in general the result, as regards form, is extremely poor, although in the historical/political field it can become, depending on the _true_ circumstances, extremely valuable.

XII

The Party must train the poet as a good militant communist, as a valuable cadre for mass revolutionary action. The poet, the artist, must contribute his utmost to the cultural education of all members of the Party. The Party, specifically, must help the poet develop into an effective agitator, a soldier with expert marksmanship—in a word, a fit cadre. The poet must acquaint all his comrades with Nazim Hikmet or Pablo Neruda and give them a clear concept of the role of cultural work within the context of general revolutionary activity. He must also make sure that the Administrative Secretary of the Central Committee, for example, loves St. John of the Cross, Henri Michaud, or St. John Perse.

XIII

It is necessary to root out the false, mechanical, destructive notion that the poet committed to his people and his time is an angry or excessively pained individual who goes through life saying, without any further ado, that the bourgeoisie is disgusting, that the most

7

beautiful thing in the world is a union meeting, and that socialism is a garden of yielding roses under an especially mild sun. Life is not so simple, and the sensitivity a Marxist needs to be truly such [i.e. Marxist] had better be grasped fully. It is the poet's duty to fight against mechanical, schematic thinking. This schematic approach impedes the development of poetry—which, as conqueror of the cosmos, must keep ever fresh its thirst for adventure—and damages the potentially positive concepts it contains.

XIV

Someone characterized the poet as one who does not live normally if kept from writing. The structure of that idea is like that of a sentiment which took root in me some years ago: that of the impossibility of doing creative work outside the ranks of the revolution. If the revolution, that is, the struggle of my people, my party, my revolutionary theory, are the pillars on which I wish to base and raise my life, and if I consider life in all its intensity as the great source and substance of poetry, what sense is there in thinking of creation if one abandons the obligations that go with being a man and a militant? Undoubtedly, it makes no sense whatever. And this, it's fitting to explain here, has nothing to do with 'expressive form' nor (if you'll pardon the redundancy) with the response of poetry itself to civic duties.

The sentiment I refer to is solidly backed by genuine objectives. I'll illustrate this point with a few lines from Roger Garaudy, written to summarize conclusions (arrived at during the "First Week of Marxist Thought" celebrated in Paris last year) that synthesized and sharply delineated the basic elements that the revolutionary position incorporates in our lives. "Marxism-Leninism," says the wise French professor, "allows us to think and live out the three greatest forces that today move the world with regard to the wonderful work of the enlightenment: the most thoroughgoing *humanism*, the most exalted conception of mankind, one with limitless horizons; the most dependable *scientific method*, that which is inferred from dialectical materialism; and the greatest force for putting this science and this humanism into action—*the proletarian revolution.*" Love of humanity, best means of arriving at the truth, and a force that guarantees hope will be realized. Can one conceive another, better basis for poetry?

8

XV

The revolutionary is, among other things, the person most useful to his epoch because he lives to bring about ends that signify the highest interests of humanity. This holds true for the revolutionary poet—as revolutionary and as poet—in that, from the publication of his first word he is addressing all people in defense of their own highest longings. Therefore it's foolish to so much as discuss the matter with those who assert that, in poetry, the social function and the humanist posture are extrapoetic elements. Foolish, mainly, because such discussion of itself implies a renunciation, *a priori,* of the universality of poetry.

XVI

It is a fine thing to think of the poet as a prophet. In itself such regard is a poetic act in that the creator of poems seems to look out, from the forested heights, over the future of humanity, and to point out the great pathways. I prefer, however, to pinpoint the poet more as a scrutinizer of his own time than of the future, because, like it or not, by insisting too much on what will come we lose our immediate perspective, and we run the risk of not being understood by all the people who find themselves immersed in everyday life. The very problem of Revolution deserves to be approached—within the poetic undertaking—from this point of view. A case in point: should we revolutionary Latinamerican poets concentrate our labor on the foretelling of socialist society before raising to the category of poetic material the contradictions, disasters, defects, customs and struggles of our present society? I sincerely believe not. I consider that the average reader in the capitalist world, in order to be convinced of the necessity for Revolution, will have to know, among other things, how the crude intellectual schemes of the bourgeoisie are structured, plus the sordidness of individual deeds in their capitalist subworld, and the clash between noble humanistic sentiments and the ambiance that comes of exploitation. Besides, I realize that the reader must be given the opportunity to become acquainted with new points of view about life, events and people, for instance about the nation's history, which has had an expurgated version imposed on it by the ruling class—a distortion that literature, through its own specific resources, would have very little difficulty in combating. Only after such labor, involving (I don't pass over it) a great deal of destructive activity, is it possible to begin constructing, without major obstacles, the prospectus of the future. And it is necessary to call attention to one essential aspect of this viewpoint: I hold this thesis to be valid in the preparatory stage, the insurrectional stage and in the triumphal stage of any Latinamerican revolution. Including when that revolution is already on the road toward the construction of socialism. Although in this latter case, obviously, it would continue only partly in effect.

XVII

Honor of the revolutionary poet: to convince his or her generation of the necessity for being revolutionary here and now, in the difficult period, the only one that has the potential to be the subject of an epic. To be revolutionary when the revolution has eliminated its enemies and has in every sense consolidated itself can be, no doubt about it, more or less glorious and heroic. But to be so when the condition of being revolutionary is usually rewarded with death, that is truly the dignity of poetry. The poet then takes the poetry of his or her generation and gives it over to history.

Translated by James Scully

ROQUE DALTON (1935-1975) was an enormously influential figure in the history of Latin America as a poet, essayist and revolutionary. As a poet who brilliantly fused politics and art, his example could be said to have permanently changed the direction of Central American poetry. Author of some dozen books of poetry, one of which (*The Tavern and Other Poems*) was winner of the Casa de las Américas poetry prize, his work combines fierce satirical irony with an humane and exuberant tenderness. His legacy extends beyond his achievements as a poet to his political writings and his work in the establishment of the ERP.

AFTERWORD ON DALTON'S ESSAY

Roque Dalton: wry, witty. Caustic. A militant communist poet whose irony penetrates, as in the sidewinding epigram on "Generál Martinez:"

> They say he was a good President
> because he allotted cheap housing
> to the Salvadorans who were left[1]

Yet "Poetry and Militancy in Latin America" has little of the irony or the razory singlemindedness of Dalton's poetry. He does persist in awkward, excoriating honesty: true to the world as he is, to himself, and to the relationship between them. But he is not inclined to mock, nor even to be companionable with that bittersweet charm of his. The voice is tentative, unassured, going from back-off academic all the way over to heroic, fleetingly romantic deliveries. So the reader may suspect the essay communicates more than it says. And it does. It is as much drama as essay, a symptom as well as a saying.

Surrounding and conditioning this are intimations of a complex, unresolved life—the life of a principled yet realistic man who no longer even dreams of an easy way out. What are the circumstances? Where and when was this published? For whom written? By whom?

In 1963 Dalton was 30 years old, had escaped imprisonment in El Salvador, and was living in exile. The essay, as most of his poetry, was published in Cuba. It must be read in terms of its audience. Or audiences. Dalton had more than one in mind, though not at the same time.

Some are Cuban fellow artists—like him, communists and party members, but unlike him in being over the threshold of a developing revolution and in a relatively safe, 'socialist' environment. Dalton himself must contend with disadvantages that this audience has no experience of. He must work in exile or survive in El Salvador under the threat of imprisonment, torture and death. Still other problems are historical in a different sense: for instance, his effort to express a country that has not yet entered into a phase even of *bourgeois* nationalism. And some disadvantages appear as advantages, such as his having been raised in privilege, amidst spectacular exploitation and poverty, and formed throughout his youth by Jesuit schooling (manifest perhaps in the intellectual impatience and acerbic militancy of much of his poetry).

He also speaks, or talks back, to the more superficial and brittle verities of the Communist Party leadership. And he becomes, by turns, patient, indirect, teacherly, defensive, aggressive, ambivalent. Aside from himself (the internal dialogue and struggle are pervasive) this seems to be the audience that he is most acutely, and uneasily, conscious of.

Here the issues he raises are especially instructive. For one, the insistence on creative freedom—on not only allowing the committed poet his or her initiative (the qualification, though implicit, is definitely present), but permitting the inclusion of all aspects of life, not just approved ones. The latter demand, of course, could be put to any establishment or academicism, whatever its ostensible politics.

Also he observes, almost in passing, that slogans and agitational verses are called-for on occasion, and that they may be truly useful, though seldom achieving the status of art.[2] Given stereotypical views of the 'Party writer' as a hack who must produce slogans, one might expect Dalton to dwell on this matter. His cursory treatment suggests that the problem, if there is one, is neither recurrent nor exceptionally intense.

The pressing issues are much subtler. For example: the injunction to describe the world dialectically, in terms of what it is becoming, and thus to present history constructively, in terms of a developing working class and its eventual triumph through socialism. The responsibility (for that is what it is) to see and understand the world in such a manner is based on profound respect for the dynamic nature of reality. But when this responsibility is accepted and projected in a mechanical way, it degenerates into just another instance of idealist thought whereby there is no 'becoming,' only the 'being' that is and the 'being' that is to come. (Such 'being,' with its false implication of stasis, and its mystification of process mechanisms, is no more than a 'seeming,' an illusion.) This is the tendency that Dalton takes seriously, and takes pains to reject, particularly as it is used to push ahistorical abstractions. For him, the poet must deal with the present as *is,* rather than try to overleap it or to project a future, an audience and a language that have not as yet been historically realized.[3] Here, anyway, he invokes a historical materialist consideration—over against the cynicism and despair of a merely assertive utopianism. He is too sincere, too practical, to imagine a goal without also imagining, and trying out, the steps by which it might be arrived at.

So he turns to his Salvadoran compatriots. These he exhorts: to teach them and win them over. His intent is to promote a socialist, or rather a modified 'anti-imperialist', national culture. Which is also why he, much like Cardenal in Nicaragua, writes so much historical verse—both of them formulating and bringing to light the suppressed histories of their respective, in fact overlapping, territories.

Yet, as often happens, the anti-imperialist outlook gives way to nationalism, in effect resolving into a non-class analysis in which 'socialism' is retained as a sentiment, a conscience, but abandoned as a guide to ongoing practice. Dalton's phrase, 'my people' is not synonymous with 'workers of all countries', but is at once less focused regarding class commitment (qualitative deterioration) and more exclusive (quantitative decline). Certainly this shift did not make him any less militant. In what he did as in what he wrote, Dalton remained a fighter. But the resulting political incoherence left his poetry, sharp and impressive as it is, somewhat at a loss. It forced him ever more deeply into the bind of an ironic attitude.

He is seldom ironic here, however, not even when responding to bourgeois assumptions, usually in order to dismiss them. Their perspective being almost entirely the reflection of an ideological warp, he does not take them seriously. The one exception occurs where he partly gives in to their assumptions, and partly reacts against the flat, self-mutilating utilitarianism of his more abstracted comrades, by asserting the need for 'beauty'. Doubtless the notion of beauty has been so abused that it needs defending. Yet even if we think we know what he means, and if we sympathize with his intent, still his claim is unconvincing because it begs the question. He does what too many others (including Marxists) have done in presuming, without analysis, the necessity for an unspecified 'artistic quality', as though 'beauty' or 'artistic quality' were self-born, self-sufficient essences rather than classbound, materially conditioned terms. Naturally he distinguishes his own use of this concept—intimating that it is historical, not metaphysical—from that of the 'art for art's sake' fantasizers of virginbirths. But the blur remains.

What is more interesting is his avowed aim of using bourgeois culture against itself in order to hasten the exhaustion of that culture's resources and, thereby, to move beyond it. In part this is a rationalization for his own reliance on critical irony. But it also stands opposed to the radical notion of destroying bourgeois culture completely, so as to start afresh.[4] Then again it does not coincide with, though more closely resembling, Lenin's position, which was to overcome cultural backwardness by incorporating and using the techniques and traditions of past culture.[5]

The incompatibility of these views raises intriguing questions. For instance the historical record shows that the bourgeois state cannot, except incidentally and temporarily, be used against itself. From this recognition comes the imperative that, before socialism can be built, the bourgeois state apparatus must be destroyed. Does this mean that bourgeois culture cannot be used against itself? Possibly. Yet what might a historically viable alternative be? Before beginning to answer such a question we need a more precise, substantiated understanding of the interrelationship between state power and the culture it both generates and absorbs.

What then are we left with? In considering most poets we suspend whole areas of awareness so as not to embarrass them or ourselves with revelations of their limits, the triviality and feebleness of their bases. Not here, though. Here we have the example of a fine, sinewy, tenacious poet and admirable human being who speaks to—who thinks aloud in front of—a number of distinct audiences *because in truth he has no audience at all*, none he can count on to be with him. This is the drama that surrounds, couches, probes and interferes with the text. "Poetry and Militancy in Latin America" is the apologia of a principled, engaged, Party-disciplined poet in exile. He does not, cannot finally, articulate a relationship between political content (or political value) and aesthetic value. Nor can he dovetail his official and heartfelt commitment to a Marxist class analysis, and to partisanship in the class struggle, with his passion for a multi-class synthesis under the banner of cultural nationalism. Between one and the other is the gap his irony, at least in the poetry, tries to fill in.

— James Scully

Notes:

1. Martinez, who ruled from 1932 to 1944, had taken power by killing 4,000 rebels (who had risen in response to overturned elections) and organizing, within weeks, the massacre of 30,000 peasants, Indians, trade unionists and members of the Salvadoran Communist Party—4% of the entire population.

2. It should be noted that, contrary to scholastic belief, slogans are not inherently inferior or simplistic. They demand extraordinary decisiveness, concreteness and lucidity. Most of all they demand realization. Their power is in the potential for crystallizing and mobilizing communities. The main difficulty, aside from the stresses of more or less collective creation, is that slogans cannot survive flaws. They stand exposed, unhedged, subject to open challenge from the reality they would confront and transform (the reality that *all* literature, whatever the form, must ultimately measure up to).

3. Of course the corrective has its own pitfalls. As Engels noted, responding to the editor of a proposed multi-volume anthology of revolutionary poetry, "In general, the poetry of past revolutions (the *Marseillaise* always excepted) rarely has a revolutionary effect for later times because it must also reproduce the mass prejudices of the period in order to affect the masses. Hence the religious nonsense even among the Chartists..." [letter to Hermann Schlüter, 15 May 1885]

4. Historically associated with some 'Left' artists in the early years of the Bolshevik Revolution; with the Proletkult, most acutely in its later stages; and with the Cultural Revolution in China.

5. See Lenin's intervention in the 1920 Proletkult Congress, as he attempts to head off not only their claim to organizational autonomy, but their move to throw out all of bourgeois culture: "Marxism has won its historic significance as the ideology of the revolutionary proletariat because, far from rejecting the most valuable achievements of the bourgeois epoch, it has, on the contrary, assimilated and refashioned everything of value in the more than two thousand years of the development of human thought and culture. Only further work on this basis and in this direction, inspired by the practical experience of the proletarian dictatorship as the final stage in the struggle against every form of exploitation, can be recognized as the development of a genuine proletarian culture." [On Proletarian Culture, 8 October 1920]

   Curiously, especially in light of the aborted Cultural Revolution a quarter of a century later, Mao at Yenan held a similar view: "We should take over the rich legacy and the good traditions in literature and art that have been handed down from past ages in China and foreign countries, but the aim must still be to serve the masses of the people. Nor do we refuse to utilize the literary and artistic forms of the past, but in our hands these old forms, remolded and infused with new content, also become something revolutionary in the service of the people." [Talks at the Yenan Forum; conclusion , 23 May 1942]

The Mayakovsky Case & Other Essays

PREFACE

These essays, written between 1928 and 1930, the years when Vallejo made three visits to the Soviet Union to confront questions revolutionary artists and writers were then facing—questions that ultimately sprang from the economic crisis and political upheaval of the time.

Within the U.S.S.R. the move to accelerate industrialization and collectivize agriculture, together with the need for internal discipline to manage this, had led to the Five Year Plan. On the cultural front, the call went out for artists and writers to rid their work of petty bourgeois manifestations, to proletarianize themselves (at least in outlook), and muster together into a cultural 'red front.' At the same time, somewhat paradoxically, the ominous development of right wing and fascist forces outside the U.S.S.R. led to the promotion of a united front policy, whereby the maintenance of contacts with 'fellow travelers' played an important role.

Conceived in the context of this historical process, these essays call for artists and writers to assimilate Marxist-Leninist theory and practice into their lives and work. For Vallejo, the mechanical adoption of new styles and techniques, new words or metaphors—no matter how 'communist' or correct—served merely as a cerebral, superficial cover imposed on the deeply human struggles of the laboring masses. Only by embracing the new revolutionary way of life corresponding to a new way of seeing, of feeling, and acting, does artistic expression of that life become possible.

"Though these conflicts between the dynamics of life and the perils of abstraction were never entirely resolved, his [Vallejo's] notebooks show his determined effort to distinguish between revolutionary thought, proletarian art, Bolshevik art, and socialist art. The need for such a distinction arose because of his conviction that art legitimately served an immediate "party" purpose at the moment of revolutionary change, but also because he looked ahead to a time when once again there would be a genuinely social art, an art which he describes as 'socialist.' While Bolshevik art belongs to the transitional stage before the establishment of a truly socialist society, and while proletarian literature is a class literature, socialist art is the great art of the past and the present and the future, that which has transcended particular interests and psychologies and attained universality." [Jean Franco, César Vallejo: *The Dialectics of Poetry and Silence*]

While the language of these essays is more abstract than that of Vallejo's poetry, it is hardly academic, for it corresponds to a lived reality. It is the language of struggle, of heartfelt revolutionary practice, not of "bright ideas from the study."

—Richard Schaaf

The Mayakovsky Case

REVOLUTIONARY FUNCTION OF THOUGHT

Confusion is an organic and permanent phenomenon in bourgeois society. With problems already muddled by the very historical terms they are couched in, the confusion is compounded. This occurs with the brand-new and, at the same time, old problem of the intellectual's responsibility with regard to revolution. As posed by historical materialism, this problem is already an involved one. But when formulated or simply sketched out by bourgeois intellectuals, it has the look of an insoluble chaos.

Let us begin by recalling the principle that ascribes to thought a nature and function which are exclusively ends in themselves. *Nothing* is thought or conceived except for the purpose of discovering the means by which the indispensable necessities and interests of life might be served. Traditional psychology, which viewed thought as a simple instrument of pure contemplation, impartial and without the concrete purpose of providing for the equally concrete necessities of life, has been radically amended. The final inflection of every act of thought is a fact of absolute scientific rigor, one whose operative effect in the elaboration of history is affirmed more and more in the modern explanation of the spirit.

Even metaphysics and philosophy, based on algebraic formulas of purely logical categories, subconsciously serve the interests (albeit 'repressed') and concrete needs of the philosopher relative to his social class, to his individuality, or to humanity in general. It is the same with other so-called 'pure' intellectuals and artists. The 'pure' poetry of Paul Valery, the 'pure' painting of Gris, the 'pure' music of Schönberg—despite an apparent withdrawal from the interests, realities and concrete forms of life—at bottom subconsciously serve these realities, interests and ways of life.

"The philosophers"—says Marx—"up to now have only interpreted the world in various ways. The point, however, is to transform it." The same can be said about intellectuals and artists in general. The end of thought has been, for them, solely to interpret (while leaving intact) the concerns and other operative ways of life that it should be helping to change. The end of thought has been conservative rather than revolutionary.

The point of departure for this transforming or revolutionary doctrine of thought lies in the fundamental difference between the idealist dialectic of Hegel and the materialist dialectic of Marx. "Under its mystical form"— says Marx—"dialectics became a German mode because it seemed to cast a halo about the existing state of things." Under its rational form, dialectics, in the eyes of the bourgeoisie and its professors, is little more than a scandal and a horror, for along with the *positive comprehension of that which is*, it encompasses at the same time the *comprehension of negation* and the necessary breakdown of the existing state of things. Dialectics conceives each and every form in the flux of movement, which is to say, in its transitory aspect. It does not kneel down before anything and is, in essence, critical and revolutionary.[1]

The object or subject matter of the transforming thought process is rooted in the things and facts of the immediate present, in tangible and all-encompassing reality. The revolutionary intellectual operates always near the life of flesh and blood, before surrounding phenomena and beings. His work is vital. His sensibility and methods are terrestrial (materialist, in Marxist terms), which is to say, of this world and none other, neither extraterrestrial nor cerebral. Nothing of astrology nor cosmogony. Neither abstract masturbations nor bright ideas from the study. The revolutionary intellectual displaces the messianic formula, saying: "my kingdom is of this world."

The revolutionary intellectual, by the transforming nature of his thought and by his acting upon immediate reality, represents a danger to all the conventions of life which gall him and which he tries to abolish and replace with others that are newer, more just and perfect. He poses a threat to laws, customs and prevailing social relations. Hence he turns out to be the target *par excellence* for the persecutions and reprisals of the conservative spirit. "He is Anaxagoras, exiled"—says Eastman—"Protagoras, persecuted; Socrates, executed; Jesus, crucified." And we ourselves add: he is Marx, reviled and driven out; Lenin, scattered to the winds. The spirit of heroism and personal sacrifice is, then, for the revolutionary intellectual, an essential characteristic of his destiny.

The transforming political function of the intellectual resides in the *mainly* doctrinal nature, and in the overriding importance, of that function—and *correspondingly*, in its being militantly carried out. In other words, the revolutionary intellectual must be, simultaneously, a creator and a practitioner of this doctrine. Buddha,

Jesus, Marx, Engels, Lenin were at once creators and practitioners of revolutionary doctrine. The ideal revolutionary intellectual struggles by writing and soldiering at the same time.[2]

"Whoever is against the bourgeoisie is with us." This is the call to order—says Lunacharsky—which must serve as the basis for the organization of the International of the Intellectuals.

Can this formula be applied to revolutionary intellectuals of every country? Evidently yes. In America as in Europe, Asia, and Africa, there is now one central, common task for all revolutionary intellectuals: the destruction of the ruling social order, whose global axis lies deep within the capitalist structure of society. *All the forces of the intelligentsia must be mustered and polarized in this action.* It is very important to take account of what must be done at any given moment. On this point, Lenin offers luminous lessons. "It is not enough"—he says—"to be revolutionary and a communist partisan: you must know how to find, at every moment, the chain-link which one must grasp in order to secure the entire chain and to seize, then, the next link." For revolutionary intellectuals, the theoretical and practical link of the moment is set in the destruction of the ruling social order. Such is the specific tactical watchword of every revolutionary intellectual.

Our revolutionary task must be realized in two synchronic and indivisible cycles: a centripetal cycle of rebellion against the standing forms of mental production, replacing them with new disciplines and models of intellectual creation, and a centrifugal cycle of precepts, propaganda and agitation in the midst of society.

Our critical and destructive tactics must march together with, inseparable from, a profession of constructive faith that is derived, scientifically and objectively, from history. Our struggle against the standing social order involves, according to materialist dialectics, a necessary and implicit movement towards the replacement of that old order with a new one. With respect to revolution, the concepts of destruction and construction are inseparable.

That new social order, which is replacing the present one, is none other than the communist or socialist order. The bridge between both worlds: proletarian dictatorship.

The Soviet phenomenon is the obvious objective demonstration, with its relentless realism, of the unavoidable dialectical road which the capitalist social system must follow in order to arrive at the socialist order. Apropos of this, we shall quote from the manifesto of the Union of Revolutionary Writers:

"An unprecedented economic crisis"—so the document reads— "is breaking up the capitalist world. The number of people out of work surpasses 50 million and continues to soar. Multitudes of the unemployed and hungry file past huge warehouses overflowing with provisions while a handful of financiers impose their arbitrary will on capitalist society, fuel their locomotives with farm crops, dump wheat and coffee and sugar into the sea, burn enormous quantities of wool and cotton, all to maintain for their own lofty personal interests a high rate of profit—the one and only engine that drives the capitalist economy. The wages of the working class and poor peasants, as well as those of clerical workers and others who do not work mainly with their hands, fall with catastrophic rapidity. The specter of hunger, of a hopeless dead-end future under capitalist rule—this is here the reality, and the horizon, of the laboring masses.

Bourgeois culture is totally decadent. The imperialist spirit has infected literature and art. So as to cloud the consciousness of the masses and so save its own class hegemony, the bourgeoisie is compelled to check the progress of science and retard the cultural development of humanity. Declaring war on its past, the bourgeoisie looks to maintain its alliance with the Catholic Church, resurrecting the mystical and feudal theories of the Middle Ages so as to mask, behind a curtain of obscurantism, the fact that it is rotting away.

In the meantime, the workers and peasants of the immense country of the Soviets, after having overthrown capitalist rule and saved themselves from famine and scarcity, are setting the bases for a new socialist society. In the fifteen years of the dictatorship of the proletariat, the enthusiasm of the liberated laboring masses has produced, from one of the most backward countries of Europe, the most advanced country in the world—the first state which has undertaken the construction of socialism. The hopes of the imperialist governments and their social-democratic flunkies, who believed it was impossible to build socialism in one country, and who thought they could squelch the heroic will of the proletariat through famine and economic blockade, have fallen by the wayside. The Union of Soviet Socialist Republics has fulfilled and exceeded the Second Five Year Plan, which its enemies had declared, only yesterday, as Bolshevik lunacy. The Soviet has eliminated unemployment, attracting new strata of the peasantry and thousands of women to socialist production. Agriculture is being reorganized on a collective basis that has won out over the old rural way of life; and the fences between the socialist city and the collectivized countryside are being torn down. Tiny villages that, under Czarism, found themselves bogged down in mud and ignorance, intoxicated by the opiate of religion, may be found now crisscrossed by a closely woven network of schools, libraries, radio stations and lecture halls. In place of church bells and the policeman's whistle, the cranking of tractors. The U.S.S.R. has definitely entered into the socialist phase.

Making use of new methods of work, work that has been made into a source of pride, of courage and heroism in the socialist state— and driven by socialist emulation and shock brigades—the Soviet proletariat creates and develops huge concerns of heavy socialist industry, expands farm technology, and transforms the old, backward, agrarian Russia into a country of iron and steel, of automobiles and tractors.

From the bedrock of this socialist economy, there springs forth and develops, at an explosive rate, a cultural revolution unknown, up to now, throughout history. Millions of illiterates have entered into a vast cultural initiation. At the end of the Second Five Year Plan, there won't be a single illiterate person left in Russia. The increase in the output of periodicals and literary material far exceeds the most rapid growth rates of the most prosperous period of German and North American capitalism. The development of the productive forces of the Soviet Union marches forward with such momentum in every branch of literature, art, and culture in general, that the problem of the museum directors becomes exceptionally acute. Thousands of new people receive the education necessary to fill the top posts of the cultural revolution.

The imperialist powers witness, with dread and much gnashing of teeth, this historic movement which is incomprehensible to them and which decides, definitively, the destiny of capitalism. Consequently the imperialist powers wish to sink this movement, which is the salvation of humanity, in a bloodbath."

EXECUTION OF BOLSHEVIK ART

Bolshevik art is principally propaganda and agitation. It is determined, by preference, to incite and instruct the revolt and the organization of the masses for protest, for the recovery of what is theirs, and for class struggle. Its purposes are didactic, in the specific sense of the word. It is an art of proclamations, messages, harangues, grumblings, rages, and admonitions. Its words thrive on accusation, polemics, and militant eloquence against the ruling social system and its historical consequences. Its mission is cyclical, even episodic, and ends with the triumph of world revolution. Its destiny embraces one cycle of history, which goes from the beginnings of the workers' movement on to the universal dictatorship of the proletariat or, possibly, as far as the introduction of communism. With the commencement of world socialist construction its aesthetic action ceases, its social influence wanes. Bolshevik art is appropriate for a periodic vicissitude of society. Once this transformation or Marxist 'leap' has taken place, however, the harangues, the proclamations and admonitions lose all their aesthetic power and, by their continuing on, it's as if in the midst of sowing seeds or harvesting wheat we should hear battle hymns, apostrophes to struggle.

Bolshevik art, through its immediate explosive presence, summons and captures the collective attention more than socialist art does. Always temporal art prevails—in the moment from which it issues, and which it serves—over timeless art.

EXECUTION OF SOCIALIST ART

The socialist poet does not reduce his socialism to the themes or technique of the poem. He does not reduce it to the inserting of fashionable words on economy, dialectics or Marxist law, to mobilizing ideas and political requisitions from invoices or communist sources, nor to characterizing the actions of nature and the spirit with epithets taken from the proletarian revolution. The socialist poet assumes, by preference, a sensibility that is organic and implicitly socialist. Only a temperamentally socialist person—whose public and private conduct, whose way of looking at a star, of understanding how a car runs, of feeling pain, of doing a math problem, of picking up a stone, of keeping silent or making a friendship, are organically socialist—only that person can create a genuinely socialist poem. Only that one will create a socialist poem, the one whose essential preoccupation does not stem *precisely* from service to a party interest or a historical class contingency, but who lives a personal, everyday socialist life (I say personal, not individual). For the socialist poet the poem is not, then, an apocalyptic moment, instigated at will, in the preconceived service of a creed or of political propaganda, but is a natural and simple function of the human sensibility. The socialist poet must be such not only when writing a poem, but in all his acts, large and small, inside and out. conscious and subconscious and even when he sleeps and when he makes a mistake and when he willingly or unwillingly deceives himself and when he corrects himself and when he fails.

But does socialist art exist right now? Sure it does. It exists. Examples: Beethoven, many tapestries of the Renaissance, the pyramids of Egypt, Assyrian sculpture, some Chaplin movies, Bach (in Russia, Bach is played), etc.

Why do these works correspond to the notion and content of socialist art? Because, in our opinion, they answer to a universal concept of the masses and to feelings, ideas and interests common to—to use, as it happens, an epithet derived from substantive communism—all human beings without exception.

Who are all these human beings without exception? Those individuals whose lives are distinguished by the prevalence of human values over those of the beast. This prevalence of essentially human traits over those of the animal state is sufficient to qualify one to represent, among "all human beings without exception," those whose sentiments, ideas and interests are common and who are mutually supportive. The person who is not represented among "all human beings without exception" is the individual whose conduct indicates a morbid state or mental inadequacy, who is situated equally far from man and beast.

The way and the means by which strictly human values arise and develop necessarily vary according to a series of conditions set by the planetary and social context, conditions that in history produce many types of humanity, diverse in their ups and downs and in the accidents of their development, yet the same in their laws and in their general destiny. When a work of art answers to, serves and cooperates with this human unity, plumbing the diversity of historic and geographic types by which it is conditioned and in which it is performed, that work is said to be socialist. It is not when, on the contrary, the work of art confines its roots and social range to the psychology and special interests of this one or that one of the human factions into which the species is pluralized according to spatial and temporal contexts.

Socialist art is not, then, a reality that will come, as some Marxist critics seem to think, but one that is already—as we have just finished saying—an existing reality. Although we are still far from a socialist society, it cannot be denied that there do exist diverse aspects of social life whose collective form, structure and radiation are manifestly socialist. Examples: the assembly line, farm technology, the industrial complex and other advanced forms of work, the *standardization* of a large number of industrial products, many everyday customs, workers' housing projects and, finally, great art. Naturally this has to do with rudimentary, incomplete socialist forms given that they're held back by the antagonisms of the capitalist system in which they occur. The masses themselves are perhaps the form most suggestive, for now, of socialist life.

Socialism is found, then, in progress, embodied in the manifold phenomena of social life.

Furthermore, not yet as a consciously and scientifically elaborated system, but as a rational law and instinct of humankind throughout history, socialism has not ceased struggling and manifesting itself in different ways in communities, from the pre-class stage,and further even, since primitive communism. Plekhanov, in "Art and Social Life," and Bukharin, in "The Theory of Historical Materialism," frequently and randomly sketch, in countless examples of vaguely socialist forms, rough drafts drawn from tribal life. Later, within the societies of the ancient Orient, we can see the same thing: in particular, the labor of the masses shows—in Egypt, in Assyria—a markedly socialist character. During the Middle Ages, the historic struggle for socialism is almost totally eclipsed, only to reappear in the early days of capitalism.

Along with this socialist winking and blinking—incongruous and embryonic, yet tenacious and increasingly assertive throughout history—many other forms of socialist art have been produced, more or less directly reflecting social life. The Colosseum of Rome holds, in its architectural interweave and in the labor of the masses who brought it to light, more of an artistic socialist aspect or element, although still crude and, above all, spoiled by the original sin of the bloodthirsty social injustice of what took place there. Doubtless it's not possible to speak of socialism or socialist art in societies where man is exploited by man. This is an undeniable truth. But here we touch, precisely, on the key point of the question.

Socialist society is not going to appear at a single stroke, overnight. It will be the result of the entire social process of history. Socialist society will be the work of an ensemble of forces and determinist laws of social life. It will not be an improvisation but a rational, scientific elaboration—slow, evolving, cyclical and revolutionary. The proof is in what we are witnessing now (concretized and defined in Russia) and have already seen in the plural and successive pasts of societies, mapped out and built stone by stone—in many five-year plans, more or less brilliant or obscure, yet all strung together by one single thread of history. What can be asserted, then, is that there have been and are more or less socialist forms of life, and that in history these forms exhibit varying, though always progressive, scales and degrees of socialism. The division of society into classes, and the empire of injustice, have impeded, certainly, even today, a more vast, profound and pure socialization of many aspects of collective life. Nevertheless, the irrefutable dialectic of history, thwarting and winning out over the ruling classes, has socialized, I repeat, certain forms of social life. So it is with the United States, bastion *par excellence* of the capitalist system—with its more refined injustices—showing in its work techniques, in its industrial structure, a growing, though stifled and subterranean, invigorating socialist air. Revolutionary in the highest degree, Russia—with its elimination of classes and suppression of social injustice—has brought to an end the cycle of sporadic, intermittent and embryonic socializations, and has opened forever the socialist era of humanity. And tomorrow, when the universal proletarian revolution has broken out and triumphed, society will be wholly socialized, not only in its production but also, and more decisively, in the distribution of its wealth.

Now then: socialist artworks are following, and will continue to follow, the same progressive development as society. Socialist artistic emotion will go on improving under socialism. The socialist music of the future will be more socialist than the symphonies of Beethoven and the fugues of Bach. These musicians succeed, in effect, in touching what is deepest and most in common in all human beings, *without cropping off the circumstantial periphery of life,* the area determined by the sensibility, the ideas and the class interests of the individual. Other musicians will work through both modes of social life: touching what is profound *and* what is contingent in every individual, which is to say, their works will be more socialist than those of Bach or Beethoven.

From what I have said, up to here, concerning socialist art and Bolshevik art, two criteria can be deduced. In the first place, Soviet art taken as a means of realizing socialism and as a dialectical force for the creation of that society—that art can be considered or, more properly, characterized as socialist. Secondly, Soviet art taken as a reflection and expression of the society from which it proceeds can also be characterized as socialist, inasmuch as it contains, we repeat, many fundamental forms, already socialized, of collective life.

But, judging matters with greater precision, it is impossible not to perceive at the base of Soviet art and literature the whole spirit and character of what we have called Bolshevik art. More than to express the forms of a new society, 25% or 30% socialized, Soviet art intends, by preference, to incite and instruct the revolt and organization of the masses of the world for protest, for retribution, for class struggle and universal revolution. Thus, then, Soviet art and literature together correspond exactly to the execution of Bolshevik art, about which we have already spoken.

Let's try to see clearly and be precise. Let's try to understand ourselves. The revolution isn't performing sleight-of-hand tricks on reality, but is calling things by their true names and looking them squarely in the face.

I am sure that most Soviet artistic and literary works (I except architecture) will be quite remote from the socialist art of the future. The Bolshevik beauty and emotions in *Battleship Potemkin*, in *Red Cavalry*, in *To Command*, in *The Red Poppy*, will dim considerably. (Nor will bourgeois aesthetics and criticism find this 'Bolshevik beauty' at all surprising. Doesn't it already speak to us of 'Greek beauty' or 'Gothic beauty'?)

PROLETARIAN LITERATURE

Burning discussions have been advanced regarding the nature of proletarian art.

The Leninist and official Soviet criterion, which would have proletarian literature be an instrument of the State to carry out the workers' dictatorship and world revolution, has been followed by that of Trotsky, who extends the proletarian criterion of art to vaster and more profound domains of the spirit, and declares that not one Russian poet of the revolution, beginning with Blok, has been able to realize those essential outlines of proletarian art. Nevertheless, proletarian literature, according to Trotsky, remains always locked-up inside the spiritual catechism of the Proletarian State. He treats proletarian art solely as a relative extension of the viewpoint of Lenin and the Soviet.

There is a second way of characterizing proletarian art. Gorky has said: "The typical line for the proletarian writer is in active hatred for all that oppresses man both within and without, preventing the free, full development of his faculties. The proletarian writer tends to intensify the readers' participation in life, giving them a more secure sense of their own strengths and of the means for defeating every internal enemy, and helping them acquire a deep feeling for life and for the great joy of work." As is seen, Gorky's position gets confused with the spirit of bourgeois literature, which tries to realize intentions literally identical to those that Gorky attributes, in a way that is all too generic and vague, to proletarian literature. Gorky does not delineate the strictly proletarian character of the art in question. What he has to say about this, bourgeois aestheticians and critics have been saying about bourgeois art for years and years.

A resolution regarding proletarian literature still has not been arrived at in Russia. Most people do not want to admit that proletarian art is nothing, in sum, but Bolshevik art itself. Once again, Lenin is right here and has it over Trotsky, who attempts to, so to speak, deflect the work of the proletarian artist and disperse it in idle humanism—and also over Gorky, who, as a writer, ought to see these problems with better technical insight than those who are not writers.

"In the face of bourgeois customs"—Lenin said—"in the face of profiteering, opportunism and bourgeois literary individualism, in the face of 'aristocratic anarchism' and the competition among bourgeois writers for their own personal benefit, the socialist proletariat must affirm, carry out, and enlarge upon, in its most wholly realized form, the principle of a proletarian literature. What is this principle? Proletarian literature must be a class literature and a party literature. It must be inspired by the socialist idea and in sympathy with the workers, who embody and struggle for the realization of that idea. This literature will enrich the final word of the revolutionary thought of humanity through the experience and living activity of the socialist proletariat."

So then, proletarian literature must serve the class interests of the proletariat and, specifically, must keep within the framework set by the directives and practical watchwords of the Communist Party, vanguard of the laboring masses. In other words, proletarian literature is equivalent to Bolshevik literature. Copnez, delegate to the Communist International before the Second World Congress of Revolutionary Writers, said:

> "The present period of worsening antagonisms within the capitalist system demands that revolutionary literature become proletarian. If the writer becomes revolutionary not from an unabashed desire for publicity, nor out of sheer demagoguery with the intention of becoming popular, but 'because he is imbued with a burning hatred of capitalist society, and because he is resolved to dedicate his talent to the destruction of this society,' then the logic of the struggle, the unflagging logic of his own striving toward revolution, must lead him to proletarian literature."

THE MAYAKOVSKY CASE

At a gathering of Bolshevik writers in Leningrad, Kolvasieff was telling me that Mayakovsky is not, as is thought in foreign countries, the greatest Soviet poet, nor anything like it. Mayakovsky is no more than a theatrical person who speaks in hyperbole. Ahead of him there are Pasternak, Biedney, Sayanof, and many others...

I know Mayakovsky's work, and I couldn't have agreed more with Kolvasieff. And when, some days later in Moscow, I spoke with the author of "150,000,000," our conversation sealed forever Kolvasieff's verdict. Mayakovsky is not, in fact, the best Soviet poet. He is only the most widely published. If Pasternak, Kazin, Gastev, Sayanof, and Viesimiensky were read more, then the name Mayakovsky would lose much of its reverberation around the world.

But why should my conversation with Mayakovsky be the definitive key to his work? To what extent can a conversation define the spirit and, what is more, the aesthetic value of an artist? The answer, in this case, depends on the method of critical thinking. If we start out from a surrealist, Freudian, Bergsonian, or any other reactionary method, we certainly cannot base our opinions on a simple talk with an artist in order to ascertain the importance of his work. According to these various spiritualist methods, the artist is instinctive or, to express ourselves in more orthodox terms, intuitive. His work flows out of him naturally, unconsciously, subconsciously. If asked his opinion of art and of his own art, he will probably reply in banalities, with everything, quite often, contrary to what he makes and does. A genius, according to this, belies and contradicts himself, or almost always ends up going astray in his conversations. To rely on these, like a fundamentalist critic, turns out to be, for that reason, a mistake. But not if we start out from the method of historical materialism, so dear to Mayakovsky and his communist friends. Marx does not conceive life except as a great scientific experiment where nothing is unconscious or blind, but where everything is reflexive, conscious, technical. The artist, according to Marx, in order for his work to function dialectically, with repercussions on History, must proceed with a rigorous scientific method and in full understanding of his means. Hence, there is no better exegete of the poet's work than the poet himself. What he thinks and says about his work is, or ought to be, more on target than any outside opinion. Mayakovsky then, in the statements that he made to me, conveyed better than any critic the meaning of his work and what it really amounts to.

Mayakovsky was speaking to me in a overtly pained, bitter tone. Contrary to what all his critics say, Mayakovsky was suffering, deep down, an acute moral crisis. The revolution had come in the midst of his youth, when his spiritual mold was already cast and even set. The effort to do an abrupt about-face, and be completely amenable to the new life, broke his back and made him lose his center of gravity, leaving him out of joint, like Esenin and Sobol. Such has been the lot of this generation. It has suffered, smack in the middle of each individual aorta, the psychological consequences of social revolution. Situated between the prerevolutionary and postrevolutionary generations, the generation of Mayakovsky, Esenin, and Sobol has seen itself literally crucified between the two faces of that great event. Within this same generation, the Calvary has been greater for those whom the revolution caught by surprise, the disinherited of every revolutionary tradition or initiation. The tragedy of personal psychological transmutation has been, then, brutal, and only the unconcerned ones wearing revolutionary masks, and the insensitive ones posing as Bolsheviks, have managed to escape it. The more sensitive and openhearted the individual as he absorbs social happenings, the deeper the personal upheaval he feels from political convulsion, and the more exacerbated the pathos of his intimate personal revision of History. The final judgment has been, then, terrible. Suicide, literal or moral, has turned out to be fated, inevitable, as the sole solution to the tragedy. For the others, on the contrary, for the insensitive, the unconcerned "bolsheviks," it has been easy: they risked nothing by their "revolutionary" cries, since for them the revolution went only skin-deep, as a phenomenon or a spectacle of State, never becoming a personal, intimate, psychological revolution. There was no difficulty or danger, then, in associating themselves with the trend followed by others, which is what most writers in Russia and other countries have done and are doing. Which writers go so far as to kill for the 'holy cause'? And what of it? ...It proves nothing. Throughout History there have been many who were made to kill for much less.

In the case of Mayakovsky we have to distinguish, right off, between his life and his work. Since his suicide, his life has been rounded off as one of the greatest and clearest individual expressions of the collective act. Doubtless his suicide was no more than one of a thousand critical moments along one long, moral Way-of-the-Cross traveled by the writer himself, uprooted by History and by a powerful will to understand, and live to the utmost, the new social relations. This internal struggle between the past—which holds up even as every point of support is, in the meantime, lost—and the present— which demands a genuine, thunderous adaptation—was in Mayakovsky long, bloody and dreadful. Deep down, the tenacious and irreducible petit-bourgeois sensibility survived with all its fundamental values in play, and only outwardly would he engage in his willful, self-driven struggle to throttle the profound essence of past history in order to replace it with the equally profound essence of the new. The grafting of this onto that was impossible. In vain he exchanged, on the day after the revolution, his futurist waistcoat for the workshirt of the Bolshevik poet. In vain he went, from then on, declaiming Soviet verses through the streets and squares, in factories, on farms, in logging camps, labor unions, the barracks of the Red Army... In vain he became the Pindar of the proletarian epic. In vain he sought in the multitudes the influence necessary to Sovietize his deeply unbalanced soul. Gigantic of body, strong, with the tough, iron-ringing voice of a loudspeaker, he would recite: "O my country! You are a beautiful adolescent. O my young Republic! You swell with pride and rear up like a filly. Our impulses go right on into the future. And you, old countries, we're going to leave you a hundred kilometers behind. I salute you, O my country! yours is the youth of the world..." In vain, all of it... In vain... The genuine inner life of the poet, shackled in the artificial formulas of an external and inorganic Leninism, goes on suffering in silence, feeling entirely the opposite to what his verses are saying. Meanwhile Mayakovsky continued going wrong in literature, with that strutting bunch of 'revolutionary' artists, those who seem revolutionary with the same facility that they might seem brave or adult or able to stay out till all hours of the night—as the inner life of the poet, in stark disagreement with an art that was not translating it into reality, kept fighting back, underground, struggling in agony. Such was the tragic, shameless rupture of every concurrence between the author's life and work. And neither the revolutionary poet nor the reactionary poet got out of it. His inner struggle totally neutralized his sensibility and its artistic expression. Mayakovsky was a mere litterateur, a simple versifier, a hollow rhetorician.

—War on metaphysics—he was telling me in Moscow. —War on the subconscious and on the theory according to which the poet sings as a bird sings...War on apolitical poetry, on grammar, on metaphor... Art must be controlled by reason...Must always serve as political propaganda, and work with clear, preconceived ideas, and must even develop into a thesis, like an algebraic theorem. Expression must be direct, point-blank...

Did his poetry answer to these strictures? Evidently yes. Except that Mayakovsky's theory served only to turn him into a manufacturer of verse 'to order,' cold and dead.

Mayakovsky's declarations express the truth about his work, confirming the fact that it is an art steeped in formulas and not in a personal, deeply felt sincerity.

By holding to an artistic program taken from historical materialism, Mayakovsky made only verses lacking intimate warmth and feeling, stirred up by external mechanical forces, by artificial heating.

Mayakovsky was a representative spirit of his medium and his time, but he was not a poet. His life was, likewise, grand in its tragedy, but his art was declamatory and empty, having betrayed the authentic, actual, critical moments of his life.

FROM THE NOTEBOOKS
from 1929-1930 [the green notebook]

Bolshevism is humanism in action. The same can be said about being revolutionary or about communism, which are humanisms in action; which is to say, the humanist idea and sentiment and the humanist ideal are fulfilled by means of humanist technique and practice—the ideal is made flesh.

Russia is reproached for having its artists produce political art. Well then: France gives gold medals to its Salon artists who have distinguished themselves in the trenches. Germany, England and Italy do exactly the same. {from 1936-1937(38'?)}

There is Russian revolutionary literature and there is revolutionary literature battling from within the capitalist world. The objectives, method of work, technique, means of expression and social material vary from one to the other. No one has yet made this distinction in Marxist criticism.

The revolutionary writer believes, erroneously, that it's necessary to produce proletarian art, considering the worker to be a pure worker—which isn't certain, because the worker is also bourgeois. The worker breathes bourgeois air and is saturated with the bourgeois spirit more than we imagine. It is very important [to be clear about this] in conceiving a proletarian or mass art.

Translated by Richard Schaaf

Notes:

1. Cite the 'creationism' of Vicente Huidobro, interpretation of thought: Don't copy life, transform it, Huidobro; but he transforms it corrupting it, misrepresenting it. It is teaching a bad boy to do good, but in the process turning him into a woolly doll with two heads or a monkey's tail, etc. This is what all the schools of art do: surrealism, etc. [C.V]

2. Cite Clemenceau: "A writer, a word is a public act." Add on Rimbaud and Lautreamont. As for us, there's no separating a man's ideas from his actions, as happens in the bourgeois world. Ideas and acts, spirit and matter—it is all one. [C V]

Autopsy on Surrealism

The capitalist intelligentsia exhibits, among other symptoms of its death throes, the vice of the literary coterie. It is curious to see how the more recent and acute crises of economic imperialism—the war, industrial reorganization, the misery of the masses, the bankruptcies and stock market crashes, the spread of workers' revolution, the colonial uprisings, etc.—correspond, at the same time, to a furious proliferation of literary schools, as makeshift as they are ephemeral. About 1914, Expressionism sprang up (Dvorák, Fretzer). Around 1915 it was Cubism (Apollinaire, Reverdy). In 1917, Dadaism (Tzara, Picabia). In 1924, Surrealism (Breton, Ribemont-Dessaignes). Not to mention already existing schools: Symbolism, Futurism, Neo-Symbolism, *Unanimismo*, etc. Finally, since the surrealist declaration, nearly every month a new literary school bursts onto the scene. Never has social thought been so broken up into so many fleeting formulas. Never has it undergone such frenetic whims and such a need to stereotype itself through recipes and clichés, as if it dreaded its own freedom, or as if it were unable to bring about its own organic unity. A like anarchy and disintegration is to be seen nowhere except among the philosophers and poets in the decadence of Greco-Latin civilization. Those of today, in turn, signal a new spiritual decadence: that of western capitalist civilization.

The last and most publicized school, Surrealism, has just officially died.

In truth, surrealism as a literary school did not make one constructive contribution. It was more a prescription for custom-making poems, as literary schools of all times do and have done. Moreover, it wasn't even an original prescription. All the pompous theory and the abracadabra method of surrealism were precipitated by a few sketchy thoughts which Apollinaire had on the subject. Based on these ideas of the author of *Calligrams,* the surrealist manifestos were limited to the constructing of clever parlor games related to 'automatic writing,' morality, religion, and politics.

Parlor games, I have said, and clever also: calculating, I should say. When surrealism came on, through the irresistible dialectic of things, to confront the living problems of reality—which do not depend, exactly, on the belabored abstract metaphysics of any literary

35

school—surrealism found itself in a tight spot. For to be consistent with what the surrealists themselves were calling 'the revolutionary and critical spirit' of this movement, it had to take to the streets and take charge of, among other things, the political and economic problems of our time. Surrealism was then anarchistic—this most abstract, mystical, cerebral form of politics, and the one that best reconciled itself with the ontological and even occultist character of the coterie. Within anarchism the surrealists could continue getting recognition, since the organic nihilism of the school could live with and even unite with it bodily.

But much later, as things got going, the surrealists came to realize that outside the surrealist catechism there was another revolutionary method, as 'interesting' as what they themselves proposed: I refer to Marxism. They read, they mused, and by a very bourgeois miracle of eclecticism and indissoluble 'permutation,' Breton proposed to his friends the coordination and synthesizing of both methods. The surrealists instantly became communists.

Only at this time—not before nor after—does surrealism acquire a certain social importance. From the simple mass production of poems, it was transformed into a militant political movement, into a truly alive and revolutionary decree regarding what must be done. Surrealism deserved, then, to be taken into consideration and to be judged one of the more vital constructive literary currents of the period.

Nevertheless, this judgment was liable to be treated with contempt. It had to continue observing subsequent surrealist methods and disciplines in order to know up to what point the content and actions were, in truth, sincerely revolutionary. Even though one knew about coordinating surrealist method with Marxism, it didn't go beyond being a childish outburst or a temporary mystification, yet the hope remained that, little by little, these brand new, unexpected, militant bolsheviks would go on being radicalized.

Unfortunately, Breton and his friends, contradicting and belying their strident declarations of Marxist faith, subconsciously, and unable to avoid it, went on being incurable anarchist intellectuals. From the very first, out of surrealist pessimism and desperation— pessimism and desperation that, in its time, was able to activate the conscience of the coterie—there came a permanent, static system, an academic configuration. The moral and intellectual crisis that surrealism was determined to stir up, and which (another failure of originality in this school) might have originated and had its first and foremost expression in Dadaism, became fossilized in writing-table psychopathy and in literary cliché, despite all the injections of Marx's dialectics and the formal, diligent adherence of the restive youth to communism. Pessimism and desperation must always be stages along the way, not ends to be arrived at. In order to rouse and enrich the spirit, they must be enlarged upon until they are transformed into constructive affirmations. Otherwise, they won't get beyond the status of pathological germs, condemned to devour themselves. The surrealists, evading the law governing the essential shape of things to come, made their famous moral and intellectual crisis academic and were powerless to overcome and go beyond it with truly revolutionary forms, that is to say, destructive/constructive forms. Each surrealist did whatever came to mind. They broke with numerous members of the party and with its press organs, and they proceeded, in all, in perpetual breach with the great Marxist directives. From the literary point of view, their productions continued being characterized by an evident bourgeois refinement. Adherence to communism had no reflection whatever in the sense or essential forms of their works. Surrealism was being found, for all these reasons, incapable of understanding and practicing the true and only revolutionary spirit of these times: Marxism. Surrealism quickly lost the only social posture which could have justified its existence—and entered, hopelessly, into its death throes.

At the present time, surrealism—as a Marxist movement—is a corpse. (As a mere literary coterie—I repeat—it was like all schools an imposter of life, a common scarecrow.) Its obituary has been issued through two documents by the party concerned: *The Second Surrealist Manifesto* by Breton, and one titled *A Corpse*, directed against Breton and signed by numerous surrealists led by Ribemont-Dessaignes. Both manifestos establish, together with the death and ideological decomposition of surrealism, its dissolution as a group or physical aggregate. This schism or total collapse of the congregation was the most serious, and the last, in an already long series of breakdowns.

Breton, in his *Second Manifesto,* reviews the surrealist doctrine, appearing satisfied with its realization and effects. Breton continued being, up to the last, a professional intellectual, a scholastic ideologue, an armchair rebel, a stubborn pedant, a polemicist in the fashion of

Maurras, and finally, a 'village' anarchist. He declares, once again, that surrealism has triumphed, because it has achieved what it was determined to achieve: "to stir up, from a moral and intellectual point of view, a crisis of consciousness." Breton is mistaken. If in fact he had read and subscribed to Marxism, I can't understand how he forgot that, according to doctrine, the role of writers is not to stir up more or less serious or general moral and intellectual crises, that is, not to make revolution 'from above,' but on the contrary to make it 'from below.' Breton forgets that there is only one revolution, the proletarian one, and that the workers will make this revolution with action, not the intellectuals with their 'crisis of consciousness.' The only crisis is the economic crisis, and it has been found to be such— as fact and not simply as a notion or as 'dilettantism'—since time immemorial. As to the rest of the *Second Manifesto,* Breton devotes it to attacking, with the outcries and personal abuse of a literary cop, his old associates—insults and hollering that show the character, bourgeois to the core, of his 'crisis of consciousness.'

The other manifesto, called *A Corpse,* presents memorable necrological passages concerning Breton:

> "At one time"—says Ribemont-Dessaignes—"surreal-ism pleased us: the youthful flings, if one wishes, of household servants. Young boys are allowed to love even the wife of a gendarme (this woman is embodied in the aesthetic of Breton). Phony comrade, phony communist, phony revolutionary, but a veritable and authentic fraud: Breton better watch out for the guillotine. What am I saying!? Corpses don't get guillotined."

> "Breton was beating around the bush"—says Roger Vitrac—"scribbling in a reactionary, sanctimonious style about subversive ideas, achieving a curious effect which never failed to astonish the petty bourgeoisie, the small businessmen and manufacturers, the seminarians and the heartstroke victims of the grammar schools."

> "Breton,"—Jacques Prevert says—"was a stutterer who got everything mixed up: desperation and liver pains, the Bible and the Cantos of Maldoror, God and god, ink and desk, the barracks and the divan of Madame Sabatier, the Marquis de Sade and Jean Lorrain, the Russian Revolution and the Surrealist revolution...lyrical steward, he passed out diplomas to the lovers who were versifying and, on days of indulgence, to those who were novices in desperation."

"Breton's cadaver"—Michel Leiris says—"makes me sick because, among other reasons, he is a man who has always lived off cadavers."

"Of course"—says Jacques Rigaud—"Breton spoke very well about love, but in life he was a character out of Courteline."

Etc., etc., etc.

It's only that these same assessments of Breton can be applied to all surrealists without exception, and to the defunct school itself. It will be said that this is the clownish, incidental side of these people and not the historical basis of the movement. Well said. Provided that this historical basis in fact exists, which, in this case, isn't so. The historical basis of surrealism is very nearly a void, from whatever angle it is examined.

Thus literary schools pass away. Such is the fate of all uneasiness that, instead of turning into an austere creative laboratory, becomes no more than a mere formula. All the thundering blurbs, the proclamations for the great unwashed, the full-color ads, in short, every sleight of hand and trick of the trade turns out to be useless then. Together with the aborted tree, all the verbiage, like too much foliage, suffocates itself.[1]

LITERATURE BEHIND CLOSED DOORS OR THE WIZARDS OF REACTION

The writer behind closed doors knows nothing about life. Politics, love, economic problems, the unmediated haphazard struggle of man with men, the minute and immediate drama of the conflicting forces and tendencies of objective social reality—none of this even reaches the desk of the writer behind closed doors.

The parlor poet is the direct descendant of the economic error of the bourgeoisie. Landowner, financier, with livings or sinecures from the state or from the family, his bread and the roof over his head are secure and he can escape the economic struggle, which is incompatible with isolation or detachment. Such is most commonly the economic situation of the litterateur. Other times, this scribe feeds his belly by means of a tacit business sense inherited through the psychology of the class from which he comes. Then he is without income, like a vulgar social parasite, yet profits from a disposition that enables him to make a literature that is much in demand. How? "The artist"—writes Upton Sinclair—"who triumphs in an era is a man who sympathizes with the ruling classes of that era, whose interests and ideals he interprets, identifying himself with them." In a society of tiresome farts and complacent exploiters who, as Lenin says, "are sick with obesity," the most gratifying literature is that which smells of desk moths. When the French bourgeoisie were happier and contented with their empire, the literature held in highest regard was that produced behind closed doors. On the eve of the war, the king of the pen was Anatole France. It's the same today, in countries where the bourgeois reaction appears most stubborn, as in France itself, in Italy, and in Spain—to mention only Latin countries—the writers in vogue are Paul Valéry, Pirandello, and Ortega y Gasset, whose works embrace, at heart, the sensibility of the drawing room. That mental refinement, that ingenious game, that parlor philosophy, that bookish emotion, wafts off in the distance to the man who masturbates, tenderly, behind closed doors.

THE DUEL BETWEEN TWO LITERATURES

However much its pontiffs and overseers may wish it, the capitalist literary process cannot succeed in avoiding the germs of decadence which emerge, after many years, from the social body on which that process rests. This means that the inherent, growing, fatal contradictions with which the capitalist economy struggles, circulate as well through bourgeois art, generating its collapse. This means, likewise, that the resistance those intellectual wheeler-dealers put up against the death of this literature is vain and useless, since we are already in the presence of an accomplished fact, on a strictly objective plane, through nothing less than the forces and forms at the base of economic production, all of which are quite remote and foreign to the sectarian, professional, and individual interests of the writer. Capitalist literature does no more, then, than reflect—I repeat, without power to avoid it—the slow, lingering death throes of the society from which it proceeds.

What are the most salient signs of decadence in bourgeois literature? These signs have been made clear enough already without our dwelling on them. They can, nevertheless, all come under one common heading: the draining of social content from words. The word is empty. It suffers from an acute, incurable case of social consumption. No one says anything to anybody. Communication between man and men is broken off. The individual's term for collectivity has been left mutilated and crushed in the individual mouth. In the midst of our incomprehensible wordiness, we are speechless. It is the confusion of tongues arising from the exacerbated individualism which is at the base of bourgeois economy and politics. Unbridled individual interest—to be the richest, the happiest, to be the dictator of a country or an oil baron—has been heaped up with pure egoism. Even the words. Terms are overwhelmed by individualism. Speech—the most human of all forms of social intercourse—has thus lost its very essence and all its collective attributes.

Implicitly, in our everyday life together, we are all aware of this social drama of confusion. Nobody understands anyone. The interests of one person speak a language that the interests of another ignore or don't understand. How are they going to understand one another: the buyer and the seller, the ruled and the ruler, the poor and the rich? We all also realize that this confusion of tongues is not, cannot be, a permanent thing and that it must end as soon as possible. And for this we know that all that is lacking is one common key: justice, the great clarifier, the grand coordinator of interests.

Meanwhile the bourgeois writer continues constructing his works with the interests and selfishness peculiar to the social class from which he proceeds and for which he writes. What is in these works? What do they express? What are people called in them? What is the social content of their words? In the themes and trends of bourgeois literature there is nothing more than egoism, and of course only egoists take pleasure in making and in reading it. The work with bourgeois meaning, or that written in a bourgeois spirit, pleases no one except the bourgeois reader. When other classes of people— worker, peasant, or even bourgeoisie no longer stuck in their classbound posture—whenever they set eyes on bourgeois literature they turn away, cold, with repugnance. The play of interests which nourishes such literature speaks, certainly, a language different from, and foreign to, the common general interests of humanity. Words appear there, incomprehensible or inexpressive. The words *faith, love, liberty, good, passion, truth, sorrow, courage, harmony, work, happiness,* and *justice* lie there empty or full of ideas and sentiments different from what such words state. Even the words *life, God,* and *history* are ambiguous or hollow. Hot air and imposture dominate the theme, the context and the meaning of the work. That reader then shrinks from or boycotts this literature. This occurs, notably, with proletarian readers regarding most capitalist authors and works.

What happens then?

By the same means that the proletariat rapidly assumes the foremost place in the organization and management of the world economic process, so also it creates a universal class-consciousness for itself and, with this, its own sensibility, one capable of creating and taking in its own literature, which is to say, proletarian literature. This new literature is springing up and developing in proportions that are correlative and parallel—in extent and depth—to the international working class and to its degree of class-consciousness. And as this population today embraces nine-tenths of humanity, and as proletarian consciousness is winning over nearly half the world's workers, it happens that workers' literature is entirely dominating worldwide intellectual production. "We have something now"—the proletarian German writer Johannes Becher says, modestly— "to put up against the masterworks of bourgeois literature in the domains of poetry, the novel, and even the theatre." But Béla Illés says, more justly: "Proletarian literature is now in a position in many capitalist countries (especially Germany) of competing with bourgeois literature."

What are the most prominent signs of this surging proletarian literature? The most important is that it restores to words their universal social content, filling them out with a new collective substratum, one that is more luxuriant and pure, and endowing them with a more diaphanous, human expressiveness and eloquence. The worker, unlike the boss, aspires to the social understanding of everything, to the universal comprehension of lives and interests. His or her literature speaks, therefore, a language that would be common to all people. For the confusion of tongues in the capitalist world, the worker wishes to substitute the hope of social cooperation and justice, the language of languages. Will proletarian literature carry out this regeneration and this purification of the word, the pre-eminent and the richest form of the human instinct for solidarity?

Yes. It will achieve it. Already it is succeeding. We don't exaggerate, perhaps, in affirming that today the workers' literary production already has artistic and human values superior, in many respects, to those of bourgeois production. I say workers' production, including in this every work dominated, in one way or another, by the proletarian spirit and interests: through the theme, through its psychological context, or through the sensibility of the writer. This is how authors with diverse class origins figure in proletarian literature, authors such as Upton Sinclair, Gladkov, Selvinsky, Kirchon, Pasternak, O'Flaherty, and others, ones whose works are stamped with a sincere, definite interpretation of the world of workers.

On the other hand, what is quite significant in this regard is the attention and respect that proletarian literature awakens in the better bourgeois writers, attention and respect that are evident in the frequency with which they deal with—even if only episodically—in their recent works the life, the struggles and the revolutionary movements of the working masses. This attitude reveals two things: at times, the 'snobbism' characteristic of byzantine 'intelligences' and, at other times, the instability and vacillation characteristic of a moribund ideology.

In sum, all these considerations attest, on the one hand, to the arrival and sweeping offensive of proletarian literature and, on the other, to the defeat and rout of capitalist literature.

The crossroads of history are, it's obvious, laid out in this terrain.

DELUSIONS OF GRANDEUR, BOURGEOIS INFIRMITY

Some writers believe in infusing their works with loftiness and grandeur—speaking, in them, of the heavenly bodies and their rotations, of interatomic forces, of electrons, cosmic storms and cosmic equilibrium—though, in truth, such works aren't inspired by the least sentiment regarding those aesthetic ingredients. At the base of these works are only numbers of things, not the sentiment or creative, deeply felt notion of things.

NEW POETRY

New poetry has been defined as verses whose lexicon is made up of the words 'cinema,' 'airplane,' 'jazz-band,' 'motor,' 'radio', and, in general, every expression of contemporary science and industry; whether or not the lexicon corresponds to an authentically new sensibility is not important. What matters are the words.

But there's no getting around the fact that this is neither new poetry nor old. Nor anything. The artistic materials that modern life offers must be assimilated by the artist and transformed into sensibility. The radio, for example, is destined (more than just making us say 'radio') to awaken jittery new temperaments and more intense emotional insights, amplifying certainties and under-standing, and intensifying love. Anxiety springs up, then, and the breath of life revives. This is true culture, bringer of progress. This is its sole aesthetic meaning, not stuffing the mouth with brand-new words. Often new voices can falter. Yet, just as often the poem, without saying 'airplane,' nonetheless conveys an airborne sensation in a way that is obscure and implicit, yet effective and human. Such is truly the new poetry.

Other times, one just manages to come up with a skillful combination of these or those artistic materials, and so achieves a more or less perfect, beautiful image. Now in this case, it isn't a question of a 'new' poetry based on new words, but of a 'new' poetry based on new metaphors. But here also there is an error. In genuinely new poetry, new images can falter—perfection being a function of ingenuity, not genius—but in such poetry the creator enjoys or suffers a life in which the new relations and rhythms of things and men have become blood, cells, anything which in the end has been vitally and organically incorporated into his sensibility.

The 'new' poetry based on new words or new metaphors distinguishes itself by its pedantic novelty and by its baroque complication. The new poetry based on new sensibility is, on the contrary, simple and human, and, at first glance, might be taken for old, or not even invite speculation as to whether it is or is not modern.

ROUNDABOUT ARTISTIC FREEDOM

"I protest"—an ivory tower poet was saying to me—"the artist and writer having to submit to the yoke of any government or social class, even if they be the Soviet government and the proletarian class. The artist and writer have nothing to do with party politics or with classes. They must work at their art with absolute freedom and independence."

"Do you believe"—I argued—"that, from this perspective, at some time in history, there have been free and independent artists and writers?"

"Of course. This very day, there's Bernard Shaw, Stravinsky, Picasso, Chaplin."

"Oh? Free from what? Independent of what?"

"From the politics of Chamberlain, Stalin, Chautemps, Roosevelt. "

"Stop right there. Let's get this straight. Suppose one day Picasso paints a cubist portrait of Laval, with the Lille police making a sabre charge against the French weavers because they demand a wage increase. What would happen? I'll tell you what...in the first place, neither M. Rosenberg—Picasso's dealer—nor any other Paris art dealer would exhibit that canvas in their galleries; secondly, the 'rue de la Boétie' crowd—the 'chic,' the rich and cultured of fashionable Paris, who can afford the dearest paintings of Picasso—would become indignant and would find the subject matter and even the technique of the painting 'ridiculous,' in bad taste, gruesome and, finally, irritating, particularly as it's not even 'very interesting' (and now we know why!); thirdly, the critics from *Le Temps*, *Le Figaro*, from *Paris Midi*, etc. would hit the ceiling; and fourthly, the famous M. Chiappe's secret police would pay Picasso a visit one evening, serving him a none-too-agreeable notice. In short, the painter would lose in both his reputation and, following that, in his wallet, not to mention his being subjected to an unspoken, vicious watchfulness, which could end with the artist off in Iran somewhere. So where is his freedom? Moreover it's certain that the subject matter of this painting would not be Picasso's invention, but actually happened in July 1930 when Laval was Minister of Labor. And it's also clear, finally, that tragedies—especially when they are social—contain artistic suggestions of the highest order."

"But that's just it"—the ivory tower poet, somewhat deflated, was saying to me—"the artist mustn't meddle in politics. Picasso would never have painted such a picture and, therefore, what you say never would have happened..."

"Sure. Of course. Picasso and the other 'free' artists don't meddle in politics because it doesn't pay. They pretend not to know Zola's phrase: 'I cannot keep silent, because I don't want to be an accomplice.' It's most convenient to sit on the fence. What does it matter that these political subjects have, in themselves, extraordinary thematic grandeur? Yet just meddle in them, and goodbye to 'freedom.'"

"But Picasso, like other great artists, is far from doing this out of cowardice or egoism..."

"Now, now. It's a matter of unconscious egoism, and an equally unconscious dependency on the bourgeois class and its state."

"Suppose it's as you say. But between that and the fully conscious submission of oneself to a state and a social class—as is done, unfortunately, by Russian writers and artists—there's an abyss, and no comparison is possible."

"Of course. There's no possible comparison. While bourgeois artists and writers are subject to capitalist states and classes—based on the exploitation of the majority by a few parasites, called bosses, and on the most notorious injustice, and on the sharpening contradictions driving these systems headlong into breakdown and irremediable collapse—the Bolshevik artists and writers acquiesce spontaneously, rationally and consciously (just as I've told you) to proletarian dictatorship and to the working class and peasantry, who struggle to bring economic equality and social justice into the world, and who bear in their life-blood the health and well-being of humanity. You've bound yourself to a cart that's plunging into the abyss and there's no turning back; we've bound ourselves to one which goes on into the future. As for freedom—which is not absolute, as you conceive it, but relative—it will attain its maximum expression in socialist society, created, indeed, through proletarian revolution."

The ivory tower poet stopped coming around.

"Don't sacrifice men to stones"—Proust urges—"whose beauty comes precisely from their having, for one moment, captured human truths." (*Time Regained.* Conversation during wartime with M. Charlus regarding a church destroyed by bombers.)

REVOLUTIONARY ART, MASS ART, AND THE SPECIFIC FORM OF THE CLASS STRUGGLE

In the present social period—owing to the acuteness, the violence, and the profundity evident in the class struggle—the inherent revolutionary spirit of the artist cannot avoid having social, political and economic problems as the thematic essence of his works. Today these problems are posed throughout the entire world so fully and with such bitter anger that they irresistibly penetrate and encroach upon the life and the consciousness of the most solitary of recluses. The sensibility of the artist, perceptive and sensitive by its own definition, cannot avoid them. It is not in our hands to keep from taking part, on one side or the other, in the conflict. Therefore to say 'art' and, what is more, 'revolutionary art,' is equivalent to saying class art, art of class struggle. The revolutionary artist in art implicates the revolutionary artist in politics.

Where is one to find the revolutionary front in today's class struggle? Which social class embodies the movement, the idea and the revolutionary force of history? I assume no one would dare consider him or herself as being on the capitalist front, in the bourgeois class. The social revolution is being seeded with the blood and battles of the proletarian class, and the front which embodies that class is none other than that of the Bolsheviks, vanguard of the working masses. In this struggle the place of the revolutionary artist is, therefore, in the ranks of the proletariat, the Bolshevik ranks, among the laboring masses.

This being revolutionary art, specifically in terms of class struggle and mass art, what should be the point of departure, the form and content, the social goals of the artwork?

The strategic and tactical positions which, in the course of class struggle, the international working class adopts in accordance with the critical twists and turns imposed by momentary circumstances, must constitute the point of departure for the revolutionary artwork. In other words: the work of art must always be grounded in the most recent incident of the struggle and must start out from the day-to-day necessities and interests of this struggle. Hence the artist and writer must follow closely the directives and guidelines of the Communist Party, and keep up, hour by hour, with events.

The form of revolutionary art must be as direct, simple and spare as possible. An implacable realism. Minimum elaboration. The shortest road to the heart, at point-blank range. Art of the foreground. Phobia of halftones and shades of meaning. Everything in the rough—angles and no curves, yet heavy, barbarous, brutal, as in the trenches.

The content of the artwork must be a content of the masses. The stifled aspirations, the turbulence, the common fury, the frailties and the driving thrusts, the lights and shadows of class consciousness, the back-and-forth swaying of individuals within the multitudes, the frustrated potential and the heroism, the triumphs and the vigils, the ups and downs, the experiences and lessons of every working day— in short, all the shapes, gaps, flaws, hits and misses of the masses in their revolutionary struggles. To this end, it is necessary to create and develop throughout the proletarian ranks a vast network of organizations and contacts involving revolutionary art—such as, among others, the factory and farm correspondents, the workers' control within the national sections of the U.I.R.E., and in the organs of the press and the revolutionary publishing houses, the peasants' and workers' reading circles, the 'Blue Shirts' theatre group, the critiques of the masses, the workers' clubs, the fairs for proletarian and peasant artisans, the roving academies, the artists' and writers' brigades in workers' organizations, in the trenches of the civil wars, etc., etc.

The concrete and immediate ends of revolutionary art will vary according to the changing needs of the moment. One must bear in mind that the audience for this art is multiple: the masses who still are not yet radicalized and who fall into line in the ranks of Fascism or AnarchoSyndicalism or even the parties of the bourgeois left; the masses without class consciousness; the masses already radicalized and Bolshevik; and, lastly, the petty bourgeoisie and the bourgeoisie itself. In this field of action one has to employ tactics which are shrewd, skillful, sharp and flexible, since the practical objective of the artistic or literary work depends on the means used with regard to each audience, and on the needs of the moment. For instance, in dealing with the bourgeoisie in general, the revolutionary end is realized either by attacking it to the death or by winning it over. The 'fellow travelers'—of whom Romain Rolland speaks—cannot be aroused or won over except on grounds that are straightforward and cordial. And we know already what a great service these liberal or sympathetic artists and intellectuals bring to the revolutionary movement, when, as in many cases, they have not completed being radicalized or even proletarianized. And lastly, we know that the majority of the members belonging to the 'International Union of Revolutionary Writers' are at present, 'fellow travelers.'

FROM THE NOTEBOOKS

from 1929-1930 [the green notebook]
What ideas will those bourgeois intellectuals develop? They believe that their country represents humanity, and that human virtues dwell solely in their kings and presidents. Their brains must be really strange. It would be interesting to analyze their works in relation to social reality, which is shaped not only by the bourgeoisie, but, above all, by the proletariat. It's not that they don't have class consciousness, but that their eyes see only their own class, never the working class. Larrea also sees the world through his bourgeois lenses and in this way judges history.[2]

How can one speak of spiritual liberation while not having made material and social revolution, and while living in the material and moral atmosphere of bourgeois productive forces and economic relations?

The intellectuals are rebels, but not revolutionaries.

Humanity, suddenly finding itself facing a problem (the worker) containing all other human problems (moral, artistic, etc.), scares itself, being able to solve that problem, through reason and conscience, only on pain of renouncing its bourgeois class rights. It is then that bourgeois thought sneaks away from reason and consciousness into the unconscious, into parapsychology and the Freudian libido. And all because it doesn't have the courage to utilize its reason justly in the solution of the great problem of the worker, which will bring about the solution of all other universal problems.

Everything comes down to knowing: at the moment, what is the greatest and most acute problem? Without doubt, it is the social problem, the worker. Why don't the intellectuals solve it?

Politics penetrates everything now. It is everywhere. Hence the intellectuals meddle in it and no longer continue in indifference as before. For there has always been injustice and the worker has starved to death, and they have let it go. And nobody said a thing. But today political consciousness is on the increase, is showing through.

from 1932
The most eloquent image of social solidarity is the sight of several
workers lifting a great stone.

from 1934
Breton recovers the human in Rimbaud as much as he does the
revolutionary. Breton believes that adherence to a revolutionary
party does not necessarily make the work of an artist revolutionary.
The opposite of Mayakovsky.

It's not necessary to deceive people by saying that the only thing [that
matters] in the work of art is economics. No. It must be said clearly
that the content of a work of art is multiple—economic, moral,
emotional, etc.—but that in these times it's necessary to *insist* above
all on the economic—because here lies the whole solution to the
problem of humanity.

from 1936-1937(38?)
Gide hopes that the revolution doesn't end simply with the
disappearance of misery. "If it ended like that"—he says—"it
wouldn't be much. The revolution must conclude by giving great joy
to humanity."

Gide is wrong. The revolution must end not only with great rejoicing,
but with one great humanity made up of *joy, but also of sorrow and
all the rest.* What's happening is that Gide, who is rich, is ignorant,
not knowing what a great source of superior humanity freedom from
hunger is.

Translated by Richard Schaaf

CESAR VALLEJO was born in Peru in 1892 and died in Paris in 1938. He is considered—along with Pablo Neruda—to be one of the most important twentieth century revolutionary poets of the Americas.

Notes:
1. Add that Aragon and Eluard remain communists. [C V]
2. Juan Larrea, Spanish writer and critic associated with the Cubists, later served as a relief official during the Civil War in Spain. In the early 20's he and Vallejo, coedited a short-lived literary journal.

VLADIMIR MAYAKOVSKY
How To Make Verse

PREFACE
by James Scully

ORGANIZING MAYAKOVSKY'S POETRY

Mayakovsky was born in the Caucasus in 1893. By 1905, at the age of 12, he was joining with other students in singing Georgian revolutionary songs during demonstrations. Two years later, after his father had died, Mayakovsky and his mother moved to Moscow. In 1908 he joined the Bolsheviks, began studying Marxist literature, and disseminated propaganda among bakers, shoemakers and printers. He was 15. Between March 1908 and July 1909 he was arrested three times, spending a total of 11 months in prison. There he read "the so called great" authors, such as Shakespeare, Byron and Tolstoy. He also began to write poetry. Along with an interest in literature, he had contracted an acute sense of the exclusions of the classical canon:

> I spit on the fact
> that neither Homer nor Ovid
> invented characters like us,
> pockmarked with soot.

> (from "A Cloud in Trousers,"
> Hayward and Reavey, trans.)

He described "great literature," actually the literature produced by ruling castes and classes, as an avalanche burying him and his kind.

In 1912 he became involved with the emerging Russian Futurism. Although avant-garde and nihilist (their slogan was "Burn Raphael"), these Futurists, in marked contrast to those in Italy, proposed a parallel between their opposition to traditional art and the rejection of traditional bourgeois society by a revolutionary proletariat. The parallel was fanciful, however. As Trotsky put it: "Futurism proclaims

52

the revolution in Moscow cafés, but not at all in the factories." Besides, few workers knew much of the old, traditional artistic culture that was under attack; they had had no access to it. Nonetheless the Futurists shared enemies with the workers and with some of the peasants. Mayakovsky's brand of Futurism was meant to speak for those who had been silenced: the tongueless street.

> Upon every achievement
> I stamp nihil.
>
> I never want
> to read anything.
> Books?
> What are books!
>
> Formerly I believed
> books were made like this:
> a poet came,
> lightly opened his lips,
> and the inspired fool burst into song—
> if you please!
> But it seems,
> before they can launch a song,
> poets must tramp for days with calloused feet,
> and the sluggish fish of the imagination
> flounders softly in the slush of the heart.
> And while, with twittering rhymes, they boil a broth
> of loves and nightingales,
> the tongueless street merely writhes
> for lack of something to shout or say.

> (from "A Cloud in Trousers")

By the spring of 1919, Mayakovsky was putting his art at the service of the Soviet government. From October 1920 to February 1922, he worked for ROSTA, the Russian Telegraphic Agency, where he made 2000 drawings and 280 posters, many with jingles and slogans, pertaining to various national and international events. From 1923 to 1925, during the period of the NEP (New Economic Policy), along with Rodchenko, he designed advertisements—for instance, for the GUM department store. Such was his way of 'forsaking trifles' (see the poem "Order #2 to the Army of the Arts"). For this he was criticized from both right and left. The avant-garde accused him of selling out, while Lenin dismissed Mayakovsky's bolshevized Futurism as "hooligan communism."

In 1923, returning from Berlin where he had met George Grosz and John Heartfield, Mayakovsky with other Futurists founded the magazine LEF, the Left Front of the Arts. The second issue had as its cover one of the first Russian experiments in photomontage. As might be expected of a group and a publication that considered literature to be "a craft not basically different from other socially useful occupations" (see Edward J. Brown, *Russian Literature Since The Revolution*), LEF graphics had a Constructivist basis. According to Mayakovsky, "one of the slogans...also, one of the big achievements of LEF—is the de-aestheticizing of the productive arts, i.e., constructivism."

LEF was not only a magazine. It was an organization whose members proposed to write for the masses. Their program:

1) To aid in the discovery of a Communist path for all varieties of art.

2) To re-examine the theory and practice of so-called 'left' art, freeing it from individualistic distortions and developing its valuable Communist aspects.

3) To struggle with decadence and aesthetic mysticism, as well as with self-contained formalism, indifferent naturalism, and for the affirmation of tendentious realism, based on the use of the technical devices developed in all the revolutionary schools of art.

Correcting a Futurist oversight, Mayakovsky and LEF realized that the revolution had produced from "the semi-literate masses" a new audience whose objective needs called for a new art. From this came the concept of 'the social command.' Artists who observed the social command produced what that new audience needed. As Dave Laing puts it in *The Marxist Theory Of Art*, "The social command...is envisaged by Mayakovsky as the artistic equivalent of the scientific socialist politics exemplified by Lenin, an intervention of the artist into social reality...The social command sums up the external relations and determinants of the production of the poem." As Laing indicates, *How To Make Verse*, which is also a polemical response to textbooks written by various pedants and hacks to instruct workers and peasants in the art of poetry, may itself be the clearest exposition of the meaning and practice of the "social command."

LEF folded in 1925. Only seven issues had been published. It was revived in 1927 as NOVY LEF, or NEW LEF, but a year later this too came to an end. The new version of LEF stressed even more that art was a socially useful skill that could be learned. In addition, NEW LEF determined that "the concern of the writer should be with facts, rather than with his own invention or fantasy." The fixation of objective fact was to be required of him rather than the creation of artistic wholes, which tend to 'destroy or disfigure the fact,' in accordance with subjective purpose."(Brown, op. cit.)

Later, responding to criticism from the left (to the effect that a purely documentary literature is passive, even static, and does little to further the revolutionary process), Mayakovsky and his colleagues disbanded LEF and in 1929 founded REF, the Revolutionary Front of Art. REF was to represent the struggle against 'apolitical tendencies,' a rejection of art-as-documentation and a move toward tenden-tiousness.

Finally in 1930, under duress, Mayakovsky joined RAPP, the Russian Association of Proletarian Writers. RAPP had developed from VAPP, the All-Union Association of Proletarian Writers, which itself went back to the Proletkult. Because the organizational lineage of RAPP was one with which Mayakovsky and his organizations had been in almost unbroken competition, his decision to join was momentous. Neither line—that of the intensely working class oriented Proletkult, nor that of Mayakovsky and his engaged Futurists—had been approved by Lenin. But now, at the beginning of the '30s, the Proletkult-informed RAPP had become the official majority organization. Many of its assumptions, not all, coincided with those of Mayakovsky. It considered art as a class weapon, but went further in defining writers as shock workers in art brigades. RAPP also insisted on complete rejection of bourgeois culture (putting it to the left of the position Lenin had taken) and aimed to organize working-class ideas and feelings toward collectivist rather than individualist goals. Ironically, two years later, the rightward-moving government would disband RAPP, accusing it of "communist conceit." At a time when the USSR was promoting nationalism at home, yet trying to gain the support of non-communist allies, especially in the struggle against fascism, RAPP was judged to be too internationalist (it's one thing to be working-class internationalist, as RAPP supposed itself to be, but quite another to promote an alliance of nationalisms, or to propose the anomaly of a socialist nationalism) and too sectarian. But that came about after Mayakovsky's suicide on April 14, 1930.

Mayakovsky was a poet who could write:
I want
the heart to earn
its love wage
   at a specialist's rate...
I want
   the factory committee
      to lock
my lips
   when the work is done...
I want
   the pen to be on a par
      with the bayonet;
and Stalin
     to deliver his Politbureau
reports
   about verse in the making
as he would about pig iron
     and the smelting of steel.

       (from "Back Home!", 1925)

He wasn't kidding. Nor being ironic, nor saying something he was forced to say. He wanted verse to be a recognized, integral part of the production process, not a superstructural appendage. The production of verse should be as important as the production of pig iron. His ambition, which sounds outlandish in the context of our own stunted cultural development, was to have "the understanding of verse" in the USSR top "the pre-war norm."

In "At the Top of My Voice" (January 1930), a colloquy with comrades of the communist future, Mayakovsky makes the case for his own political good faith, contrasting his commitment with that of careerists who, unlike him, may have had a Communist Party membership card, but had no appreciation of what communist commitment entails:

When I appear
>before the CCC*
>>of the coming
>>>bright years,
by way of my Bolshevik party card,
>>I'll raise
above the heads
>of a gang of self-seeking
>>poets and rogues
all the hundred volumes
>of my
>communist-committed books.

*Central Control Commission of the CP.

HOW TO MAKE VERSE

I.

I have to write on this subject

In the course of various literary discussions, in conversation with young workers from various productive literary associations (RAP [2], TAP, PAP, etc.), in giving short shrift to the critics I often had, if not to destroy, at least to discredit the old poetics. The old poetry itself, which was blameless, was of course left almost intact. It drew fire only when spirited defenders of old junk hid themselves from the new art behind the backsides of monuments.

On the contrary—pulling down the monuments, breaking them up and overturning them, we showed the Great to the readers from a totally unexplored and unknown point of view.

Children (like young literary schools) are always interested in what is inside a cardboard horse. After the work done by the Formalists[3], the insides of paper horses and elephants are clearly visible. And if the horses have got a bit damaged in the process—sorry! There is no need to quarrel with the poetry of the past, to us it is material for study.

Our chief and unrelenting hatred comes crashing down on the sentimental-critical philistines: on those who see all the greatness of poetry of the past in the fact that they, too, have loved, as Onegin loved Tatyana[4] (souls in harmony!), because they too have an understanding of the poets (they learned them at school!), because iambics caress their ears. We abhor this foolish pandemonium because it creates around the difficult and important craft of poetry an atmosphere of sexual transport and swooning, of belief that immortal poetry alone is not undermined by dialectics and that the only method of production is an inspired throwing back of the head while waiting for the poetry-spirit to descend on one's bald pate in the guise of a dove, a peacock, or an ostrich.

It isn't hard to expose these gentlemen.

It's enough to compare Tatyana's love and "the science sung by Ovid" with the draft marriage laws, to read about Pushkin's "disenchanted lorgnette" to Donetz miners, or to run in front of the column in the May Day parade yelling: "My uncle is of most honest principles!"[5]

It is hardly likely that after such an experiment any youngster burning to dedicate his energies to the revolution would feel a genuine desire to take up the ancient craft of poetry.

Much has been written and said about this. The tumultuous approval of the audience has always been on our side. But straight after this approval skeptical voices were heard:

—You only destroy, and you create NOTHING! Old textbooks are bad, but where are the new ones? Give us the RULES of your poetics! Give us textbooks!

The excuse that the old poetics has existed for fifteen hundred years, and ours for only thirty, is of little help.

You want to write and you want to know how to do it? Why is a work written according to Shengeli's rules[6] with exact rhymes, iambics and trochees, not accepted as poetry? You have the right to demand that poets should not take the secrets of their craft to their graves.

I want to write about my craft not as a dogmatist but as a practitioner. My article has no scholarly value whatsoever. I am writing about my work, which, according to my observations and convictions, differs very little on the whole from the work of other professional poets.

Once again I must make a very definite reservation: I am not giving any *rules* which will make a man into a poet and enable him to write poetry. Such rules do not exist. The poet is precisely a man who creates these poetic rules for himself.

For the hundredth time I quote my tiresome example and analogy.

A mathematician is a man who creates, amplifies and develops mathematical rules, a man who contributes something to mathematical knowledge. The man who first formulated "two and two make four" was a great mathematician even if he arrived at that truth by adding two cigarette butts to two more cigarette butts. All those who followed, even if they added much larger things together, for example, a railway engine and another railway engine, are not mathematicians. This assertion in no way detracts from the labor of the man adding up the engines. When transportation is disrupted, his labor may be hundreds of times more valuable than the naked arithmetical truth. But one should not send the accounts for railway engine repairs to a mathematical society and demand that they be considered on the same level as Lobachevsky's geometry. This would enrage the planning commission, puzzle the mathematicians and stump the traffic controllers.

They'll tell me that I am battering my way through a door which is already wide open, that all this is obvious. Nothing of the kind.

Eighty percent of the rhymed trash printed by our publishing houses is printed either because the editors have no understanding of the poetry of the past, or because they don't know what poetry is for.

The editors only know what "I like" or what "I don't like," forgetting that taste, too, can and should be developed. Almost all editors have complained to me that they don't know how to return poetry manuscripts, or what to say when they do.

A competent editor should say to the poet: "Your verses are quite correct, they have been constructed according to the third edition of M. Brodovsky's manual of poetry writing[7] (or Shengeli's, or Grech's,[8] etc., etc.), all your rhymes are well-tried rhymes, long included in the complete dictionary of Russian rhymes by N. Abramov[9]. Since at present I have no good new verse, I shall willingly take yours, paying what we pay a qualified copyist, three rubles a signature, provided you submit three copies."

The poet will have no recourse. Either he has to give up writing poetry, or he has to approach poetry as a craft which demands more effort. At any rate, the poet will stop turning up his nose at the reporter who, for his three rubles per item, does at least report new events. The reporter wears out his pants while following up scandals and fires, while the poet of this kind expends nothing more than saliva—to turn the pages.

For the sake of raising the qualifications of poets and for the sake of the future flowering of poetry, one must stop isolating this easiest of crafts from other types of human labor.

A reservation: the formulation of rules is not in itself the aim of poetry, otherwise the poet could degenerate into a pedant drawing up rules for nonexistent or unnecessary things and situations. For example, it is futile to think up rules for counting stars while racing along on a bicycle.

Situations requiring formulation, requiring RULES, are created by life itself. The methods of formulation and the purpose of the rules are determined by class and by the demands of our struggle.

For example, the Revolution threw out into the street the uncouth speech of millions, the slang of the suburbs flowed along central thoroughfares; the enfeebled language of the intelligentsia with its emasculated words: "ideal," "principles of justice," "divine origin," "transcendental image of Christ and Anti-Christ"—all of these whispered restaurant conversations—have been trampled. This is the new element of language. How can it be made poetic? The old rules with their "moons and Junes" and their alexandrines won't do. But how can one introduce everyday speech into poetry and how can one eliminate poetry from everyday speech?

Should one damn the Revolution for the sake of iambs?

> We've become evil and reconciled,
> We can't get away.
> The Railway Board has already separated
> The tracks with its black hands.[10]
> (Z. Gippius)

No!

It's a hopeless task to try to pack the explosive thunder of the Revolution into a four-foot amphibrach designed for whispering!

> Heroes, wanderers of the oceans, albatrosses,
> Table guests at thunderous banquets,
> Tribe of eagles, sailors and sailors,
> To you a fiery song of ruby words.
> —from "To the Sailors" by V. T. Kirillov[11]

No!

Let's give all the rights of citizenship to the new language immediately: to a shout instead of a melody, to a thundering drum instead of a lullaby:

> Keep the revolutionary step![12]
> (Blok)

> Deploy on the march![13]
> (Mayakovsky)

It is not enough to give examples of the new verse, of rules for acting upon revolutionary crowds by the use of words; it is necessary that this action should aim at maximum support for one's class.

It is not enough to say that the "untiring enemy is always alert."[14]

It is necessary to show exactly what the enemy looks like, or at least give an unmistakable impression of him.

It is not enough to deploy on the march. It is necessary to deploy according to all the rules of street fighting, so that the telegraph office, the banks, the ammunition depots fall into the hands of the insurgent workers:

> Gobble your pineapple,
> Chew at your grouse,
> Your last day is coming, you bourgeois louse...
> —"Gobble Your Pineapple" by V. Mayakovsky

It is hardly likely that this sort of verse would have been acceptable in classical poetry. Writing in 1820, Grech knew nothing about *chastushki*,[15] but even if he had, he would probably have written about them in the same vein that he wrote about folk verse—that is, scornfully: "These verses know neither meter nor harmony."

Yet the streets of Petersburg have taken these lines to heart. The critics can try to discover at their leisure the basic rules according to which all this was done.

Novelty is obligatory in a poetic work. The material of words and word-combinations that the poet comes across must be reworked. If, for the making of verse, old scraps of words are used, they must be in strict correlation with the quantity of new material. Whether or not this alloy is fit for use will depend on the quantity and quality of this new element.

Novelty in no way presupposes the constant uttering of unprecedented truths. Iambs, free verse, alliteration, assonance are not created every day. It is also possible to work at extending, deepening and widening their usage.

"Two twos are four" does not exist on its own and cannot do so. We must know how to apply this fact (rules of application). We must make this fact easy to remember (rules again) and we must show its infallibility in a number of cases (example, content, theme).

It is clear from this that description, the representation of reality, has no independent place in poetry. This kind of work is needed but it should be rated on a par with the work of the secretary of a vast assembly. It is the simple "proposal put; decision taken." In this lies the tragedy of the fellow-travelers:[16] it not only takes them five years to become aware of the proposal, but their decision is also rather belated—after all, the others have carried it out!

Poetry begins with tendentiousness.

In my opinion the poem "I go out alone into the road..." is an incitement to get girls to walk with poets. It's dull on one's own, you see. Oh, if only such a powerful poem were to be written urging people to combine in cooperatives!

The old manuals for writing verse were definitely nothing of the kind. They were only descriptions of historical, traditional ways of writing. The correct title for these books should not be "How to write," but "How they used to write."

I'll be honest about it. I know neither iambs nor trochees, I never could make them out and never will. Not because it is a difficult task, but because in my poetic work I never had anything to do with things like that. And even if bits of such meters did crop up, they were simply something heard and written down, because these tedious rhythms recur much too often—like: "Down the mother-river Volga."

Many a time I took up the study of these things, understood the mechanics of them, and then forgot them. Such things, which take up ninety percent of the poetry manuals, take up less than three percent of my practical work!

In practice, there are only a few general rules for beginning a work of poetry. And even so those rules are pure convention. As in chess. The first moves are almost monotonous. But with the next move one is already beginning to plan a new attack. The most brilliant move cannot be repeated in any given situation in the next game. It is the unexpected move that confounds an opponent.

Just like the unexpected rhymes in verse.

What then are the fundamental requirements for beginning poetic labor?

First. The presence in society of a problem which can only conceivably be solved through a work of poetry. A social command.[17] (An interesting theme for a special work would be the disparity between a social command and a real action.)

Second. An exact knowledge of, or more precisely, an exact sense of the wishes of one's class (or the group one represents) in this matter, that is, pragmatic orientation.

Third. Material. Words. The constant restocking of the storehouses, the granaries of your mind, with all kinds of words, necessary, expressive, rare, invented, renovated, manufactured, and others.

Fourth. Equipment. The business equipment and tools of the trade. Pen, pencil, typewriter, telephone, a suit for visits to the doss-house, a bicycle for riding to editorial offices, a well-arranged table, an umbrella to write under in the rain, living space which allows the particular number of strides necessary to one's work, a connection with a clipping agency to send you information about matters causing concern in the provinces, and so on and so forth, and even a pipe and cigarettes.

Fifth. The skills and methods for processing words, infinitely personal, achieved only after years of daily toil: rhymes, meters, alliterations, images, an inelegant style, pathos, endings, titles, outlines, etc. etc.

For example: social task: providing words for songs of the Red Army men going to the Petersburg front. Pragmatic orientation: to defeat Yudenich. Material: words from the soldier's vocabulary. Tools of the trade: a chewed-up pencil stump. Method: rhymed chastushka. Result:

> My lass gave me a long felt cloak
> and a pair of socks of woolen twine.
> Yudenich[18] bolts from Petersburg,
> like he was oiled with turpentine.

The novelty of these four lines, which justifies the making of this chastushka, is in the rhyming of "woolen twine" and "turpentine." This novelty makes it relevant, poetic and a model of its genre.

For its impact, the chastushka needs the device of rhyme involving total disparity between the first two lines and the second two. Moreover, the first two lines can be called subsidiary.

Even these general elementary rules for poetic labor will provide more possibilities than there are now for evaluating and describing poetic works.

Features of the material, of the equipment, and of the method can be directly taken into account.

Is there a social command? Yes. Two units. Pragmatic orientation? Two units. Is it rhymed? One more unit. Alliteration? Another half a unit. And for rhythm—one unit, because the peculiar meter required journeys by bus.

Critics may smile, but I would rate the verse of an Alaskan poet (given the same ability, of course) higher than, say, the verse of a man from Yalta.

Indeed I would! The Alaskan has to freeze and spend money on buying a fur coat, and the ink in his fountain pen keeps freezing. Whereas the Yalta man writes against a background of palm trees in a spot which is pleasant even without verse.

The same clarity is also introduced into the description of works.

Demyan Bedny's[19] verse represents a correctly understood social command for today, a precise pragmatic orientation—the needs of the workers and peasants, a vocabulary of semi-peasant usage (with an admixture of obsolescent poetic rhymes) and the device of the fable.

The verse of Kruchenykh:[20] alliteration, dissonance, pragmatic orientation—helping future poets.

Here there is no need to concern ourselves with the metaphysical question as to who is better: Demyan Bedny or Kruchenykh. These are poetic works made from different components, on different levels, and each of them can exist without supplanting the other and without competing.

From my point of view, the best poetic work will be that which is written according to the social command of the Comintern, with its aim—the victory of the proletariat—communicated in a new vocabulary, expressive and comprehensible to everyone, made on a table equipped by N.O.T.[21] and delivered to the publishing office by airplane. I insist—by airplane, since the poet's way of life is also one of the most important factors of our industry. Of course, the process of accounting and discounting in poetry is considerably more delicate and complicated than I have shown.

I deliberately emphasize, simplify and caricature my ideas. I emphasize them in order to highlight more sharply the fact that the essence of contemporary works on literature lies not in the evaluation of certain ready-made works from the point of view of taste, but in a correct approach towards the study of the productive process itself.

The present article is not a discussion about ready-made models or methods, but an attempt to reveal the very process of poetic production.

How, then, is verse made?

Work begins long before one receives and becomes aware of the social command.

Preliminary work goes on continuously.

A good poetic work can be made to a deadline only if one has a large reserve of ready poetic stock. Now, for example (I am only writing about what occurs to me at the moment), a good surname, "Mr. Gliceron," derived accidentally from some garbled talk about glycerine, throbs in my brain.

There are also good rhymes:

>(And in the sky the color of) cream
>(Arose the austere) Kremlin
>(God to Rome, to the French) to the Germans,
>(There seek shelter for) Bohemians.
>(To the sound of the horse's) snort
>(One day I'll ride all the way to) New York.
>New York's
>A morgue.

Or:

>(Rich and) raucous
>(Are the days and nights) of August

I also like the meter of a certain American song, still requiring alteration and Russification:

>Hard-hearted Hannah
>The vamp of Savannah
>The vamp of Savannah
>Gee-ay.

There are also well-tailored alliterations suggested by the surname "Nita Jo" glimpsed on a poster:

>Where's the joint of Nita Jo?
>Nita's joint is just below.

Or in connection with the dye-works of Lyamina:

>Mummy's job needs lots of stamina—
>Mummy's name is Mrs. Lyamina.

There are themes of varying clarity and obscurity:

(1) Rain in New York.

(2) A prostitute on the Boulevard des Capucines in Paris. A prostitute with whom it is particularly smart to go to bed because she is one-legged, the other having been cut off, it seems, by a tram.

(3) An old male attendant at the lavatory in a huge Hessler restaurant in Berlin.

(4) The vast theme of the October Revolution, which one cannot complete without spending some time in the country, etc., etc.

All these items of poetic stock are stored in my mind. The particularly difficult ones are written down.

How they are to be used in the future I don't know, but I do know that everything will be used.

All my time goes into this storing. I spend between ten and eighteen hours a day on it, and keep muttering something almost incessantly. Concentration on this explains the proverbial absent-mindedness of poets.

For me this labor of storing is done with such intensity that in ninety cases out of a hundred I even know the place where, during my fifteen years of work, certain rhymes or alliterations, images, etc., came to me and took final shape:

Astride.
Ride as...(On the tram-ride from Sukhareva Tower to Sretensky Gates, 1913).

The sullen rain screwed up its eye.
It sighed...(Strastnoy Monastery, 1912).

Caress the wasted soot-black cats. (The oak in Kuntsevo, 1914).

Bereft.
Left. (In a cab on the Embankment, 1917).

Son of a bitch, d'Anthès. (On a train near Mytishchi, 1924).

Etc., etc.

This "notebook" is one of the main requirements for the making of an AUTHENTIC work.

People usually write about this notebook only after the death of the writer. For years it lies about amid rubbish, it gets printed posthumously and after "the finished works"; but for the writer this book is everything.

Naturally, beginners have no such book, just as they have no practice and experience. MANUFACTURED lines are rare, and therefore their poems are thin and long-winded.

Whatever his abilities, a beginner cannot write an impressive work straight away; on the other hand, the first work is always "fresher" because it embodies the poetic stock from the whole of his past life.

It is only the presence of well-thought-out poetic stock that enables me to finish a work, because, when I work hard, my normal production is eight to ten lines per day.

Whatever the circumstances, a poet values each meeting, each signboard, each event solely as material to be formed into words.

I used to get so stuck into this work that I was even afraid to utter words and expressions which seemed to me likely to be needed for future verse; I used to become sullen, boring, and taciturn.

About 1913, returning from Saratov to Moscow, I said to a woman traveling in the same carriage, in order to prove my respectability, that I was "not a man, but a cloud in trousers."[22] Having said this, I realized at once that it might come in handy for a poem and what if it were spread by word of mouth and wasted to no purpose? Terribly anxious, I spent half an hour plying the girl with leading questions and was only reassured when I satisfied myself that my words had gone in one ear and out the other.

Two years later, "a cloud in trousers" came in handy as the title for a whole long poem.

I spent two days thinking about words for the tenderness of a lonely man towards his only love.

How would he cherish and love her?

On the third night I went to bed with a headache, not having thought of anything. In the night the definition came:

> Your body
> I shall cherish and love,
> as a soldier maimed by war,
> unneeded, nobody's,
> cherishes his one remaining leg.

I jumped up, half-awake. In the dark I wrote down "one remaining leg" on a cigarette pack, using a burned match, and I went back to sleep. In the morning I spent two hours wondering what this "one remaining leg" jotted on the cigarette pack meant and how it could have gotten there.

A rhyme which can almost, but not quite, be pinned down poisons one's existence: you talk without understanding, you eat without appetite and you cannot sleep, almost seeing the rhyme floating before your eyes.

Following the trend started by Shengeli, we began to treat the labor of the poet as a mere trifle. There are even smart lads who have improved on the professor. Here, for example, is one of the advertisements from the Kharkov "Proletarian" (No. 256):

> "How to become a writer.
> For details send 50 kopeks in stamps to Slavyansk
> Station, Donetz Railway, P. O. Box No. 11."

How do you like that!

However, this is a pre-revolutionary product. Already, as a supplement to the periodical *Entertainment,* a booklet has been sent out, and it's called "How to Become a Poet in Five Lessons."

I think that even my small examples place poetry among the most difficult tasks, which indeed it is.

One's attitude to a line should be like one's attitude to a woman—as in Pasternak's brilliant quatrain:

> That day, like some provincial actor
> in a Shakespearean play, I roamed the town
> lugging you with me, rehearsing you
> and I knew you by heart from combs to toes.[23]

In the next chapter I shall try to show the development of these preliminary requirements for making verse, using the writing of one of my own poems as a concrete example.

69

II.

My most effective piece of recent verse is, I think, "To Sergei Esenin."[24] For this poem there was no need to look for either a magazine or an editor—it was copied by hand before it was printed, it was secretly sneaked out of the composing room and printed in a provincial paper; the audience itself demanded to hear it, and while it was being read you could have heard a pin drop; after the reading people shook my paws, they raved in the corridors and praised it to the skies, and on the day of its publication a review appeared consisting at once of curses and compliments.

How was this poem worked out?

I had known Esenin for a long time—about ten or twelve years. When I met him for the first time he was wearing bast shoes and a peasant's shirt with some kind of cross-stitch embroidery. The meeting took place in one of the better apartments in Leningrad. Knowing how gladly a real, as opposed to a stage, peasant changes his garb for shoes and jacket, I did not trust Esenin. He appeared to me theatrical, like a character from an operetta. Even more so because he was already writing appealing verse and clearly could have found the money to buy a pair of boots.

As a man who, in his time, had worn and discarded the yellow blouse,[25] I inquired in a businesslike manner about his clothes:

"What's this? Publicity?"

Esenin answered me in a voice like icon-lamp oil brought to life. Something like:

"We're village folk...we don't understand these ways of yours...we get by somehow...in our homemade old things..."

His very capable and very rustic verse was inimical, of course, to us Futurists. But he was still a funny and endearing fellow.

On leaving I said to him in passing:

"I bet you'll soon drop all these bast shoes and this folksy embroidery!"

Esenin objected with passionate conviction. Klyuev[26] led him aside, like a mother leading away a daughter whose virtue is endangered because she fears the girl won't have the strength or will to resist.

I caught sight of Esenin now and then, but it was only after the Revolution that we came face to face at Gorky's[27] house.

With all my innate tactlessness I yelled at him at once: "Pay up, Esenin, you're wearing a jacket and tie!"

Esenin got mad and started to pick a quarrel. Later I began to come across lines and poems by him which one couldn't help but like, such as:

My dear, dear funny fool...etc.[28]

The sky a bell, the moon its tongue...

And others.

Esenin was freeing himself from his idealized rusticity, but not, of course, without lapses, and side by side with: "My mother is my Motherland, / A Bolshevik is what I am..."[29] there appeared an apologia for "a cow." Instead of a "monument to Marx" there was a compulsive need for a monument to a cow. Not to a dairy cow, but to a symbolic cow, a cow thrusting its horns against a railway engine. We often had rows with Esenin, blaming him mainly for the Imagism which grew around him like dank undergrowth.

Then Esenin left for America[30] and other places, returning with a marked enthusiasm for things new.

Unfortunately, during this period we came across him more often in police records than in poetry. Quickly and surely he was breaking away from the ranks of healthy workers in poetry (I speak of the minimum which is demanded of a poet).

At this time I met Esenin on several occasions; our meetings were elegiac and without the slightest disagreement.

I watched with pleasure Esenin's evolution from Imagism to VAPP.[31] He spoke with interest of other people's verse. There was a new side to the conceited element in Esenin; he felt a certain envy toward all the poets organically welded to the Revolution and to the workers, who saw a great and optimistic road ahead.

This is, I think, the root of Esenin's poetic touchiness and his self-dissatisfaction, while his excessive drinking and the harsh and clumsy attitudes to those around him did not help matters.

Toward the end Esenin even showed some obvious sympathy for us (members of LEF[32]): he called on Assev,[33] rang me up at times, and contrived to run into us.

He became a little soft and flabby, but remained elegant in his own Esenin way.

Our last meeting made a painful and profound impression on me. At the cashier's desk of the State Publishing House I met a man who rushed towards me, his face swollen, his tie askew, his hat precariously held in place by a lock of fair hair. He and his two sinister companions (at least from my point of view) reeked of alcohol. I literally had difficulty recognizing Esenin. With difficulty I evaded his immediate desire to drink, which he reinforced by waving a thick wad of ten-ruble notes. All day I kept recalling how he looked sick, and that evening I argued with my friends at length that something should be done about him (unfortunately, such matters never go beyond this). Both they and I blamed his "milieu," and we parted convinced that Esenin was being cared for by his friends—the Esenin crowd.

It turned out differently. Esenin's end saddened us with the sadness common to all humanity. But this end immediately appeared completely natural and logical. I heard about it in the night, and my sadness would have probably remained sadness and abated towards morning had not the morning papers carried his last lines:

> In this life there's nothing new in dying,
> But in living there is nothing newer.[34]

After these lines, Esenin's death became a fact of literature.
It immediately became clear how many unstable people this powerful poem, precisely a poem, VERSE, would bring to the noose and the revolver.

And no newspaper analyses or articles could ever erase this poem.

One can and should counter this poem with a poem, and NOTHING BUT A POEM, verse.

Thus the poets of the USSR were given a social command to write verse about Esenin. An exceptional command, important and urgent, because Esenin's lines began to take effect quickly and unerringly. Many accepted the command. But write what? How?

There appeared verse, articles, reminiscences, literary sketches, and even plays. In my opinion ninety-nine percent of what was written about Esenin was either simply claptrap, or else damaging claptrap.

The verses written by Esenin's friends are trivial. You can always recognize them by the way they address Esenin familiarly as "Seryozha" (this is where Bezymensky[35] found this unsuitable word). "Seryozha" as a literary fact does not exist. There is a poet—Sergei Esenin. And as such we ask you to speak of him. Introducing the familiar "Seryozha" immediately disrupts the social command and overall design. The word "Seryozha" reduces a grave and important theme to the level of an epigram or a lyric. And no amount of weeping by his poetic kinsmen will help. Poetically these verses cannot impress. They provoke laughter and irritation.

Although Esenin's "enemies" were placated by his death, their verses are pious humbug. They simply refuse him a poetic burial because of the very fact of his suicide:

> We never thought that even you could be
> Such a wicked hooligan as this...[36]
> (Zharov, I think)

These are the verses of those who hastily fulfill a poorly understood social command, the pragmatic orientation of which is entirely unconnected with the method, and of those who adopt a feuilleton style which is totally ineffective in this tragic instance.

Torn out of its complicated social and psychological circumstances, Esenin's suicide with its unmotivated moment of negation (what else could it be?!) is depressing in its falsity.

The prose written about Esenin is of little help in fighting against the harmfulness of his last poem.

Let's start with Kogan,[37] who in my opinion tried to deduce Marxism on his own, not from studying Marx, but from Luka's dictum: "Fleas are not so bad, they are all black and they all jump," which truth he considers the height of scientific objectivity, and who, therefore, in Esenin's absence (after his death) wrote a laudatory article now no longer needed; and let's end with the stinking little books by Kruchenykh, who instructs Esenin in elementary political theory, as though Kruchenykh himself had spent all his life in a forced labor camp suffering for freedom and as though it were a great effort for him to write six (!) booklets[38] about Esenin with a hand still bearing the marks of jangling fetters.

So what and how should one write about Esenin? Having examined his death from all points of view and delved into other people's material, I formulated and set myself the problem.

Pragmatic orientation: deliberately to neutralize the effect of Esenin's last poem, to make his end uninteresting, to replace the bland beauty of death with another kind of beauty—because working humanity needs all its strength for the Revolution which has started, and because in spite of the hardship of the road and the painful contradictions of the NEP,[39] it demands that we glorify the joy of life, the happiness of the immensely difficult march to communism.

Now that I have the poem in front of me, these things are easy to formulate, but how hard it was when I started writing.

The work coincided with my travels in the provinces where I was giving lectures. For about three months I kept returning to the theme, day in, day out, but I could not think up anything worthwhile. All kinds of evil nonsense teeming with water pipes and livid faces crowded into my mind. In three months I hadn't come up with a single line. From the daily sifting of words some stock rhymes emerged, such as "in some/hansom," "Kogan/blowgun," "Napostov/ boast of." When I was already on my way back to Moscow I realized that the slowness and difficulty of the writing was due to the excessive similarity between what I was describing and my personal environment.

The same hotel rooms, the same water pipes, the same enforced solitude.

This environment wrapped itself around me, did not let me escape, did not yield either sensations or the words needed to damn and deny, and did not provide me with the essentials for evoking optimism.

From this one can almost draw a rule: to make a poetic work, a change of place or time is essential.

Just as, for example, in painting, when sketching an object one must walk back to a distance equal to three times its size. Unless you do this, you simply will not be able to see the object you are depicting.

The bigger the object or event, the greater the distance you will have to walk away. The feeble cool their heels, waiting for an event to pass them by so that they can reflect it, the powerful run just far enough ahead to give the pull to the times, which they have understood.

The description of contemporary events by those taking part in the struggles of the day will always be incomplete, even incorrect, at any rate one-sided.

It is obvious that such labor is the sum, the result of two kinds of work—the records of a contemporary, and the generalizing labor of tomorrow's artist. This is the tragedy of the revolutionary writer: he can present a brilliant report, for example *The Week*[40] by Libedinsky, and yet be hopelessly wrong in drawing general conclusions with perspective. If not the perspective of time and place, at least mental perspective.

Thus, for instance, deference to "poetry" at the expense of facts and news reports prompted the workers' correspondents to issue the collection *Petals*[41] with verse like:

> I am a proletarian gun,
> I fire about come rain or sun.

There is a lesson in this: (1) let's drop the delirious ramblings about unfurling "epic canvases" while fighting on the barricades—all the canvases will be torn to shreds, (2) the value of factual material (hence the interest in the reports of the workers' rural correspondents) at the time of a revolution should be rated higher, or at least no lower, than a so-called "poetic work." Premature poeticization only emasculates and distorts the material. All handbooks of poetry à la Shengeli are harmful because they do not elicit the poetry from the material, that is, they do not give the essence of facts, do not compress facts to the point where the result becomes a concentrated, compact economical word, but merely dress up new facts in any old form. More often than not, the form is the wrong size: either the fact is completely lost like a flea in a pair of trousers, as, for example, Radimov's piglets[42] get lost in his Greek pentameters better suited to the Iliad, or—the fact sticks out from the poetic clothing and becomes ridiculous instead of sublime. That's how, for example, "The Sailors" look in Kirilov's poem, walking in procession in his worn-out, overstuffed, amphibrachic tetrameters.

A change of surroundings, away from the one where this or that fact took place, a certain distance, is essential.

This does not mean, of course, that a poet should sit by the sea waiting for good weather, while time goes by. He must urge time onward. He must substitute a change of place for the slow passage of time and, in his imagination, must let a century pass in the space of a day.

For slight, short pieces this substitution can and should be made artificially (and in fact this happens of itself).

It is good to begin writing a poem about the First of May in November or December, when the desire for May is desperately strong.

In order to write about gentle love, take the No. 7 bus from Lubyanskaya Square to Nogin Square. The terrible jolting is the best way of making you appreciate, by contrast, the charm of another kind of life. Jolting is essential for comparison.

Time is also needed to perfect already written works.

All of the poetry I wrote in the white heat of inspiration on topical themes pleased me when I was writing it. Nevertheless, a day later it seemed petty, unfinished, one-sided. I always wanted to alter something.

That's why, when I have completed a work, I lock it up in my writing desk for a few days, after which I take it out and see at once the defects that were not previously apparent.

I'd been overdoing it.

This does not necessarily mean that one should write only non-topical works. No. Quite the contrary—they should be topical. I am merely focussing the attention of poets on the fact that rhymed propaganda slogans, which are considered easy, in reality demand the most intensive effort and the most varied devices to make up for the lack of time.

Even when preparing an urgent piece of propaganda one should, for instance, make a revised copy in the evening and not in the morning. In the morning one can see at a glance many things which can be easily corrected. But if one makes a revised copy in the morning most of what is bad will be left there. The know-how for creating distances and organizing time (but not the iambs and the trochees) must be included as a basic rule in every effective handbook of poetry.

That is why during the short drive from Lubyansky Passage to the Tea Marketing Boards in Myasnitskaya Street (on my way to redeem an advance payment) I was able to do more of my poem about Esenin than during the whole of my journey. Myasnitskaya Street was a sharp and necessary contrast: after the solitude of hotel rooms—the crowded Myasnitskaya Street; after the provincial quiet, the excitement and liveliness of buses, cars and trams; and all around, as a challenge to the old rush-lit villages—the electrified engineering offices.

I walk about, gesticulating, mumbling still almost without words, now shortening my steps in order not to impede my mumbling, now mumbling more quickly in time to my steps.

Thus is the rhythm hewn and shaped: the rhythm, which is the basis of all poetic work and which goes through it like a rumble. Gradually from this rumbling one begins to squeeze out single words.

Some words simply rebound and never return, others linger, turn over, and twist themselves inside-out several dozen times until one feels that the word has fallen into place. (This feeling, developed through experience, is called talent.) First, and most frequently, the main word becomes apparent—the main word which characterizes the meaning of the verse or the word which is to be rhymed. The remaining words come and arrange themselves in relation to the main one. When the fundamentals are done, there suddenly emerges a sensation that the rhythm has been violated—some tiny syllable or small sound is lacking. One begins to tailor all the words anew, and this work drives one to distraction. It is as though for the hundredth time a crown is being unsuccessfully fitted to a tooth and, finally, after the hundredth attempt, is it pressed and falls into place. The similarity for me is strengthened, moreover, by the fact that when, finally, that crown "falls into place", tears gush from my eyes (literally)—from pain and from a sense of relief.

It is not clear where that basic "rumble-rhythm" comes from. To me it is any repetition within me of a sound, noise or slight rocking, or even, generally speaking, the repetition of any phenomenon which I connect with sound. The repetitive surge of the sea; the maid who slams the door each morning, and, repeating herself, plods along, shuffling in the back of my mind; and even the revolving of the earth which, for me, seems inevitably connected, in a funny way, with the repeated turning of a globe in a shop for visual aids, in the whistling of a rising wind.

The endeavor to organize movement, to organize sounds around oneself, discovering their nature, their peculiarities, is one of the main unceasing poetic tasks—the stockpiling of rhythms. I don't know whether rhythm exists outside of me or only within me, most likely—within me. But, to awaken it, there has to be a jolt: thus some unknown creaking noise starts rumbling in the belly of a grand piano; thus, too, a bridge begins to rock, threatening to collapse from the synchronized steps of many ants.

Rhythm is the basic force, the basic energy of verse. It is impossible to explain it, one can only talk about it as one talks about magnetism or electricity. Magnetism and electricity are forms of energy. There can be a single rhythm in many verses, even throughout the whole work of a poet, and this does not make the work tedious because rhythm can be so complicated and difficult that one cannot get at it even with the aid of several long poems.

The poet must develop in himself precisely this feeling of rhythm and not memorize other people's rhythms: iambs, trochees, or even the canonized free verse—all are rhythms adapted for some precise occasion and fitted exclusively for this precise occasion. Thus, for instance, the magnetic energy given to a horseshoe will attract steel filings and cannot be used for any other purpose.

As to meters, I don't know any of them. For myself, I am simply convinced that for heroic or majestic assignments one should use long meters with a large number of syllables, and for light-hearted ones, short meters. For some reason, ever since my childhood (from the age of about nine) all the former kind have been associated in my mind with: "Victims you fell in the terrible fight..."[43] and the latter with: "We'll defeat the decadent order..."[44]

Curious. But I give you my word it is so.

In my case, meter is arrived at as a result of overlaying this rhythmic rumble with words, words prompted by the aim and orientation one has in mind (one keeps asking oneself: is this the right word? to whom shall I read this? will it be understood correctly? etc.), words controlled by the highest degree of sensitivity, abilities, and talent.

To begin with, the poem to Esenin started as a kind of rumbling which went something like this:

> Da-da-dá/da dá/da, da da, dá/da dá/
> da-da-di/da da da/da da/da da da da/
> da-da-da/da-da da da da dadi
> da-da-da/da da-da/dada/da/da da

Later words emerged:

> You have gone da da da da da another world.
> It may be you fly da da da da da.
> Neither advance for you, nor skirt, nor pub.
> Da da da da da da da/sobriety.

I kept repeating this dozens of times, listening carefully to the first line: "You have gone da da da to another world," etc.

What is this damned "da da da" and what can replace it? Perhaps I should leave out the "da da da" altogether:

You have gone to another world.

No! Some verse I heard before immediately comes to mind:

The steed fell on the battlefield.[45]

Who wants a steed! We are not talking of horses, but of Esenin. And even without these syllables some kind of operatic gallop is arrived at, whereas this "da da da" is much more exalted. One cannot drop this "da da da" at any cost—the rhythm is correct. I begin to try out words.

You have gone, Seryozha, to another world...
You have gone beyond return to another world.
You have gone, Esenin, to another world.

Which of these lines is best? All rubbish! Why?

The first line is false because of the word "Seryozha." I never addressed Esenin in this grossly familiar way, and this word is inadmissible even now, since it brings in its wake a lot of other false words foreign to me and uncharacteristic of our relationship, such as: "thou," "gentle," "brother," etc.

The second line is bad because the words "beyond return" are not inevitable but accidental, put in only for the sake of meter: they not only fail to help, and explain nothing, but they just get in the way. Indeed, what does "beyond return" mean? Has anyone ever died not beyond return? Is there a death with a return ticket?

The third line is no good because of its utter seriousness (the orientation I had in mind gradually drums it into my head that this is the failing of all three lines). Why is this seriousness unacceptable? Because it permits people to ascribe to me a biblical-sounding belief, which I do not hold, in the existence of an afterlife. This is one reason, and another is that this seriousness makes the verse simply funereal instead of tendentious, and it obscures the pragmatic orientation. This is why I introduce the words "as people say."

"You have gone, as people say, to another world." The line is done; "as people say," while not directly mocking, subtly reduces the pathetic element of the verse and simultaneously removes any suspicion about the other believing in some beyond-the-grave nonsense. The line is done, and at once becomes the basic one, determining the whole of the quatrain, which must be made to serve a dual purpose, neither breaking into dance on the sorrowful occasion nor, on the other hand, indulging in a tearful whine. The quatrain must be split in half straightaway: two solemn lines and two colloquial, popular lines, each set enhancing the other by contrast. That's why, because of my conviction that for light-hearted lines one should have fewer syllables, I immediately tackle the ending of the quatrain:

> Neither advance for you, nor skirt, nor pub,
> da da dá da da dá da dá sobriety.

What shall I do with these lines? How shall I cut them down? The words "nor skirt" must be taken out. Why? Because these "skirts" are living people. It is tactless to call them this when the greater part of Esenin's lyrical verse is dedicated to them with great tenderness. And that's why it's false, that's why it lacks resonance. What remains then? "Neither advance for you, nor pub."

I attempt to mutter it to myself—it doesn't work. These lines are so different from the first ones that the rhythm does not change, it simply breaks and tears. I have cut out too much. What then is to be done? Some absurd syllable is missing. This line, in breaking away from the rhythm, has become false. It is false from another point of view, too—that of its meaning. There is insufficient contrast and, moreover, it blames Esenin alone for all the "advances and pubs," whereas they apply equally to all of us.

How then can I make these lines even more contrasting and at the same time more generalized?

I take the most common saying:

> —There's no floor for you, nor roof
> —There's no advance for you, nor pub.

In the most colloquial, the most vulgar form they say:

—no floor for you, no roof
—no advance for you, no pub.

The line fell into place as regards meter and meaning. The familiar mode of address "for you" (in Russian tebe) is in even greater contrast to the formal mode of address in the first lines of the poem. The formal address in the first line, "You have gone..." (in Russian, Vy ushli and the familiar form "for you" [tebe] in the third line at once show that advance payments and pubs are not brought in to degrade the memory of Esenin, but as a general phenomenon). This line turned out to be a good point of departure for discarding all the syllables before "sobriety," and this sobriety itself turned out to be something like a solution to the problem. Therefore the quatrain attracts the sympathy of even the keenest supporters of Esenin, while remaining essentially almost a sneer.

The quatrain is basically ready, with only one line still left to be filled in with rhyme.

You have gone, as people say, to another world,
it may be you fly da-da-dá-da.
No advance for you, no pub—
sobriety.

Perhaps one could leave it unrhymed? No. Why? Because without rhyme (meaning rhyme in a broad sense) the verse falls to pieces.

The rhyme sends you back to the previous line, makes you remember it, makes all the lines shaping one thought hold together.

A rhyme is usually defined as a consonance of the last words in two lines when the same stressed vowel and the sounds following it approximately coincide.

Everybody says this, but all the same it is rubbish.

Consonance at the end of lines, rhyme, is only one of the innumerable ways of tying lines together and, by the way, the simplest and crudest.

It is also possible to rhyme the beginnings of lines:

astride—
ride as the grand land owner...etc.

One can rhyme the end of a line with the beginning of the next line:

> the sullen rain screwed up its eye,
> it sighed, the while behind...etc.

It is possible to take the ending of the first and second lines and make the final word of the third or fourth lines rhyme with both of them at once:

> from a scholarly angle
> barely
> could Russian verse be made out by Shengeli

etc., etc., ad infinitum.

In my quatrain it is necessary to rhyme the word "sobriety." The first words that come into my head could be words such as "impropriety" for example:

> You have gone, as people say, to another world,
> it may be you fly...I know your impropriety!
> No advance for you, no pub—
> sobriety.

Can one leave this rhyme as it is? No. Why? First of all because this rhyme is too exact, too transparent. When you say "impropriety" the rhyme "sobriety" thrusts itself forward and when uttered it does not surprise nor arrest one's attention. This is the fate of almost all cognate words, if a verb is rhymed with a verb, a noun with a noun, when they have the same roots or cases, etc. The word "impropriety" is also wrong because, even in the first lines, it introduces the element of derision, and in this way it weakens all subsequent contrasts. Perhaps it would be possible to make one's task easier by replacing the word "sobriety" by some word which rhymes more easily, or not to place "sobriety" at the end of the line but to fill out the line with several syllables—for example, "sobriety, stillness"?...In my opinion this should not be done; I always place the most characteristic word at the end of a line and find a rhyme for it at all costs. As a result my rhyming is almost always unusual, or at any rate my rhymes have not been used before and are not in the rhyming dictionary.

Rhyme ties lines together, therefore its fabric should be even stronger than the fabric used for the remaining lines.

Taking the most distinctive sound "briet"—of the word

"sobriety" which is being rhymed, I repeat it lots of times to myself, listening carefully to all its associations: "briet," "bright," "brighter," "rioter," "rightly," "vitally," "mightily." An apt rhyme has been found. An adverb, and, moreover, a solemn one!

But there's the rub: in the word "sobriety" the sounds "s" and "t" can be heard. What can be done with them? It is necessary to introduce analogous letters in the previous line too.

That's why the words "it may be" are replaced by the word "emptiness" with its "t" and "s's" and we keep the word "fly" which, with its soft "I" sound, offsets the sound of the "t."

And here is the final version:

> You have gone, as people say, to another world.
> Emptiness,—you fly, sundering the stars mightily...
> No advance for you, no pub—
> sobriety.

It is self-evident that I am oversimplifying, schematizing and subjecting poetic labor to a selective mental process. Obviously, the process of writing is more circuitous, more intuitive. But all the same the labor, basically, follows a scheme like this.

The first quatrain defines all the subsequent poem. Now that I have this quatrain before me I can estimate how many of them will be needed for the given theme, and how to distribute them to the best effect: the architectonics of poetry.

The theme is big and complex: as well as quatrains it will be necessary to use six-line stanzas and two-line stanzas—in all, about twenty to thirty bricks. After manufacturing almost all these bricks, I start trying them for size, fitting them now in one place, now in another, listening carefully to the way they sound and trying to imagine the impression they create.

Having done some of this fitting, and having thought it through, I make the following decision: to begin with, I must capture the interest of every listener by means of ambiguity, so that it is not clear whose side I am on; then I must take Esenin away from those who exploit his death for their own profit, I must praise him and exonerate him as his admirers "driving their flat rhymes into the mound" failed to do. One must finally win the sympathy of the listeners by heavily coming down on all those Sobinovs[46] and Kogans, those who vulgarize Esenin's work—even more so because they vulgarize any other work they tackle—while carrying the listeners along with what are, by now, easy couplets. After winning over the listeners, and having wrested from them the right to speak about the achievements of Esenin and his group, I must then suddenly direct them towards a conviction of the complete worthlessness, insignificance and unimportance of Esenin's end by rephrasing his own last words, giving them a contrary meaning.

As a simple figure, one comes up with the following diagram:

When you've got the quatrains, the basic building bricks, and when you have devised a general plan of construction, the basic work can be regarded as over.

Next comes the relatively easy technical processing of the poetic work.

The expressiveness of the verse must be taken to its utmost limits. One of the chief ways of making the poem expressive is the use of images. Not the basic image or vision, which arises at the start of the work as an indistinct initial response to the social command. No, I am speaking of the auxiliary images which help the main one to grow. This image is one of the usual devices of poetry, and certain movements such as, for example, Imagism, made it their goal, thereby condemning themselves in essence to developing only one of the technical aspects of poetry.

There are innumerable ways of manufacturing images.

One of the elementary ways of making an image is by the use of comparisons. My first works, for example, "A Cloud in Trousers", were built entirely on comparisons—always "like, like, and like." It is, perhaps, this primitive element which makes later critics consider "A Cloud" the "culmination" of my work. In later works and in my "Esenin", this primitive element is eradicated. I found only one comparison: "tediously and at length like Doronin."[47]

Why like Doronin, and not, say, like the distance to the moon? First of all, the comparison is taken from literary life, since the whole theme is that of a man of letters. And secondly—"The Iron Ploughman" (did I get that right?) is longer than the road to the moon, because the road does not exist, whereas "The Iron

Ploughman" unfortunately does; and then again the road to the moon would seem shorter because of its novelty, whereas four thousand lines by Doronin startle one with the monotony of a verbal and rhyme landscape which has already been seen sixteen thousand times. And then, the image itself must be tendentious; that is to say, in developing an important theme, one should, for the sake of the struggle and literary propaganda, exploit all the minor independent images one comes across along the way.

The most widespread method of making an image is that of using a metaphor, i.e., transferring definitions which up to now have belonged only to certain things to other words, things, phenomena, and concepts, as well.

For instance, the metaphor in the line: "And they carry the funereal scrap of verse."

We are familiar with iron scrap, food scraps. But how does one define the poetic trash which has remained unused, left over from poetic works? Of course, it is the scrap of verse, verse scrap. Here this scrap is of only one kind—funereal, it is the funereal verse scrap. But this line cannot be left as it stands because it becomes "funeral verse scrap," i.e., "scrap" which can be read "crap" and this so-called "shift" distorts the whole meaning of the verse. This kind of carelessness occurs very often.

For instance, in the lyrical poem by Utkin, which recently appeared in *Projector*, there are the lines: "He will not come, just as/ The summer swan alights not on winter lakes."[48]

The word "snot" is clearly heard in the second line.

The first line of a poem published by Bryusov in the early days of the war in the magazine *Our Times* is most effective: "We are veterans, our wounds are hurting us." [49] [Note: Mayakovsky's non-existent comment on this line is hardly necessary here since the sequence of syllables in the Russian makes up the passive participle of the verb "to shit."]

This shift is disposed of and, at the same time, the order of the words gives the simplest and most clear-cut definition: "the scrap of funeral verse."

One of the methods of making images that I have been using more and more recently is the creation of utterly fantastic events— incidents emphasized by the use of hyperbole:

> So that Kogan should rush away in all directions
> crippling everyone he met with the spears of his
> moustaches.

In this way Kogan becomes a collective image which makes it possible for him to rush in all directions, and for his moustaches to turn into spears; and to enhance this "spear quality," people lie around crippled by his mustaches.

Methods of image construction are varied, as is all the rest of the verse-making technique, depending on the extent to which the reader is surfeited with one or another of the forms.

In addition, there may be imagery of the opposite kind, that is, imagery which, far from mentally extending what has been said, tries on the contrary to condense the impression given by the words into a deliberately limited framework. For example in my old poem *War and the World*:[50]

> In a rotting truck forty men—
> and only four legs.

Many of Selvinsky's[51] works are based on such numerical images.

Next comes the labor of selecting verbal material. It is necessary to take into account with great precision the milieu in which the poetic work develops, so that no word foreign to this milieu gets in by accident.

For example, I had the line: "You had the skill, my friend, to do such things."

"My friend" is false, firstly because it cuts across the severe denunciatory treatment of the work; secondly, we never used this term in our poetic milieu. Thirdly, it is a weak term, habitually used in insignificant conversations, rather more to conceal feeling than to throw it into relief; fourthly, it is natural for a man truly overcome by grief to conceal this with coarser words. Moreover, this term does not define what things the friend had the skill to do—what was it you could do?

What did Esenin have the skill to do? Today there is a great demand for and an intent and admiring focusing on his lyrics; Esenin's literary development moved along the line of so-called literary scandal (not an offensive thing but exceedingly respectable, an echo, a side-effect of the famous public appearances of the Futurists). And it was precisely these scandals which, during his lifetime, were Esenin's literary milestones and stages.

How unsuitable the following would be to the living Esenin: "You had the skill to sing such things to the soul."

Esenin did not sing (in essence he is, of course, the gypsy-guitar type, but his poetic salvation lay in the fact that, at least during his life, he was not taken for such, and that in his volumes there are a dozen or so poetic innovations). Esenin did not sing, he was rude, he used bad language. It was only after long consideration that I put down "bad language," however annoying such a term might be to those brought up in literary brothels, hearing nothing all day but "bad language" while dreaming of unburdening their hearts in poetry about lilacs, bosoms, trilling nightingales, harmonies and tender cheeks. Without any comment I shall now demonstrate how the words in one line were gradually worked out.

1. our times are poorly equipped for gaiety;
2. our times are poorly equipped for joy;
3. our times are poorly equipped for happiness;
4. our life is poorly equipped for gaiety;
5. our life is poorly equipped for joy;
6. our life is poorly equipped for happiness;
7. for merrymaking our planet is poorly equipped;
8. for merriment our planet is poorly equipped;
9. our planet is not specially well equipped for merrymaking;
10. our planet is not especially well-equipped for gaiety;
11. our puny little planet is not well-equipped for pleasures;

and finally, the last, twelfth line:

12. for gaiety our planet is poorly equipped.

I could deliver a whole speech in support of the last of these lines, but for the present I shall simply content myself with copying the lines from my rough notes in order to demonstrate how much labor it takes to produce a few words.

The sound-quality of a poetic work, the linking of word with word, is also included in the technical processing. This "word magic," this "perhaps everything in our life is but a means for brightly singing verse,"—this sound element also seems to many to be the aim of poetry, which once again reduces poetry to the level of technical labor. If one overdoes alliteration, consonance, and so on, one creates an impression of satiety after a minute's reading.

For example, Balmont: "I'm a wandering wind and I wend to the west weaving a way through the waves,"[52] etc.

It is necessary to use doses of alliteration with extreme care and as far as possible without ostentatious repetition. An example of clear alliteration in my Esenin poem is the line: "Where is it, the resounding bronze, the grinding edge of granite...".

I resort to alliteration to frame and underline even more strongly the word which is of importance to me. One can resort to alliteration simply in order to play with words, for poetic amusement; poets of the past (who for us are the old poets) used alliteration mainly for melodiousness, for its verbal music, and therefore often used the type of alliteration I most hate—onomatopoeia. I have already spoken about such methods of alliteration in connection with rhyme.

Of course, it isn't obligatory to pack one's verse with fancy alliteration and to rhyme it throughout in improbable ways. Always remember that the policy of economy in art is the most important rule for every production of esthetic value. Therefore, when one has completed the basic work, of which I spoke at the beginning, many aesthetic passages and fancy bits must be deliberately toned down, so that other passages will gain in brilliance.

It is possible, for example, to half-rhyme lines, to connect a verb which grates on the ear with another verb, in order to lead up to a brilliant thunder-clap of rhyme.

This serves to underline, once again, the relativity of all rules for writing verse.

The technical labor also includes the intonational side of poetic work.

It is impossible to work at a poem that is to function in an airless void or, as often happens with poetry, in a void that is only too airy.

It is necessary to have constantly before one's eyes the audience to whom the poem is addressed. This is particularly important when the chief means of contact with the masses is the auditorium, the public platform, the voice, the spoken word.

It is necessary to adapt one's tone to suit the audience—to make it persuasive, pleading, commanding or questioning.

Most of my poems are constructed in a conversational tone. But despite careful consideration this tone is not strictly fixed, but is a method of address which I frequently change during a reading, depending on the composition of the audience. Thus, for example, the printed text says, rather indifferently, counting on a well-qualified reader:

Happiness has to be snatched from the days to come.

Sometimes at public readings I amplify this line to a shout:

Slogan:
snatch your happiness from the days to come!

Therefore, there is no need to be surprised if someone puts out the poem, even in its printed form, with the words arranged to suit several different moods, and with particular expressions for each occasion.

When one has made a poem intended for print, one must take into account how this printed poem will be understood as a printed poem. It is necessary to take into consideration the ordinariness of the reader; it is necessary in every possible way to make the reader's interpretation approximate the very one which the poet intended to give his poetic line. Our usual punctuation, with its full stops, commas, exclamation marks and question marks, is too poor and inexpressive compared with the shades of emotion which today's more sophisticated man puts into a poetic work.

The meter and rhythm of a poem are more significant than the punctuation, and the punctuation is subordinated to them when it is used in its old form. Nonetheless, everyone reads these lines by Alexei Tolstoy:[53]

Shibanov said nought. From the wound in his foot
The scarlet blood flowed in a stream...

as:

Shibanov said nought from the wound in his foot...

And again:

No more, ashamed I am
To lower myself before the haughty Pole... [54]

89

reads like provincial chit-chat:

No more ashamed I am...

In order that this be read as Pushkin intended it, one must divide the line as I do:

No more,
        ashamed I am...

With such a division into half-lines there will be no muddle either as to meaning or as to rhythm. The division of lines is often dictated, moreover, by the necessity of hammering out the rhythm with absolute precision, because our condensed, economical verse structure frequently makes us discard the intervening words and syllables, and if, after these syllables, no pause is made—often a bigger pause than between the line—the rhythm will snap.

That's why I write:

Emptiness...
        You fly,
                sundering the stars, mightily.

"Emptiness" stands alone, as the sole word characterizing the celestial landscape. "You fly" stands alone to avoid the imperative meaning: "fly sundering," etc.

One of the important features of a poem, particularly a tendentious, declamatory one, is the ending. The most successful lines of the poem are usually put in the ending. Sometimes one has to recast the whole verse to justify such an arrangement.

In my poem about Esenin this ending naturally consisted of a rephrasing of Esenin's last lines. They sound like this:

Esenin's: In this life there's nothing new in dying,
           But in living there is nothing newer.

Mine: In this life there's nothing hard in dying.
          To make one's life have meaning is much harder.

During my extensive work on the whole poem I constantly thought of these lines. While working on other lines I kept returning to these—consciously or unconsciously.

It was utterly impossible to forget that this was the only way to do it; therefore I did not write down these lines but made them in my head (as I previously used to make all my poems, and still make the most striking ones).

That's why it is not possible to reckon the number of versions, but in any case there were no fewer than fifty or sixty variants of these two lines.

The methods by which words are technically processed are infinitely varied, and to talk about them would be pointless since the basis of poetic labor, as I have frequently mentioned here, consists precisely in inventing methods for this processing, and it is exactly these methods which make a writer a professional. The Talmudists of poetry will probably make a wry face over this book of mine because they like to give ready-made poetic recipes. Take a certain theme, clothe it in poetic form, iambs or trochees, rhyme the ends, slip in a dash of alliteration, stuff with images—and the poem is ready.

But in every editorial office they throw this simple handiwork into the wastepaper basket over and over again (and a good thing, too).

A man who picks up his pen for the first time and wants to be writing poetry a week later will not need this book.

My book will be of use to the man who, despite all obstacles, wants to be a poet, the man who, knowing that poetry is one of the most difficult productive processes, wants to acquire and hand down certain seemingly mysterious methods of this craft.

Conclusions:

1. Poetry is a productive process. A most difficult, most complicated one, but still a productive process.

2. Training in poetic labor is not a study in the preparation of a definite, limited type of poetic work, but a study of the methods used in any poetic labor and of the productive skills which help to create new skills.

3. Novelty—novelty of material and of method—is obligatory for every poetic work.

4. The labor of a verse-maker must be practiced daily to improve one's craftsmanship and to collect one's poetic stock.

5. A good notebook and the ability to use it are more important than the ability to write faultlessly in meters which have kicked the bucket long ago.

6. There is no need to start a vast poetic factory in order to make poetic cigarette lighters. One should turn one's back on such irrational poetic trivialities. One should take up one's pen only when there is no other way of speaking except in verse. One should produce finished verse only when one feels a clear social command.

7. To understand the social command correctly, the poet should be at the center of things and events. A knowledge of economic theory, a knowledge of the realities of life, a grounding in the study of scientific history, are more important for the poet—in the early stages of his labor—than are the scholastic textbooks of idealist professors who worship old junk.

8. To fulfill the social command most satisfactorily, it is necessary to be in the vanguard of one's class; it is necessary, together with one's class, to struggle on all fronts. The fairy tale about apolitical art must be smashed to smithereens. This ancient fairy tale is now emerging in a new form under cover of idle chatter about "wide epic canvases" (first epic, then objective, and finally non-Party), about a grand style (first grand, then elevated, and finally, spiritual) etc., etc.

9. Only by regarding art as a productive process can we eliminate the accidental, the lack of discrimination in taste, and the subjectivity of evaluation. Only this will bring into harmony the various types of literary labor: both verse and the report of the workers' correspondent. Instead of mystical discussions on a poetic theme, this will give us an opportunity for a precise approach to the immediate problem of how to rate and assess poetry.

10. One should not attribute an independent value to workmanship, the so-called technical processing. But it is precisely this workmanship which makes a poetic work fit for use. It is only the difference between the methods of processing that makes the difference between poets; it is only knowledge, a striving for perfection, the accumulation and variation of literary methods, that make a man into a professional writer.

11. The poet's everyday circumstances influence the creation of a real work of art in the same way as do all the other factors. The word "Bohemian" has become synonymous with commonplace artistic philistines. Unfortunately, a struggle was waged against the word Bohemian and only against the word. In reality we are faced with the old atmosphere of individualist literary career-mongering, of petty malicious group interests, of mutual intrigue, the notion "poetic" being supplanted by "loose-living," "boozy," "lout," etc. Even the poet's clothes, even his conversations with his wife at home, must be different, determined by his entire poetic activity.

12. We, the members of *LEF*, never say that we are the only possessors of the secrets of poetic creation. But we are the only ones who want to reveal these secrets, the only ones who do not want, for the sake of profit, to surround creativity with artistic-religious worship.

My present effort is the weak attempt of one man alone, using theoretical works written by my comrades, the students of literature.

It is necessary for those students of literature to adapt their work to contemporary material and directly help the future development of poetic labor.

But this is not enough.

It is necessary that the authorities for mass education should give the teaching of old esthetic junk a thorough shake-up.

Translated by Valentina Coe

Notes:
1. CCC: Central Control Commission of the CP
2. RAP: see preface.
3. Basically the Formalists held that literature as literature could be analyzed solely with reference to the formal properties of texts. As Terry Eagleton encapsulates it, the Formalist injunction was that "criticism should dissociate art from mystery and concern itself with how literary texts actually worked: literature was not a pseudo-religion or psychology or sociology but a particular organization of language." This aspect of Formalism was adopted by Mayakovsky and members of LEF; to it, however, they added the notion of the "social command" (see Preface). JS
4. Onegin and Tatyana are the hero and heroine of Pushkin's *Eugene Onegin*. VC
5. "my uncle is of most honest principles" is the first line of *Eugene Onegin*. VC
6. G. A. Shengeli (1894-1956), minor poet and translator, wrote a variety of handbooks including *How to Write Essays, Poems, and Stories* (M. 1926), and one book (in 1927) attacking Mayakovsky. VC
7. M. Brodovsky's *Guide to Versification* (1907). VC
8. Nikolai Grech's *Textbook of Russian Literature* (1820). VC
9. N. Abramov's *Complete Dictionary of Russian Rhymes* (1912) was, from Mayakovsky's point of view, very incomplete. VC
10. A garbled citation from Zinaïda Gippius's poem "Now" ("Seichas"). VC
11. Kirillov (1889-1943) was a "Smithy" poet, singer of a machine-tooled future (approved by Mayakovsky) but in old forms (not approved). VC
12. From Blok's narrative poem "The Twelve" (1918). VC
13. The first line of Mayakovsky's poem "Left March." VC
14. A line from Blok's "The Twelve." VC
15. Chastushki: a popular rhymed jingle or song, originally folkloric, normally very diversified. VC
16. Fellow-travelers: members of the non-Communist but liberal intelligentsia who would go along with the revolution, or with the Soviet government, either generally or with respect to specific campaigns, e.g. later, in the united front against fascism. JS
17. For more about social command, see Preface.
18. Yudenich: a general in the White Army.
19. Bedny (1883-194S) was a Communist Party poet who wrote in variations of folk genres, updating fables and fairy tales for propaganda purposes. VC
20. Alexei Kruchenykh (1886-1968) along with Mayakovsky (but far less talented), a Futurist poet. VC
21. N.O.T.: Russian initials for the Scientific Organization of Labor bureau. VC
22. Mayakovsky's most famous long poem is entitled A Cloud in Trousers (1914-15). For a translation see Pat Blake and Max Hayward (eds.) *The Bedbug and Selected Poetry* (Bloomington: Indiana University Press, 197S). VC
23. Mayakovsky slightly altered the first quatrain of Pasternak's "Marburg" (1917). VC

24. "To Sergei Esenin" was written in early 1926, published in April. In the early morning of Dec. 28, 1925, Esenin hanged himself in a Leningrad hotel. Roughly twenty-four hours before this he had written his last poem—in blood from his arm. A literal translation follows:

> Goodbye, my friend, goodbye. My dear, you are in my heart. Predestined separation, Promises a future meeting.
>
> Goodbye, my friend, without handshake and words, Do not grieve and sadden your brow,—In this life there's nothing new in dying, But in living there is nothing newer.

This was to end a very disorderly and colorful life which included marriage to Isadora Duncan, political turnabouts, and frequent antisocial behavior. But Esenin was, and is, an extremely popular poet, a worthy rival of Mayakovsky in this respect. VC
Mayakovsky's response to Esenin's world-weariness and negativism was summed up in his own lines:

> In life it is not difficult to die, To make life is far more difficult... Why increase the suicide rate? Better to increase the flow of ink!

25. The yellow blouse was worn by some of the Futurists who, according to Trotsky, represented the revolt of Bohemia—that is, of the semi-pauperized left wing of the intelligentsia—against the closed-in and caste-like aesthetics of the bourgeois intelligentsia...The proletarian revolution caught Futurism in a certain stage of its development and pushed it forward. Futurists became Communists. By this very act they entered the sphere of more profound questions and relationships which far transcended the limits of their own little world.
Robert C. Williams. in *Artists in Revolution: Portraits of the Russian Avante-Garde 1905-1925* (Indiana University Press 1977) has a less critical characterization of Russian Futurism: "words were declared to be independent of their meaning, new rhythms and rhymes were created on the basis of sight and sound, and a trans-sense language emerged subject to the poet's own will and often designed to shock middle-class audiences. The futurists took to the streets wearing outlandish dress: Mayakovsky's yellow tunic, Burliuk's top hat, and spoons and radishes in buttonholes. They issued manifestoes and painted their faces, employing all means to antagonize the philistines. They threw tea at their audiences, read poetry on street corners, glorified the modern city, and made their life into public theatre."
By the time he had produced this particular essay, of course, Mayakovsky had outgrown such Futurism—having realized, as Williams describes it, that "the gap between the Futurists and the average Soviet citizen was wide. The

Futurist journal *Iskusstvo kommuny (Art of the Commune)*...functioned more as a haven for the avante garde than as a service to the revolution. When Mayakovsky proclaimed in an article that 'the streets are our brushes, the squares our palettes,' the 'our' obviously referred to the Futurists rather than to the worker artists of Proletkult. Proletarian Art, Brik noted rather cleverly, "is neither 'art for the proletarians' nor 'art of the proletarians' but 'art of the artist-proletarians.'" JS

26. Nikolai Klyuev (1887?-1937), gay Russian 'peasant' poet, Esenin's mentor at one time. VC

27. Maxim Gorky (1868-1936) the novelist, playwright, Soviet functionary and person of letters.

28. "My dear, dear funny fool...": a line from Esenin's long poem "Sorokoust" (1920). VC

29. "A Bolshevik is what I am": from Esenin's poem "Jordan Dove" (1918). VC

30. In 1922-23 Esenin visited the United States with Isadora Duncan.

31. VAPP: acronym for the All-Union Association of Proletarian Writers. VC

32. See preface.

33. Poet Nikolai Aseev(1889-1963), a member of LEF.

34. Apparently because of the newspapers, it was widely believed that Esenin slashed his wrist, wrote the poem cited, and then hung himself all on the same night. But this is not true. VC

35. Alexander Bezymensky (1898-1973), a Communist Party, proletarian poet, wrote a poem called "An Encounter with Esenin." VC

36. From A. Zharov's poem "On Esenin's Coffin" (1926). VC

37. P. S. Kogan, a literary critic, wrote several panegyrical pieces after Esenin's suicide. VC

38. Kruchenykh published a steady series of brochures about Esenin in 1926. VC

39. NEP: acronym of the New Economic Policy, which was instituted in 1921, toward the end of the Civil War, and extended into 1928. Under the NEP some private trade was restored, including trade involving agriculture. Small business was revived, etc. Conceived as a practical response to the chaos and shortages brought on by the war, the NEP was in effect a step back from socialism. Some considered it a betrayal of the Revolution, while others defended it as a way to preserve socialist movement by temporarily abandoning socialist tenets. This is one of the 'painful contradictions' Mayakovsky speaks of. Another was the fact that, according to Gail Harrison (in Rodchenko and the Arts of Revolutionary Russia, Pantheon, 1979), "among the many impediments to the creative construction advocated by LEF was taxation introduced under the NEP. Mayakovsky voiced his scornful opinion of the new taxes in his poem "A Conversation with a Tax Collector," published in 1926. JS

40. *The Week: a short novel* (1922) by Yuri Libedinsky (1898-1959) showing ruling Communists in a favorable light. VC

41. *Petals*: a 1924 collection of writings by workers. VC

42. Radimov's piglets: an allusion to A. S. Radimov's poem "Herd of Pigs;" Mayakovsky also made fun of him for using archaic forms for modern poems. VC

43. "Victims you fell in a terrible fight...": a line from a popular revolutionary song ("Funeral March"). VC

44. "We'll defend the decadent order": a popular revolutionary song from the 1870's by P. L. Lavrov. VC

45. "the steed fell on the battlefield": a line from Glinka's opera *Ivan Susanin*. VC

46. L. V. Sobinov, an opera singer who sang about Esenin's death at memorial gatherings. VC

47. I. I. Doronin wrote a long poem called "The Iron Ploughman" (1926). VC

48. "He will not come, just as/The summer swan alights not in winter lakes": from I. P. Utkin's poem "The Burial Mound" (1926). VC

49. "We are veterans, our wounds are hurting us": imprecise quote of a Bryusov translation of a Verhaeren poem. VC

50. "War and the World": a long poem by Mayakovsky, the title of which, in Russian, is a homonym for War and Peace. VC

51. Ilya Selvinsky (1899-1968), a well-known Constructivist poet. VC

52. "I'm a wandering wind and I wend to the west weaving a way through the waves": from Balmont's "Snow Flowers." In the original there is a ludicrously heavy alliteration of 'v' and 'e.' VC

53. Alexei Tolstoy: (1917-1875), poet and dramatist. His ballad "Vasily Shibanov" is the source of the quoted lines. VC

54. In Pushkin's tragedy *Boris Godunov* the Pretender says these words. VC

Art Is in Danger!

PREFACE
by Paul Gorrell

On December 31, 1918, the artists George Grosz, John Heartfield, Wieland Herzfelde and Edwin Piscator joined the Communist Party of Germany (KPD). This was at the founding congress of the party, which had formed partly in opposition to the Weimar Republic, itself less than two months old. To many, the Weimar Republic appeared to have a genuinely revolutionary character. The abdication of Kaiser Wilhelm II was hailed as the beginning of a socialist era. At the time, the socialists were divided between the Socialist Party of Germany (SPD), the Independent Socialist Party (USPD) and the Spartacus League. The SPD was the majority party and headed the new government. It saw its role as primarily that of preserving order after the strikes and uprisings which led to the establishment of the Republic. The Spartacus League, however, whose members included Karl Liebknecht and Rosa Luxemburg, pushed for a continuing revolution with the goal of establishing a proletarian dictatorship.

The lines were clearly drawn in December when the SPD formed an alliance with the old imperial army in order to put down worker demonstrations and strikes. One manifestation of this alliance was the appointment of Gustav Noske as Minister of the Interior. He accepted the position, saying, "someone has to be the butcher." From this alliance emerged the Free Corps, ex-soldiers under the command of reactionary generals. The Free Corps was especially brutal, shooting "even the wounded...and Red Cross nurses," as one member boasted. The Free Corps left no doubt as to the nature of the new government. It was similar to the old, with the same rulers, only without the Kaiser.

In 1919 alone there were about 5000 strikes in Germany. Most turned into battles between the workers and the Free Corps. The Spartacus League re-formed as the KPD in open opposition to the government. In January of that year a large uprising of workers was crushed by Free Corps troops using machine guns. On January 15, Liebknecht and Luxemburg were captured and murdered.

While the brothers Heartfield and Herzfelde had been early supporters of the Russian revolution and the Spartacus League, it was the SPD's betrayal of the people to the ruling class which transformed Grosz from a cynical caricaturist of bourgeois life into a committed revolutionary artist: "There were the fascists and there were the people; I chose the people."

When the Weimar Republic was first proclaimed in 1918 many artists saw their role as that of promoting 'radical art.' Grosz and Heartfield belonged to *Novembergruppe*, which was comprised of artists who sought to make art responsive to the needs of the new society. But the group lacked direction. Its politics, though generally radical, were not sharply defined. The KPD had only recently been founded and had only a few thousand members. Soon Grosz and Heartfield, among others, became dissatisfied with these radical artists, much as they had already grown disgusted with the new government. They wanted to promote an art responsive to the workers' growing class-consciousness. Works such as Grosz's *The Face of the Ruling Class*, a small book of fifty-five political drawings which sold 30,000 copies in the early 20's, marked the beginnings of a more revolutionary art. But it was not until a few years later, when the KPD had gained in strength, that Communist artists formed a group within the party. Their program and goals were concrete, having been clearly and specifically outlined in the *Red Group* manifesto. The party helped focus the work of these artists in the class struggle.

In January of 1920, a mass demonstration in Berlin was put down with machine guns. In the days and weeks that followed, protest strikes erupted all over Germany. But the Free Corps, with the support of the SPD and the old imperial powers, was strengthening itself to respond to the challenge of the workers. For the duration of the Republic, the SPD and the Free Corps would continue to play the 'good cop/bad cop' routine, the "excesses" being blamed mostly on the Free Corps, while the SPD was "urging restraint." In reality they were two faces of the same dictatorship. The role of the SPD was to legitimize that dictatorship and give it breathing room, by promising reforms that never came. A contemporary saying—"The Kaiser is gone, but the generals stay put"—succinctly characterized the Weimar Republic.

In March the Free Corps felt powerful enough in their own right to stage a coup (the Kapp Putsch). It held power for four days before a general strike by the trade unions forced it to capitulate. Still, the Free Corps was given what it wanted: a free hand in staging an all-out offensive against the Communists.

During the days of the Kapp Putsch (the *Kapptagen)*, a battle between soldiers and workers took place in front of the Zwinger art gallery in Dresden. A painting by Rubens ("Bathsheba") was damaged. Oskar Kokoschka, Dresden artist and professor of art, appealed to the "public" to do their fighting away from the galleries, so that "the sacred possessions of the German people" might not suffer further damage. This appeal, presuming the privileged separation of art from struggle, typified all that artists such as Grosz and Heartfield felt was wrong with the bourgeois conception of art and artists. Kokoschka's concern was the work of art, not the struggle of people needing food, shelter, jobs. The artists of the KPD, on the other hand, located the value of a work of art in its potential usefulness in the class struggle.

The two approaches to art can be expressed as the difference between formalism and tendency art *(Tendenzkunst)*. Tendency art is committed, political, an art consciously in the service of the class struggle. Formalist art seeks to avoid tendency; its illusory goal is to remain aloof, free from the demands of everyday life. It looks to the eternal, the mysterious. To Grosz and Heartfield, the dichotomy was a false one, because all art has a tendency of some sort or other. Art and artists, too, exist and function in a social context. For those artists who joined the KPD in 1918, Kokoschka's appeal epitomized the narrow formalism of bourgeois art. "The Art Scab," which first appeared in 1920, shortly after the *Kapptagen,* is not only an attack on Kokoschka and bourgeois art, but also an appeal for artists to commit themselves, on the side of the workers, in the class struggle.

"The Art Scab" appeared originally in the monthly journal *Der Gegner* (The Adversary). *Der Gegner* was published by Malik Verlag, the publishing company founded by Heartfield. "Instead of a Biography" discredited bourgeois artists' preoccupation with formal devices and religious motifs. It challenged them to use their talent in support of the proletariat. In this it continued the theme of "The Art Scab," that all art was in fact a tendency art. "Art Is in Danger!"— which came out in 1925—considers how deeply art is influenced by new technologies as well as by class struggles. What is art in the context of photography and motion pictures? How can a painting of an ocean compare to a film of it? How is art to be judged? Fine art is doomed, incapable of escaping key developments of the twentieth century: technology and class struggle.

Heartfield was one of the first artists to exploit the new technology for propaganda purposes. His photomontage method, combining parts of different pictures and drawings into one, made connections that would elude simple photographs. According to

Heartfield, the photomontage method had its origins in the fact that traditional graphics methods were too slow to keep pace with the rapidity of events and the readiness of the bourgeois press. As a revolutionary artist, he had to find a way to keep up with the progress of the proletarian struggle. The photomontage, then, was the technical aspect of a solution to a political problem. The impact of Heartfield's photomontages was as clear and immediate as a powerful slogan. By the 1930's, the Nazis were making political attacks not only on Heartfield's politics, but on his technique—focusing on its analytical/ critical, pieced-together character—calling the photomontages "corrupt, degenerate, broken apart" (explicitly associating these characteristics with "Jewishness") while contrasting that with the Nazi's own corporativist aesthetic and politic, the "unification of the people."

Unlike Heartfield's, Grosz's style and method were not determined by his Communist politics. He had drawn, and he continued to draw, caricatures of bourgeois life. One noticeable difference, after he had joined the KPD, was that his drawings increasingly ridiculed the SPD leaders, a favorite target being Interior Minister Noske. While working within the Communist Party, Grosz had direction, focus and positive political purpose.

The strongest art of both Grosz and Heartfield drew its power from their understanding of, and commitment to, class warfare. Art had a new, urgent meaning, one given it by the revolutionary struggle that was then being waged. Art was not for contemplation or for museums but for action and the streets. This new attitude toward art is clearly expressed in the short poem by Hanns Eisler (a composer and early collaborator with Bertolt Brecht) which appeared, in the 20's, in an advertisement for a proletarian book club:

WHAT DO WE READ?

> How and why do we read?
> And how and why do the
> bourgeoisie read?
> The bourgeoisie read for fun,
> for diversion.
> We read to learn, to concentrate.
> In their books, the bourgeoisie
> seek illusion, escape
> from reality.

In our books, we seek reality,
          so as to change it.
  The bourgeoisie want a "trip,"
       an "experience."
We want to stimulate our minds,
       broaden our awareness.
  For the bourgeoisie, art is for
      pleasure, for consumption.
For us, art is for thought, for
     learning, for struggle.

ART IS IN DANGER!

THE ART SCAB

The bourgeoisie and the petite bourgeoisie have armed themselves against the rising proletariat with, among other things, "culture." It's an old ploy of the bourgeoisie. They keep a standing "art" to defend their collapsing culture. Bible in hand, they wield their deadly weapons to further the interests of oppression. With Goethe's *Faust* in their knapsacks, with vicious lines of stupefying poetry in their mouths, they strike the pose of "moral balance" so necessary for robbery, oppression and ruthless exploitation.

In public buildings set aside for the care and maintenance of the goods of the Middle Ages, a staff of civil-service art attendants praise all the dead, irrelevant scribblings and scrawlings that, at best, have only historical interest for idiots and layabouts. Here hang 'works' by Rubens and Rembrandt which haven't the least significance for us today. They're just bourgeois investments. Even today, in a time of widespread hunger, they invest their surplus capital in the accumulation, the hoarding, of works by painters whom they consider stupid, and in acquiring the masterpieces of master "creators" (don't insult such maestros by calling them workers!). They're only interested in these paintings as investments and as something to hang in the unused rooms of their houses. Incidentally, there's an additional benefit for the bourgeoisie. All the glitter and glory of art make this seem an unselfish endeavor—it gives the bourgeois status as a patron of the arts, a position from which he can sit back, puff on his expensive cigar, and look down on the merely utilitarian work of the "uncultivated" masses. You can see, when they acquire a prized new possession, how beside themselves they are! For example (to name but one) what a thrill to be able to enter the mansion of the Berlin millionaire Mendolsohn-Barthody, and under the dazzling, feudal, candelabra-lit staircase, right by the coatrack, see a painting by Henri Rousseau! It seems so *incidental,* as if it cost hardly anything (it cost, of course, a fortune). What a thrill to see your fur coat, as you hang it up, touch such a painting and to hide this immortal, costly work behind your coat that's still dripping wet from the rain.

Here all is liberal, open-minded. Here one is awed, as well, by the fat man of the house, the one who oppresses so graciously. Here is a cultured atmosphere in which one may blissfully contemplate the world. Here, the very essence of life unfolds. All the world's beauty reveals itself. Here one discovers what our culture values most. One is inspired, committed to protect all this from the purposeful devastation of those culture-smashing Bolsheviks, and from the mob mentality which is so symptomatic of the breakdown taking place in modern times. And yet it's heartwarming to behold a painting that costs 200,000 marks and find, next to the finest paintings of the old masters (Rubens' pompous paintings of women's thighs, high and mighty generals with medals and stars, all masterfully painted, and today irreplaceable; plus Rembrandt's *Descent from the Cross* and *Man with Gold Helmet)*—to find, as I say, modern works of art, perhaps the young professor Oskar Kokoschka's highly profitable drawings and paintings, perhaps even his picture, "The Actress Margarete Kupfer with Her Pet Dog," which can be painted left or right without taking a stand regarding the evils of the bourgeoisie, and which can be painted with a revolutionary splurge of cobalt blue, and which, if by chance that blue runs out, can be carried on as Prussian blue, thereby achieving a "classic" effect. It might even be disturbing to the sensibilities of Frau Bienert-Dresden, who owns a large mill. As disturbing as some petty bourgeois art, e.g. "Blue Garden Fence," "Primeval Forest #3," "Child with Ball," "Forest with Zeppelin."

Yes, this is where the great works of art belong. High over the splendid wainscoting on the walls! Or might they belong in some worker's cramped apartment, crowded by the daily misery of the workers. Perhaps they should be hung over his lice-ridden bed?

What would a worker do with art?

What? When he must struggle hourly for the most basic necessities of life. When he labors under the most miserable conditions, seeing his comrades, his family, all who struggle alongside him, foundering—all because of the bourgeois bloodsuckers, the overstuffed owners. What? When he feels compelled to spend every minute freeing this world from the clutches of the capitalist system.

When he has to watch out, always, for the crimes, the tricks, the lies and deceptions, the smears with which the bourgeois society tries to undermine his attempts to change the world.

When he has to keep confronting capitalism, which at every turn institutionalizes oppression. When he sees people selling out the revolution. When he sees education, along with hand grenades, heaved in his way. What *could* a worker do with art when—despite all the horror—art continues to project an ideal, untouchable world, when it continues to overlook the crimes of the owners and to mislead him with its bourgeois representation of the world as a peaceful and orderly place. An art that delivers him into the teeth of his oppressors, rather than one that agitates against those dogs.

What should a worker do with poets and thinkers who, despite the oppressive conditions he lives under, don't feel the least obligation to join the struggle against his oppressors?

And what should art do for the workers? Have painters painted in accord with the needs of the working class in its struggle for freedom? Have they painted so that workers might learn how to throw off the thousand-year yoke of oppression?

They have, despite all the atrocities, painted the world in a peaceful light. The beauty of nature, the forests with their chirping birds, the late afternoon sunlight! Show the forest in the grubby hands of profiteers! The hands of those who have claimed the forest as their own private preserve. They alone have the right to exploit it, to sell the lumber to those who can afford it, while those who have none are left out in the cold.

Meanwhile, of course, art has no "tendency" whatsoever. O no, not at all!

That's why they go on painting that old baroque religious fraud: baroque angels and apostles, and nobody knows what to do with them! Crucifixions of every sort, with "originals" to hang over the Junker's dinner table, and reproductions to stupefy the masses.

That's why, in their art, they preach escape from thoughts and feelings. Escape from earth, with its intolerable conditions, to the moon and the stars. To permit the machine guns of democracy to hold sway, they hold the image of a blest afterlife before the eyes of the poor. That's why a wimp like Rainer Maria Rilke, whom one of the perfumed idle rich put up with, could write: "Poverty is a wondrous glow from within" *(Book of Hours).*

Workers! It's you whom they've given Christian ideals, you they want to disarm, so as to turn you over to the murderous machinery of the state.

Workers! In their pictures they depict a wealth and beauty that the bourgeoisie can hold to, and that can deceive you. They strengthen the bourgeoisie and undermine your class-consciousness, your will to power.

You're excluded from their art, yet they write of "the art of the people." They would tempt you to believe in a "good" that only they and your oppressors possess—tempt you to give up the *real* struggle, that you might embrace their world. They want their "spirituality" to domesticate you, make you docile, impress upon you your own insignificance in relation to the wonders of the human spirit.

Fraud! It's a fraud!

No, art belongs in museums, where it can be gaped at by the petite bourgeoisie on vacation. Art belongs in the palaces of the bloodsuckers, where it may hide their wallsafes.

Workers! *You* create the surplus value that makes possible the very existence of exploiters who load their walls with "aesthetic" luxuries; you guarantee the artist a living standard far above what he has had in the past. Now listen, workers, to how such artists take a stand with respect to your struggle.

After the *Kapptagen,* when, to the chagrin of the antimilitarists and pacifists, you had taken up arms—then, frankly, they'd rather have had you dressed in long white robes, a candle in one hand and Frank's book, *God Is Good,* in the other, driving away the White Witch with weapons of the spirit. During this time even an artistic type such as Oskar Kokoschka, a republican professor at the art academy, not only kept his distance from the struggle (the traditional response of intellectuals) but offered the following terse manifesto to the people of Dresden:

I SAY TO ALL WHO ARE CONCERNED ABOUT THE FUTURE—YOU WHO ARE NOW ARGUING POLITICAL THEORIES (WHETHER LEFT OR RIGHT OR MIDDLE-OF-THE-ROAD) WITH GUNS—I MOST URGENTLY IMPLORE YOU TO STAY CLEAR OF THE MUSEUM AND TO RESTRICT YOUR WARLIKE ACTIVITIES TO THE FIRING RANGE. ON MONDAY, THE 15th OF MARCH, AN IMPORTANT PAINTING OF RUBENS WAS DAMAGED BY A BULLET. THESE PAINTINGS ARE NOT SAFE IF THEY DO NOT ENJOY OUR PROTECTION. AND WHILE IT MAY BE CLAIMED THAT WE HAVE NO NEED FOR THIS ART, THE ART AUTHORITIES OF DRESDEN WHO, WITH ME, ARE APPREHENSIVE AND NERVOUS, CONSIDER SUCH MASTERWORKS TO BE RARE CREATIONS. AND WHEN

WE'RE RESPONSIBLE FOR PROTECTING THEM, AND THEY'RE DESTROYED, IT'S WE WHO ROB THE POOR PEOPLE OF THE FUTURE OF THE HIGHEST GOOD. WE MUST DO EVERYTHING POSSIBLE TO PREVENT THIS. THE GERMAN PEOPLE OF THE FUTURE WILL CERTAINLY FIND MORE MEANING IN THESE PAINTINGS THAN DO THE POLITICIZED PEOPLE OF TODAY. I HARDLY DARE HOPE THAT MY COUNTERPROPOSAL WILL BE HEARD, WHICH STATES: IN OUR GERMAN REPUBLIC, AS IN CLASSICAL TIMES, FEUDS SHOULD BE DECIDED BY DUELS BETWEEN POLITICAL LEADERS. THIS SEEMS LESS HARMFUL AND LESS CONFUSING THAN THE METHODS EMPLOYED AT PRESENT.
—Oskar Kokoschka, Professor, Academy Of Visual Arts, Dresden

We say to all who aren't too nauseated after reading this, all who despise the statements of this *art scab*, we urgently implore you to take a stand against this. We call on all who feel it a trivial concern that bullets damage paintings, who know that bullets tear human beings apart. We call on all who will risk their lives to save themselves and their comrades from the claws of the parasites.

The "highest good," when one speaks of art, culture, the fatherland, etc., is nothing more than what is man-made. And when you are called upon to struggle, realize that for people like Oskar Kokoschka and Wilhelm II, the highest good is for them to keep their possessions, their investments, in their own hands. But you who want, at any cost, to keep "the poor people of the future" from being robbed, will welcome it when, instead of serving at the pleasure of cultural luminaries like Kokoschka, these paintings are sold in order to feed the malnourished children of the coming generation.

"The poor people of the future" need more than the opportunity to stand before undamaged paintings on crippled legs. The German people will find more significance in the cultural ignorance of our art than in the honoring of Rembrandt. The struggles of "the politicized people of Germany" are the logical expression of a desire to survive and to create better living conditions, something which now only people like Kokoschka can conceive of. He who has eaten his fill and who can joke about the hungry. Naturally, sated people need peace and quiet in which to digest, and they find it disturbing when they have to take notice of unimportant people. And when it comes to pistols and machine guns, this one tries to hide his dependence on his own kind, the intertwining of his fate with theirs. He's a gross lump who wants his artistic endeavors to be admired as the workings of a spiritual quest. Yet today there is more meaning in a Red Army soldier cleaning his rifle than in the sum total of the metaphysical works of all the painters combined. The notion of art and artist is an invention of the bourgeoisie which can be used only to support the ruling class, that is, the bourgeoisie itself.

The title "artist" is an insult.

The category "art" is a denial of human equality.

The idolization of the artist is the same as self-idolization. The artist stands no higher than his society. It's not his own little head which produces the contents of his works; he only puts out the world-image of his public, the way a sausage machine packs meat.

Of course Oskar Kokoschka, the creator of "psychological" portraits, doesn't waste his insights on the soulless mob. His aloof, academic awareness is enough for him. It allows him to be reasonable, to call upon the left, the center, the crooked and the right-wing radicals to confine their arguments to the combat zone.

And though he stands above the quarreling of political parties, as do all the great prostitutes of art, at the same time he tries to prevent the poor deluded mob from mindlessly pursuing the new political consciousness. The political arena should be where the leaders fight as gladiators do, so that no conflagration may break out, so that guards can protect the borders, so that Rembrandt and Rubens won't turn over in their graves.

Herr Professor, do you know any means by which Rembrandt and Rubens, who can't even use a telephone, might reach us, might rise from the grave with their tri-cornered hats, pointy shoes and all the rest, appearing as if in their own paintings? Doubtless they would cause the German soul, now so torn, to heal over, so that peace and order might be restored to our troubled Fatherland, and a better future be ushered in. A future, certainly, in which the Treaty of Versailles has been revised.

Such angels down from the moon, from the meadows of metaphysics, are symptoms. Their conception of art is geared to the art market. So whenever we come up against this conception of art, we attack it—attack also the stupidity, the arrogance and clubbiness which it conceals. The whole shameless artistic and cultural fraud of our time!

Kokoschka's statements are a typical expression of the sentiments of bourgeois society. This society places its art and culture above the lives of the working class. The conclusion is this: there can be no reconciliation between the bourgeoisie, with its culture and standard of living, and the proletariat.

Workers! We see proletarian reconstruction of the world in the attempts to change this culture and its deceptive conception of art. We anxiously await a response from Felix Stossinger who, in *Free World,* exhibited for you, the workers, the work of Oskar Kokoschka, and who demonstrated its importance to you. He has also demonstrated the importance of the theological crap of the *Isenheimer Altar* and the individualistic artistic creations of Van Gogh. Egocentric individualism rose hand in hand with the development of capital, and so must fall with it.

WE WELCOME THE NEWS THAT BULLETS ARE BEING FIRED INTO MUSEUMS AND PALACES, INTO THE WORKS OF RUBENS, INSTEAD OF INTO THE HOUSES OF THE POOR IN WORKING-CLASS NEIGHBORHOODS!

We welcome it when open struggle between capital and labor takes place where art and culture feel at home. The art and the culture that gag the poor, that delight the bourgeois on Sunday and accommodate oppression on Monday.

There is only one task: to accelerate, through every available means, the downfall of this oppressive culture.

Every expression of indifference is counterrevolutionary!

We will never permit the Kokoschkas to survive, to go on using the future to justify the present. (What is a futuristic painting—"A Woman's Hat Goes Down the Steps"—when there isn't enough butter to go around?)

We call on everyone to take a stand against this masochistic awe regarding historical worth. To take a stand against culture and art!

We especially ask that you express your opposition to the proposal of Oskar Kokoschka! We need to speak in a collective voice against such scabs and those who hide beneath them.

Workers! As you alone, with your own hands, have created organizations for class struggle, you alone will create a workers' culture.

(1920)

INSTEAD OF A BIOGRAPHY

The art of today depends on the bourgeoisie and will die with it. The painter, even if unaware of it, is a cash factory, a machine for producing profit, who is used by wealthy exploiters and aesthetic jackasses so they may invest their money more or less profitably and be called, therefore, patrons of the arts. Art is, to many, a kind of flight away from this "vulgar" world into a shining sphere where they may fantasize about a paradise free and clear of civil strife and factionalism.

The cult of individuality and personality, which promotes painters and poets only to promote itself, is really a business. The greater the "genius" of the personage, the greater the profit. How can an artist reach such heights among the bourgeoisie? Through swindle. Most artists start out in proletarian circumstances, in shabby studios, yet have an amazing, if unconscious, adaptability when it comes to finding a way out. Before long the artist finds some influential bigwig to "sponsor" him, which means: paving his way to the marketplace. Occasionally a patron comes along and gives him 100 marks a month in exchange for handling his entire artistic production; or he becomes the property of an art dealer whose job is to convince bourgeois collectors that they need these artworks. With an eye to what's fashionable, the artist does exactly what the market demands; to that end, all the old props of sacred and divine fraud, as well as the cosmic and metaphysical ones, are paraded out, heralded by heavenly trumpets. Behind the scenes, one can spot the cynical manipulation of insiders. This contrasts with the outward show of cultural advancement. This is what's called "the star system". It's what the system demands, and what the business thrives on. The artists themselves, whether super sophisticated or still rough around the edges—artists whose exalted status arose from their discontent with the world—are mostly brainwashed, and fall in line behind the reactionary fraud called art criticism, a criticism that is utterly subjective and eclectic. They think themselves "creators" who, at the very least, tower above the average philistine who laughs at the "deeper meanings" in a painting by Picasso or Derain. Yet their "creations" are entirely in accord with the so-called spirit of art: they are thoughtless, hostile to reality, and removed from struggle. Just go to art exhibits and see what radiates from the walls! The present is so idyllic, dreamlike, so ready to accommodate some sacred Gothic cult, or primitive beauty, or red circles, blue squares, any farcical inspiration: "Reality, argh! It's ugly. The turmoil disturbs our inner equilibrium, it distracts the soul."

Or look at those with more contemporary diseases—how tense they are, how afflicted with their own grandiose visions. We really need such a marasmus, don't we...indigestible chunks of Gothic and ancient Greek, and don't forget Egyptian! Just look at the great Grünewald, or Cézanne, so proud of his honors—or Henri Rousseau, that dear, old, ignorant customs official intoxicated with his own blest innocence. Today all that seems so desolate, cold, empty. And the current revolution is so straitlaced, so mute and listless. The only struggle is the struggle for more money, but that's neither real nor saintly. Men have utterly forgotten that they are "descended from God."

It's a mistake to think it necessary for a small circle of artists to paint cubes or a profoundly tangled mass, even if such painting *is* in opposition to Makart. Sure he's a bourgeois painter. He paints bourgeois passions, values, bourgeois history. But what about you? What are you but a pathetic satellite of the bourgeoisie? Your snobbish ideas, your bizarre thoughts, where did you get them? Are you going to work for the proletariat, the bearer of the coming culture? Are you taking the trouble to experience and understand the ideas of the proletariat—to form, together with the exploited and oppressed, an opposition? Ask yourself if it isn't time, finally, to be done with your precious awards. You pretend to be timeless, to stand above party and faction, you in your ivory tower. You claim to paint for the people. Where are the people!? What is your cultivated indifference, your abstract nonsense about timelessness, but ridiculous, senseless speculation about eternity? Your brushes and pens, which should be weapons, are nothing but slips of straw.

Come out of your studios, even if it's hard on you. Stop being individualistic and defensive. Give yourself over to the ideas of the proletariat. Help them in the struggle against this rotten society.

"A human being is nothing, a beast." Actually, men have created a vicious system, one with a top and a bottom. A few earn millions while thousands upon thousands lack the bare necessities of life. In South America trains are powered by corn distillates while in Russia millions die of hunger. Yet we speak of culture and discuss art. But perhaps the well-set table, the handsome limousine, the stage and the furnished parlor, the library and the gallery, all that the rich screw manufacturer treats himself to at the expense of his slaves, perhaps, just perhaps, this is not really culture at all?

But what does all that have to do with art? Precisely this, that many painters and writers continue to tolerate this state of affairs without taking a clear stand against it. Today, when all this needs to be flushed away, they continue to stand aloof, cynical as ever—today, when there's a need to lead the way in opposing all this pettiness, this cultural hypocrisy, this damned callousness.

Now the prevailing belief is in self-satisfying private initiative. The purpose of my work is to shake this belief, to show the oppressed the true face of their oppressor.

It is the duty of revolutionary artists to propagandize in two ways. To purge our world-view of the supernatural powers, of superstition, of God and angels. To open men's eyes that they may see their actual relationship to their environment. The traditional symbols and mystical transports of the stupidest religious frauds still clutter today's artworks. What should we do about this? The demands of life are too pressing to allow this painted nonsense to go on.

Go to meetings of the proletariat. Sit and listen how the people, people like you, discuss how to make the smallest improvements in their lives.

Understand, these are the masses working toward a world organization. No, *you* are not. But you *can* build this organization with them. You can help, if you have the desire to do so. In your artworks take the time, trouble yourself, to formulate the revolutionary concepts of the workers.

I'm trying to be understood by everyone. I renounce those profound depths which no one can ever get to without a diving suit pumped full of cabalistic mumbo jumbo and academic metaphysics.

There has got to be an end to expressionistic anarchism. Today, painters indulge in it because, being out of touch with the workers, they are ignorant. Yet the time is coming when artists will no longer be overblown Bohemian anarchists but bright, healthy workers in a collectivist society. As long as the goal of the working masses still lies in the future, the intelligentsia will continue to waver this way and that, riddled with doubt and cynicism.

I write this instead of the expected, more popular biography. To me it seems more important to speak of my perceptions—and what are, I believe, valid judgments based on my experience—than to enumerate the stupid, superficial, accidental events of my life, such as birthday, family background, schooling, first pair of long pants, the artist's travels from cradle to grave, creative impulses and inspirations, first success, etc. etc.

All that self promotion is utterly beside the point.

(1920)

RED GROUP

Painters and draftsmen, organized activists in the Communist Party, have united in a 'communist art group' recognizing that (1) a good communist is primarily a communist, and only secondarily a skilled worker, an artist, etc., and that (2) all knowledge and ability are instruments in the service of the class struggle.

This group has set itself the task (working closely with central local organs of the Communist Party) of increasing the effectiveness of communist propaganda through the media of writing, the graphic arts and theatre. This is to be carried out as follows:

1. By organizing evenings of ideologically coherent propaganda.
2. By giving practical aid to all revolutionary organizations.
3. By speaking out against the dregs of 'Free German' ideology (nationalist, patriotic, romantic) that still remain in proletarian organizations.
4. By teaching art in local workshops, helping with the design of wall posters and the making of placards for demonstrations; also, giving support to the as yet amateurish attempts of party members to articulate their revolutionary will by means of art.
5. By organizing wall displays.
6. By conducting ideological and practical instruction among revolutionary artists themselves.
7. By speaking out and taking a stand against manifestations of counterrevolutionary culture.
8. By subverting attempts to present the works of bourgeois artists as being neutral.
9. By exploiting bourgeois art exhibits for propaganda purposes.
10. By keeping in touch with art students in the schools, so as to revolutionize them.

We consider the *RED GROUP* the core of a consistently expanding organization of all proletarian revolutionary artists in Germany. So far many writers, associates of comrade Edwin Piscator, have joined the communist art group. We extend an invitation to all painters and writers to join us and work with us to carry out our program. Correspondence should be sent to Rudolph Schlichter, Berlin, Neue Winterfeldstr. 17.

Berlin, June 13, 1924

RED GROUP
Union of Communist Artists
Chairman: George Grosz. Vice-chairman: Karl Witte. Writer, Secretary: John Heartfield

ART IS IN DANGER!

Anyone considering the art of today will find it a crazy, confusing subject. It's not easy to criticize it correctly.

These days, with their contradictions and pitched battles, give rise to comparable struggles in art. How does art appear today?

Let's enter the arena of art! A bizarre crowd—ranging from the pathetic to the eccentric buffoon, often cheerful and content, yet at times bickering and combative to the point where there are broken brushes and bent compasses—a great commotion everywhere. We find business, advertising, sound effects, but also noble detachment, resignation, escapism. A whole range of individuals in the heart of the academy. And art publications of every form—triangular, square, oblong—each combating the other, and all filled with problems and theories. One picks them up and asks, which of these *does* know the true meaning of art: "Der Sturm?" "Der Kunstwart?" "Der Cicerone?" "Kunst und Künstler?" "G?" "Das Kunstblatt?"

There's one group which defies all tradition. Wildly ecstatic, they brandish their instruments and paint as barbarically as aborigines. Others are overwhelmingly Gothic, or zealously Catholic, while another bunch will declare itself Zionist or Buddhist. Others go back to old Tuscany. Stimulated by the old masters, they revive the elegant and the slender with a slight Parisian sauciness. Even the Cubists with their eternal guitars are reluctant to die out. Lately, though, the

Classical has gone up in price, and Ingres, Flaxmann, Poussin and Genelli have begun to rise from the grave. Also the Futurists, worshipers of simultaneity and sound effects. Still others put together a cosmopolitan conglomeration of old Russian ikons and Cubism. And many (honesty being the best policy) dispense with innovation and experimentation altogether; they stick to home cooking. The research into optics and color by the Impressionists (e.g. the *detail* method of the Japanese: Mount Fuji as seen through a fishnet). The experiments of Pointillism and Neopointillism are ever new. Others swear by Lübl, Lehnbach, Menzel or Defregger. And the pasty stroke of Trübner is, especially in southern Germany, highly valued. Even painters of the soil, such as Eichler, Putz, Erler, and the 100% German painters Karl Vinnen and Hans Thoma, as well as recluses like Kubin, Ensor, and Doms, still believe in hexes and fairies despite the automobile and the radio. And not to be forgotten are those painters who dwell in the great exhibits, the masters of oversized society portraits, of representational paintings, of life-sized horses and madonnas; they are honored, given medals and ribbons, recognized and valued by the elite. And, last but not least, the panoramic and gallery painters. They too are called artists. And why not? It's only a small circle that would deny them that designation.

Whose opinion is correct? Which viewpoint will be confirmed? How do artists, the 'sensitive antennae of society,' express themselves today? How and where does one determine their influence?

Never has art been more off-putting than it is now, especially for the common man of today, who claims he can live without art. Whatever one understands art to be, it's clear that its overriding task is to satisfy man's living *Bildhunger* (yearning for images). This *Bildhunger* persists today, more than ever, within the masses. And it's going to be satisfied in an unprecedented way, but not by our display-window conception of art. Photographs and motion pictures will be sufficient to meet this need.

The twilight of art began with the invention of photography. Art forfeited its right to report the world. The romantic longings of the masses are satisfied at the movies, where they can get their fill of love, ambition, the exotic unknown and nature. Whoever enjoys newsreels or historical splendors pays his own way in: the sovereign with or without silk hat; the murderer and thief, Haarman; gymnastics exhibitions and memorial services, our wonderful countryside—it's all there. Hindenburg's sorrow-through-fear countenance is a humanity no Rembrandt or Dürer ever captured. No Michelangelo created Dempsey's muscles.

The objection will be raised that this is not the essence of art— how the artist's eye sees, and how he translates what he sees—but a matter of heart, of soul. This objection holds that journalism has no role in art today. And that therefore, to see today's world, one should go to the movies, not to an art exhibit. And that at the movies you will only find half of art. Yet for most people it is the more important half, and it is more complete than ever. The other half is limited to the subtleties, the spiritualities and nobilities of our forefathers' art, an art which reported as much then as it does now. Very little.

Technologically, man is progressing at a brisk pace. The film-half of art is no longer confined to a rectangular canvas. Neatly confined to a rectangular canvas, neatly packaged, today's artworks lie in a small cylinder and can appear (another advantage) simultaneously in New York, Berlin, London, Paris, and just as easily in the most remote village. In comparison, how laborious and antiquated the creation of an oil painting appears. How quaint. In film the work is also fresher, and its making does not depend on the talent of one individual. Many minds work on it, and thereby the film more easily achieves a social character than the individual handiwork of an artist does. Incidentally, problems of light and motion, which were only partly solved by painters, present no difficulty in film. How can a painting compare, really, with a film of a moving ocean? The painting is a boring affair; at best it is only more or less well done.

Many of our painters have observed this. Some have recognized the superior reproductive capacity of the technical sciences and have therefore assigned them the task of imitating nature. Immersed in their own worlds, they imagine themselves beyond the world of reality, and so they follow after the "orphic resonances" of their own souls. The soul should win that particular race.

Many expressionists have started from this point: honorable, somewhat richly talented men. Kandinsky made music, projecting the music of the soul on canvas. Paul Klee crocheted tender girlish handiwork on the Biedemeyer sewing table. The only representational subject matter that remained for so-called pure art was that of the painter's own emotions. Consequently, the true painter had to paint his inner life. Here the disaster began. The result: 77 directions for art, everyone claiming to paint the true soul.

There were also groups that saw that this wouldn't work (the soul is too vacillating an image) and so, with burning zeal, they set themselves to work on other problems: simultaneity, motion, rhythm! Naturally this turned out to be a futile sort of idealism: simultaneity and motion cannot be expressed adequately on canvas.

And here lay the beginnings of new perceptions. Some pressed on and began to "construct." Although some spoke of dynamics, in short order they discovered that the most immediate expression of *that* was in the dry drawings of the engineer. So the soul and metaphysical speculation were driven out by the compass and the ruler. Constructivism came into play. It *saw* with greater clarity. It didn't go off on metaphysical flights. Its aims were free of archaic, outworn prejudices. The Constructivists wanted objectivity, wanted to work in terms of concrete necessities. They upheld an art whose goals and method could be construed, perceived and verified.

Unfortunately the Constructivists have a practical failing— they're falling short of their goal. In most cases they're still confined within the traditional sphere of art. They forget that, as a rule, there is only one type of constructivist: the engineer, the architect, the welder, the carpenter. In a word, the technician. They set out to be leaders—but were, it turns out, only a reflex. The more honest among them put so-called art aside and focused their energy on the real basis of constructivism: the industrial economy. But in trying to save the precious word "art," they have compromised it. Furniture from the Weimar Bauhaus is probably well-constructed. But one would rather sit on a chair factory-produced by anonymous carpenters; it would be more comfortable than one designed by a romantic, decadent Bauhaus engineer. Constructivism logically led to the engineer. Constructivism logically led to the downgrading of artists. It led to the occupations of construction engineer, architect, and design engineer, the real creators of our time. In Russia, this constructivist romanticism has a deeper meaning and is more thoroughly socially conditioned than in western Europe. In Russia, Constructivism is, in part, a natural reflex of the powerful machine-oriented offensive of industrialization. For the farmer, the experience of electric power, of red-painted tractors of the Kees Company, of turbines, is utterly novel and unheard of. There, the canvasses combining spiritual and mechanical construction are not as purposeless as in western Europe. The suggestive power of the machine aesthetic, the (to the layman) almost supernatural secrets of technology, served as a starting point for the masses, who have responded more emotionally than rationally. The artist is (even if unconsciously) a mediator and recruiter for the ideas generated by industrial development. I *(George Grosz)* am personally persuaded that, in the state academy in Moscow, a study section has been established where there is instruction in physics and mechanics so that, in many cases, these artists are called "technical students." In this way a more genuine "constructivist" will be made of the art student whose primary attraction to the beauty of technology has been emotional.

In the West, art can no longer fulfill such tasks. Here technology does not have to be detoured through art. For the masses, both in the city and in the country, technology has long been commonplace.

Then what's to be done? Everything said so far leads to one conclusion: the liquidation of art. Of course, this is not a satisfactory way to resolve the situation. But why so? The aforementioned introspective nature of art seems capable of another focus, one that doesn't demand that the artist have an antiquated mind. Art is not just a mood; it's an ancient impulse which man, often in dire need, persists in. Man believes wholeheartedly that there is yet something to be said that only an artist can say, something that must be said. Even if an artist's contemporaries will not hear him, there is the consolation that perhaps, after his death, a future generation will grant recognition to his work. Even today, a centennial exhibit suddenly thrusts some name into the light of day, and the art market is taken by surprise—caught out by the fame of one who was, in his own lifetime, misunderstood.

Genuine self-confidence in their ability to create something of lasting value gives those artists the strength to endure the indifference or rejection of their contemporaries. It's an astonishing fact that any number of highly accomplished men will work a lifetime, fruitlessly, clinging to the twin concepts of future and eternity. (Presumably, by overlooking the cares and petty details of daily life, one grasps the "essential.") The lucky ones see, in their own lifetime, their work hung in a private gallery or two, possibly even in a museum.

Should this be the end we work toward: to be admired in galleries? The very idea (Grünewald had his *Isenheimer Altar* exhibited near Cassirer) shows quite blatantly the problematical situation of artists in contemporary society. Material deprivation bespeaks an idealism, a passion for the future, for eternity.

The point is, then, to figure what the artist imagines the future to be (eternity is really just an extension of the present). Obviously he isn't hoping for recognition from a future that is distinct from the people of that future. If people in the future are unchanged from what they were during the artist's lifetime, then he has no reason to expect the posthumous recognition that he hopes for. For the future to be different, the people must be different. Yes, the unspoken hope of every artist who strives for future recognition is that mankind will discover new standards and form new opinions. And surely the artist will help in this. For his own sake and for that of his work, he will help bring about this change. Many are convinced that, in some mysterious way, this will come about.

And so we have a paradox: those anemic, long-haired, peculiar men in their studios, men who couldn't throw a stone at a cat, who live in dread of the cleaning lady, and who are devastated by the bind their work is in...those very same men are furthering progress!?

I too have been one of those peculiar people. I want to discuss the revolutionary aspects of my development now, to encourage artists to work independently of contemporary reaction.

For a long time it has been acceptable to say that a real painter must be ignorant. Must he be? Don't we consider the artist's knowledge of the world to be the most advanced in the nation? Should "the most worldly-wise in the nation" confine themselves to the cultivation of their feelings while leaving the rest to ignorant clods, who have neither information nor understanding? And even if the artists *are* correct—to be a revolutionary, is it enough to paint year in and year out hoping for a better future? My own opinion is that artists don't have the right to do that. An artist must expand his knowledge and understanding, and do so personally, in response to the danger we face. It is no longer sufficient to love; one must also learn to hate.

When I began consciously to experience the world, I soon found that there wasn't a whole lot to the gaiety or glitter of life. Nor, above all, to my fellow human beings. Consequently I became a vague idealist and a true romantic; I felt cut-off, isolated. Unwittingly, I overrated art and came to have a distorted view of it. I had blinders on both eyes. I despised mankind. I saw everything from the perspective of my little studio. I was surrounded by smalltime merchants, homeowners and shopkeepers whose talk and ideas disgusted me. I became a righteous misanthrope and a skeptical individualist. Foolish and misinformed as I was, I felt I had a monopoly on knowledge and awareness. I was proud of myself. I even believed I could see through the stupidity that lay all around me, like a fog. The sketches I did in those days express that hatred. For example, I drew a *Stammtisch* (daily gathering of friends at a table set aside for them) in a beer hall where men sat packed together like thick red masses of flesh in ugly gray slacks.

To achieve a style that would render clearly and bluntly the harshness and coldness of my subjects, I studied the crudest manifestations of the artistic impulse: I copied graffiti, the folklore of men's rooms. They struck me as the most direct expression, and succinct translation, of strong feelings. Even children's drawings stimulated me with their single-mindedness. Thus I gradually developed the knife-edged line I needed to record my observations, which at that time were misanthropic. Herein lay the danger: to get bogged down in the stylization of the drawings. As a countermeasure I tried fluid nature studies, which I'd neglected for a long time. I admired the Japanese, who observed nature with an unbroken ease. I found their woodcuts full of life. It was especially gratifying that most depicted daily life. Even so, it was Toulouse-Lautrec who inspired me. But I also enjoyed ancient woodcuts, where I found striking expressions in the simplest of lines. I made jottings on the street, in cafés, in music halls, and afterwards I analyzed my impression in writing. Once, before the war, I'd planned a large three-volume work, *The Grotesqueness of the Germans.* But I couldn't get an advance to get started on it, and Malik Verlag didn't yet exist.

I was in Paris for a short time. Paris didn't make any special impression on me, and I never shared others' overestimation of that city.

In the time before the War my views could have been summed up as follows...people are pigs. All talk of ethics is a fraud, meant only for the stupid. Life has no purpose except to satisfy one's hunger for food and women. There is no soul. All that matters are the necessities of life. Most important, man has no worth. It is necessary to shove and elbow your way through life, but it's also disgusting. So, my work expressed a strong loathing of life, and this was overcome only by my interest in the works themselves. When the loathing got to be too much, I got drunk.

The outbreak of the War made it clear to me that the masses, who were marching, cheering wildly, through the streets, were under the influence of the press and the military and had no will of their own. The will of the politicians and generals dominated them. As for myself, I was aware of these overpowering forces, but I was not cheering, because I saw that my individual freedom was now threatened. I wanted to live apart from mankind and its demands. Instead, against my will, I was forced into the military along with the rest.

My hate focused on the cause of all this. I considered the war a monstrous, degenerate manifestation of the everyday scramble for possessions. This war was, in its particulars, repulsive to me, and in general it was even more so. But I could not keep myself from being turned into a Prussian soldier. To my astonishment I discovered that the people were not as enthusiastic about the war as I'd thought. I despised them a little less. And my sense of isolation began to diminish somewhat. My life as a soldier inspired many of my drawings. A few comrades clearly enjoyed these. As they shared in my feelings, I found their attention preferable to the recognition of this or that collector who would appraise my work only from the standpoint of a speculator.

Because I had made friends I was, for the first time, drawing with the awareness that others shared my views and experiences. I began to realize it was better to work for more than myself and my art dealer. I wanted to become an illustrator, a journalist. High art, insofar as it's concerned with depicting the beauty of the world, interested me less than before. I began looking to tendency artists and moralists: Hogarth, Goya, Daumier, and similar artists. Although much occupied with the lively conflicts taking place among new art trends, I couldn't share in the general indifference which people in those circles had regarding social events. I sketched and painted, beset with contradictions, and tried through my work to picture the world in its utter ugliness, sickness and despair. I had no apparent success at that time. I considered myself an out-and-out revolutionary. I imagined my resentment to be awareness.

Yet the war didn't bring about any fundamental changes. Again I mistrusted friendship. Anything like camaraderie didn't suit my world. I didn't want to have any illusions. Then I began to hear of revolutionary movements, but unfortunately I had no direct contact with them and so remained skeptical: one needed only look at the SPD, which was supporting the great brotherhood of man *and* war credit allocations, and all in one breath. That was the reality. I saw it. No more Swedenborgian hell and demonic power for me! I was seeing the real devils: men in trousers, with beards, with and without medals and ribbons. As for the hopes many of my friends had for peace and revolution, I considered them groundless.

Once again a civilian, I experienced the earliest days of the Dada movement in Berlin. Its beginning coincided with the turning point of Germany, winter 1917 known in popular terms as the "Turnip Winter" *(Die Zeit der Kohlrübe)* because of the food shortage.

This German Dada movement had its roots in the awareness (which I and most of my comrades had come to) that it was irrational to believe that "spirit" ruled the world. Imagine Goethe in a barrage of gunfire, Nietzsche with a field pack, Jesus in the trenches! Yet there are still people who hold that spirit and art are powers unto themselves.

Dadaism has been the only substantial artistic movement in Germany in the past hundred years. Don't laugh. Compared with this movement, all other "isms" in art seem like minor studio affairs. Dadaism was not a made-up movement; rather it was an organic reaction to the head-in-the-clouds tendency of so-called high art, whose devotees meditated over Cubism and "the Gothic" while the field marshals did their own painting with blood. Dadaism forced all those who were really interested in art to do the same.

What did Dadaism do? It held that it doesn't matter whether one simply bats the breeze or recites a sonnet by Petrarch, Shakespeare or Rilke; or whether one polishes boot heels or paints madonnas: there will still be shootings, still be profiteering, still be hunger. What is art for? Was it not the height of deception to pretend that high art creates spiritual values? Were not artists incredibly ridiculous, taking themselves seriously when no one else would? "Hands off high art!" cried the opponents of Dadaism. "Art is in danger! The spirit will be defiled." How could they babble on about spirit, when such spirit as there was was worthless? The press was writing: Buy War Bonds. As far as art and artists are concerned, they are happy when they have only to repaint, daily, with beauty and fascination, the increasingly exposed face of *Anno 13.*

I, along with the other founders of German Dadaism, know today that our main error was to have been too preoccupied with so-called art. Dadaism was a mocking break with a narrow, overrated milieu that was too highly regarded. But it only swayed in midair, suspended between the classes. It could not assume the responsibilities of both classes at once. At that time we saw the mad end-product of the ruling social order, and we burst out laughing. We didn't see, yet, that there was a system underlying the madness.

The nearby revolution made us gradually aware of this system. There was no further occasion for laughter; there were more pressing problems than those regarding art. The problem of art must be put into perspective. Having overcome the rhetoric of art, we found we had lost a number of our Dadaists, mainly in Switzerland and France. They had experienced the social upheavals of the past decade through—from the perspective of—the newspapers. The rest of us saw our work cut out for us: to produce tendency art in the service of the revolutionary cause.

In the art world today, the call for tendency is still met with indignant, disdainful protest. This happens to be the case now, perhaps, even more than in the past. True, it is conceded that in every era there have been artworks with a tendentious character. Yet still such works are judged not with regard to their tendency but to their formal, "purely artistic" qualities. The people who make such judgments fail utterly to understand that every work of art in every era embodies a tendency; all that has been changed is the clear-cut character of this tendentiousness. A few rough, sketchy examples: the Greeks promoted "the beautiful man;" sports, physical culture, served as a cohesive factor; Eros, their religious outlook. In a word, this comprised the "100% Greek." The Gothic was instructed by Christian propaganda. In the Middle Ages, artists created what pleased the kings, the patricians and the merchants. The primitive caveman, the aborigine, have their idols, their hunting and sexual art. Today we understand, and adhere to, what is material. We may distinguish countless tendencies. A few examples: Menzel is the painter of Prussia and of early German industrialization; Defregger idealizes retail merchants, and loyalty to the home, and brings forth cheerful stories. Delacroix paints what is cosmopolitan, what is supported by history and tradition, and is for heroism, progress, and a powerful France. Toulouse-Lautrec saw through the celebrated French tourist/pleasure scene, revealing it as bourgeois eroticism. Gauguin, tired of civilization, believes like Seume in "Better Game," and propagandizes for romantic individualism. Angelo Jank paints the equestrian pastimes of the aristocracy. Hodler promotes spiritualism, metaphysical monism, respect for historic exploits and heroic passions. Kokoschka propagandized for the "sublime," complicated, decadent "Last Citizens," the bourgeoisie and their problems. Hans

Thoma is enamored of harmless, rustic, dreamy men, idealized nature and homelife. He advocates complete indifference to concrete interests and social questions.

These examples should be sufficient to show that tendency in art is the rule, not the exception. Of course artists are not always conscious of the tendencies in their work, but this doesn't lessen the effect. One may determine the tendencies of any artist simply by knowing his or her works in relation to the world in which that artist lived. There are also artists who deliberately try to avoid every tendency they're aware of, in particular renouncing those that are troublesome. Often they believe one should create instinctively, without premeditation, as nature does, which gives form and color to plants, crystals, stones, to all that exists. They give their paintings incomprehensible names or just plain numbers. Clearly, what underlies these tactics is the attempt (similar to that in music) to limit all possible reactions to a work of art to one reaction: simple fascination. The painter is nothing but the creator of form and color. Whether these artists believe that their work has no "deeper meaning," or that it is given an emotional or metaphysical significance by the observer, the fact remains: they deny the very possibility that artists are influenced by ideology (be it eroticism, religion, politics, aesthetics, morals, etc.). Regarding social events, they're silent as well as indifferent and irresponsible; or, in those cases where it's not intentional, they work in ignorance and impotence.

Assuming these artists enter the service of industry and the applied arts, there is little to object to. As in the case of a politician who keeps busy, proving himself a hard worker, the question is simply one of aptitude: how well he does what he does.

To the extent that this form of art (so appealing to the literal-minded) is self-generated, it will serve as propaganda for blasé indifference and irresponsible individuality.

So the relation of the artist to the world is excluded from his work and, without fail, denied altogether. When one accuses an artist of being tendentious in his work, this accusation can be justified only to the extent that the tendency contradicts the unconscious views of the artist as revealed in and through his style—or when he tries to compensate for ineptitude by tacking on a tendentious motif or title. It seems everyone with insufficient talent advocates a tendency which he is fully convinced is right. But one cannot point to insufficient ability as reason to oppose, across the board, tendency in art.

One almost never hears that Grützner has painted propaganda for German beer or for the contentment of the monastic life, or that Grünewald's theme is based on his Christian beliefs. When critics try to belittle a work by calling attention to its tendentiousness, they're not criticizing the work of the artist but the idea for which it stands.

The artist, even if he neither wants it nor knows it, lives in a constant interrelationship with the public and with society. He cannot escape the laws which govern their development, especially not today when these laws are determined by class struggle. When distinguished artists remain aloof from society, their indifference and other-worldliness automatically support the class which is in power. In Germany, that class is the bourgeoisie. Moreover, large numbers of artists consciously support the world bourgeois order; only within that world order does their work have any value.

In November 1918, when the tide seemed to turn, suddenly the most isolated, esoteric brushes discovered their hearts were beating for the working masses, and for a few months red and pink allegories and pamphlets were turned out in great numbers. And they held their own in the art market. But soon law and order were restored, and what do you know...our artists made their way, as quietly as possible, back to the higher spheres. "What do you want from us! We're still revolutionary. But the workers, they've given up! They're all philistines. There's no way to make a revolution in this country!" And so they brood in their studios over the "real" revolutionary problems: form, color and style.

Of course, formal revolution had long ago lost its purpose. The modern bourgeois has digested everything; from him, nothing is safe. The merchant of today is different from the merchant of Gustav Freytag's time. This one is cold, distant. He hangs radical works on the walls of his apartment. The catch phrase is, don't be old-fashioned, adapt quickly and without thinking. His art must be in the latest style. He lacks any notion of responsibility or mission. He's sober, realistic to the point of proceeding in a stupor, skeptical, without illusions, greedy. He understands only his goods. There are specialists for understanding the rest: philosophy, ethics, art, all the stuff of culture. Exports determine what is fashionable and the rest accept it. The formal revolutionary, the "wanderer in a void," hasn't done too badly. Despite superficial differences, he and the merchant are closely related, sharing the same indifferent, arrogant perspectives.

125

Anyone to whom the revolutionary concerns of the workers are not merely an expression (or "a beautiful, but unfortunately impractical, idea") cannot be content to work on harmless or formal problems. He will struggle to express the revolutionary ideas of the workers, to measure the worth of his work in terms of its social usefulness and effectiveness—not according to some arbitrary, individualistic principle of art, nor by the work's "success."

To summarize: the meaning, essence and history of art stand in direct relationship to the meaning, essence and history of society. The prerequisite for awareness and criticism of art in our time is awareness of the realities and relationships of real life in all its upheavals and tensions. Humankind has been in control of the earth's means of production, on a large scale, for a century now. At the same time, the struggle for possession of these means has grown ever more inclusive, drawing all men, without exception, into its storm. On one side there are workers, paid employees, civil servants; on the other there are shareholders, entrepreneurs, merchants, and financiers. The rest form a buffer zone between the two fronts. This struggle for existence, which divides humankind into exploiting and exploited halves, is called in its clearest and final form: class struggle.

Art is, indeed, in danger.

The artist of today, if he doesn't want to evade the issues, or become an empty shell, must choose between technology and service in the class war. Either way, he must give up "pure art." Either he joins the ranks of architects, engineers, and admen whom the industrial powers employ and the world exploits, or he becomes a depicter and critic who critiques the face of our time, becoming a propagandist and defender of revolutionary ideas and of their supporters in the army of the oppressed—those who struggle for their just share of the world's resources, and for a meaningful social order.

(1925)

THE WORKING ARTIST

Under the influence of the imperialist war of 1914-18, the pillars of bourgeois culture and morality began to collapse. The artists could not keep pace with events. The pencil turned out to be too slow a medium: it was overtaken by the lies spread by the bourgeois press.

Revolutionary artists couldn't keep up and were left behind. They never succeeded in following along in the tracks of the proletarian struggle...

The proletarian artist must face the fact that photography has developed further...if I can assemble photodocuments and skillfully juxtapose them, then the agitation/propaganda effect on the masses will be enormous. And this is what is most important to us. It is the foundation of our work. Therefore, our task is to have a powerful, intensive impact on the masses.

If we are successful in this, we will have brought a true art into being.

(1931)

Translated by Paul Gorrell

Bibliography

"The Art Scab" (Der Kunstlump) first appeared in *Der Gegner* (The Adversary) Vol. 1, nos. 10-12. Malik Verlag, Berlin. 1920. It was reprinted in *Die Aktion* Vol. 10. Verlag der Wochenschrift Die Aktion, Berlin. 1920.

"Instead of a Biography" (Statt einer Biographie) first appeared in *Der Gegner* Vol. 2, no. 3. Malik Verlag, Berlin. 1920. It was reprinted in *Die Kunst ist in Gefahr!* (Art is in Danger!) Vol. 3. Malik-Bucherei, Malik Verlag, Berlin. 1925. "Red Group" appeared in *Die Rote Fahne* (Red Flag), official organ of the Communist Party of Germany (KPD), in 1924.

"Art is in Danger!" (Die Kunst ist in Gefahr!) appeared as the title piece of Vol. 3 Malik-Bucherei, Malik Verlag, Berlin. 1925.

"The Working Artist" (der Operierende Künstler) is from a speech John Heartfield gave in Moscow in 1931.

A Note on the Authors
Malik Verlag was a collective effort. Because of this it is difficult to determine exactly who wrote what. The essays in this volume were written by Grosz, Heartfield and Herzfelde. There were probably others who contributed as well. The title page of the 1925 edition of *Art is in Danger!* has Grosz and Herzfelde as authors. "Instead of a Biography," which appears in this edition, was credited to Grosz alone when it originally appeared in *Der Gegner.* "The Art Scab" was written primarily by Grosz and Heartfield.

Theory & Practice of a Cinema with the People

BY WAY OF A PROLOGUE

Well, I'm going to speak: I think things should come out as they are felt. First, on behalf of my *compañeros,* I want to thank you for this work you are doing for the good of the peasants, all the peasants, inside and outside Ecuador. I don't know how to speak too clearly, I can't read, I never read or wrote anything. I am like a blind man— with words, that is—but I know suffering! Shit, how we peasants suffer! Outside and inside our country we suffer. Tonight we have seen something that brings us painfully back to Ecuador, our land. But it gladdens us to see other Indians who know how to struggle and who are fighting to correct the problems and injustices. Right now you make us want to return and join with our brothers, but this is difficult for me because I don't have papers, since I came to Colombia on foot, crossing the border.

But I tell you, I'd be ashamed to stand in front of the peasants of Riobamba or the other communities we saw in the film, who are standing up firmly to the cops and the government. Here I am selling things, not doing things like them who are fighting for us.

In the film we see well-informed peasants, with clear heads, well-read and courageous, who begin to unify the community. I lived for a time in the house of a good shoemaker friend named Damián. He is a really good friend who knows many things. He knows about Che and Camilo, the priest who died for the poor. He tells me things and I listen, but now I am kind of old—how I wish I could be young so I could know and do things. I am old but something that my friend, who was a fighter before, gave me always remains...that the youngsters, our children, must return to Ecuador to join with the peasants, weavers, shoemakers and students, like the ones who have brought us this film, with the consciousness to demand justice.

They say Ecuador is big and beautiful; I really don't think it's like that. I think there are sufferings for the peasants, that we suffer from hunger. I don't see anything going to the poor. There is oil, they say, but we don't see any; that is for the rich, for the military, the landowners. The film shows our life.

I congratulate the peasants in the film, the old woman who talks about her deep pain. Her pain is the pain of our poor women. That's why we have to learn more. This shows us, makes us see as one sees through clear water, our enemies; it lets us know their plans, their deceitful ways of exploiting us. It is easy to understand...with the film one quickly learns and discovers...

We must win respect for our ponchos, our weavings, here and wherever we are.

Thank you for showing our life, our land, and our brothers. This is making us think hard. I will talk about the film with my friend Damián. I know that if he had come, then he'd know about Ecuador, my land. This little thing would have shown him; he is so good, he teaches me so many things. I am deeply sorry he didn't come.

I like the film. I never go to see these things. I couldn't go to the cinema when I was young either. This is the first time I've seen these machines.

Now let the young men and ladies here speak. I said what I feel, what more can an old man say?

Juan Chimbo, Bogotá, April 1978

[Transcript of a taped interview made on the occasion of a showing of the film *Get Out of Here!* in the city of Bogota. The man interviewed: a 53 year-old weaver from Otavaleño, Ecuador.]

INTRODUCTION

The idea of explaining our cinematic work in the Ukamau Group led us to compile some theoretical essays, articles and interviews, and to order them in such a way as to provide a full-blown vision of the process of development of our cinema. We have no pretentions to presenting these writings as a book. We simply think that, by reading them, our concerns and thoughts about committed cinema, as well as our experiences which have always been the fundamental source of every theoretical inquiry, will become known.

Our first film saw the light of day in 1963. Fifteen years of cinematic work, which at the same time has been political work, have elapsed. The majority of our "thought of" or "dreamt of" films still remain on paper or locked deep in our minds, waiting patiently for the day when they can come into existence. Nevertheless, a few have managed to reach their audience and have provoked considerable unrest and reflection.

The opinions of Latin American workers and peasants who have seen and used our films have been and are the best reward in our search for a popular cinema that can be made into an instrument of struggle by the people themselves. Also it has been a principal concern that these works, themselves embedded in the culture of the people, become part of that very culture, representing in their own small way a dynamic expression of the expansion and growth of the cultural task of our Indian America.

Our work has only been made possible thanks to the creative participation and collaboration of workers and peasants, as well as intellectuals and filmmakers who understand the need to work together with the people, contributing their life experiences and knowledge to a dialectical and human interrelationship of mutual spiritual enrichment.

I am deeply indebted to these *compañeros,* both as a man and a filmmaker, for their many ideas and many examples of unselfishness and sacrifice. I would like to mention each and every one of them; however, I must resign myself to calling up their memory for the very reason that it would be impossible to mention all the many peasant and worker compañeros who gave so much of themselves, often aware that they were placing their personal security at risk. In gratitude to all of them, we would like this collection of writings to serve and be of use in the same sense the films they helped to create serve and are of use, since we know that that would truly make them happy.

To conclude this brief introduction it remains for us to say that we are convinced our work with the *compañeros* of the Ukamau Group is an attempt to clear pathways in the great search for a revolutionary cinema: conceived, realized and utilized by the people in the construction of the Great Liberated Country of our America.

La Paz, June 1978
Jorge Sanjinés Aramayo

HISTORICAL ANTECEDENTS OF SOCIAL CINEMA IN BOLIVIA

Bolivia is a country with a turbulent history, a nation that fights to seize its own destiny, which is impeded by imperialist aggression and by the alienation of an enemy dominant class which not only exploits its own people but against whom it is racist. The real Bolivia exists clandestinely; it lives, breathes and grows spiritually in the anonymity of a vigorous and creative people who have woven an extraordinary history, dignifying themselves in their struggle for freedom. The dominant class of Spanish ancestry has been ousted on more than one occasion and has regained its dominance mainly thanks to the economic and police support that North American imperialism has provided it. Its deep bonds within the metropolis, its controlling interests of our raw materials, as well as our geopolitical position, have been principal factors behind this vested support.

Nevertheless, the Bolivian people have resisted in different ways, and when they were powerless to take to the streets and fields and take up arms, they have tenaciously and steadfastly continued to develop their own culture in contrast to the dominant class that speaks Castilian and thinks like North Americans. The working class of Bolivia, considered among the most outstanding and experienced on the continent, has continued its advance and is today the principal front of resistance against fascist power.

We have wanted to give this brief overview because militant cinema in Bolivia was born precisely as a result of a revolutionary process that convulsed our country, a process that changed for a brief period the relations of production in the people's favor, and that in turn has created a social consciousness among intellectuals who have committed their work to the service of the people.

In 1952, after terrible fighting, the Bolivian people defeated the oligarchy. Thousands of people died in the streets of La Paz and Oruro. Workers, peasants and a sector of the petite bourgeoisie organized by the nationalist party—which expressed the people's aspirations in slogans calling for agrarian reform, nationalization of the mines, universal suffrage—seized the Government Palace and began a process that in its first years was carried forward in practice through the avenues of popular power. The last parade of the oligarchy's army was held in the central plaza: the officers taken prisoner marched in front with their caps on backwards, and the workers and peasants came behind them, armed. That frenzied, chaotic scene was particularly meaningful for all those who were conscious of the extent of the exploitation and suffering of those peasants and workers, whose life expectancy was a mere 27 years. Popular militias were created, and the traditional standing army was eliminated. The peasants, aided by the miners and directed by their leaders, rose up to recover their stolen lands and felt they had ended almost 500 years of slavery begun with the Spanish colonizers. The reform measures taken by the vanguard petite bourgeoisie were exceeded by the masses and it frequently had to subordinate itself to the surging number of popular leaders. A great euphoria was experienced in the first two years. The *latifundio* was liquidated and the *latifundistas* who weren't able to flee had to face the people's tribunals.

These first two years of revolutionary exuberance on the brink of chaos demonstrated the organizational ability of the Bolivian people, and demonstrated the absence of rancor on the part of the peasants, who, despite centuries of shameless exploitation that had reduced them to a state of slavery, showed tolerance and an abundance of good will towards their oppressors. It is a fact that on many *haciendas* the liberated peasants ate the beef from thoroughbred cows, but it is a fact that their hunger went back thousands of years and those cows, which were treated better than they were, deserved their hatred. And it is also a fact that the peasants organized themselves and began working collectively, and thus were able to build in those first two years more than 600 rural schools and 200 roads without state support; but they lacked teachers, which the government was unable to provide.

That state of things couldn't last for long: the limitations of the petite bourgeois leadership that could only advance the process as far as the limits of a bourgeois-democratic revolution, the maneuvers by *yanqui* imperialism—that crippled the government by means of partial blockades and that obtained, with the support of the oligarchy who controlled in absentia the tin works, a drastic reduction in the price of that mineral—were weakening the process, and the revolution of 1952 found itself on the brink of economic ruin. Corruption and the political naiveté of the people themselves, as well as of their leaders who didn't have a real understanding of their power (until it was too late!), caused them to cede positions to the petite bourgeoisie that ended up making a pact with imperialism and handing over the country. Nevertheless, the whole experience has not been lost, and this is why the working class of Bolivia today is not only courageous but mature.

SOCIAL CINEMA IN BOLIVIA

We believe social cinema in Bolivia was born and forged in that atmosphere of struggle, in those years of popular euphoria, of massive mobilizations in which the filmmakers saw history actually being protagonized and directed by the people. Much later on, that social cinema would have to give way to a militant cinema in Bolivia.

Among the first documentaries of importance made in Bolivia through the official organism established by the revolutionary government in 1952, namely, the Bolivian Institute of Cinematography, we can find images that record key moments of the popular mobilization: the presence of thousands of peasants from all over the country who, armed, watch over the fields of Ucureña during the signing of the Agrarian Reform Decree; the marches of the bold, courageous and feared miners who, with dynamite strapped to their cartridge belts, carry the arms they seized from the oligarchy's army. These films were made by people who knew little about cinema at the time and who alone attempted to produce political propaganda material; however, their images are filled with the living presence of the people.

In that effervescent Bolivia during the years that followed the popular triumph in April, 1952—more specifically, during the decade of the 50s—cinematic activity was minimal. Filmmakers, from scriptwriters to cameramen, comprised no more than 10 persons. We think their most important films would not have been possible had it not been for that sociopolitical process. Their vision fits in with a country in search of itself within the depths of the people and their culture.

Today's militant cinema finds its clearest origin in that period. And although, later on, popular control of power was lost, anti-imperialist ideas and positions, which have their practical origin back then, spread and took root among the people. While subsequent governments betray the nationalist and revolutionary postulates of April, revolutionary ideology continues its advance, and the need to implant an anti-imperialist liberation dictates the revolutionary tasks. As a result of this evolution, a revolutionary cinema has developed that situates its works within the anti-imperialist struggle.

(Excerpts from a paper presented by Jorge Sanjinés in a symposium of the XXXIII Congress of FIAF, June, 1977.)

ELEMENTS FOR A THEORY AND PRACTICE OF REVOLUTIONARY CINEMA

REVOLUTIONARY CINEMA, ANTI-IMPERIALIST CINEMA

It is all too obvious today that the military-economic machinery of imperialism (the interrelation of the multinationals, the covert operations agencies, the military and political machinery of the system, is perfectly synchronized) is linked to and planned in conjunction with the policy of the means of mass communication, whose function it is, on the one hand, to spread disinformation, and, on the other, to consolidate the ideology of the system.

This ideology of an individualist society that does not see any reason for living other than the accumulation of things and possibilities—power, influence, privilege, money, etc.—needs to destroy every politically or culturally opposed ideology so that it can expand. And in this last area, the destruction of all cultural resistance smooths the way for the installation of its political system.

In categorical terms, capitalism's philosophy of life is so brutally simple that it is, through its own intrinsic stupidity, a sinister threat to all humanity. What a crude, disinformed, tough and pragmatic Texas oilman thinks is what imperialism propounds as life. It doesn't matter, in the vastness of the system's inertia, if fascist theoreticians, like Kissinger, with particularly sophisticated backgrounds, exist; both he and the cold scientific *yanqui,* who is anxiously searching for a better way to depopulate the Third World, are advancing the same policies at the service of the same concepts so as to resolve that uncultivated, capitalist Texan's problems. Does capitalism propose something better?

Has North American society developed more and better goals within its own framework? Don't the majority of North Americans think Ford can make a better President than the others because he is able to lead an orchestra for the fun of it, or because he puts on a Mexican sombrero, or swims every day in his pool?

A deep critical thought evidently exists in North American society, but it gets lost for the most part amid *the widespread broadcasting of the ideology of capitalism.*

When the television show *Sesame Street* shamelessly indoctrinates our Latin American children with the egotistical values of private property, it is instilling one of the most sacred ideological concepts of the capitalist system and attempting to win over their minds into thinking as capitalists do, in order to accept their system and become consumers in it. It pacifies any sense of resistance and insidiously promotes submission. The capitalist ideological position conceives the life of man as a mad race to obtain more. Look: aren't the representatives of that power the ones who generally have more; or better still, the ones who best represent those who have more? Naturally, then, we will encounter everything in this system as playing a part in the complex process of forming and consolidating such an ideology, which does not originate from some aristocratic section in Boston but begins in the very moment private property is born, which goes back before the first legislation by Solon, some 2500 years ago. Engels wrote that "vulgar greed has been the driving force of civilization from its first day to this; wealth and again wealth and once more wealth, always wealth, not of society but of this single miserable individual—here was its one and final aim."[1] We can say today that the evolution of that tendency to expand capitalist society beyond its natural borders and to consolidate itself as the common objective, with consumption and accumulation as definitive goals, has passed from the individual to society as a whole.

Now then, the consequences of a system with these objectives is what ought to concern us, since it is a system that organizes all its power to expand beyond its territorial borders, "enlightening" the world to its way of seeing and conceiving life.

Revolutionary cinema is an anti-imperialist cinema for ideological reasons. Its basic assumptions are fundamentally opposed to imperialism. The ideology of imperialism is the ideology of the most extreme form of individualism. Its view of the world stems from idealist positions about man and reality: from the idea of the ontological aloneness of man, which conceives him as an isolated being devoid of any social or real human interaction, and which gives him the right to exist before everything else, even before the nihilist, fatalist or clearly fascist convictions of capitalist thought. In the last instance, it is a matter of the irreconcilable contradiction between the love of life and the total dehumanization of life, which is death.

Imperialism is determined to exterminate us at all costs. At work behind this sinister attitude are its brutal convictions, its belief in our inferiority that, in its eyes, denies us the right to live and morally justifies wiping us off the face of the earth. Its host of religious hypocrites preach to the Indians of Latin America not to consume protein; they sterilize our women by different means, and they disseminate viruses in strategic areas in order to turn the inhabitants into paralytics—as happened with the tribe of Aucas Indians in Ecuador—contaminated by missionary translators of the Bible who have paved the way for the *yanqui* oil companies to penetrate the jungle. On the other side of the coin, by manipulating pure and innocent ideas, they sow confusion and passivity in the minds of the simple inhabitants who accept them, preparing them for their death, seeing how the "Last Judgment" is so close at hand! "The fewer who live, the fewer who sin," they tell our women just before sterilizing them.

To them we are mice in what they call "their storeroom," and therefore the mice must be eliminated in order to preserve their supplies. But as mice are easier to fight because they are incapable of organizing themselves and developing political consciousness, their methods of eliminating us go from organizing entire epidemics to administering doses of ideological venom, from starvation and malnutrition to spitting out distorted "messages" on the television set.

Because of all this, to expose these tactics and explain their ideological content is an urgent and peremptory task.

Although it is impossible to separate ideology and culture without losing their meaning, we can, out of necessity, more concretely specify their elements.

We referred briefly to the expansionist and monopolizing work of imperialism that destroys all ideological resistance, and, since culture is the human expression of ideology, the destruction of culture as an agent of resistance is imperialism's favorite operation.

Not for nothing have conscientious anthropological, ethnographic and sociological studies been financed, and still are being financed, by North American universities that later hand their conclusions over to experts in the Pentagon or to interventionist agencies which, furnished with scientific data, know what they have to do to crush all resistance. They have unleashed a sweeping offensive to supplant customs, ways of thinking, of behaving, of conceiving things, dressing, combing one's hair or even sitting down. They aren't the first ones who realized that the conquest of a people or the "swallowing up of a people"—if you can call it that—must involve the destruction of indigenous cultures. The Spanish, who were driven by their urgent desire to satisfy their unbridled ambitions with gold and power, and by their total incomprehension of the remarkably advanced universe they trampled under, ended the eighteenth century by systematically planning and carrying out the destruction of the indigenous culture. The visitor Areche, owing to the great Indian insurrection that broke out almost simultaneously in most of the territory controlled by the Spanish, and which was led by Tupac Amaru in 1781, advised the viceroy to destroy the dominant culture as a way of ensuring the lasting power of Spain in America: banning indigenous customs, dances, dress, names, hair styles, language, religion, etc. Of course, they couldn't totally realize their sinister intentions; the Spanish didn't possess today's means of mass communication and, although they managed to destroy the political organizations of the American peoples and completely crush their civilization, they couldn't eradicate the deep-rooted habits of thought of the Indians, who resisted the onslaught and preserved their culture, often at the price of having to retreat into a stifling and immobilizing isolation.

Anti-imperialist revolutionary cinema must do the important work of exposure, clarification, recovery and exaltation. It must promote a renewed consciousness of the validity of national cultures, contributing to their development through its participation in them.

Imperialism's lethal campaign is most successful in countries where there is the least cultural resistance: I am referring to those countries that were totally deprived of their aboriginal roots through the brutal extermination of their original inhabitants. Today, cerebral conditioning is carried out by remote control, from television sets and movie theaters, and this operation is facilitated when these conquered peoples have been formed solely within western culture, that carrier of imperialism's ideological viruses.

In Puerto Rico, isn't this nearly total conditioning of minds responsible for the sterilization of more than 50% of working women between the ages of 20 and 40? The alarming thing is that they have been sterilized with their consent; these humble women can no longer make decisions for themselves. Thus, without putting up any resistance, they are easily led by the means of mass communication that tells them to get sterilized. They might as well tell them to commit suicide as a quick formula to happiness! Having "informed" them to get sterilized is almost the same thing! If the liquidation of our people's cultural expressions is preparation for our actual physical liquidation, can we filmmakers remain disengaged? What more important task is there than to struggle for the life of our peoples? If imperialism wants to deliver our death blow at all costs, our duty is to know on what fronts it is acting so that we can fight it precisely there!

The enemy knows that to strip a people of its culture is to disarm it, and that, oppositely, a people with a national identity, with its own conceptions and means of resolving reality, is a potentially dangerous enemy. Let's remember Vietnam! Could all the weapons and incredible technology of the enemy defeat a people who were ten times less armed with heavy artillery and rifles?

We can no longer make films that, though they may look upon the culture of our peoples with respect, actually prevent them from fighting back. Our work must not only be in support of the people, sympathetic in parallel fashion, but it must also enter into dialectical interaction *with* them, because culture and tactics are woven together to form the strategy of the anti-imperialist struggle.

In graphic economic terms, imperialism is devouring us in gigantic mouthfuls! We have raw materials that are in the process of being exhausted. There are species of South American fauna that are extinct or are on the verge of extinction due to the greed of the *yanqui* or European exporters. And it is the same with our flora. Our forests are being stripped for their wood, without being reforested, and in less than ten years important varieties of trees will appear only in specialized text books and encyclopedias! Agriculture in countries driven by imperialism toward monopoly-production or toward dependent industrialization is disappearing, as in Venezuela, or has disappeared, as in Puerto Rico. Every imperialist economic policy is disposed to finance access routes to manufacturing centers, yet at the same time prohibits these products from being manufactured in the very countries that produce the raw materials. It suffocates national economies, specializes them into areas that are more profitable for the imperialists. It sets and fixes the prices of products, causing economic dependence and misery. It loans money at high interest rates that imperialism itself uses in studies of studies carried out by its experts, it demands the acquisition of *yanqui* machinery, the use of its technicians, etc. It helps itself to our national capital to operate North American businesses. It extracts the surplus-value from millions of South American workers exploited by the multinationals that not only profit from the starvation wages but also from their political influences, from the natural resources they expropriate and from the commercial operations they set up. It corrupts functionaries, bribes and perverts government officials, etc., etc. Which is to say, it has established itself as the worst of economic scourges on our peoples, who have ended up working for the U.S., feeding millions of uninformed North Americans—when we ourselves go hungry!—who patronize us and actually think they are helping us. The U.S., with a population of only 6% of the total world, consumes more than 50% of the food produced by the world!

When you get right down to it, we are the principal providers of raw materials, surplus-value and favorable investment climates. We are the ones who sustain the gluttonous economy of imperialism. If we were to paralyze all *yanqui* activity in Latin America or set our own prices for our own products, the monster would be disarmed and perish. They are dependent on us; not the reverse, as they want us to believe. We are poor because the U.S. is rich!

To expose and denounce the whole assembled, corrupt, economic machinery is, well, an absolutely essential task, without which it becomes almost impossible to orchestrate the liberation struggle.

If imperialism pursues the political submission of our peoples through pressures, threats, military pacts, mutual defense treaties, and proceeds to intervene directly with its troops or indirectly by manipulating the flunky bourgeoisie or the military, trained and organized by the imperialists, then we will never be able to conceive of the development of our own political life except in relation to imperialism's influence or intervention.

What are the chances today of a Latin American country installing a popular socialist government without imperialism intervening? Facts and events indicate to us that there is no longer any chance of this happening. Imperialism would intervene directly, occupying that country, as it did in Santo Domingo, or indirectly by applying pressure, by boycotting and undermining that government's resistance, or by organizing sectors that support it, like the army in most instances, in order to bring about its collapse. Isn't imperialism threatening countries like Italy, where it is faced with the possibility that the communists may seize power?

For this very reason, we must regard imperialism as the most powerful enemy to our sovereignty, the principal obstacle, and the most basic political analysis that a revolutionary cinema can attempt to make about our reality cannot ignore this presence, but must expose and denounce it.

From everything set forth up to here, we can conclude this first section by saying that the identification of revolutionary cinema with anti-imperialist practice is, well, the vital essence of revolutionary cinema during the actual struggle for liberation, and is its mode of existence. A cinema considered to be revolutionary that is indifferent to the anti-imperialist struggle is a contradiction, and is not only an absurdity but must be viewed as being uncommitted and even in complicity with the enemy, which also tries to give the impression that it has nothing to do with our basic dilemma.

PROBLEMS OF FORM AND CONTENT IN REVOLUTIONARY CINEMA

Revolutionary cinema must seek beauty not as an end but as a means. This proposition implies a dialectical interrelation between beauty and the objectives of cinema, which must be correctly aligned in order to produce an effective work. If that interrelation is missing, we end up with a pamphlet, for example, which may well be perfect in its proclamation, but which is schematic and crude in its form. The lack of a coherent creative form reduces its effectiveness, destroys the ideological dynamic of the content and merely locates for us what is, on the surface, the superficialities, without giving us any of the essence, the humanity, the love—categories that can only issue from a sensitive and responsive means of expression, capable of revealing the truth.

COLLECTIVE WORK

Revolutionary cinema is in the process of formation. Certain conceptions about art that bourgeois ideology has deeply instilled in those artists who have been formed within the parameters of western culture are not so easily or quickly changed. Nevertheless, we think it is a process that will succeed in purging itself through contact with the people, by integrating them into the creative process, by elucidating the aims of popular art, and by abandoning individualistic positions. Today there are many group efforts and collective films, and, what is very important, there is the participation of the people who act, who come forward, who create directly, determining the form of the film in a process where the immutable script is disappearing or where the dialogue, during the act of filming, spontaneously issues from the people themselves and from their prodigious capacity. Life begins to be expressed in all its power and truth.

As we already maintained in an article on this question, revolutionary cinema cannot be anything but collective in its most complete phase, since the revolution is collective. Popular cinema, in which the fundamental protagonist will be the people, will develop individual histories when these have meaning for the collective, when these serve the people's understanding, rather than that of one individual, and when they are integrated into the history of the collective as a whole. The individual hero must give way to the popular hero—numerous, quantitative—and, in the process of elaboration, this popular hero will not only be the internal motive of the film but its qualitative driving force: participant and creator.

LANGUAGE

A film about the people made by a screenwriter isn't the same as a film made by the people *through* a screenwriter, inasmuch as the interpreter and translator of that people becomes their expressive vehicle. With a change in the relations of creation comes a change in the content and, in parallel, a change in the form.

In revolutionary cinema, the final product will always be the result of individual abilities organized toward one same end, where the spirit and life-breath of a whole people, and not just the problems of one man alone, is captured and transmitted. The problems of the individual, which assume overblown proportions in bourgeois society, are resolved within revolutionary society through the process of confronting the problems of society as a whole, and are reduced to a normal level because their solutions are encountered in the course of being integrated into revolutionary society, where the aloneness that causes all psychological neuroses disappears forever.

The loving or apathetic treatment by a filmmaker of an object or of men becomes evident in his work, mocking his sense of being in control. What the filmmaker thinks and feels is manifested in the expressive means he chooses to use. His selection of language forms reveals his attitude and, therefore, a film tells us not only something about the subject it treats but also something about the filmmaker.

When we shot *Blood of the Condor* with the peasants in the remote community of Kaata, our purpose deep down—though we desired to contribute politically with our work by denouncing the *gringos* and showing a social picture of Bolivian reality—was to achieve recognition for our abilities. There's no denying it, just as we can't deny that during the filming our relationship with the peasant actors was still a vertical one. We were employing a formal treatment that led us to select scenes according to our personal likes, without taking into account their communicability or their cultural meaning. Scripts had to be memorized and repeated exactly. Though the soundtrack played an important role in the resolution of certain sequences, we didn't give importance to the needs of the viewer for whom we said we were making that film, who required clear, visual images and who later complained when the film was shown.

Thanks to the confrontation of our films with the people, thanks to their criticisms, suggestions, advice, protests and confusions due to our misunderstanding of the ideological relationship between form and content, we were slowly distilling a language and incorporating the creativity of the people themselves, whose notable expressive and interpretative abilities demonstrate a sensibility that is pure, free of stereotypes and alienations.

While filming *The Courage of the People,* many scenes were shot in the same place as the events discussed, with the actual protagonists of those historical accounts we were reconstructing, with those who at bottom had more of a claim on deciding how things ought to be reconstructed than we did. On the other hand, they were interpreting things with a force and conviction that was unattainable by a professional actor. These *compañeros* wanted not only to transmit their experiences with the intensity they possessed, but they knew what were the most important political objectives of the film and, therefore, their participation brought to it a fresh militancy. They possessed a clear consciousness of how the film was to serve, spreading its enunciation of the true facts throughout the country, and they were prepared to make use of it as they would a weapon.

We, the components with the film equipment, became the instruments of the people who were expressing themselves and fighting through our medium!

The dialogue was drawn from their precise memory of the events, or else became the expression of their thoughts about the events, as in *The Principal Enemy*. The peasants used the scenes to liberate their repressed voice, and they told the judge or boss in the film what they really wanted to say about the truth. Cinematic reality and actual reality are interwoven and merge as one

What is artificial has to do with mere extraneous factors, but through the revealing, creative actions of the people the cinematic re-enactment meshes with actual reality.

When we decided to use sequence shots in our latest films, we were spurred on by the surging demands of the content. We had to use shots that integrated the participation of the viewer. Jumping right away to close-ups of the assassin (in *The Principal Enemy)* in the crowded plaza where the popular tribunal was held didn't serve our purposes, because the surprise that is always produced by directly cutting to a close-up was opposed to what we were trying to develop in the sequence shots, which was to engage the participation of the viewer by means of the internal power of the people's collective participation. The simple movement of the camera interpreted differing points of view, the dramatic demands of the viewer that would enable him to quit being a viewer so as to become an actual participant. Occasionally the sequence shots would lead us into a close-up, sparing what distance is in fact possible in the approach, or else would open up the field between shoulders and heads in order to bring us physically closer to see and listen. To cut to a big close-up is to brutally impose the viewpoint of the filmmaker, his own interpretation of reality, on the viewer. To move from a general shot with other people in it to a close-up has a different meaning, embodies a different attitude, which is more coherent with what is taking place, with the actual content. While filming *The Principal Enemy*, we often felt compelled to break with this kind of treatment because of purely technical limitations; failures in the sound equipment through overuse, noise from the "blimp," or the camera's noise filter, hampered our shooting in sequences, and we had to break the filming up into parts. Also, the high degree of improvisation that goes along with popular participation made it difficult to conceptualize successive cuts with any degree of continuity.

Somehow, though, that experience was for us totally justified, because the whole process of making the film became, simultaneously, a rich process of discovering new elements (at least they were new to us). It was a totally different school of cinema than the one in which we had learned our ABCs, and we were often amazed by what was taking place before our very eyes!

Put another way, there is the subjective treatment of things that goes hand-in-hand with the needs and attitudes of a certain individualist cinema as opposed to an objective, non-psychological, sensorial treatment that facilitates the participation and needs of a popular cinema.

The presence of a collective protagonist, rather than an individual protagonist, informs the objective treatment and distance needed to engage the viewer in reflection. Not only did the search for an ideological coherence help convince us of the need to do away with the individual protagonist—the hero and focus of every story in our culture—but also our observation of the primordial and essential characteristics of indigenous American culture. Indians, through their social traditions, tend to conceive of themselves first as integral members of the group and then as isolated individuals. Their way of living is not individualistic. They understand reality as the complex integration of everything and everyone, and they act on the basis of this understanding very naturally, since it is an inseparable part of their world view. At first it is bewildering to understand what it means to think of oneself in this way, because it is a whole other way of thinking and involves a dialectic opposite to that of individualism. The individualist exists alone and above everything and everyone; the Indian, on the other hand, exists solely in interaction with everything and everyone. When that equilibrium is upset, the Indian becomes disoriented and nothing makes any sense. The great Peruvian political thinker, Mariátegui, referring to concepts of freedom, said that the Indian is never less free than when he is alone. I remember an interview we recently filmed where a peasant was demanding the presence of his *compañeros* from the community so that he could feel confident and comfortable about what he was saying. Exactly the reverse would happen with an ordinary citizen, who would want to be alone in order to feel secure!

In revolutionary art we always encounter the stylistic mark of a people and the life-breath of a popular culture that embraces a whole community of men and women, with their particular way of thinking

145

and conceiving reality, and their love of life. Its aim is to arrive at the truth *through* beauty, and this is what differentiates it from bourgeois art, where beauty is pursued even at the cost of lying. By observing and incorporating popular culture into our work, we will be able to fully develop the language of a liberating art!

DISTRIBUTION OF REVOLUTIONARY CINEMA

The distribution of revolutionary films constitutes a major problem and raises questions that require urgent solving.

Militant anti-imperialist films are the object of special persecution and censure in the majority of countries where their purpose is most likely to be fulfilled. This situation has greatly discouraged whomever doesn't view the work of a revolutionary filmmaker as being done simply when the work of filming and editing is done, that the problems of distribution are problems of realization that cannot be dismissed because of the immediate impossibility of resolving them. Similarly a film must not cease to exist because it may be impossible to distribute it at that precise political moment. From the moment the problems of one dominated country become the problems of other dominated countries, that pretext is invalidated.

We must remember that the political dynamic of our countries, at least the majority of them, is constantly changing, and that the ebb and flow of the internal contradictions of each country create favorable periods when these films can be widely distributed. It is a matter then of struggle! And in the struggle you must know when and where to shoot, and when to keep your head down in the trenches.

To censor ourselves, to disguise our film's content, to symbolize it, is to fall into opportunism and into operations dangerously useful to the enemy, which knows well how to manipulate materials that do not confront it head-on to its advantage.

A true revolutionary film has the right to exist, and the necessity of distributing it is implicit in its essence. Revolutionaries today can fight the same enemies wherever they are. Naturally, they could wage this struggle under better conditions through the enemy's own controlled means of communication, but when this isn't possible they must take up another position on the battlefield, which is the world exploited by imperialism. What cannot be tolerated is

146

remaining in Paris, comfortably vegetating. Revolutionaries don't have vacations nor does the revolution take a break.

Nowadays revolutionary films can be seen in many European countries, generally through some television networks or in specialized movie theaters. This distribution, as well as screenings at frequent film festivals, reaches viewers who can be classified *grosso modo* into two groups: the passive viewer and consumer of culture or entertainment who is in the majority, and that other viewer whose attitude towards this cinema is consistent with his advanced thinking and who extracts information to be used in the formation of new ideas and concepts. We believe this last type of viewer is each day becoming more numerous in Europe, and, therefore, the distribution of our films in Europe is justified (one could also justify this distribution on the basis of the economic support it provided, which meant selling copies to television networks and movie theaters, even though filmmakers in nearly every instance received next to nothing from these dealings).

In the United States, in the very bowels of the imperialist enemy, revolutionary cinema is being distributed. Many films are shown by universities and progressive organizations, shedding light on the problems of our peoples and showing the real workings of the system, the atrocities it commits against the world it subjugates. This has resulted in a deepening of solidarity with our peoples and a strengthening of the anti-imperialist struggle raised by progressive North American sectors which are well-acquainted with the exploitation, the dehumanization, the racism in the U.S., all of which are also caused by capitalist ideology.

Nevertheless, we Latin American filmmakers are mainly interested in distributing our cinema in our countries, whether they be our own or our brother countries. We have said that this task is very difficult and also dangerous: Carlos Alvarez, the screenwriter of *What is Democracy?*, was jailed along with his *compañera* by the Colombian military, accused of subversion for his cinematic work! Walter Achugar was detained and tortured in Uruguay; Félix Gómez, of the Ukamau Group in Bolivia, spent close to 18 months in a concentration camp for having in his possession a case containing props for our film, *The Courage of the People*. Antonio Eguino, director of photography for the same film, was arrested and detained for 15 days, during protests by university students and broad progressive sectors, for the offense of having in his possession a copy of *The Courage of the People*. Filmmakers and actors on the left have been imprisoned by Pinochet, and today we still know nothing of their fate! A good part of the most committed Latin American filmmakers have been prohibited from returning to their countries. But, despite the persecution and repression, Latin American cinema continues to be produced and, in some countries, there exists a true effervescence that will quickly bear fruit in new values and new experiences. The circulation of Latin American films, though restricted, has never been stopped, and it is even increasing where conditions are favorable. In Venezuela, Colombia, Panama, Peru, Ecuador, Mexico, film festivals have been organized and Latin American cinema is widely distributed. In Venezuela and Panama they have even held festivals for Cuban cinema. What is mainly lacking in these countries where distribution is possible is a more systematic and organized effort to consistently bring this cinema to the people. This is why the present Ecuadorian experience, which we will talk about in more detail, is so important.

In Bolivia, before the ominous outbreak of fascism, the films of the Ukamau Group were widely distributed. *Blood of the Condor* was seen by close to 250,000 people! We weren't satisfied with its distribution through the conventional commercial channels, so the film was brought to the countryside using a portable generator and equipment in order to screen it in villages that were without electricity. The result was uplifting: the film contributed to the ousting of the Peace Corps of *yanqui* imperialism, because it caused a stir and led to the formation of university and official commissions that studied its suspect activities and thus called for its expulsion.

In Chile, before and during the government of the Popular Unity, our films were being distributed through commercial channels, as well as being shown in factories and in the countryside. In Argentina, there have been interesting distributing experiences by organizations like the Cinema Liberation Group, which distributed its materials widely among the workers.

Right now, in the present political moment, we think Ecuador is where one of the most interesting political experiences of anti-imperialist cinema is taking place. At the moment, films such as *What Is Democracy?, Cerro Pelado, The Hour of the Furnaces, Compañero President, NOW, Revolution, That's the Way It Is, Blood of the Condor, The Courage of the People,* and *The Principal Enemy* have been widely distributed in the universities and workers' centers. For reasons of cultural identity and the fact that the people of Ecuador face the same problems as the rest of Latin Americans, some of these films have reached a surprising number of viewers: in two and a half months *The Courage of the People* was seen and discussed by nearly 40,000 workers in the area of Quito alone! Based on statistics we collected, and taking into account the work of distributing our films among the peasants in the countryside, we calculate that in just one year approximately 340,000 workers, peasants and students came to see the films of our group. We feel very pleased and proud that our films have reached so many people in a country as small as Ecuador. This fact is in large part due to the efforts of the cinema department of the Central University, and the enthusiasm of the *compañeros* of the Cinema Club of the National Polytechnic School. Both institutions have concentrated their work in the mass-based organizations and in the trade unions, but they have also brought films into the interior of the country and to the countryside. Other universities, trade unions and peasant organizations, as well as priests committed to truly helping the poor, are also openly distributing this material with an intensity that is remarkable. In the case of the films by the Ukamau Group, it is possible that factors of cultural identity, like the fact that Quechua is spoken in parts of the films, greatly influence their being accepted and widely distributed. However, we think this is due chiefly to an identification with the socio-political dilemma that these films confront. The discussions and interviews we had with viewers were characteristic: they either insisted on their identification with the problems of Bolivia and Ecuador, or they simply didn't give any importance to the question of nationality in the film and discussed it as something in its own right.

We are going to conclude this article by citing the opinions of workers and peasants who are actually seeing and demanding to see these films, but first we want to call attention to the Ecuadorian experience and call for cinema to be immediately brought to the people in those countries where it's possible to do so. The attitude and practices of movie theaters and institutions that show these materials must change, in order to transform the static movie houses devoted to sterile pleasure contrary to the meaning of this cinema, by using portable equipment that can be set up in factories and in communities, initiating a dialogue with the people that benefits both the viewers and those showing the film, because that relationship will change during the process of interaction itself, and also because a give-and-take exchange of information will be facilitated.

WHAT THE PEASANTS HAVE TO SAY

"Who are the actors in this film, *compañeras?* They are the very people of Bolivia, of Ecuador! It is the people who cry out as only they know how to do. It gives us a lot of courage and when we grasp this courage we must hold on to it tight! We don't have arms, but we can sure unite ourselves, organize ourselves, because to be organized is like waking up (...) This film is like putting arms in the hands of the people! This must make the rich furious!"

(Compañera from the Organization of Washerwomen in Quito, August, 1975.)
Film: *The Courage of the People*

"You don't need to know Quechua or Spanish, or be an Evangelist or a Catholic, to realize that what we saw in the film is the misery of someone who lives on the edge. He looks for bread in the garbage, he lives like a rabbit, he begs in the cities, and they don't give him a thing. But we see the cops wearing good clothes, fine boots, with rifles for mowing down the poor workers who don't have weapons (...) but shit, in the film they take their rifles away and kill the cops, it's fantastic! The politician talks and talks and he can't take up the rifle...but the factory workers walk away from their lathes and go around uniting themselves to fight with sticks and iron bars! With great sadness we see barefoot, hungry children. Shit! It's like a photograph of Ecuador! Exactly as it is! I saw the film twice and I want to see it again and again."

(Peasant in the interior of Ecuador, 37 years old November, 1975.)
Film: *Revolution*

"Now we understand what these *gringos* from the United States who have come to Ecuador are up to. They want to force their way into our communities with their skills and know-how. It seems like they are doing us a favor but it isn't true; these *gringos* are tricking us. The lie is that they come to help us, the lie is that they come to learn Quechua, or so they say; these *gringos* come to defend their profits, their businesses, they come to teach us the Gospel in order to divide the Community! They come to castrate us! This film should be shown in all the communities now!"

> (Elderly peasant, province of Chimborazo, February, 1976)
> Film: *Blood of the Condor*

"Holy shit! I didn't know this before! My brothers from other lands have problems just like us, they have a *patrón* almost the same as us. I am poor but I still have the strength to fight the bosses. We have to talk with our *compañeros* in order to get organized like in the film, and really, I tell myself, things can't go on like this in Ecuador! There are many things the same: they killed the leader Pajuña just about a year ago; they murdered him. Of course he was fighting for us. The *patrón* ordered the killing, paying off an assassin. They machine-gunned poor Pajuña in cold blood and in his own little house. In the film the same boss murders the leader Julián. The film makes us think that we must unite to fight against these murderers who receive help from the *gringos!* With the force of our unity we can make the icy, windswept plateaus tremble!"

> (Peasant from Santa Rosa, September, 1975)
> Film: *The Principal Enemy*

"Now is the time to kick out the *gringos* and the rich who haven't the eyes to see the people and who only have eyes to murder and get rich. We must unite and organize ourselves—all the poor, peasants and workers—as the dear old leader in the film says. And just as the music rises at the end of the film, so we will rise up free if we organize and fight back, and never again will we have to break our backs hauling their silver."

> (Peasant from Chibuleo, 62 years old, January, 1976)
> Film: *The Principal Enemy*

"Speaking frankly, this is as much for the poor whites as it is for the peasants; that is, we have to organize ourselves at the level of all the poor—white, black, Indian, mestizo, every exploited man—we have to be *one single fist* in order to attain our victory, in order to defeat the exploiters. If we do this, we have power; if we don't, we will never triumph. If we are divided amongst ourselves, assuming we peasants are the only ones who have to organize, I don't think we are powerful, and we would never attain our victory. We Indians need the workers, the students—that is, everyone, right?—organized against the exploiters! All the men, all the women, all the exploited: we must raise *one fist!* The film is for everyone, not just for the Indians but also for the whites and all the poor. The rich who have all the silver won't pay much attention to these things, but they are going to know that this film is *ours!*"

(Peasant from Imbabura, October 11, 1977)
Film: *Get Out of Here!*

ABOUT A CINEMA AGAINST THE PEOPLE AND FOR A CINEMA WITH THE PEOPLE

BOURGEOIS CINEMA AND POPULAR CINEMA

1. Bourgeois Cinema

Bourgeois cinema, in its best works, is the cinema of the screenwriter who gives us a subjective view of reality, and of the film director who attempts to seduce us with his own world, with his personal world, or who projects himself at us without any intention whatsoever of making himself understood; that is, the only thing that matters to him is that we acknowledge his existence. Bourgeois cinema is also the cinema of the principal protagonist, of the complex or simple hero. It is the cinema of the individual and individualism, of the artist who, looking down from Mount Olympus, makes films so as to indulge his personal obsessions, or to keep himself busy, or to go out on a limb with others. The problems with which he deals are the problems that interest, preoccupy, or concern him. This attitude is, moreover, very characteristic of concepts about art promoted by the ideology of the bourgeoisie. Its validity is relative to the historical period that determines it and, for that very reason, it exists solely within the contradictions and boundaries of that ideology. In the economic system, where the bourgeoisie makes its home, the margin of alleged freedom that the artist believes he has is circumscribed by the demands of profitability, which, in turn, are tied to the habits and appetites of the public, habits and appetites these very economic demands have created. Compromise and self-censorship are operations inseparable from the production process, which heeds and submits to the canons of the market. Hence, it turns out that the individualism generated by the passivity of bourgeois thought encounters its dissolution not only in the social demands of life but also in the economic ones.

The capitalist system, which can produce exceptional works within the definition of art for art's sake, which can somehow exercise self-criticism in isolation, which can "put its own finger on its own wound," is at the same time incapable of handling its own venom that qualitatively and quantitatively saturates the air—like air pollution. The massive production of films and television programs transmitting ideological viruses are infiltrating the brains of half of humanity, and this phenomenon, which in part may be unconscious, is also organized and directed by capitalism, which has a clearly developed consciousness of its own *evilness*. The economist Lerner maintained that the degradation of the popular mentality was necessary in the interests of mercantilism. Modern capitalist advertising is the best demonstration of that pernicious thesis.

On the one hand, we encounter a bourgeois cinema driven to make money and to make a shining name for itself, and on the other we encounter the cinema of the system itself, transporting its perverted cargo, the annihilator, whose tactic it is to condition minds in order to transmit not only what serves the bourgeoisie but what serves imperialism. Imperialism has everything to gain from this cerebral conditioning which numbs all resistance and turns its victims into its accomplices. Amid the ups and downs of this twofold operation of converting a victim into an accomplice, we can make out those intellectuals and artists who feel at odds with the system and who fire mere pingpong balls at it. Their "revolutionary" positions turn out to be deeply contaminated by the ideology against which they pretend to fight, to such a degree that they are as obvious as they are self-destructive.

Now then, where do these intellectuals in capitalist society come from? They mainly come from the bourgeoisie and petite bourgeoisie, and, therefore, we have to be constantly on our guard against the enemy that to a greater or lesser extent has infiltrated our brains if we don't want to serve it, even when our intention is to destroy it. But, as happens with every complex human process, psycho-social factors intervene. Nothing can be as difficult to distinguish for the revolutionary intellectual as knowing where precisely the enemy is influencing his behavior and thinking. And it is a fact that this conditioning process begins long before we become conscious of it. Only continual self-criticism will prevent us from falling into its grasp and provide us with a clear understanding of the role the revolutionary artist must play.

Nowadays there are many important commercial films of "revolutionary" content. On the whole, ideological elements that correspond to the capitalist system, but not to the revolution, will end up producing a work that is useful to the system in the last analysis. The capitalist system certainly knows how to make the best use of its products: it finances with the greatest pleasure those products that show it to be an open and democratic system, those that don't damage its vital interests and, what's worse, those products where the process of self-castration has been so extensive that they not only yield cash profits but ideological ones.

Faced with this situation or with the existence of artists previously neutralized by this process of indoctrination, we also have an audience which is no less indoctrinated. We have a public addicted to ideological dope, deeply corrupted and perverted, whose attitude has remained almost on the level of a conditioned reflex. This public has remained and remains within the enemy's grasp, uncontested, without being able to compare and choose. This battlefield of the ideological struggle is like a free and open laboratory where resistances are broken down and where submission to ideas that pursue, in their deepest content, the destruction of humanity is conditioned. This itself explains why the system is often tolerant of certain works that, because of their lack of continuity, dissolve uselessly upon reaching this audience, like a small grain of sugar in a sea of salt. Only by flooding the marketplace with films that expose the evils of the capitalist system will qualitative changes come about. But to unleash such an offensive assumes a clear notion of the language that must be employed.

2. Form and Content: An Ideological Relationship

When we realize that a cultural product, alleged to be "revolutionary," is formally saturated with reactionary ideology, we discover the ideological inconsistency of those creators who, at times, fall into this trap. It is impossible to conceive of a revolutionary work of art where there exists a dichotomy between form and content.

A commercial North American film is consequently expressing capitalist ideology without at all intending to be a vehicle for any political awareness. A revolutionary film that propounds revolution using the same language as a commercial film will be selling-out its content, formally betraying its ideology. The same thing occurs with the screenwriter who writes his "honest," "noncommercial" screenplay, and who believes he has saved his film and won the right to employ subjective elements in it. Who cares? Is all that production effort, that expenditure of resources and money, justified so that some person tells us about his frustrations and confusions, so that some individual attempts to toy with our intelligence, so that we are presented with dilemmas whose solutions lead nowhere? What is going on is that these works are vicious manifestations of an ideology that has to be fought with no let up or second thoughts, and that must be stamped out. No one sits on the bench during the revolution if he calls or feels himself a revolutionary. No one has the right to place himself above historical events that have to do with the life of his society and of humanity. Nor does anyone have the right to proclaim himself a leftist intellectual and preoccupy himself exclusively with himself.

We believe form and content correctly exist in one ideological relationship. They correspond permanently, and the phenomenon of truth occurs when the integration of both categories exists. We cannot make revolutionary cinema if we program it on the basis of a suspenseful police plot. The treatment of the story, its form, will resist such a definition and impose concessions such that the "revolutionary" content will remain on the surface (this occurs with the films of Costa Gavras, for example). Glauber Rocha, in a correct analysis of this kind of cinema, said that it is a cinema that deals with effects and never gets at the deep causes of things. This is so. This cinema will always remain on the surface, merely exposing the symptoms, not because it isn't interested in digging deeper but because its form prevents it from doing so. The analysis, the getting to the bottom of things, demands forms that engage our reflection, which must be permanently activated: no other interests must disturb that inquiry into the truth, no distractions can get in the way, and balance and beauty must be at work.

3. From the Inside To the Outside:
From the People To the People

We can distinguish two paths or methods of accomplishing a creative work: the first is from the outside to the inside, and the second is from the inside to the outside. When we say from the outside to the inside, we are referring to an individualist art which believes it is based solely on individual ability, on the talent and intuition of the artist, and which feels qualified to apprehend reality and penetrate deeply into it, without realizing, as we now observe, that the individual is determined in social interaction with others. Nevertheless, this method, which bases the discovery of truth on the talent of an individual removed from life's experiences, is not the method most suited to attaining a popular cinema, since its own contradictions stand in the way. Furthermore, the fraction of reality it endeavors to show us will invariably be a rendering of that artist's personal view of the world, which he has observed through his own tinted glasses.

This method no longer interests us. Man cannot exist outside the history of his people. Time has run out, and we refuse to continue down the path of an ideology which we are only interested in fighting.

The second method, from the inside to the outside, is part of a presupposition of ideas and, perhaps more than from theories, follows from consistent action. This method is in keeping with the search for a popular art and has the aim of serving, of aiding the struggle. Through it, we discover the dialectical relationship between popular art and the liberation struggle: the people are fighting and the art that expresses the people today unavoidably expresses that fight and is itself another weapon in that struggle against the oppressor. Within this context, the point of view of the individual loses all meaning and ends up being obsolete. The masses are the ones who protagonize history. It becomes vitally important to unite with the people, to go forward together, and to create with them: the history of the people is history, they are its principal protagonist. This in no way suggests that the individual gets lost in the revolutionary process. On the contrary, his permanence is indissolubly linked to his people. His realization is the realization of his people and, since he is no longer living in isolation but in social interaction, his egocentric condition disappears, his individualism

156

gets dropped so that he may become a particular expression of the masses.

4. Popular Cinema, Revolutionary Cinema, Collective Cinema

Popular art is revolutionary art is collective art, and, within it, we always encounter the collective stamp of a people, of a culture that embraces a whole community of people, with their general and particular conception of reality and their way of expressing it. This popular art is revolutionary because its basic aim is the truth, and this truth is shown to us with the undying power of what is beautiful. Revolutionary popular cinema takes this principle into account and is created with the people, serving as *their* expressive instrument, completely. The result in the long run will be the same as that of the other popular artistic expressions, because just as we encounter in popular ceramics a collective stamp and spirit and not just the particular style of one individual, so also, in this cinema, when it reaches its full development, we will encounter the life-breath of a people and their profound truth. This is why its methods must discard every individualistic tendency which seeks its own ends and thus furthers individualism instead of pursuing an integration with the group. Here is where it will reach its full realization, because it does not try to stifle or confound the particular creative power, but to integrate it properly to allow its total splendor; and this complete realization can only occur healthily and fully in the bosom of the collective, as a part of the integrated participation of the others. The isolated tendencies necessarily implicate psychological imbalances, frustrations, neuroses, which can become forces that move society, eventually. Bourgeois art is plagued with solitary, neurotic and even demented artists who didn't find creative integration and had to release their creative energies interpreting, in isolation, the reality from the outside to the inside.

OUR AIM: TO MAKE A CINEMA THAT WORKS FOR THE PEOPLE

It seems obvious that each man seeks the vehicle most akin to his inner self in order to express his world: his interests, his pain or his happiness and humanity. I prefer not to be standing up here looking down, lecturing at you in a cold, formal manner; rather, I prefer dialogue and simple discussion. Therefore I invite you to interrupt me to ask questions or to exchange ideas about any point that may interest you.

To present a film by our cinema group here, in Ecuador, has immense meaning for us, both as Latin Americans and as Bolivians. Ecuador—with its Indian blood, with its culture that goes back thousands of years, with its past history, like our own, with the Incas and Liberators—is, well, like our own land, like breathing in the same icy, rarefied air of the *cordillera* of my distant country that I encounter here not just in the past and common traditions, but in the hospitable look of those Ecuadorians who equally think of themselves as Bolivians, Peruvians, or Argentines. I thank you for this, brothers of my own blood and hope!

When, in 1960, we began our first cinematic work that, before shooting films, consisted of drawing up plans, researching themes and screenplays, we had to answer one all-important question: for whom are we going to make films? That is, to whom did we want to direct our work? The answer was tied to the social unrest felt by our small group of intellectual and artist friends of which Oscar Soria and Ricardo Rada formed a part—the first was an outstanding short story writer and the second a philosophy professor and enthusiastic publisher. During our talks until dawn over coffee, we were obsessed with the strength of our people and with their tragic, bloody destiny. Their history full of vicissitudes, heroisms and ceaseless struggles deeply disturbed us. When we went out into the city streets or walked around the dirt roads of the *Altiplano* looking for images, with our eyes wide-open to the objective reality that was all around us, we were struck by one pitiless, undeniable truth: the pain of our people, the differences, the terrible contrasts. In short, we were really witnessing with our own eyes the Bolivia for which we felt so much pain. But we also saw the resolve of the people to liberate themselves, their capacity for organization, their combat experience, their courage and dignity. Therefore, the answer to that all-important question didn't have to wait and we decided to make a cinema aimed at the Bolivian people, a cinema that was useful to them, that would serve them.

Thus the Ukamau Group was born with the clear aim of fulfilling a social task which, while the group was solidifying, had to acquire the form of a political task.

In the second phase of our production (after *Revolution, Landslide!* and *That's the Way It Is)*, which comprises the principal part of our work, we tried to deepen our vision and penetrate beneath the surface of things, exposing the problems and pointing out their causes. *Blood of the Condor* was written with that aim in mind, one which we would have to develop further in succeeding films to the point of attempting a dismantling of the mechanisms and organized structures used for exploitation and domination.

It was very gratifying for us to learn of the words uttered by an outstanding Colombian peasant leader who, in 1968—the very same year we presented these plans at the First Meeting of Latin American Filmmakers in Mérida, Venezuela—addressed a group of technocrats who had come to Peru for a seminar on agrarian reform in Latin America. In addition to reminding them that they didn't have the right to determine how agrarian reform should be implemented from comfortable, spotless desks to which they commute in their cars, without knowing or suffering life in the fields, without having calloused their hands in the soil or having an inkling of what were the peasants' most urgent problems and needs, he said to them: "What the peasants want to know is where their enemies are, how they act, how they maneuver, what are their strengths and weaknesses, because so long as we peasants don't know how to identify our enemies we will not be able to free ourselves from them!" Words that spring forth from the people themselves, that we should not only salute but humbly follow.

Well aware of the power of *Blood of the Condor,* imperialism has tried to check its distribution in several countries, but the greater their efforts the more the film spreads. Thus we have the case of the Cinemateca in Bogotá, which was closed down after refusing to submit the film to the censorship board. It was the first time that that criminal procedure was exacted on culture. Nevertheless, 16mm copies of the film were widely distributed and shown throughout Colombia! For the only thing that that dumb Goebbelsian method served was to awaken the people's curiosity and promote the film's distribution. And the fact of the matter is, this enemy cannot understand that the truth is like a sun and he cannot cover it up with one hand!

In Chile, during the Allende period, the fascist group "Patria y Libertad" tried scaring people away by planting a bomb in a movie theater where the film was being shown. Despite this, however, *Blood of the Condor* was shown from one end of this long and today-martyred brother-country to the other.

In Ecuador, last year, a 16mm copy of *Blood of the Condor* was stolen from us after a showing for a few people in the Central University. The alleged thieves also made off with a new projector that belonged to the German television station. The theft was reported to the police. In seven days they returned both the copy and the projector, and they showed us a photograph of the thief. But when we went to show the film, we were surprised to discover that this thief had entertained notions of being a censor, because the film was practically useless: they had cut out fifteen minutes, they burned images with a cigarette, and there was a scratch made with a razor blade on sections of the sound track. The *gringo* characters in the film had disappeared and the unsettling texts were erased!

It is because of all this that it gives us such great satisfaction to present *Blood of the Condor* today in this movie theater of the Central University. We know about the anti-imperialist tradition of this outstanding place of study, we are aware of the respect it has for the culture of our peoples and for their right to express themselves, we feel the solidarity of the students and professors with the task of unmasking the exterminators of our peoples and we are certain that nothing will prevent the film from spreading beyond this theater and the Cinema Department, whose members we warmly congratulate for having taken on the urgent task of making the movement of Latin American cinema known in Ecuador. It's time we focused on our own powerful values in terms of their human and cultural significance.

Latin American cinema exists! But, generally speaking, this cinema is excluded from the normal distribution channels because these channels are controlled by the multinational monopolies that not only specialize in spreading ideological venom but also close their circuits to a cinema that tells the truth and combats social alienation. This Latin American cinema, considered to be very significant and important in the world today, is widely known throughout Europe. It is influencing cinema all over the Third World and is changing concepts that are held in Europe itself about political cinema.

In Latin American countries, however, where we don't have a particularly knowledgeable audience, this cinema barely figures in the scheme of things. This is why the existence of a theater like this one, which has the autonomy and freedom to schedule films of real cinematic interest and bring to Ecuador the cinematic voice of Latin America, which delves deep into its historical, cultural roots and struggles for its liberation, takes on singular importance!

We are convinced that powerful reactionary forces will fight to destroy this theater's independence by transferring its administration to one of the many commercial monopolies on the pretext that it will bring in more income. And it is a fact that one free voice intimidates and alarms the enemy, who fears the dissemination of the truth! But we are also convinced there is sufficient consciousness within the university environment that views the existence of an independent movie theater as a victory and will block every maneuver by the enemy with the dignity and honesty that has distinguished the Central University throughout its 150 years of existence! The defense of this movie theater is an inseparable part of the defense of university autonomy!

Blood of the Condor is the first anti-imperialist film by our cinema group. It initiates a series of films that confront the enemy, that see in him the fundamental contradiction of our peoples. If, in *Blood of the Condor,* Ignacio's family desperately searches for human blood to save his life, the foreign sterilizers work to cause his death; and this conflict, in allegorical terms, is also the conflict between the oppressed peoples of the world and their principal enemy. The sterilization carried out against innocent, humble women is only possible because another kind of sterilization process has already been carried out within the country which conditioned the minds of the dominant class to consent to foreign intervention, to the manipulation of their reality in favor of interests that are not exactly those of the country itself. These men who belong to the Bolivian bourgeoisie—alienated through the consumption of capitalist ideology, inheritors of prejudices fabricated by the first colonizers— zealously accepted the job of genocide from the new colonizers, who were not only better informed but equipped with modern technology. Not only are they eliminating Latin Americans before being born, but today they weaken our population by means of false religious groups that indoctrinate them to abstain from eating the meat of certain animals—such as domestic rabbit and boar—thus depriving them of their only source of protein. And not only do they preach total passivity and resignation but they divide them internally, separating through the medium of religion the traditionally unified indigenous groups; not only are they sterilizing our peasant children with vaccines which they say are for measles, but they also let loose strange epidemics to shrink our population! All this work of murder is endorsed by a submissive and collaborating class of people who disown the percentage of Indian blood circulating through their veins and who believe, as one Bolivian military man stated, that the solution for our peoples is the insemination of Indian women with semen from North Americans!

What kind of people act and think this way? The stupidity of these ideas that pretend to deny the existence of the majority of the population, who are the very ones who labor for and feed with their hunger that racist minority, becomes palpable daily in the pitiless and discriminatory treatment that these ideologically indoctrinated men dispense to the people. In *Blood of the Condor,* these gentlemen leave Ignacio to die, bleeding to death in the same way they contribute to, with their attitude towards and support for, the practices of the exterminators.

This is why in the film's treatment we also wanted to expose the cultural conflict, the impact of concepts and attitudes on reality, because to the extent that a country is possessed mentally, the possibilities for its destruction and genocide are increased. A popular culture nourished principally by the indigenous culture is what gives Bolivia its identity and definition, and even when the racist dominant class itself wants to boast of cultural nationalism, it must refer to that identity because there remains no other way of distinguishing itself from the rest!

No country can remain frozen in its traditions and customs. These must serve to shape its cultural identity, to develop valid, lasting concepts of its own culture. But when development is unequal and survival means retreating into isolation, to repeat over and over again the constants of one's identity thereby proclaiming it to be invincible, it is by the same token understood that the force of the revolution will let loose a new current enriched by the memory of a culture teeming with humanity and love, that will set in unstoppable motion a people who possess an extraordinary ability to act collectively. This is why, in *Blood of the Condor,* what affects one person deeply affects all the rest.

We believe that these very concepts and ideas feed the revolutionary potential of the people, who, when they win their liberation, will unavoidably embark on building a beautiful and just country because their ideology profoundly coincides with the ideology of revolution!

It is necessary to make certain distinctions because there is a danger in confusing the need to revitalize and extol national culture with the tendency—deeply racist—to fall into a kind of indigenous chauvinism as a current of struggle. In *Blood of the Condor,* the return of Sixto—the brother turned worker who denies his indigenous condition in the beginning of the story—and his reverting back to wearing peasant clothing do not signify an exaltation of what is Indian because he is Indian. No. Sixto's entire experience during the course of the story—his conflict with the bourgeoisie who refuse him blood for Ignacio, his becoming aware of what really happened to his brother in the countryside—contributes to his gaining social consciousness, and he returns to the countryside to take the place left by Ignacio in order to carry on the struggle from the depths of his nationality, from the roots of his identity. Sixto does not renounce his condition as a worker, but assumes his national identity mainly as a weapon of resistance against the enemy. His return is also a symbol of the unity of peasants and workers. The class struggle is stated in no uncertain terms.

The screenings of *Blood of the Condor* in the popular peasants' and workers' centers were essential in helping us to elaborate a language consistent with what we think popular cinema ought to be. The peasants and workers did more than those critics who are particularly impressed by technical perfection. The main weaknesses of *Blood of the Condor* were pointed out to us by these folks. And from a close analysis of *their* observations, we were able to elaborate a language nearer to and consistent with revolutionary cinema, a language which demands the creative participation of the people, which views them as the principal protagonist, which serves as *their* instrument of expression, and not just as an expressive vehicle at the service of one screenwriter or film director but at the service of the whole community. From this standpoint, *Blood of the Condor* is a decisive step forward to a new cinema that our group is creating, where form and content are established in ideological relation to one another, where the distance necessary for any possibility of reflection is provided through the objective treatment of the camera and the collective protagonist, but which also gives importance to the elaboration of an emotional life-breath so necessary for engaging reflection.

Our aim is that this cinema serve, that it contribute, that it be at work for the people and that they use it. We learned many things from the people and we want to return the favor by placing this cinema at their service, because this cinema exists and has developed primarily due to the creative contribution of the peasants and workers who gave us their experiences, their marvelous naturalness, their warmth and passion, their advice and ideas!

[Lecture on the occasion of the showing of *Blood of the Condor* in Ecuador, 1976]

POLITICAL CINEMA MUST NEVER ABANDON ITS PREOCCUPATION WITH BEAUTY

IGNACIO RAMONET: Faced with the emergence of dictatorships, many Latin American filmmakers have emigrated to Europe. You are one of the few who, under such circumstances, have preferred to continue working and producing in Latin America—in democratic countries, but lacking cinematic infrastructures. Is your decision rooted in a desire to continue transmitting, whatever the cost, the problems and culture of the Andean peoples?

JORGE SANJINÉS: Yes, of course. The filmmaker who wants to transmit the struggle of his people cannot separate culture and revolution; therefore, in order to film *Get Out of Here!* we went to Ecuador (just as before, we had gone to Peru to film *The Principal Enemy*), because we have common cultural borders. Ecuador is a country that possesses a mixed-Indian population very similar to the Bolivian population, where the majority of people also speak Quechua. It is a country that has the same roots as ours, since we mustn't forget that the Inca Empire included Ecuador as a province. It is a matter then of the same people, with very similar problems.

IR: In all your films you pay particular attention to the interrelationship between culture and revolution. To what degree is this politically essential?

JS: I think one of the major problems that pervades our Latin American left is rooted precisely in its disregard for the importance of that interrelationship. Many leftist leaders in our countries are unaquainted with this problem and have not assigned it real importance. The reason for this attitude is that they have had little or no actual contact with the people, with the life of the peasants whom they have underestimated culturally. The underestimation of our culture goes back to the conquistadors and the Spanish colonizers, was inherited by the Republican Epoch, and has lasted up to now. Many leftists are condescending towards our culture. They don't know it, they underestimate its richness, both what it is and what it may become. And that is extremely grave. Many leftists continue to be racists. The political vanguard of petit bourgeois extraction ignores our culture and doesn't even speak the language of the majority of the people, because the reality is that the majority of the population possesses a culture that does not correspond to the culture of the minority who are in the vanguard of the movement of the left. I once said to a *compañero* that those of us who have been formed by a western culture seem to be more Spanish, for example, in our ways of being, thinking and speaking. We have more of a relation with them than with the men of the Bolivian *Altiplano*. And anyone, no matter how "left" he may be, who doesn't speak the language of these people and who isn't familiar with that cultural world will be as much of a foreigner on the *Altiplano* of La Paz, in Bolivia, as would a Spaniard. And this is tragic. It's a reality that demands profound rethinking, since it can lead some Indians to think that their problems cannot be raised in terms of the class struggle, that it's impossible for others to understand them and that their problems are purely and specifically of a racial order. This indigenous position is even held by *compañeros* who are studying here in Europe, who, on returning to their countries, are capable of leading racist, indigenous, and extremely pernicious movements, and who are lavishly received and even financed by imperialism because they weaken and divide the liberation movement.

IR: In *Get Out of Here!* you denounce certain practices by North American religious sects and, particularly, the sterilization they carry out surreptitiously among the Andean population. You already accused North American Peace Corps volunteers of sterilizing, by surgical means, the Andean Indians in another of your films, *Blood of the Condor*. Why return, almost ten years later, to treat the same theme?

JS: As we continued using cinema as an instrument of struggle, we realized that this cinema must offer the viewer more. Back then, *Blood of the Condor,* denounced the work of forced sterilization being carried out by the Peace Corps, but it did not fully explain why. We discovered this fact when the film was shown here in Bolivia: the peasants were very impressed with its statement, but they were always asking why the sterilization was being done. And the answer to that question was missing. We then decided to provide a more complete explanation in another film, because the work of destruction and genocide that North Americans in Latin America are carrying out reaches truly staggering proportions. And you must remember that when we denounced these practices in *Blood of the Condor,* in 1968, the sterilization centers were barely a year old. Now they have been in operation for ten years, carrying out genocide.

One of the consequences of *Blood of the Condor* was the expulsion of the Peace Corps from Bolivia, although that didn't put a stop to the sterilization of the population, since a little later those bodies were replaced by the religious sects. We know this because in a meeting that took place in 1971 (when General Torres[2] was still in power), some miners met with and recognized old members of the Peace Corps, expelled from Bolivia, who had returned and were passing themselves off as members of religious sects. That was one of the first indications we had that there was something else, something very wrong, behind these religious sects.

IR: What is the real power of these sects?

JS: They control extensive regions of Peruvian territory (even though the government of Velasco Alvarado[3] gave them a time limit in which to get out of the country), as well as territory in Ecuador and Colombia in the Amazon zones, where only citizens authorized by these sects have access. The Summer Language Institute obtained from these Latin American governments a certain number of prerogatives under the pretext of "studying indigenous languages," but it turns out that the study of these languages involves, curiously enough, the operation of planes, ships, private airfields where planes take off and land unimpeded by state controls.

It is significant to note that these religious sects find clever, intelligent formulas for tempering the resistance of the Indians. The reason for this is that the most important anthropological studies of these human groups are made by North Americans under the auspices of universities, and we know that these studies, these theses, are going to end up at the Pentagon.

IR: With respect to this, in your film, the resistance of the people manifests itself without nuance: it's either ingenuous, spontaneous, or radically brutal. Why?

JS: The purpose of the film, within a framework of exposing and explaining things, is to dismantle a concealed mechanism which is able to operate precisely because it isn't visible. The forms of struggle against that mechanism have come from the people themselves, as well as from the political organizations that struggle for their liberation. Faced with an enemy that carries rifles, the people have developed their own forms of struggle. Now they will have to develop others. The important thing is to dismantle the present mechanism of intervention being used by the enemy. We cannot do anything more: we cannot offer concrete solutions to problems of how to struggle, because we don't have sufficient political authority to do so. We can only contribute by exposing and explaining how the enemy operates: our contribution ends at that point.

The last scene in the film where the peasants get together to discuss the problem and analyze their mistakes is interesting because it represents the meeting of two contending positions: a spontaneous, indigenous position and a more politicized, much more developed position, but which isn't manipulated by us—that is the interesting point. It's apparent they are not merely mouthing a script, but are indeed thinking about these matters. And there is a nucleus of leaders who raise issues in terms of the class struggle.

IR: Did the actors in the film actually experience the interventions of the religious sects?

JS: We were working with a community that had suffered things much more horrifying than those we put in the film. We had to make a synthesis so that the film wouldn't end up being too long.

When we arrived, they had already expelled the religious sects. They had realized on their own that they posed a danger to the community. They observed how the sects divided the community, which was what they had to fear the most since their sense of collectivity is vital to them. They understood that the aim of the sects was to divide the people, to destroy any sense of collectivity, to prevent that human group from conceiving of itself as a collective, from acting collectively.

IR: Although their themes are closely related, your films *Blood of the Condor* and *Get Out of Here!* are different with respect to the concept of the "hero," the "protagonist." In *Blood of the Condor* the individual is the hero, while in *Get Out of Here!* the hero is the collective. What importance does that difference hold for you?

JS: For us, the difference is crucial. Contact with the people to whom we directed our cinema was always teaching us things, demonstrating little by little that the kind of individualistic cinema we were still making until *Blood of the Condor* didn't produce the result or have the effect we intended. The peasants resisted a work like *Blood of the Condor* because of its formal structure. We were asking ourselves what had happened, why this film wasn't working among the peasantry as it had among the petite bourgeoisie, and we discovered that it was simply a cultural problem, that we had to develop a language capable of expressing a collective conception of things, consistent with a collective culture. And, little by little, we were finding solutions. In *The Principal Enemy,* for example (which, in this respect, gave us the most satisfaction), the participation of the peasants is truly wonderful and, unlike what occurred with *Blood of the Condor,* as soon as the film ends the peasants spontaneously start asking questions, desiring a dialogue, and we have observed, curiously enough, that they don't talk about the virtues or defects of the film, but instead discuss the virtues and defects of the story, of history. And we must pay particular attention to this, because we believe the form for realizing our cinema must be the result of very close, serious observation of the culture of the people. In that way we also began to feel, for example, that the use of the "close-up" presented an obstacle to a correct understanding of our purpose. We were becoming aware that the form of the film was alienating them from reality, creating an obstacle for them. Therefore, we now use sweeping shots, generalized shots, that permit a greater degree of freedom in which the popular actors can act, and that also discourage an authoritarian manipulation of reality through the use of props, staging, casting, etc., so characteristic of bourgeois cinema.

IR: Aesthetically, *Get Out of Here!* possesses an impressive rigor, a kind of austerity that gives it a very particular beauty, that I would call classic. Do you think that the concept of beauty should be taken into account at a time when political cinema is being elaborated?

JS: Political cinema, to be more effective, must never abandon its preoccupation with beauty, because beauty, in revolutionary terms and as we understand it, must be a means and not an end, in the same way that the creator of a film in a revolutionary society must be a means and not an end. Beauty has to have the same function that it has for the indigenous community, where everyone is able to create very beautiful objects; where someone makes a weaving and that weaving not only serves as clothing but also as a beautiful work of art that expresses the spirituality of the whole community. And this is what we want for ourselves: that our films also represent in some way the spirituality and beauty of our people. Through the film's imagery, music, dialogue, etc., we attempt to be consistent with that culture; we pose the question of aesthetic coherency. We believe we have to give our utmost attention to this all-important question. We reiterate that a beautiful film will be, in effect, more revolutionary since it will not remain at the level of a pamphlet. A cinema as a weapon, as the cinematic expression of a people without cinema, must preoccupy itself with beauty, because beauty is an indispensable element. Also, we are struggling for the beauty of our people, that beauty which imperialism today attempts to destroy, to desecrate, to enslave...The struggle for beauty is the struggle for culture is the struggle for revolution.

Note: We believe that only those who correctly understand the dialectical interrelationship between culture and revolution take up the struggle for the liberation of countries like Bolivia, where different indigenous groups live side by side. To try to apply political methodologies and programs alien to the cultural character of Bolivia will only serve to turn back the process of liberation. Those in the vanguard who schematically rely on external ideological prescriptions can actually become obstacles to the development of that process, because their mistaken actions sow confusion among the masses and their failures are manipulated by the enemy to distort the image of the revolutionary struggle.)

We cannot ignore the fact that we live in a country, Bolivia, where the cultural majority is comprised of the Quechuas and Aymaras. Making revolution and winning liberation must be tasks *totally at one* with the spirit of that majority. Thus the struggle will be a way of belonging to the people, of representing them, but not with words and proclamations, not with theories and declarations, but through consistent daily practice, even to the point of sharing the popular, collective vision of reality; so that, in this way, with the right that authenticity confers, one can engage in the struggle from within the very bosom of the people.

The revolutionary experience and theory of other peoples should help us to build and enrich the revolutionary work itself, but it must never leave off being the expression of the majority. Each revolutionary act, if it corresponds to the will of the collective, will be infused with a genuine cultural breath; thus, each measure, each step, will be consolidating the *national identity*.

(Interview conducted by Ignacio Ramonet for the Spanish magazine, *Triunfo*, Paris, July 1977)

Translated by Richard Schaaf

JORGE SANJINÉS studied philosophy and filmmaking in Chile in the 1950s before returning to Bolivia where he began working with "natural" rather than professional actors during the production of *¡Aysa!* (*Landslide!*, 1965), and of *Ukamu* (*That's the Way It Is*, 1966). The group renamed itself after this last film and began production of its most acclaimed film *Yawar maliku* (*Blood of the Condor*, 1969), the last of their films to have a script per se. *El caraje del pueblo* (*The Courage of the People*, 1971) is the first example of the onsite re-enactment of historical events with the original participants that characterizes Sanjinés' mature work.

Between 1971 and 1979, Sanjinés was forced to live in exile. Yet, despite this alienated condition, he maintained his engagement with his people through the "popular memory" of the Andean peasantry. *El enemigo principal* (*The Principal Enemy*, 1973) was filmed in Peru; and *¡Basta ya!* (*That's Enough!*, 1979), in Colombia and Venezuela. And the documentary *Las banderas del amanecer* (*The Banners of the Dawn*, 1984) chronicles political events in Bolivia in 1983.

Notes:
1. Frederick Engels, *The Origin of the Family, Private Property and the State.*
2. The regime of General Juan José Torres (October 1970-August 1971) was one of the most extraordinary governments in Bolivian history. This idealist military man initiated a radical and left-leaning process of social and economic transformation that for a brief period freed Bolivia from its former exclusive dependence on European and North American largesse. By nationalizing the tin mines, constructing Bolivia's first tin smelter, accepting East European and Russian economic assistance for the first time, and creating a "Popular Assembly" to replace the old parliament, General Torres sought to provide the political space needed by the radical left and labor groups to organize their mass base. While peasant and worker federations and unions sprang up quickly during this brief euphoria, General Torres never succeeded in unifying their support for his regime. He was toppled in a bloody coup led by Colonel Hugo Banzer in August of 1971.
3. General Juan Velasco Alvarado came to power in a bloodless coup in 1968. His military regime instituted a genuine social and economic transformation of Peruvian society, breaking with the norms set down at the time of the Spanish conquest. This fleeting (the government of Velasco Alvarado was toppled in a bloodless coup in 1975 by Army Commander General Francisco Morales Bermudez, amidst an economic crisis instigated by the policy of imperialism) yet left-military regime pushed a sweeping agrarian reform program and it began a process of recovery of Peru's natural resources usurped by foreign capital. Velasco Alvarado succeeded in nationalizing firms in mining, agro-industry, fishing, banking, utilities, transport, and communication. He pushed through many social reforms, such as the reorganization of the education system, a subsidized medical program, and extension of the social security system. Nevertheless, all this amounted to a form of state capitalism that lacked genuine trust in democratic mass organizations and which became increasingly anticommunist.

JAMES SCULLY

Scratching Surfaces
the social practice of tendency poetry

CLANDESTINE POEMS

Roque Dalton was a Marxist-Leninist militant of the Salvadoran Communist Party and of the People's Revolutionary Army (ERP). His poems, especially in *Poemas Clandestinos* (preferred source of these newly translated collections), are discursive, politically explicit.[1] They are what poems are not supposed to be. Worse, they're encouraging: heartening rather than consoling. They raise gritty issues with brio and devastating humor. Their clandestinity is a function of their outspokenness (the public, or eminent, domain having been claimed by social silence). I'm not about to address the articulated issues, however, nor the translations themselves. I'm concerned with the aesthetic ruins scattered about the feet of these resurrected, transfigured, unbowed poems. They so unsettle our aesthetic presumption that we have to ask what, in our notions of poetry, we have refused to admit. What poetry have we buried under our own dust. And why? The answer, or a clue to it, may be found where most are found: just beneath the surface of what seems too obvious for words. In this regard what seems self-evident is the incompatibility of didacticism and/or ideas, historically specific ideas, with what is designated "poetry."

PREACHING, DIDACTICISM, ETC.

For many contemporary poets the injunction against preaching makes good aesthetic sense. It is also a moral imperative. It must be wrong "to tell people what to think." To believe otherwise will lead you to violate art *and* humanity. Will make you cold, hard: a hammerhead. That anyway is the conventional wisdom. It makes sense. But how much, and whose sense is it?

What for now I'll call preaching (didacticism? sloganeering? pamphleteering? poetically indecorous prosiness?) is a catchall for a

172

range of social practices, written and spoken. When "preaching" is charged against texts that are direct and impassioned, explicitly engaged with politics or social justice, we might ask what then is recommended: indirection? not saying what we think? not addressing certain aspects of life?[2] But tempting as this might be, even such questions as these, with their transparent effort to pass as answers, only deepen the mystification. Their terms are like those of a formal debate: the options share an internal logic, a common discourse, which is sustained by a sea of exclusions and suppressions. The seeming alternatives are no more than variations within an effectively monolithic social set. Here, for instance, by momentarily putting the conflict in terms of "content"—saying or not saying "what we think," talking or not talking "about certain things"—we have raised a pressing issue, but with it we have papered over what is more problematically at issue. More troubling and crucial than the isolatable issues of "content" or "reference," there is the indissociable matter of conduct.

The provocation may be less what preaching is about than what it does. Any so-called preaching, especially within the precincts of the "aesthetic," may be condemned for reasons having less to do with subjects of preaching, encapsulated themes or contents, than with preaching as social practice. And that may be the problem. Preaching is discourse constituted as unembarrassed social practice. It confronts, troubling the hegemony of social silence. Even status quo preaching is met with ambivalence—because it strains the status quo, and in addressing ideology (which is by definition unconscious, pervasive, a way of naturalizing and living the web of social relations, and doing so in the self-serving terms of class interest), it mortifies ideology, laying it open to critical analysis. The distinction of preaching is in the degree to which it admits its own condition as social practice.

SAYING

As we ordinarily use the word, preaching patronizes. But the opprobrium cast on that also smears poetries that are discursive, explicit about the social values that inform them. It would be more appropriate to call this, not preaching, but saying. *Saying* is what this is about.

What is the moral or aesthetic flaw in *saying?* Who says? And why? Must poetry be only symptomatic, a social function rather than social practice? A nonsaying comparable to hack teaching whereby a "problem" is posed and an "answer" (momentarily, yet in that moment signaling *power over*) is withheld? What poetic universe does that imply? One where motifs, themes, genres and dehistoricized forms drift in a void, occasionally having their numbers painted in. They might as well, because nothing adds up in such a world. And that's the point: nothing is supposed to. What is produced is not knowledge or social practice (which are transformative: "if you want to know the taste of the pear, you must change the pear by eating it yourself") but commodity exchange. A kind of dark ages filling up with sensible dead matter. Yet this commodity exchange is of lives frozen in social silence:

> Here in the University
> while I listen to a speech by the President
> (in each doorway there are state police
> making their contribution to culture)
> pale with disgust I recall
> the sad peace of my native poverty,
> the gentle slowness of death in my village.
>
> My father is waiting back there.
> I came to study
> the architecture of justice,
> the anatomy of reason,
> to look for answers
> to the terrible abandonment, the thirst.
>
> Oh night of false lights,
> tinsel made out of darkness:
> where should I flee
> if not into my own soul,
> soul that wanted to be a flag returning home
> and that now they want to turn into a filthy rag
> in this temple of thieves?
>
> —Roque Dalton
> "Remembrance and Questions" (Richard Schaaf, trans.)

SOCIAL SILENCE

What does social silence signify? Withholding what we think from what we say, we treat thoughts as objects, things. (If we cannot think without language—a debatable assumption anyway—we can and do think without speaking or writing.) In so doing we commodify thought, making it a property. Though what's behind the hoarding, the metaphorical greed, is fear. Social silence is fear.

Jameson has said that "the profound vocation of the work of art in a commodity society [is] *not* to be a commodity, *not* to be consumed...." It might seem that by withholding, or trying to withhold, we refuse commodification. But what is withheld, and from whom? In truth this is not the powerful leaden silence of a Bartleby squatting in the nerve center of commodity exchange, up against the wall, defiant to the end. This silence signifies accommodation, not resistance. Silence is job, career, acceptance. Silence, this silence, is golden.

Consumption occurs through our eating our own thoughtful words: self-censorship.

Language generates a more reverberant, spellbinding, insidious silence than "silence itself" does. Social silence may be projected as speech, writing, data or news. Then words are used reflexively, as screens, walls, mirrors facing in on their own ideological garden, which is what they cultivate. They become like Milton's serpent, the silence *within* speech.[3] Social silence may be called law, poetry, torture or tolerance. Or it may be named beauty, harmony, civilization, history (how much unimaginable silence is there in these). Whatever, it is the silence pressuring all lives to be opaque, self-preoccupied, impersonal, interchangeable and, it follows, redundant. Lives become commodities that they may be, in the perverse logic of this system, valuable. Meanwhile, socially sanctioned language mediates and shares that degradation—the language of love no less than that of politics or "educational" (i.e., domesticating) systems:

FOR A BETTER LOVE

'Sex is a political category" (Kate Millett)

Everyone agrees that sex
is a category in the world of lovers:
hence tenderness and its wild branches.

Everyone agrees that sex
is a category within the family:
hence children
nights together
and days apart
(he, looking for bread in the street,
in offices or factories;
she, in the rearguard of household work,
in the strategy and tactics of the kitchen
allowing them to survive in the common battle
at least until the end of the month).

Everyone agrees that sex
is an economic category:
it's enough to mention prostitution,
fashion,
sections of the newspaper for her only
or only for him.

Where the trouble begins
is the moment a woman says
sex is a political category.

Because when a woman says
sex is a political category
she can cease being woman in itself
and begin being woman for herself,
constituting the woman in woman
starting from her humanity
and not from her sex,
conscious that magical lemon-scented deodorant
and soap that voluptuously caresses her skin

are made by the same corporation that makes napalm
conscious that the tasks belonging to the home
are tasks belonging to the social class to which that home

belongs,
that the difference between the sexes
shines much brighter in the deep loving night
when all those secrets that kept us
masked and strangers, become known.

—Roque Dalton
(Schaaf, trans.)

Our life is socially complex, specific, struggling to be realized. We need a lucid, conscious language to articulate it. Instead we're given parody complexity: complication, the surging maze. This takes many forms—such as the floating island of Laputa, with its too-familiar academy, in *Gulliver's Travels*—but all are surrounded by, rest upon, silence. Complication, the labyrinth, disorients to no end that is not a dead one. It turns only on itself. It's not harmless either, but intimately, pervasively, oppressive.

We speak the obvious or succumb to it. There *is* an obvious:

Don't ever forget
that the least fascist
among the fascists
are also
fascists.
    —Roque Dalton
    (Schaaf, trans.)

AUTHORIAL DISCRETION:
AUTHORITATIVE IRRESPONSIBILITY

Still there are poets who say, "I don't tell the reader what to think," as though they were making a sensitive gesture in the cause of social/ political freedom and freedom of thought (not to mention preserving the miraculous autonomy of art). But no one is prisoner

177

of a poem. Poems can be persuasive, not coercive. What *will* crimp "freedom of thought" are the desires, needs, exclusions, the fears and mystifications, constituted by the conditions under which we live and make our living.

The argument for stonewalling is self-deceiving as well as presumptuous. Poems do not exercise power as even TV ad campaigns do, or as the only newspaper in town does. Poems are not the propaganda encirclement of free speech celebrated by the owners of the free press, who freely express themselves and their dominion through it:

> He came to us
> and said
>
> you are not responsible
> either for the world or for the end of the world
> the burden is taken from your shoulders
> you are like birds and children
> play
>
> and they play
>
> they forget
> that modern poetry
> is a struggle for breath

> —Tadeusz Rozewicz
> "The Deposition of the Burden" (Czeslaw Milosz, trans.)

Authorial discretion, hand over mouth, seems considerate of the reader.[4] No one gets breathed on. The reader's "freedom" or sensibility is left intact. Yet stonewalling, which here might be called sandbagging, renders the poet a subject (capable of social practice) while reducing the reader to an object (a social symptom, a thing). The reader is projected as passive—seen, known, acted upon— whereas the poet appropriates and reserves the privilege, to herself or himself, of acting, seeing and knowing. Authorial discretion assumes individual autonomy (author as transcendental subject). That assumption is rooted in the ideology of private, or antisocial, property, which is in its furthest reaches the ideology of property itself.[5] Though such discretion has a veneer of humaneness, its antisocial basis comes through in that the humanization of some, especially of the "self," is predicated on the dehumanization of others. The poet is person; the reader, a kind of ward. Beyond that lies the inadmissible: that "the humanization of some" is predicated on the dehumanization of all, "self" included.

Then there is the poststructuralist project. Its managed disappearance of the historically-situated subject seems opposed to the humanist project, whose "author" is sublimated from social being into a sensibility innocent of all but "self" (its innocence of ramification and consequence making it anything *but* innocent). But by desituating and dehistoricizing the work, poststructuralism ends up in line with the humanist position. The results are all too familiar. Telegraphing self-fulfillment, the work's specious authority will derive from the illusion that it is not valuebound, not historically conditioned, not responsible. Not in fact authored but "inspired": the passed-on product of a muse or maybe a "narrative," but not the production of a historically specific, socialized subject. The work's "authoritativeness" will depend not on the masking of its particular human source but on the implicit denial that it comes from anywhere at all, or that it is class couched. The traces of production will be obliterated; the work itself, naturalized. It will *be* ideology.

Where does that leave *us*?

> I must learn to hide
> from my persecutors
> and am thereby
> in double danger
>
> Perhaps not well enough
> hidden from them
> and perhaps by now
> hidden too well from myself
>
> —Erich Fried
> "In Hiding" (Stuart Hood, trans.)

TENDENCY WRITING

During the last century, progressive literature associated with the Young Germany Movement was called *Tendenz,* "the tendency."[6] Defined in opposition to so-called pure art, it was also called committed writing. The significance of *Tendenzpoesie* lay in its concrete historical engagement, at least up through the Revolution of 1848. Also, *Tendenz* was practiced by associates of Marx and Engels and was commented on by those two, especially by Engels, who was critical.

The novelty of tendency writing came from its being a politically gestated "aesthetic" practice. *Tendenz* was cast in political struggle. There seems, on a superficial look-through, no precedent for it. Not the polis art of an Aeschylus wedged into philosophical fissures at the core of its world, nor the hit-and-run satire and invective in Greek and Latin literature. It doesn't match up with the moral, social satire of much 17th- and 18th-century European literature either. Nor with the decent-minded, overreaching and idealist social response of isolated, individually activist English poets, though it's tempting to make exceptions of Blake and Shelley. Are Dante and Milton precursors? Whatever, *Tendenz* was not sideline or Olympian commentary, but engagement with actual political power.

In time, *Tendenz* would refer to insistently politicized art committed to revolutionary struggle. Now the term suggests art that is engaged, didactic and developed from a consistent political perspective, usually socialist or communist.[7] Unlike protest art, tendency art has a focused, positive aspiration—not simply a notion of social injustice, say, based on the standard-of-justice of an unjust system, but a working concept of concrete, *systemic* remedy.

REALISM & PARTISANSHIP

Tendency art articulates latent historical tendencies. Or, to put this negatively, it's an art that refuses the harmonizing, the glossing and freeze-framing, of bourgeois ideology. *Tendenz* is as much a function of realism—not any convention of realism, but realism as revelation of, and contention with, the dynamics and ramifications of social interrelationship—as of partisanship. Realism and partisanship are inseparable. It's not simply that partisanship without realism may be toothless, but that the dependency is the other way round: there can be no realism without partisanship.[8] (We can't describe anything accurately without entering into a relationship with it and accounting for that relationship in our description. This doesn't mean we must be "subjective" rather than "objective," though those are question-begging terms, but that we must struggle to be objective about our subjectivity. For instance, Yeats attempted this in his Doctrine of the Mask as well as in individual works such as "Easter 1916".) But the partisanship has to be conscious. Unconscious or unavowed partisanship is a bottomless pit, precisely the condition of "apolitical" art. In *that* there is no present, no future, no living history. Only compulsions, reactions, postures, tableaux.

FORM & ENGELS

Tendency writing cannot consist of sheer assertion. Willful partisanship is a function of idealist presumption (one of the more notorious, historically, being the idealist stance of Zhdanov). If tendency writing is to amplify and unravel contradictions informing the current growing and decaying social configuration, it has to proceed from materialist assumptions. That is also why tendency art does not prescribe formal criteria, even though it is, must be, suffused with formal considerations. The realism of tendency writing is not conceived as a particular form or style, but as social practice. This is the realism of demythification (of phenomena) and demystification (of consciousness). It owes nothing to received conventions of realism or to the parody realism of representation.[9]

Still, tendency writing has had a poor press. Engels himself, maintaining a metaphysical rather than a materialist distinction between form and content, was hostile toward it. This from one letter: "The more the opinions of the author remain hidden, the better for the work of art."

He attacked "Schillerism" as "making individuals into mere mouthpieces of the spirit of the times." Though in a late (1885) letter to Minna Kautsky he did qualify his rejection of *Tendenz*:

> I am not at all an opponent of tendentious writing as such. The father of tragedy, Aeschylus, and the father of comedy, Aristophanes, were both strong tendentious

poets, as were Dante and Cervantes.... But I believe the
tendency must spring forth from the situation and the
action itself, without explicit attention being called to it;
the writer is not obliged to offer to the reader the future
historical solution of the social conflicts he depicts...

To salvage something from this, Raymond Williams suggested
that Engels's criticisms relate to "'applied tendency'—the mere
addition of political opinions and phrases, or unrelated moral
comments." In other words, the "tendency writing" that is
editorialization, the fault being that it is *formally* intrusive. And it's
true that Engels usually has novels or plays in mind—novels and
plays, moreover, as conceived and practiced in *his* time. He objects to
the tendentious violation of fictive constructions, or of the fiction
conventions with which he was familiar. In this respect his opposition
is based on narrowly formalist concerns. It's significant that neither
he nor Marx, as far as I know, complained of the poet Heine's
tendentiousness, though they did make caustic comments on its
political thrust.

Some of Engels's criticism does seem based on a Romantic appeal
to "organic form," but one honed by the contempt that a dedicated
political activist is likely to have for politically dabbling literati. Early
on (1851), referring to the Young Germany Movement, he says:

A crude Constitutionalism, or a still cruder Republican-
ism, was preached by almost all writers of the time. It
became more and more the habit, particularly of the
inferior sorts of literati, to make up for the want of
cleverness in their productions by political allusions
which were sure to attract attention. Poetry, novels,
reviews, the drama, every literary production teemed
with what was called "tendency," that is with more or
less timid exhibitions of an antigovernment spirit.

This characterizes literature which, although *about* social or
political conditions, has no penetrating social analysis and so falls
short of effective social practice. Nor does the work itself constitute
social practice. It is only protest literature, the groans and
exclamations of an uneasy liberalism. And yet, as happens, attacks
on such literature extend to tendency writing as well, caricaturing it,

making it beneath comment not only for the ruling class and its cultural support system but for much of the culture-working left also, which continues to mark time in the lockups of bourgeois "aesthetics."

RESPONSIBILITY: FROM THE VIEWPOINT OF PRODUCTION

Using terms that are unself-critical yet suggestive, Morawski calls tendency writing "the projection by essentially discursive yet poeticized means of an idea of history and of the attitudes, feelings, conflicts, etc. of the artistic personality (the author) about this idea." When we look at it from the inside out, we find that "tendency poetry" obliterates the illusion of distance between poet and poem. Not formally, but with respect to assumed responsibility. The illusory distinction between poet and poem dissolves, but does so *only from the viewpoint of production,* not necessarily from that of critical reception or consumption. For the critic there may be no poet, only a work or a boundary-shifting text. But for the poet or producer, even the producer as a socially defined "discourse-medium" rather than a metaphysically posited "source," there is social being, and some sort of self-identity, and therefore social implication and critical juncture and decision. There is responsibility.

There is responsibility not only in the writing but also in the being of the writing, even when that writing is well out of hand. It remains a gesture of the producer, whatever is made of it. It's in this sense, the only meaningful sense from the perspective of production, that the tendency poet contends with values enacted by and through the work. There is no lyric washing of the hands, no signaling: "don't hold me accountable for what I say and do, I'm only a symptom, or I'm only a site where saying takes place, where meaning emerges with its slow thighs to trouble the sight...I'm only saying what is, passing it on..."

RESPONSIBILITY: SOCIALIZING EXPERIENCE

This does not mean that responsibility is individually determined (the miserable niche that the *moral* carves out of the *social),* or that it may be sufficiently informed by sheer personal experience.[10] Responsibility, like experience, must be socialized. Accordingly, tendentious writing would not restrict or deny personal experience but enhance and extend it. *Tendenz* begins by fulfilling the conditions of an art, referred to by Jameson and others, which prepares us to learn, really learn, by permitting us "to grasp the essentially historical and social value of what we had otherwise taken to be a question of individual experience." More significantly, tendency writing would not simply contextualize or *typify* personal experience but would expose that experience as being, of itself, an isolation pit. Personal experience, privileged, degenerates into a cultivated ignorance: another walled garden.[11]

All poetry, like language itself, is social. Open to the world. Tendency poetry takes this condition literally and seriously, as an opportunity rather than an inconvenience. An opportunity not to "preach" but to sing—to a socially rather than an individually defined someone—even if the song must often be rueful:[12]

> For $140,000
> you can scratch your back
> with Brancusi's *Bird in Space.*
>
> Just $17
> and you'll receive *Fortune* magazine
> for twelve months.
> Poor peon
> who barely makes $55 a year:
> the worth of modern sculpture
> is an unresolved matter,
> and *Fortune*
> comes out only in English,
> so why kid yourself?
>
> May eternal spring be with you, compatriot
> of our Central American soccer (junior division)
> champions!
>
> —Roque Dalton
> "60% of El Salvador" (Schaaf, trans.)

This the most consciously social of poetries turns on the second person, you, the pronoun of intimacy and division we are given to struggle with—though its welling subtext is the collective *we* which is partly assumed, still to be realized. Of course that collectivity cannot be realized without struggle. Nor without going well beyond current political definitions and boundaries. Any tendentiousness is disturbing, even to people whose interests and values approximate those of the work itself, because it forces recognition of living issues. Issues *of* living. And that is scary.[13] Not only is struggle inescapable: in tendency poetry, struggle, largely class struggle, is declared *and* engaged.

BRINGING LANGUAGE BACK TO LIFE

Granted that the *materia* of social problems are already raised and defined. It does not take tendency poetry to do that. However, they are raised and defined in terms of the dominant, empowered class. Social contradictions and conflicts are mythified as symptoms of a "condition" (a fact of life, a dehistoricized situation without historic cause and therefore without remedy) rather than revealed as problematical and as socially originated (therefore actionable and solvable):

> There have been good people in this country
> ready to die for the revolution.
> But the revolution everywhere needs people
> who are ready not only to die
> but also to kill for it.
>
> About those good people Che said:
> "They are capable of dying in torture chambers
> without letting out a single word,
> but they are incapable of taking out
> a machine gun nest."
>
> And the class enemy as is well known
> uses not only torture chambers
> to defend exploitation

185

but also machine gun nests
and all sorts of such things.

In short:
only those who are ready to die and kill
will end up being people who are good
for the revolution.

Because it's through *them* the revolution will be made.

Though the revolution ends up being for
all good people.

—Roque Dalton
"Old Communists and Guerrillas" (Schaaf; trans.)

This is not an image-generating language. Nor does it have the forked tongue of complication and indeterminacy. The subtlety is in the precision, the discrimination, the transparent respect vesting the gesture. And it is in the fine-tuning not of the self-congratulatory obvious, but of the unassuming: here, the prepositions:

En resumidas cuentas:
sólo aquellos que estén dispuestos a morir y matar
llegarán hasta el final siendo buenas personas
para la revolución.

Porque será por ellas que habrá revolución.

Aunque la revolución termine por ser para
todas las buenas personas.

The generative contradiction of the poem is manifest in the sibling *por* and *para (through/by* and *for)* that play off one another, with sly wit, down to their hospitable and remarkably gentle conclusion. The idealist assumption that what is for all decent people must transpire *through* them, through all such regardless—as though dehistoricized ends might constitute historical means—is stopped in midflight and seen (read) through.

Tendency poetry realizes a *lived* poetic. This is not just a matter of taking poetry seriously. Rather, here is a poetry conscious of living social context: what it is becoming and what it is coming up against. In idealist poetries the awareness of limits induces fatalism, cynicism, sentimentality. It reinforces the stupefying belief that truth is relative, that the fragments of experience cannot be added up—as they cannot be if experience is conceived subjectively, in isolation, rather than socially. But in tendency poetry the encounter with limits is an encounter. It produces historical specificity. The fact is that truth isn't relative, it's historical. This isn't something that can be learned. We have to keep on learning it. *Truth is not relative, it's historical.* It is arrived at through personal social struggle. There are no shortcuts. The almost transpersonal optimism of tendency poetry flows from the understanding that there are no truths, not even scientific ones, that are not historically conditioned.

How assume otherwise? How assume that poetry may be exempt from the historicity of its, and our, world? All language is of life, social life. It's remarkable how little curiosity many poets have regarding their own language. How much they give up on, and how readily. There's interest in deracinated etymology, in words "untimely ripped," but little or none in the concrete historical content of the language they use, nor in its social function. Nor in whose language it is:

> Render unto God the things that are God's
> and unto the fascist government of President Molina
> what belongs to the fascist government of Pres. Molina.
>
> I don't pretend to know, from my limited perspective,
> all that belongs to God
>
> but, yes, I'm sure about what we ought to give
> the fascist government of Molina.
>
> —Roque Dalton
> "Variations on a Phrase by Christ" (Schaaf, trans.)

TENDENCY POETRY IMPERFECT

Tendency poetry assumes a present not sealed off, like one time capsule addressed to another, but activated with the reader. Rather than close on itself like an archive, where life is congealed, objectified, no longer becoming, it *enacts* socialization. That's why tendency poems are not self-contained but generative. They hang around, resist being finished off:[14]

ARS POETICA 1974

Poetry
pardon me for having helped you to understand
you are not made of words alone.

—Roque Dalton
(Schaaf, trans.)

Tendency poetry would not simply manifest social being. It would constitute, and be constituted by, social transaction. From the perspective of production, tendency poets and poetries are especially obliged to look and listen, because "the world" goes on talking back, surrounding and impressing, returning the challenge posed by Rilke's archaic torso of Apollo and demanding that the poet (poetry) change his or her life and understanding of life and "art." Here's Brecht on a lesson learned from workers/actors staging *Die Massnahme (The Measures Taken):*

The workers judged everything according to the truth of its content; they welcomed every innovation which helped the representation of truth, of the real mechanisms of society.... Anything that was worn out, trivial, or so commonplace that it no longer made one think, they did not like at all ("you get nothing out of it"). If one needed an aesthetic, one could find it here. I shall never forget how a worker looked at me when I replied to his suggestion that I should add something to a chorus about the Soviet Union ("It has got to go in— otherwise what's the point?"), that it would destroy the artistic form. He put his head on one side and smiled. A whole area of aesthetics collapsed because of his polite smile. The workers are not afraid to teach us and they were not themselves afraid to learn.[15]

Tendency poetry is risky. Even subjectivity and self-identity (or self-misrecognition) are at hazard:

THE PETITE BOURGEOISIE
(one of its manifestations)

Those who
in most cases
want to make revolution
for History for logic
for science and nature
for next year's books or the future
to win arguments and even
to appear finally in the newspapers
and not simply
to put an end to the hunger
of those who are hungry
and the exploitation
of those who are exploited.

It is natural, then,
that in revolutionary practice
they only concede before the judgment of History
morality humanism logic science
books and newspapers
and refuse to concede the last word
to the hungry the exploited
who have their own history of horror
their own implacable logic
and who will have their own books
their own science
nature
and future

       —Roque Dalton
       (Schaaf, trans.)

TENDENCY & SOCIALIST REALISM

Tendency poetry entails the realism of demystification and demythification, not of representation.[16] Which is why tendency poetry doesn't hole up, becoming merely one kind of form (i.e., a style). It engages becoming.

Socialist realism was also supposed to engage becoming. That potential was squelched: by the revolutionary romanticism, if we may call it that, proclaimed by Zhdanov—a romanticism so utopian that even he had to insist it was not; by the inertia of a bourgeois past, which was also a present, and by the demands of a politically temporizing present, a future-dominated present, whereby the frontier fluidity of proletarian internationalism was being displaced by a united front of (static, bourgeois) nationalisms. Socialist realism flaked off into the sorry thing characterized by Trotsky in the late Thirties: "The 'realism' consists in the imitation of provincial daguerreotypes of the third quarter of the last century; the 'socialist' character apparently consists in representing, in the manner of pretentious photography, events which never took place." The potential of socialist realism now goes unrecognized, if not unrealized, though some of the more mature 20th-century poetry follows from the philosophical (not, repeat, the historically effected) bases of socialist realist art.[17]

The Turkish poet Nazim Hikmet went so far as to use socialist realist principle to question the stultifying exoskeleton that socialist realism had become historically:

I have some questions for the cosmonauts
did they see the stars much larger
were they like huge jewels on black velvet
        or apricots on orange
does it make a person feel proud to get a little closer to the stars
I saw color photos of the cosmos in Ogonek magazine now
                                            don't get
        upset comrades but nonfigurative shall we say or abstract
        well some of them looked just like such paintings which is
        to say they were terribly figurative and concrete
my heart was in my mouth looking at them

they are the endlessness of our longing to grasp things
looking at them I could think even of death and not feel one bit
                                                                    sad
I never knew I loved the cosmos

> —Nazim Hikmet
> "Things I Didn't Know I Loved"
> (Randy Blasing and Mutlu Konuk, trans.)

The poem is dated April 1962, when such issues were being aired. Seven or eight months later Khrushchev made his notorious attack, at the scene of a Moscow art exhibit, on nonfigurative or "modernist" tendencies in Soviet art.

PARTISAN POETRY & PARTY POETRY

It has been noted that tendency poetry is partisan poetry.[18] Certainly all literature is partisan, a compounding of interests, perspectives, class values, ends. But tendency poetry acknowledges its partisanship. It does not make a virtue of being at the mercy of unconscious bias (though no poetry or language, including this one, escapes that entirely). Still, partisanship is one thing. Lenin's *partiinost*, "party-spirited" literature, is something else: an extension of partisanship, but so intensified in degree that it becomes different in kind. The questions raised by *partiinost* are provocative, not least because they are bound up with the necessities of revolutionary transformation. Serious, prolonged struggle requires organization and discipline. There's no way around that. The question, which for us in the U.S. still awaits an answer, is, what kind of organization? Discipline how constituted?

Tendentious literature does not have to be party-spirited literature. Usually it is not. But what happens when it is? Problems arise when "party-spirited" cools into "party-outlined"—when the literature is abstracted in accord with ephemeral aspects of a policy that at any given moment must be, no matter how hard it tries not to be, blindly literal.[19] And so, blind to itself and its consequences... more attuned to tactics than to strategy. Or mistaking the relationship between them. That will happen, of course. That's the chance taken by any movement or organization engaged in revolutionary struggle. Yet that same chance has also to be taken by literature and, as regards revolutionary organizations, *with* literature. There has to be that good faith. Brecht had something of the sort in mind when he accused Lukacs and others of being "enemies of production": "Production makes them uncomfortable. You never know where you are with production; production is unforeseeable. You never know what's going to come out. And they themselves don't want to produce. They want to play the *apparatchik* and exercise control over other people. Every one of their criticisms contains a threat."

CROCK LOGIC

"Criticism of the Soviet Union
can only be made by one who is anti-Soviet.

Criticism of China
can only be made by one who is anti-China.

Criticism of the Salvadoran Communist Party
can only be made by an agent of the CIA.
Self-criticism is equivalent to suicide."

—Roque Dalton
(Schaaf, trans.)

Party-spirited literature is written in free association with a party or it is nothing, least of all effective. It must be produced by party-committed human beings, not functionaries. But this is a problem to be worked out by those who have the experience and competence to do so. The issue may not seem pressing now, when local revolutionary organizations are weak and undeveloped. But sooner or later there will be no way around it. History tends to eliminate options, or the illusion of options. (Objectively. Subjectively, as we've seen, that illusion can be carried into the teeth of any reality.) There will have to be a party-spirited literature. Not the literature of ad hoc or issue-bound groups—which are theoretically and practically self-incapacitating—but of fundamentally principled, ultimately mass-revolutionary organizations. At some point it should be clear that there are no sidelines to stand back of: no "aesthetic" area sealed off from a "political," no knowing apart from doing, no moral values dissociated from actual conduct:

DEATH CERTIFICATE

"Because it's all no use
They do as they please anyhow

Because I don't want to get
my fingers burnt again

Because they'll just laugh:
it only needed you!

And why always me?
I'll get no thanks for it

Because no one can sort this out
One might only make things worse

Because even what's bad
may have some good in it

Because it depends on how you look at it
and anyway whom can you trust?

Because the other side too
gets wet when it rains

Because I'd rather leave it
to those more qualified

Because you never know
what you let yourself in for

Because it's a waste of effort
They don't deserve it"

These are the causes of death
to write on our graves

which will not even be dug
if these are the causes

—Erich Fried
(Georg Kapp, trans.)

So, tendency poetry. Or something of it. The case of *Tendenz* needs to be reconsidered, especially by those developing a language adequate to engage it. There's already enough tendency poetry to support such an undertaking.[20] An undertaking, note, that has been denigrated and suppressed for the very reasons that revolutionary parties have been put down (not piecemeal, relative to weaknesses or questionable policies, but categorically, in their entirety): because they cannot be pocketed or otherwise contained. They are systematically subversive practices.

JAMES SCULLY, the author of seven collections of poetry—as well as translations (with Maria Proser & Arlene Scully)of *De Repente/All of a Sudden* and translative adaptations (with Maria Proser) of *Quechua Peoples Poetry*, and the book of cultural essays, *Line Break: Poetry as Social Practice*— was the founding editor of Curbstone's *Art on the Line* pamphlet series. He currently lives in San Francisco.

This essay is reprinted from the book of essays by James Scully, *Line Break*, published by Bay Press.

Notes:

1. At the time this was written, two translated selections of Dalton's poetry were about to come out: *Poems* (Willimantic, Ct.: Curbstone Press, 1984), translated by Richard Schaaf, and *Clandestine Poems / Poemas Clandestinos* (San Francisco: Solidarity Publications, 1984), translated by Jack Hirschman. Appropriately, money to help publish the latter was raised through a community activists' dance in the Mission district of San Francisco.

2. Granted that a saying or a writing "signifies" in more ways than one, and that no one wraps this up. Granted too that what we think means more than we realize, and that (language being historical) what we say means more and less than we intend, and that meaning does not entirely preexist but is produced also in the saying. But 'meaning' in that sense is not at issue here. What is, is what happens as we exercise intentions and are, in consequence, socially accountable. Any discourse is specifically produced. There must be a producer. The question is *where* the producing, the speaking, is from.

   In certain respects the assumptions of this discussion are untenable. It's not possible to have a thought independent of the language realizing it, nor independent of the social context where that language is played out, and whereby that language is itself in part constituted. But this only means that thought, however intimate or fleeting, is socially constituted.

3. A silence that, in a prefatory, tellingly aestheticized show of power, exposes itself as thick, unbroken, coldly palpable. In context the silence materializes not as an 'it' but as 'he' who

                        toward Eve
   Addressed his way, not with indented wave
   Prone on the ground, as since, but on his rear,
   Circular base of rising folds, that towered
   Fold above fold a surging maze; his head
   Crested aloft, and carbuncle his eyes;
   With burnished neck of verdant gold, erect
   Amidst his circling spires, that on the grass
   Floated redundant....

4. It hardly matters whether the text is "written" or "spoken," or whether a critic may divine an author behind, or describe an author produced by, the text. This discussion is of the production of texts from the perspective, the subject-position, of the immediate producers of texts. It's irrelevant whether authorial self-identification is achievable, or that self-identification must necessarily be self-misrecognition. Though self-identity is problematical in that it is social, historical—ever a *becoming*—the fact is, every producer does adopt, conceive, or misconceive a functionally effective identity.

5. The notion of a process whereby one is liberated from the condition of an "object" (seen, known, acted upon) so as to assume the condition of a "subject" (seeing, knowing, acting upon) has been engaging and useful. Nonetheless it has been criticized, partly on the grounds that its positing of

a "self" is metaphysical. There is also the criticism that *any* concept of self is a concept of property, and so must necessarily constitute human relations as property relations (witness the "love" songs on the pop music charts). Yet such criticism often replaces that self or subject with an easily paradoxical "decentered subject" which is itself metaphysical and corresponds, politically, to liberal ideology. One may be everywhere, and has to be nowhere. *Has to* be nowhere.

6. The Young Germany Movement was liberal, nationalist, constitutionalist. The general push was for a German national state with a representative assembly. This meant, of course, opposition to divine right. On a popular level there was also opposition to medieval restrictions on apprentices, artisans and peasants. The intellectuals agitated for free speech and trial by jury.

7. For this and other reasons it makes no sense to include someone like the Greek poet Cavafy—whose considerable work is often tendentious and socially dimensioned—as a tendency poet. Nor, say, the 17th-century poet George Herbert, who beneath a transparency of dramatic meditation is remarkably persistent in pressing a religiously ideological (smoothing over, harmonizing) tendentiousness.

8. "All of our descriptive statements move within an often invisible network of value-categories.... It is not just as though we have something called factual knowledge which may then be distorted by particular interests and judgments, although this is certainly possible; it is also that without particular interests we would have no knowledge at all.... Interests are *constitutive* of our knowledge, not merely prejudice which imperils it. The claim that knowledge should be 'value-free' is itself a value-judgment." Terry Eagleton, *Literary Theory, An Introduction* (Minneapolis: University of Minnesota Press, 1983), 14.

   In *Reception Theory: A Critical Introduction* (New York: Methuen, 1984), Robert C. Holub summarizes Hans-Georg Gadamer's extension of Heidegger's rethinking of being. "While previous theory had advocated a purging of preconceptions, Heidegger claims that it is precisely our being-in-the-world with its prejudices and presuppositions that makes understanding possible.... Gadamer takes up this issue most thoroughly in his discussion of prejudice [*Vorurteil*]. The word in German, like its English equivalent, although etymologically related to prejudging or merely forming a judgment about something beforehand, has come to mean a negative bias or a quality that excludes accurate judgment. The enlightenment, Gadamer claims, is responsible for this discrediting of the notion of prejudice. But this discrediting, he continues, is itself the result of a prejudice that is linked to the methodological claims to truth proposed by the natural sciences. Prejudice, because it belongs to historical reality itself, is not a hindrance to under-standing, but rather a condition of the possibility of understanding" (40-41).

   For a related, "politicized" view, read the comments on prediction, impartiality and partisanship in Antonio Gramsci's *Selections from the*

Prison Notebooks (New York: international Publishers, 1971), 170-72.

9. Not the stagnant, flattened "realism" of idealist thought, but the demystifying realism of dialectical materialism. It has become fashionable to pass over dialectical materialism, or to dismiss it without having the vaguest notion as to what it might (rightly or wrongly) mean. To the ancient Greeks, 'dialectics' meant disclosing contradictions in an opponent's argument. But for Lenin dialectics is "the splitting of a single whole and the cognition of its contradictory parts." What in nature or society seems a homogeneous whole contains internal contradictions. It is by means of (not in spite of) these contradictions, struggling oppositions, that the seemingly stable whole develops and is transformed.

   Among Marxists there are differing interpretations and applications of the term. What's more, dialectical materialism may be deconstructed (provided the deconstructor, assuming a liberal position, levitates). Nonetheless even raw generalizations indicate something of its richness and power. Dialectical materialism is defined in opposition to metaphysical idealism. The basic assumptions of the dialectical method, as schematized under Stalin's name, are: a) that everything is an interconnected and integral whole; b) that everything in the world is in a state of continuous movement and change; c) that imperceptible quantitative changes at some point become qualitative (i.e., categorical) ones; and d) that contradiction is inherent in all things. These contrast with idealist assumptions: a) that things are unconnected and independent of each other; b) that nature is basically immutable; c) that process is a simple development of growth, wherein quantitative changes never become qualitative ones; and d) that contradictions, if any, are among things rather than within them.

   Historical materialism extends the principles of dialectical materialism to the study of social life. These are the terms of the realism we speak of in connection with tendency poetry

10. The question is, what constitutes "personal experience"? What *is* such experience actually *of*? As Raymond Williams points out, "Ideology…is very much more than the ideas and beliefs of particular classes or groups. It is in effect, with only limited exceptions, the condition of all conscious life. Thus the area to which most students of literature normally refer their reading and their judgment, that area summarized in the decisive term 'experience,' has in fact to be seen as within the sphere of ideology—indeed, experience is seen as the most common form of ideology. It is where the deep structures of the society actually reproduce themselves as conscious life." Raymond Williams, "Crisis in English Studies," *Writing in Society* (London: Verso, n.d.), 207.

11. The privileging of individual personal experience has led to, or abetted, the marked visual-reference bias of so much modern poetry in English. Fetishized visual phenomena represent, project, a sense-bound version of the "concrete" or substantial. As one dissenting theorist remarks: "The apparently concrete, the text, turns out, on further inspection, to be an abstraction whereas the apparently abstract, the system of relationships

between texts, proves to be the concrete or, more accurately, a necessary abstraction through which it is alone possible to encounter the text in its particular, determinate and historically varying concrete forms. The concrete, Marx remarks in the *Grundrisse,* is the result and not the point of departure for thought." Tony Bennett, *Formalism and Marxism* (New York: Methuen, 1979), 175.

A similar observation is made by Michael Ryan: "The semblance of 'being as presence'—a perceptible plenitude in the present moment—is thus simply an effect of complex chains of relations whose texture is never 'present' as such. As Marx would have put it, had he lived to be a critic of phenomenology, to privilege perception is to limit oneself to "things," at the expense of the imperceptible social relations that produce them." Michael Ryan, *Marxism and Deconstruction* (Baltimore: Johns Hopkins University Press, 1982), 22.

The fetishizing of sensory experience and of "things" has its broad rationale in empiricism. But traces of this bias (which having broken through one superstition has, in time, become a succeeding superstition) are evident even in the limited course of modern American poetry. E.g., William Carlos Williams: "...what actually impinges on the senses must be rendered as it appears, by use of which, only, and under which, untouched, the significance has to be disclosed. It is one of the major problems of the artist." Despite some hedging, the first Imagist principle— "direct treatment of the 'thing' whether subjective or objective"—underwrites the same priority, with its assumption of a transparent or self-canceling language. At the aesthetic extreme, the poem itself is fetishized, as in MacLeish's metaphysically materialist "A poem should not mean / But be," at which point the social silence is deafening.

Pursuing the matter we find that the roots of this empiricist bias are not materialist, as might be assumed, but idealist. The drive is toward *dehistoricized* being. The attempt is to render the dehistoricized 'thing.' Not incidentally, it is also an attempt to purge language ("to purify the dialect of the tribe"), to free it from the implication of history. The following passage, from an article on photography, is suggestive: "E. H. Gombrich has traced the lineage of the belief in the ineffable purity of the visual image. Plato puts into the mouth of Socrates a doctrine of two worlds: the world of murky imperfection to which our mortal senses have access; and an 'upper world' of perfection and light. *Discursive speech is the tangled and inept medium to which we are condemned in the former* [my italics], while in the latter all things are communicated visually as a pure and unmediated intelligibility which has no need for words. The idea that there are two quite distinct forms of communication, words and images, and that the latter is the more direct, passed via the Neo-Platonists into the Christian tradition. There was now held to be a divine language of *things,* richer than the language of words; those who apprehend the difficult but divine truths enshrined in things do so in a flash, without the need for words and arguments. As Gombrich observes, such traditions 'are of more than antiquarian interest.

They still affect the way we talk and think about the art of our own time."
Victor Burgin, "Photography, Phantasy, Function," *Thinking Photography*
(London: Macmillan, 1982), 214.

What's "wrong" with discursive language, with speech itself, is that it is
historical. (We may detect an affiliated bias in current attempts to privilege
Lacan's prelinguistic "mirror phase.") The impulse that promoted, in
photography, the "ineffable purity of the visual [i.e., nondiscursive] image"
coincided ideologically and to some extent historically with the Imagist
impulse (in fact reaction) to minimize or repress discursive language in
favor of "things" or "images." Considering what those and allied aesthetics
exclude—a Wilfred Owen, for instance, despite his sensuous "imaging"—it's
not difficult to figure their social function.

12. "Every literary text is built out of a sense of its potential audience, includes
an image of whom it is written *for:* every work encodes within itself what
Iser calls an 'implied reader,' intimates in its every gesture the kind of
'addressee' it anticipates.... It is not just that a writer 'needs an audience': the
language he uses already implies one range of possible audiences rather than
another." Eagleton, 84.

13. "Nothing about the problems of Negroes was ever taught in the
classrooms at school; and whenever I would raise these questions with the
boys, they would either remain silent or turn the subject into a joke. They
were vocal about the petty individual wrongs they suffered, but they
possessed no desire for a knowledge of the picture as a whole. Then why was
I worried about it?" Richard Wright, *Black Boy.*

14. Walter Benjamin links the "unfinished character" of such work with the
necessity of changing the production apparatus rather than simply
providing grist for its mill. I quote at length because his modest,
companionable subtlety is helpful in ways that cannot be summarized. He
notes that Brecht; "was the first to address to the intellectuals the far-
reaching demand that they should not supply the production apparatus
without, at the same time, within the limits of the possible, changing that
apparatus in the direction of Socialism. 'The publication of the *Versuche*,' we
read in [Brecht's] introduction to the series of texts published under that
title, 'marks a point at which certain works are not so much intended to
represent individual experiences (i.e. to have the character of finished
works) as they are aimed at using (transforming) certain existing institutes
and institutions.'...Here I should like to confine myself to pointing out the
decisive difference between merely supplying a production apparatus and
changing it.... To supply a production apparatus without trying, within the
limits of the possible, to change it, is a highly disputable activity even when
the material supplied appears to be of a revolutionary nature. For we are
confronted with the fact—of which there has been no shortage of proof over
the last decade [*Benjamin presented this paper in 1934*]—that the bourgeois
apparatus of production and publication is capable of assimilating, indeed
of propagating, an astonishing amount of revolutionary themes without
ever seriously putting into question its own continued existence or that of

the class which owns it. In any case this remains true so long as it is supplied by hacks, albeit revolutionary hacks. And I define a hack as a man who refuses as a matter of principle to improve the production apparatus and so pry it away from the ruling class for the benefit of Socialism. I further maintain that an appreciable part of so-called left-wing literature had no other social function than that of continually extracting new effects or sensations from this situation for the public's entertainment....

"I have spoken of the way in which [the New Objectivity, a literary movement] has turned *the struggle against misery* into an object of consumption.... The characteristic feature of this literature is the way it transforms political struggle so that it ceases to be a compelling motive for decision and becomes an object of comfortable contemplation; it ceases to be a means of production and becomes an article of consumption....

"An author who has carefully thought about the conditions of production today... will never be concerned with products alone, but always, at the same time, with the means of production. In other words, his products must possess an organizing function besides and before their character as finished works. And their organizational usefulness must on no account be confined to propagandistic use. Commitment alone will not do it.... The best opinion is of no use if it does not make something useful of those who hold it. The best 'tendency' is wrong if it does not prescribe the attitude with which it ought to be pursued. And the author can only prescribe such an attitude in the place where he is active, that is to say in his writing. Commitment is a necessary, but never a sufficient, condition for a writer's work acquiring an organizing function. For this to happen it is also necessary for the writer to have a teacher's attitude.... *A writer who does not teach other writers teaches nobody.* The crucial point, therefore, is that a writer's production must have the character of a model: it must be able to instruct other writers in their production and, second, it must be able to place an improved apparatus at their disposal. This apparatus will be the better, the more consumers it brings in contact with the production process—in short, the more readers or spectators it turns into collaborators." *Reflections* (New York: Harcourt Brace Jovanovich, 1978), 220-238.

15. The identification of dehistoricized "form" (codified or prescribed style) with "quality" has been one of the more effective ploys in securing, philosophically at least, ruling class cultural hegemony as regards the arts.

In one of his talks at the Yenan Forum, Mao Zedong outlined a class-cognizant, historically grounded approach to the issue of "artistic" quality: "We must popularize only what is needed and can be readily accepted by the workers, peasants and soldiers themselves. Consequently, prior to the task of educating the workers, peasants and soldiers, there is the task of learning from them. This is even more true of raising standards. There must be a basis from which to raise...From what basis, then, are literature and art to be raised? From the basis of the feudal classes? From the basis of the bourgeoisie? From the basis of the petit bourgeois intellectuals? No, not from any of these; only from the basis of the masses of workers, peasants and soldiers. Nor does this mean raising the workers, peasants and soldiers to the 'heights' of the feudal classes, the bourgeoisie or the petit bourgeois intellectuals; it means raising the level of literature and art in the direction in which the workers, peasants and soldiers are themselves advancing, in the direction in which the proletariat is advancing. Here again the task of learning from the workers, peasants and soldiers comes in." Mao Zedong, "Talks at the Yenan Forum on Literature and Art" in *Mao Tse-tung on Literature and Art* (Peking: Foreign Languages Press, 1967), 16-17.

The authors of a recent article on cultural policy in Sandinista Nicaragua also break the ideological linkage between prescribed, dehistoricized "form" and quality: "Since they are premised on an awareness of how historical self-consciousness is a precondition for cultural self-determination, the advances in Nicaraguan art have necessarily gone beyond formalism, because formalism is, above all, historical ignorance raised to the level of an aesthetic principle. Mainstream notions of aesthetic 'quality' in the United States and Europe—which largely isolate art forms from history and then fetishize those forms as all-important, with a few concluding remarks about the 'ineffability' of 'good taste'—are transparently self-contradictory to those who are recovering from historical amnesia, not to mention the political and economic causes of it. Hence 'quality' in the visual arts, far from being ignored, has been detrivialized by the Nicaraguans to mean something much more complex than self-serving remarks about 'good taste.'" David Craven and John Ryder, "Nicaragua's Revolution in Culture," *Arts*, January 1984.

16. What this might entail beyond our present political context remains to be seen. In *Literature and Propaganda* (New York: Methuen, 1983), A. P. Foulkes notes that "a demystifying art... is by its nature a subversive and questioning art. It challenges habits and modes of perception, and produces new ways of seeing and interpreting processes and relationships. To do this successfully, it must be unpredictable, surprising, even shocking, and it must be inventive enough to avoid being submerged by an integration propaganda which will naturalize its techniques in the guise of reproducing them" (p. 56). He also cautions that "newly established post-revolutionary sciences, whose integration propaganda tends to be clumsy and authoritarian, will usually react with hostility towards a literature which seems capable of producing this demystifying consciousness, as opposed to works which specifically expose the false consciousness resulting from capitalism" (p. 59).

17. For a standard but adequate characterization of socialist realist art, see Moisei Kagan's "The Formation and Development of Socialist Art" in *Socialist Realism in Literature and Art* (Moscow: Progress Publishers, 1971) 56-178.

18. See Lukács's 1932 essay "Tendency or Partisanship?" in *Essays on Realism*, R. Livingston, ed. (London: Lawrence & Wishart, 1980), 33-44. Although he prefers the term "partisanship" to "tendency" (the latter he considers compromised by idealist, undialectical, bourgeois origins), Lukacs gives a tenable account of the interdependence of "a correct dialectical depiction of

reality" and "partisanship," the latter being a precondition for such a depiction. But he is sharper in exposing the roots of the split between the Marxist sense of the word— "tendency" as social development *itself* made conscious by the poet—and the so-called tendency which is merely subjective "desire" on the part of the author.

19. For a different interpretation of Lenin's intended application of *partiinost* to literature, see Ernst Fischer's *Art Against Ideology* (New York: Braziller, 1969), 176-82. "Lenin's demand for party-mindedness was not meant to apply to literature in general but to political writings.... [According to Krupskaya] Lenin's articles *On Proletarian Culture, Party Organization and Party Literature* and *The Tasks of the Youth Leagues* do not concern literature as a fine art."

20. See *Bertolt Brecht: Poems 1913-1956*, John Willet and Ralph Manheim, eds., with Erich Fried (New York: Methuen, 1976), the best-translated, most comprehensive collection of Brecht's poetry. Four fine collections of poems by Nazim Hikmet, translated by Randy Blasing and Mutlu Konuk, are *Things I Didn't Know I Loved* (1975), *The Epic of Sheik Bedreddin* (1977), *Human Landscapes* (1982) and *Selected Poetry* (1986), all published by Persea. A smaller, earlier selection of Hikmet's poems, *The Moscow Symphony*, was translated by Taner Baybars (Chicago: Swallow, 1970). By the Polish poet Tadeusz Rózewicz there are *The Survivor and Other Poems*, translated by Magnus J. Krynski and Robert A. Maguire (Princeton: Princeton University Press, 1976) and *Conversation with the Prince, and Other Poems*, translated by Adam Czerniawski (London: Anvil, 1982). A strong selection of poems by Erich Fried, *100 Poems Without a Country*, has been translated by Start Hood (New York: Red Dust, 1980). A selection of earlier poems by Fried, *On Pain of Seeing*, was translated by Georg Rapp (Chicago: Swallow, 1969). The work of other poets also helps focus and extend the issues raised here: e.g., that of Ernesto Cardenal, Otto René Castillo, Leonel Rugama, Javier Heraud, Alejandro Romualdo, Nicolás Guillén, René Depestre, Kim Chi Ha, Mahmoud Darwish, Sidney Sepamla, and others. It would be well to reconsider—seriously, respectfully, not through the mind-boggling prism of anticommunism—the much-patronized Mayakovsky, and to develop a critical language that will do justice to the less romanticized, more tendentious works of Neruda and, especially, to the mythified *and* mystified Vallejo.

Freedom of the Artist:
People's Artists Versus People's Rulers

In its origins, the word *art* meant science, knowledge, or learning. But it now connotes more than that: it refers not simply to learning and knowledge but to learning and knowledge in ways different from those associated with science. Art is a way of seeing, or apprehending, the world of man and nature through visual, aural or mental images. Through these images, the whole conglomerate of skills that we call art or the arts assaults our consciousness to make us take a certain view of the World of Man and Nature. Let me illustrate this with a few examples.

In the *Daily Nation* of July 10, 1980, there was a letter from a Zarina Patel, Mombasa, calling upon the authorities to name the bridge linking Mombasa to the north mainland, Me Katilili Bridge. The following is the picture she painted of this Kenyan nationalist leader:

> Me Katilili has a very important place in the history of Kenya's Coast Province. She was a Giriama who fought courageously and relentlessly against the British colonial forces in the early part of this century. She and the warriors whom she led refused to accept British imperialist subjugation and exploitation. They attacked the colonialists at every possible opportunity. Finally in 1914, the British, with their superior weaponry, captured Katilili. So powerful and influential was she that they had to deport her from the area. It is time we at the Coast requested the government to recognize concretely the nationalism and bravery of Me Katilili.

That is how a Kenyan patriot described Me Katilili. But in another description written on November 23, 1913, the British Colonial District Commissioner, Arthur M. Champion, painted a very different picture of Me's organized resistance to British imperialist occupation:

> The witch Me Katilili and the witch doctor Wanji wa Mandora about the end of June 1913 did stir up sedition amongst the natives...and with this object held a large gathering of men determined to make a common cause with (other) disaffected natives to make a spell or Kiroho for the purpose of defeating a successful Government Administration. I would therefore recommend that both the woman Me Katilili and Wanji Wa Mandora be deported from the district and be detained as political prisoners at His Majesty's pleasure.

Thus to a Kenyan, Me Katilili is a nationalist who heroically resisted the British occupation of Kenya; to the British imperialist, she is a witch. In Zarina's description, acts of resistance to foreign occupation are linked to qualities of courage and heroism which deserve national recognition and pride. To Champion, acts of resistance to foreign occupation are linked to negative qualities of witchcraft and savagery. Both have used word images to persuade us or make us unconsciously or consciously adopt a certain attitude towards Me Katilili and towards imperialism: resistance to imperialism is good, noble, heroic—Zarina's nationalist patriotic view; acquiescence and accommodation to imperialism is good, noble—Champion's colonialist's view.

If you have read Haggard's *King Solomon's Mines*, you'll have seen how another African woman leader of resistance against the British occupation of South Africa is described: Gagool is a most revolting picture of a human being. But the same type of medicine man in the character of Mkomozi is painted very differently but positively in Peter Abraham's novel *The Wild Conquest*. In Karen Blixen's (Isak Dinesen's) book *Out of Africa*, all Kenyans are described in terms of beasts utterly divorced from civilization. This is her description of Kamante, her cook:

> Kamante could have no idea as to how a dish of ours ought to taste, and he was, in spite of his conversion, and his connection with civilization, at heart an arrant Kikuyu...He did at times taste the food that he cooked, but then with a distrustful face, like a witch who takes a sip out of her cauldron. He stuck to the maize cobs of his

forefathers. Here even his intelligence failed him and he came and offered me a Kikuyu delicacy of a roasted sweet potato or a lump of sheep's fat—as even a civilized dog, that has lived for a long time with people, will place a bone on the floor before you, as a present.

Out of Africa was first published in 1937. Karen Blixen was describing the life of the Kenyans whom she had robbed of vast acres of land near Ngong Hills. Jomo Kenyatta's *Facing Mount Kenya* was first published in 1938. He concludes thus:

As it is, by driving him off his ancestral lands, the Europeans have robbed him (the Kenyan) of the material foundations of his culture, and reduced him to a state of serfdom incompatible with human happiness. The African is conditioned, by the cultural and social institutions of centuries, to a freedom of which Europe has little conception, and it is not in his nature to accept serfdom forever. He realizes that he must fight unceasingly for his complete emancipation; for without this, he is doomed to remain the prey of rival imperialisms, which in every successive year will drive their fangs more deeply into his vitality and strength.

Well, two very different images of the Kenyan realities under colonial rule: to Karen Blixen, Kenyans are dogs and colonialists are gods; to Kenyatta, a Kenyan is a civilized being and the colonialist is a beast of prey with bloody fangs.

In religious art you'll find that colonialist paintings tend to depict Satan as a black man with two horns and a tail, with one leg raised in a dance of savagery; God is a white man with rays of light radiating from his face. But to the African, the colonialist was a devil, a *Mzungu hasa*, for he had no human skin.

It is the same story in cinematic arts and even in music: they assault our consciousness by giving us certain images of social realities. The musical arts are even more direct in their impact on the consciousness: certain songs create a sense of fear, of an impending doom, while others, like those used in the recent Tamaduni production of *Mzalendo Kimathi* (the Swahili translation of *The Trial of Dedan Kimathi)* create a mood of patriotic courage and anti-imperialist defiance. Missionary Christian songs created a mood of passivity and acceptance—*"Ndi Mwihia o na wanyona"* ("I'm a sinner") or "Wash me, redeemer, and I shall be whiter than snow," cried the African convert to his Maker. Liberation music created a joyous, aggressive mood, a sense of inevitable triumph over the enemy—"Twathiiaga tukeneete, tugacooka o tukeneete" ("We joyfully and fearlessly went to battle"), or "When our Kimaathi ascended the mountain, he asked for courage and strength to defeat the British imperialist"—so sang the Mau Mau guerrilla fighter as he went to fight in the forest. Both the Christian colonialist and the resistance music sang of the same reality—the foreign occupation of Kenya—but from two conflicting and opposed perspectives.

The arts then are a form of knowledge about reality acquired through a pile of images. But these images are not neutral. The images given us by the arts try to make us not only see and understand the world of man and nature, apprehend it, but also see and understand it in a certain way, or from the angle of vision of the artist. The way or the angle *of* vision is itself largely affected by the margin of natural, social and spiritual freedom within which the practitioner of the skills (the writer, the musician, the painter) is operating.

Let me put it another way. The arts present us with a set of images of the world in which we live. The arts then act like a reflecting mirror. The artist is like the hand that holds and moves the mirror, this way and that way, to explore all corners of the universe. But what is reflected in the mirror depends on where the holder stands in relation to the object. Other factors come into it too: whether or not the hand has chosen, consciously or unconsciously, a concave or convex mirror, a broken or an unbroken mirror. Any factor or factors that limit the capacity of the mirror to give us correct and illuminating images of the world are themselves limitations on the exploring hand, the hand of the artist, and they have to do with the margin of natural, economic, political, social and spiritual freedom within which the explorer is operating. These factors may be either internal or external to the artist, or they may be both.

So while there are many ways of approaching this difficult problem of the freedom of the artist, I shall pose three questions around which I shall introduce a discussion of the issue:

1. Has the artist equipped himself with a world-view which enables him to see as much of the world as it is possible for him to see and to make us see? For as charity begins at home so must the freedom of the artist: has he or not first accepted to liberate himself from certain inhibiting angles of vision? In other words can an artist adopt and defend the viewpoint of an oppressing class and still be free? Were Karen Blixen, Elspeth Huxley, Robert Ruark really free when they put their art to the service of imperialist exploitation and oppression of Kenyans? And here we can compare the limitations of these artists with the largeness of vision of artists like Balzac or Tolstoy who, although they came from oppressing classes, distanced themselves sufficiently to see and expose the reality of brutality behind both bourgeois and feudal class dictatorships.

Brecht, in a poem called *Driven out with Good Reason*, could as easily have been describing a Tolstoy or a Balzac when he wrote:

> I grew up as the son
> of well-to-do people. My parents put
> A collar round my neck and brought me up
> In the habit of being waited on
> And schooled me in the art of giving orders. But
> When I was grown up and looked about me
> I did not like the people of my own class
> Nor giving orders, nor being waited on
> And I left my own class and allied myself
> With insignificant people.
> Thus
> They brought up a traitor, taught him
> All their tricks, and he
> Betrayed them to the enemy.
> Yes, I give away their secrets. I stand
> Among the people and explain
> Their swindles, I say in advance what will happen, for I
> Have inside knowledge of their plans.
> The Latin of their corrupt clergy
> I translate word for word into the common speech, and then
> it is seen to be humbug. The scales of their justice
> I take down so as to show
> The fraudulent weights. And their informers report

207

to them
That I sit among the dispossessed when they
Are plotting rebellion.

Will the artist choose the angle of vision of the possessing classes? Or will he choose the angle of vision of the dispossessed and therefore struggling classes? Each artist has to make a choice. For this is the area of spiritual freedom. Or call it the area of self-liberation!

2. Is the artist operating in a situation in which he is continually being harassed by the state, or continually under the threat of such harassment? Has he the democratic right to practice his art without fear of state intervention by way of censorship or prisons or detention camps? Even if the artist is not actually placed in a maximum security prison for a year or more, is he really free when he practices self-censorship for the very well-founded fears of such an eventuality? This is the area of democratic freedom.

3. Is he operating within a social structure that inhibits all social systems? In other words, even if an artist had adopted a world-view that allowed him to see all and had the democratic right to speak out without fear of certain death or prison, is he free in a class-structured society where a few give orders and the majority obey, where a million toil and only a few reap? Is he free for as long as he is, for instance, living in an imperialist-dominated world where the "third" world peoples produce and the barons of profit in New York, Bonn, London, Paris, Stockholm, Rome and Tokyo dispose? Here we are talking of much more than the freedom of the artist; we are talking about the freedom of all the toiling masses as the very condition of a true creative freedom! This is the area of human freedom to be free to become even more human: the freedom of human labor, the final artist! In the case of us Kenyans, can an artist be free as long as our economy and culture are dominated by imperialist foreigners and their local allies?

Let me briefly examine the three areas of an artist's freedom:

1. Throughout history, there have been two conflicting world-views. The first view sees the world of nature and man as static and fixed. Or if it moves at all, it is in cycles, repetitions of the same motions.

Any concession to evidence or demonstration of previous movement in history is twisted to prove that the logic in all the previous movements was to arrive at the present fixed status quo. This is the world-view of all the ruling classes in all hitherto class-structured societies: We have arrived at the best of all possible worlds. A few examples will do:

(a) The feudal ruling classes in Europe for centuries held to the Ptolemaic view of the universe: that the earth was fixed and all the stars including the sun revolved round the earth, with the feudal monarchs and clergy at the center. People arguing against this were burnt alive as heretics; how could they question that which was sanctioned by God?

(b) The British ruling classes said that the slave system (that is, the buying and selling of Africans, which produced such profitable sugar, tobacco and cotton) was the best of all possible social systems for the slave (he now had a chance of acquiring a Christian name, James or Charles) and for the slave dealer: he could bank his millions on earth and buy a mansion in heaven for afterlife.

(c) The U.S. ruling circles will concede that there was a time when colonialism was not quite so good for Euro-Americans and they fought for independence from London. Every July 4, they pay annual tribute to their forefathers, who fought for an America free from British colonial rule. But now that U.S. imperialism dominates and rules most of Africa, Latin America and Asia, they argue that the world has arrived at the final system: the rule of financial monopoly capital guaranteed by American guns and yellow corn!

(d) And finally some well-placed Kenyans will concede that the different precolonial stages of communal and feudal developments in Kenya caved in to the colonial stage of imperialism; that patriotic Kenyans in turn fought bravely to end the colonial stage of imperialist domination, but since midnight December 12, 1963, we have arrived at the best of all possible world systems!

The second world-view sees that movement (or change) is inherent in nature and society. In this view, nature and society are in perpetual motion; nothing is really static, fixed, final. Life is motion and motion is life. In this view, no social system is really final and fixed but each contains the germs of a future society. But motion involves contradictions, for, as Blake once stated: without contrariness there is no progression. This broadly is the world-view of the downtrodden, of the oppressed, of the dominated: change is

209

inevitable even if it does not necessarily occur in a smooth line from one stage to the other.

The two world-views have been in mortal conflict, for the old never willingly gives place to the new. Those who profit from the old do not want anything that would disturb what they see as a well-founded stability.

This conflict is well captured by Bertolt Brecht in his play the *Life of Galileo,* in which he dramatizes the struggle between the Ptolemaic and the Copernican systems. Galileo, a great mathematician, philosopher and astronomer is able to demonstrate by a newly invented telescope that the earth is not the fixed center of the universe, that the sun does not in fact move round the earth. At one stage he goes back to Florence naively believing that once the Pope and all the defenders of the old system look into the telescope, they will see the proof with their own eyes and abandon the old views about the immutability of the universe. Some look through the telescope but refuse to believe the evidence. Others refuse even to look, which drives Galileo to plead with them: "Gentlemen, I beseech you in all humility to trust the evidence of your eyes." It is one of Galileo's friends who tells him the truth:

> Galileo, I see you setting out on a fearful road. It is a night of disaster when a man sees the truth. And an hour of delusion when he believes in the common sense of the human race. How could those in power leave at large a man who knows the truth, even though it be about the most distant stars? Do you think the Pope will hearken to your truth when you say he is in error? Do you think that he will simply write in his diary: January the tenth, 1610—Heaven abolished?

What is at stake, as Galileo discovers too late, is not the truth about the movement of distant stars, but the threat to the feudal system of inequality, corruption, oppression and privileges, a system in which the Ptolemaic view was a mere philosophic defense and rationale. In other words the world-view that nothing ever changes suits those profiting from the social status quo: "Good Morning, Mr. Dispossessed," says Mr. Possessing. "A bad morning," replies Mr. Dispossessed "I'm truly sorry about your condition," adds Mr.

Possessing. "But it's you who are sitting on my back," replies Mr. Dispossessed. "That's the Law of Nature and God," says Mr. Possessing, adding helpfully, "Let's all live in harmony and brotherly togetherness. Let's not disturb the universal law of stability." Tolstoy has put it succinctly:

> I sit on a man's back choking him
> and making him carry me, and yet assure myself and others
> that I am very sorry for him and
> wish to ease his lot by any
> means possible except getting
> off his back.

But Mr. Dispossessed is not likely to accept that being sat upon is in accordance with a fixed law of God and Nature. The world-view corresponding to his objective position of wanting the burden off his back is the one that says that motion (or change) is inherent in nature and human society.

The two world-views have produced two types of artists: the poet laureate or the court singer to the status quo, and the trumpeter of a new world. The first type is not really free—he is in a state of self-imposed slavery—while the second type is free of illusions about the present because his adopted world-view—that change, with all the contradictions involved, is inevitable—has liberated his faculties of observation.

2. But when we come to the area of political or democratic freedom, the situation of the two types of artists changes. He who holds the world-view of the ruling classes is free to write, to sing, to paint, to dance the dance of the times. The spiritual slave becomes free to sing the virtues of slavery and is given accolades for it. But the artist with a questioning spirit, the trumpeter of possibilities of a better social order, now becomes unfree to write, to sing, to paint, to dance about the heralds of a new dawn. If he should persist in his heretical position, he is persecuted, accused of a thousand and one crimes. Socrates was accused of corrupting the youth of Greece, and he was hounded to death.

Aristotle at one time had to flee into exile arguing: "We shall not let Athens offend twice against philosophy."

Galileo had to publicly abjure or recant what he knew to be the truth. Those three—death, exile, or renouncing the truth—are often the cruel choices open to the second type of artist.

I am not of course suggesting that if an artist has not been killed or jailed or exiled or had his works banned, he does not belong to the second category of artists. You may perhaps know the amusing poem of Bertolt Brecht on the burning of books: a certain regime once commanded that all books with harmful knowledge should be publicly burned. But one of the best writers, moreover one who had been in trouble with the regime to the extent of being exiled, happened to see the list of books put to the bonfire and he was shocked to find that his books were not on the list:

> He rushed to his desk
> On wings of wrath, and wrote a letter to those in power
> Burn me! he wrote with flying pen, burn me!
> Haven't my books
> Always reported the truth? And here you are
> Treating me like a liar! I command you:
> Burn me!

So I am not asking that African artists rush to the authorities and say "please persecute me," for this is not necessarily proof that the artist is painting images of truth.

Nevertheless, I would like to illustrate the state of the relative freedom and unfreedom of the two types of artists by quickly looking at Kenya's record in this matter, both before and after independence.

All the writers, dramatists, actors, dancers and singers who supported colonialist oppression and exploitation of Kenyans by the British imperialist bourgeoisie and its local Kenya settler representatives were always free to practice their art. Karen Blixen could describe Kenyans as dogs, hyenas, jackals and the like and be canonized for it. She was once a likely recipient of the Nobel Prize for Literature. In her book of memoirs, *Shadows on the Grass,* published in 1960, three years before Kenya's independence, she could still write about Kenyans in terms of beasts of burden:

> The dark nations of Africa, strikingly precocious as young children, seemed to come to a standstill in their mental growth at different ages. The Kikuyu, Kawirondo,

and Wakamba, the people who worked for me on the farm, in early childhood were far ahead of white children of the same age, but they stopped quite suddenly at a stage corresponding to that of a European child of nine. The Somali had got further and had all the mentality of boys of our own race at the age of 13 to 17.

Today independent Kenya still honors her name by naming a whole district in Nairobi after her. Karen is still one of the most fashionable residential areas in the city.

Elspeth Huxley, who depicted Kenyans as children perpetually amazed at airplanes and razor blades, was always on every Royal Commission of Inquiry into grievances of natives—whether on land or education matters. Her latest book, *Nellie,* in which she describes Mau Mau Freedom Fighters as beasts, is currently a bestseller in Nairobi bookshops. The present Kenyan authorities allowed the film of her racist memoirs, *The Flame Trees of Thika,* to be shot in Kenya, and, when the film is done, I have no doubt it will be shown in Nairobi cinemas.

Robert Ruark, who always described Kenyan Africans as wogs in his two anti-Mau Mau novels, *Something of Value* and *Uhuru,* was the he-man version of Hemingway in Kenya. His books still grace the shelves of our libraries and bookshops.

The same story is true of theater: European colonial theater has thrived on such stages as Little Theater in Mombasa, Donvon Maule Theater in Nairobi, the Kenya National Theater, and other theaters in Nakuru and Eldoret, since the Fifties.

Among Africans, those who sang and composed Christian songs in praise of a white God were always free to do so a thousand times over. A colonial government commissioned an African artist to paint some murals in a church in Murang'a in memory of those Kenyans who opposed the Mau Mau struggle. He went ahead with the grand task. In detention camps, those singing Christian songs and writing Christian pro-colonial plays—what J. M. Kariuki once described as Marebe Theater—were free to do so. In fact, they were very highly encouraged and rewarded for their anti-Kenyan artistic efforts.

The story changes when we come to the patriotic artistic tradition among Kenyans.

Around 1930, the *Ituika* revolutionary Cultural Festival among the Aagikuyu was banned. This was a festival of songs, dances, poetry and theater that took place every 25 years as a memorial to an earlier revolutionary overthrow of a feudal dictatorship by the Iregi generation.

At about the same period, the Muthirigu dancers, composers and singers were banned, with most being shipped off to jails. Their songs and dances were anti-imperialist, and they talked of a new Kenya to come. It's the same story about Mumboist artists and those associated with the anticolonial *dini Ya Musambwa* movement. Is there in Kenya today a shrine erected in honor of Muthoni Nyanjiru, who sang of a new Kenya even as she was mowed down by colonialist bullets outside the Norfolk Hotel on the very same ground where this university stands?

But the repression of patriotic Kenyan literature and art reached its climax in the Fifties. Mau Mau publishing houses, as well as Mau Mau poetry and songs and drama, were banned. Writers and publishers of this patriotic literature, like Gakaara Wanjau and Kimuthia Mugia, were sent to detention camps in Manyani. Kenya's patriotic theater, like Kimathi's Gicamu Theater movement in Karuna-ini, were either banned or stopped under the general colonialist violence and repression in the land. In place of this, the colonial government appointed a European Kenya-wide drama and music officer, Mr. Graham Hyslope, to channel Kenyan African drama and music into idiotic directions of pointless clowning and drumming in community halls, schools and churches. I could extend the same story to journalists: freedom and honor for those in praise of colonialism; jail, detention or exile for patriotic ones.

I am afraid that the political fate of the two types of artists has not been very different in an Independent Kenya.

European and foreign theater, even when it has been racist and anti-Kenyan, has flourished freely, often under government protection. In the process, some European theater critics have become so arrogant that one of them, Mary Hayne, had the audacity as late as 1979—and in a Kenyan newspaper—to describe Kimathi as a terrorist.

Foreign, particularly European, music is the order of the day in Kenyan churches and schools. Can we imagine the amount of money the Kenyan government is spending in organizing the current primary schools' music competition? And this in order that impressionable Kenyan children shall sing in praise of a rich White Lady riding a White Horse:

Riding on a horse
To Banbury cross
To see a White Lady
Ride on a White Horse
With rings on her fingers
And bells on her toes,
She shall have music
Wherever she goes.

When I myself wrote plays and novels that were only critical of the racism in the colonial system, I was praised. I was awarded prizes, and my novels were in the syllabi. But when toward the Seventies I started writing in a language understood by peasants, and in an idiom understood by them, and I started questioning the very foundations of imperialism and of foreign domination of Kenya's economy and culture, I was sent to Kamiti Maximum Security Prison.

But it's wrong, as *The African Perspective* of February-March 1978 was, to claim that I was the first writer to be jailed in an independent Kenya:

> "Ngugi's own detention came as a shock because of Kenya's enviable record in this regard. The government has always allowed its intellectuals the freedom to express their criticisms of society as it is presently constituted and no writer or artist has ever been jailed, with or without trial."

The great Kenyan poet Abdilatif Abdalla, the author of *Sauti Ya Dhiki,* was jailed for three years at Kamiti Maximum Security Prison (between 1969 and 1972) for writing a pamphlet simply asking: *Kenya: Twendapi? (Kenya, where are we heading to?) The African Perspective* was also wrong in implying that I was the first artist whose freedom of expression had been curtailed by the government. Richard Frost, in his unwittingly illuminating book about the working of cultural imperialism in Kenya, called *Race Against Time,* cites, though in praise, one of the earliest cases of artistic suppression:

215

"A month or two before independence the members of
an African boys' club in one of the poorest districts of
Nairobi wrote a play which they wanted to act in the
Uhuru Stadium during the Independence celebrations
or, if that were not possible, on successive evenings in
social halls in the various parts of the city. The play was
an ignorant travesty of history and was intended to create
hatred of Britain and the colonial administration. The
matter was brought to the attention of Tom Mboya, the
minister responsible for the independence celebrations.
He asked to see the script and immediately banned its
performance anywhere. 'That,' he said, 'is not the spirit in
which we want to enter independence.'"

The suppression of Kenyan artists in post-independence Kenya
is contained in a Kenya Writers' Association memorandum on the
status of the artist submitted to UNESCO. I will not go into details
but I could mention a few cases: Micere Githae Mugo (poet,
playwright, short-story writer, critic) was arrested in 1977 and
tortured in police cells. Ngugi wa Mirii (composer, playwright) lost
his job with the University of Nairobi. Many Kenyan journalists have
been locked up in police cells or questioned for their critical writings
and exposure.

FREEDOM OF THE ARTIST

But there's one case which should come to the eyes of the Kenyan
Public and the concerned authorities and which ought to be the
concern of every Kenyan patriot. I am referring to those girls from
Riara Loreto Secondary School in Kaimbu District who in 1979
wrote a play: *What a World My People!* or *There Are Two Worlds.*
Under the patronage of their brilliant drama teacher, Sister Agnes
Wanjiku Mukabi, they wrote and produced the play for the 1979
Kenya Drama School Festival. It won several regional prizes before
being "defeated" at the provincial level. But the play was sufficiently
popular for it to be demanded by several schools and colleges around.
I understand that it was even performed at the Kenyatta College
Cultural Festival, which was launched by President Moi in 1979. But
when the girls translated the play into the Gikuyu language and

performed it to their peasant parents, the police moved in, questioned the headmistress and the drama teacher, and the play was subsequently stopped. Now I understand that five or seven of the girls involved in the play, including the author, were later expelled from the school. I understand that the Catholic Church hierarchy was not slow in following the lead. The drama teacher, a nun, was not allowed to take her final vows. Instead, she was unceremoniously thrown out of the Catholic order and shipped to America.

I ask myself: What effect has this kind of action had on the creative development of such children? Should such a tremendous initiative by mere Form Three girls have been encouraged or suppressed? And this at a time when imperialist theater, foreign critics, foreign music are being actively encouraged. Even foreign embassies are freer to organize Kenyan theater, art and music on our own soil than patriotic Kenyans themselves!

What we are asking for is very simple: Not that the Karen Blixens, the Elspeth Huxleys and the foreign theater groups be stopped. No, we are not asking for special state protection, we are asking that Kenya patriotic theater not be suppressed. Let a hundred schools of drama compete in the villages, in the cities, in the schools and colleges, and we shall see which will win the day. I do not need to be a prophet to say that foreign music, foreign cinema, foreign art has no future in this country, no matter how much freedom and state patronage it is accorded. But why should an African government in an independent Kenya see its role as that of protecting foreign antinational interests and suppressing the voices of Kenyan people? Allow your striptease artists, your Elspeth Huxleys, your *Dallas* television programs and so on, but also allow Kenyans equal freedom.

But in another sense Kenyan artists are themselves to blame for their present plight because of their complacency and indifference to their democratic rights as Kenyans. We have in the past adopted the attitude: everyone for himself and even a separate God for each of us. We have never come together to voice those interests that bind us together as Kenyan patriotic artists. Do we as writers, musicians, painters, expect engineers to come out and speak for our legitimate self-interests? Democracy is possible only when various self-interest groups in the country, whatever their outlook, begin to voice their legitimate self-interests as groups. Only on that basis can there even be a dialogue about the freedom of the artist.

There is a poem by Martin Niemoeller that should be of interest to all those desirous of an extension of democratic rights to artistic expression:

> First they came for the Communists,
> but I was not a Communist
> so I did not speak out.
> Then they came for the Socialists and the Trade Unionists,
> but I was neither,
> so I did not speak out.
> Then they came for the Jews,
> but I was not a Jew so I did not speak out.
> And when they came for me,
> there was no one left to speak out.*

Let us Kenyan artists raise all our voices in unison against repression of artists and our cultural initiatives. Now!

3. Finally I want to be very brief on the third area of an artist's freedom. Even if a writer or an artist had a liberated vision and was allowed to write freely, can he be said to be free when the very society in which he lives is a class-structured society with a few living on the labor of millions? The artist, to the extent that he is a member of a given society, is caught up in the contradictions of that society. In the advanced Western capitalist democracies, many artists, unable to face the extreme contradictions of capitalism and the impoverishment of human life under the same economic system, have been driven to individualism, cynicism, abstractionism, despair, and often suicide. In the branch capitalisms of the third-world countries, the contradictions are multiplied: not only is there internal exploitation and oppression, but there is also external exploitation and oppression of the whole nation by the imperialist bourgeoisie. In such a situation, no artist can consider himself free, for the condition of his freedom is the freedom of the vast majority of the population.

Let me put it another way. The real artist in the world is human labor. It's human labor which has created the social environment out

---

* For this quotation, often cited incorrectly, the source of the phrasing above is Martin Niemoeller's wife. The remark was made in reply to a student's question, "How could it happen?" [Ed. note]

218

of the natural environment. All the modern technology and science and the arts are products of human labor. When the product of that social human labor becomes the property of an idle few, can the artist be said to be free? And remember that the situation is worse when the products of the human labor of a given country are controlled by foreigners. The liberation of human labor is the only condition for the true liberation of the human being, the artist.

For the Kenyan artist, the most minimal step towards his own freedom is a total immersion in the struggles of Kenyan workers and peasants for the liberation of the products of their labor for the benefit of Kenyans. Imperialist foreign domination of a people's economy and culture is completely incompatible with the freedom of the artist in the third world.

Here we come to another contradiction. It is precisely the artist who realizes the need to struggle against foreign imperialist domination and against every form of internal and external exploitation and oppression that is likely to find himself without the democratic freedom to express this. In other words, it is precisely this kind of artist who is likely to be persecuted, to be cowed into succumbing to a neocolonial culture of silence and fear. But in this the persecuting authorities are mistaken. It is very difficult to suppress the truth. There is a legend that as Galileo rose from his knees after he had abjured and sworn that the earth did not turn round the sun, he nevertheless muttered: "Yet it does turn." After the imprisoned Kenyan poet Abdilatif Abdalla came out of jail, he published *Sauti Ya Dhiki,* in which he writes:

> Kweli ilipowatoma, kama dasturi yake
> Wao wakaona vyema, afadhali wanishike
> Wanishike hima hima, hima ndani waniweke
> Ngomeni n'adhibike, nijute kusema kweli

And virtually each verse of the opening poem ends with the defiant refrain: *N'shishiyelo ni Lilo* (The truth I held, I still hold on to even more firmly.)

Abdilatif's defiant position is reminiscent of the Palestinian poet Mahmoud Darwish who, in his poem "On Man" from his book *The Music of Human Flesh,* has written the following lines of defiant immortality:

219

Oh you with bloodshot eyes and bloody hands
Night is short lived,
The detention room lasts not for ever,
Nor yet the links of chain.

Abdilatif and Darwish are right: the correct response to those who would butcher life and truth is defiance. The only answer to fascism is resistance. Fascism, autocracy, authoritarianism, work by striking fear in the population, to scatter organized opposition. Therefore the first thing to resist is fear itself.

There is a fine instructive poem by Brecht on Hitler's Germany, *Anxieties of the Regime:*

A foreigner, returning from a trip to the Third Reich
When asked who really ruled there, answered:
Fear.
Anxiously
The scholar breaks off his discussion to inspect
The thin partitions of his study, his face ashen. The teacher
Lies sleepless, worrying over
An ambiguous phrase the inspector had let fall.
The old woman in the grocer's shop
Puts her trembling finger to her lips to hold back
Her angry exclamation about the bad flour. Anxiously
The doctor inspects the strangulation marks on his patient's
throat.
Full of anxiety, parents look at their children as at traitors.
Even the dying
Hush their failing voices as they
Take leave of their relatives.
But likewise the brownshirts themselves
Fear the man whose arm doesn't fly up
And are terrified of the man who
Wishes them a good morning.
The shrill voices of those who give orders
Are full of fear like the squeaking of
Piglets awaiting the butcher's knife, as their fat arses
Sweat with anxiety in their office chairs.

Driven by anxiety
They break into homes and search the lavatories
And it is anxiety
That makes them burn whole libraries. Thus
Fear rules not only those who are ruled, but
the rulers too.

Our pens should be used to increase the anxieties of all oppressive regimes. At the very least the pen should be used to "murder their sleep" by constantly reminding them of their crimes against the people, and by letting them know that they are being seen. The pen may not always be mightier than the sword, but used in the service of truth it can be a mighty force. It's for the writers themselves to choose whether they will use their art in the service of the exploiting oppressing classes and nations, articulating their world-view, or in the service of the masses engaged in a fierce struggle against human degradation and oppression. But I have indicated my preference: Let our pens be the voices of the people. Let our pens give voices to silence.

For the artist who has chosen the side of the struggling millions, he or she should work in a strong organization with others of his kind to ensure the maximum freedom for the hand that moves the pen.

Freedom, even for the artist, was never given on a silver platter.

NGUGI WA THIONG'O is the internationally known Kenyan poet, playwright and author of *Barrel of a Pen*, which contains essays on the cultural resistance to oppression by neocolonial powers. This work, in the tradition of previous collections of essays, *Homecoming* and *Writers in Politics*, has established him as one of the world's most insightful interpreters of the relationship between culture and revolution.

This essay is reprinted from *Barrel of a Pen: Resistance to Repression in Neo-Colonial Kenya*, published by Africa World Press.

ERNESTO CARDENAL
Democratization of Culture In Nicaragua

[This is an edited version of a speech delivered by Ernesto Cardenal at the UNESCO Conference in Paris on April 24, 1982. This version, in an English translation by Amy Edelman of Berkeley's People's Translation Service, was published in *Left Curve* #8, 1982-83.]

PART ONE

The community of Mesquite Indians, a very poor population situated on a riverbank, had been gathered together so that I could talk to them. While the interpreter was translating my words, I observed lack of interest, indifference, and boredom in their faces. I told them that I was the Minister of Culture who had come to visit them (and I noted that this interested none of them), and I commenced to explain that this new Ministry was created by the Revolution for dance (there I noticed their sudden interest), for music, for ancestral traditions (and the interest in their faces was more noticeable), for the different languages we spoke (since their language is something we must preserve and defend), for crafts. I had to explain that this meant using our hands to make beautiful things more useful. As examples, I showed them some very primitive drawings that they had carved on some maracas, I showed them a "tuno" that they had just given me, a canvas that they had made from the bark of a tree, and I explained to them how they could paint these canvases. I have recounted this story before speaking of political culture in Nicaragua. Why is it important? For me, its importance is that these people, who were exploited over several centuries and did not have anything except their culture and their own language (and what they had, they were also about to lose), had just realized that the Ministry of Culture was especially for them; and the Ministry was especially there to oppose cultural ethnocide of all those segregated like them.

The destruction of indigenous culture and language was attempted in other American countries. The people were killed, hunted on the plains like deer, sent donations of sugar laced with arsenic, of clothing contaminated with cholera. But we have made them literate in their languages. We believe that they enrich our cultural identity. And we want them to progress within their culture, without remaining stagnant in it, but also without losing it. A language that is lost is an irreparable loss for humanity, since it is a people's particular vision of the world that is lost.

I founded a small community on Lake Nicaragua in the archipelago of Solentiname, inhabited by poor and isolated peasants. We developed crafts, primitive painting, and poetry with them. The crafts and painting were greatly appreciated abroad, and were sold in Paris, Switzerland, Germany, New York. Much later, the community joined the Sandinista Front's struggle for liberation. As a consequence, the Somozan forces destroyed all of the community's installations, the great library we had, archaeological pieces, records, pictures, kilns full of ceramics and enamel, everything. And peasants all over the archipelago were repressed because of us. And the police prohibited them from painting. And peasant girls went up into the mountains to paint in secret. If a policeman saw a picture inside a hut, he slashed it with his bayonet. Why do I tell you this? Because I want to present an image to you of how Nicaraguan culture was repressed. Literature, music, and theater were repressed—because we had an eminent literature of protest, a politically committed music, a popular street theater that stirred things up and yet had to be at times clandestine. And they banned books. First it was certain books that were considered most dangerous; finally it was all books, since all books were considered subversive.

THE CULTURE OF LIBERATION

When the Revolution triumphed there was a great thirst for reading in our nation. A mobile bookseller, who previously sold books in the street at great risk, began to sell his books in the pavilion of the Ministry of Culture. Such street vendors appeared all over, until there was one who set up his booth in the Transit Headquarters, in front of the police! The many copies which were published—very many for our means—sold very rapidly. A street vendor, who once sold 300 pesos worth each day, now sold 2,500 pesos worth each day. And a student exclaimed enthusiastically, "Now we are definitely free. Now we can read what we like. Before it was so difficult."

And the police who banned those books were so feared that the people closed their doors and did not even want to show their heads when the police passed. Their green uniforms and green helmets were symbols of terror and death. Now policemen, and soldiers in the army, and members of State Security forces in the Ministry of the Interior are writing poetry—and very fine poetry.

A young woman in an infantry battalion wrote this poem:

To the Soldier Juan Bustamente of the Southern Front

It was six in the afternoon the 17th of
          February 1980
when I fell in love with you, Juan.
With your camouflage uniform
and your GALIL on top of the desk
completing your twenty-four hours of duty
I approached you
and touched your chocolate-colored skin.

A police officer wrote this poem:

As Free as the Birds

Looking through the barred window
at the front of my room
I see how the sun rises
and its light between the leaves of the
guanabana tree.
On the floor it forms figures.

A zanate alights and sings in the branch
of a jocote.
It jumps. It jumps.
It returns to the same branch singing.
I think about that bird
of Nicaragua.
The Salvadoreans, the Guatemalans,
the Belicians,
all Latin America
will be free as that bird.

The second point I wanted to express is that, in the past, we had a culture of oppression, and now we have one of freedom. There was oppression in everything, so also in the culture. One cannot have oppression of a people without oppression of their culture as well. Now we have freedom in culture, and in everything.

AN ANSWER TO IMPERIALISM: CORN

Last year the United States government brusquely refused us the purchase of wheat. Our people were to be without bread. The Ministry of Culture planned a Corn Fair, with the theme, "The Corn, Our Roots," the idea being to promote all the national dishes made from corn. The Fair was celebrated in local villages all over the country, and culminated in a national gathering in the indigenous settlement of Monimbo, legendary for its heroism in the battle against Somoza. The plaza and street of Monimbo were not big enough for the 250,000 people who came to sample Nicaraguan food and drink made from corn. Junta Commanders of the Revolution, Ministers, and heads of famous restaurants made up the jury that awarded the best tortilla (our corn bread), tamales (corn mash wrapped up in leaves which one eats with cheese), *indio-viejo* (an Indian dish that is a stew of corn with meat and many condiments and lard), *cosas-de-horno* (different biscuits made of corn), *pinol*, our national drink (cornmeal with water), *cusuza* (a very strong corn liquor), *chicha* (Indian wine made from fermented corn), and innumerable desserts and tidbits made from corn. Dishes arrived from some remote regions of the country, dishes which not even we knew of and which now we have discovered.

We named the Fair "Xilonem," after the Indian goddess of tender corn. According to the myth, she sacrificed herself for her people and with her blood she produced a great crop of corn in a year of drought. For us this was also a symbol of all the martyrs of the Revolution who sacrificed themselves for the well-being of their people. One of our top researchers, Dr. Alejandro Davila Bolanos, who had studied this myth of Xilonem, was one of those who spilled his blood in the struggle for liberation.

Our culture, as well as that of all Central America, has been a culture of corn. According to Popol-Vuh, the Mayan Bible, the Gods created man from corn—the truth is that man created corn, from a wild ear of corn two or three inches in length—as one can see in the

Museum of Anthropology in Mexico—Central American man was able to cultivate the ear of corn we know today, since, unlike other grains, like wheat, which are dispersed by the wind, the ear of corn falls to the earth covered by a strong wrapper, and in order to germinate, it must be unwrapped by human hands. Man created corn and corn created our culture, and we are THE CORN PEOPLE/THE MEN OF CORN. An old Nahuatl poem says that "the tender, blond ear of corn is a light to us." And the great Corn Fair allowed our people to reaffirm their national identity, their cultural identity, and their defense of the Revolution, and to reject imperialist aggression. Furthermore, this gave our people their own food, something that was part of their own culture. And after the triumph of the Revolution, Nicaraguan food has been much more appreciated, together with everything else that originates from our own Nicaraguan past: a native past, a Spanish colonial past, an English past on our Caribbean coast, and above all, a culturally integrated past. "A people with a kitchen is a people with culture" is a French saying. And I have come to talk of the kitchen because this is a third point that I wanted to present to you: our Revolutionary culture has been a re-exploration of origins. And this re-exploration has involved the creation of a new kind of life. This was already indicated in the name of the Corn Goddess that, according to the ancient Nahuas, meant "delicate and tender, like a tender and fresh ear of corn."

But beside the French saying that a people with a kitchen is a people with culture, I want to add the words of our great poet, José Coronel Urtecho, who says that a good society and a good kitchen always walk hand-in-hand, and that decadence of the kitchen is a product of the dissolution of the society: it is a reference to the extremely bad nourishment in great masses of the population in the impoverished and underdeveloped countries, all victims of capitalism. Our present culture, embodying the rediscovery of our origins and the rescue of our own identity, of our food and myths, is a soldier of liberation.

PEOPLE'S CULTURE

These different things I have recounted serve as an introduction to the subject that I come to discuss here at UNESCO, that of the Democratization of Culture in Nicaragua. Why do I come to you to talk of some practical and theoretical aspects of a small country like

Nicaragua, which was until recently very dependent? Because Nicaragua is one of those countries in Latin America, Africa, and Asia, recently liberated or in the process of liberation, which contain more than half of the world's population. Countries in which powerful social transformations occur, which embrace all spheres of life. The terrible problems of ignorance, sickness, hunger, and misery can only be solved by our countries quickly developing their economies and creating new social structures. This is an eminently cultural matter, since our country is effecting rapid change not only of traditional social structures, but also of cultural values and cultural needs. I believe it is useful to become acquainted with our experience.

I also have come to talk to you of Nicaragua's cultural tasks, because in our political development and in our immense effort to take leave of economic underdevelopment, we have united cultural transformations with the idea of creating a society free of violence, and now this is seriously threatened.

In Nicaragua, cultural liberation has been part of the national struggle for liberation. This past February, on the anniversary of his birth, our great poet, Rubén Darío, was proclaimed Hero of Cultural Independence, and that day was named Day of Cultural Independence. The cultural heritage, actually the anticultural heritage, left by a dictatorship imposed and maintained by the United States since mid-century, could not have been more catastrophic. When the Revolution triumphed on 19 July 1979, more than half of all Nicaraguans were illiterate. And the dominant classes considered their cultural center to be Miami.

Our Revolution is concerned with the present and is above all concerned with the future, but is also concerned with the past. Our past has been revolutionary, too. In the first place there was a resurrection of the dead (in our people's consciousness). Our history immediately was different. Our heritage, which before was not visible, was declared publicly. National traditions flourished. The entire nation was always united with the liberation movement, but liberation has been the precondition under which the nation might become a good community.

Artistic skills had been decaying more and more during the long Somozan reign; at the end, Nicaragua was a country of very poor craftsmanship, and it was seen as something irretrievably lost. The Revolution came to its rescue, and in very little time the ancient lost arts reappeared in many parts of the country, and there is a new, popular art as well. It is an expression more of our identity, of the Nicaraguan nature, of our own selves, because it struggled against foreign domination, and it was achieved with the triumph of the Popular Sandinista Revolution.

The hammock is the cradle of the Nicaraguan and the cradle of American mankind. In the city of Masaya where the war ended, the hammock is woven tirelessly in gay colors, and in Europe it is said that the Masayan hammock is the best hammock in the world; sometimes our hammocks have been presented as gifts to heads of State. They are works of art—these tapestries of sisal fiber from Masaya and Camoapa, woven in luminous colors and pre-Colombian and modern designs. In San Juan de Oriente, a small village that has traditionally done pottery, replicas of pre-Columbian ceramics or newly inspired creations are precluded. In Matagalpa and Jinotega a very delicate black pottery is crafted, the clay made black by pine smoke. The only ones who still made it when the Revolution triumphed were two families, and the Revolution, through the Ministry of Culture, saved the craft from extinction. Only an old woman still knew how to carve the fine designs delicately into the white mugs. We have saved that craft, producing students who have learned to carve the intricate mosaic of birds, butterflies, and flowers. In Masatepe and Granada the ancient art of making furniture out of fresh *mimbre* (a plant) has been revived, its delicate and resistant tiling so well adapted to our tropical climate. And an important change is no longer to prefer furniture from Miami over Nicaraguan furniture. In the northern part of the country there is a mountain of soft rock of various tones and veined like marble, which the local peasant population converts into birds, fish, women's bodies. We have sent the best sculptor and the best professor of sculpture in Nicaragua to them and now San Juan de Limay is a village of sculptors. Much of what they produce is not folkcraft, but modern sculpture. On the Atlantic Coast, site of our gold mines, we have revived the lost art of goldwork. And our Caribbean coast has become a virtual jewelry store, with marine turtle shells, black coral, shark skeletons, and pearls. The Mesquite Indians carve precious wood, converting it into figures which, like their dances, represent their work: fishing, hunting and farming. The most advanced Indians now have returned to making drawings with brown, yellow and red plant dyes on the "tuno" canvas, which they make from the bark of a tree.

For all this rich and varied and previously unknown art, the Ministry of Culture has established different stores, and the best samples are exhibited in what we call "The Gallery for the People's Art" in Managua—which was previously the branch office of a bank. *cool*

PART TWO

The craftperson's hardships are due to cultural, economic and political reasons. Because of this we have forged our own road—not capitalist—leaving out the intermediaries and having the state financially support its artists. It is a fact that in our countries the penetration of capitalist civilization converts crafts into business; it takes it from the plaza to the marketplace; it strips it of its traditional functions, converts it to the product of a "boutique." The peasants, deprived of their pottery craft, eat from plastic plates; the sisal fiber is no longer used, and the craftperson depends more and more on money for his or her work. In Nicaragua, we seek out another, completely different, route. The destiny of our masks is not only to hang from the walls as adornments; the masks continue to live, and the craftpeople organize themselves into cooperatives.

The masks continue to live. One day the indigenous population of Monimbo, a population of craftpeople, rose up against Somoza. They fought with pistols and .22 rifles, with machetes, sticks, and stones. With iron rods used for construction, they made lances, with pipes they made bazookas, with gunpowder from their festival fireworks they invented an extremely powerful bomb. They launched the rockets from their festivals against the helicopters, their marimbas playing war songs from the Black dance, and they gave press conferences with festival masks on, so that they would not be *wow* recognized. (From this the soldiers in the cities got the idea of fighting with a handkerchief over their faces.) And the festival masks are the pink and red faces of the Spanish conquerors—they danced with masks from the Spanish Conquest in order to ridicule the conqueror. Those masks showed that they were a people that had never been defeated by domination. They invented an entire craft out of war. And an army could not bend them with machine guns, tanks, planes, and helicopters.

The enemies of the Revolution, from within and without, try to oppose religion. But popular religious traditions are encouraged by the Revolution. Thus it has become accustomed to "La Purísima" and "La Gritería," which are Marian traditions deeply rooted in our nation; the Patron Festivals, some of which are widely celebrated, like that of Santo Domingo of Managua and San Jerónimo of Masaya; and Christmas. In 1980, the Junta, stating "that along with the changes in fundamental structure effected by our Revolution, the Christmas celebration must recover its true popular and Christian feeling," decreed: "All kinds of advertisements and commercial promotions that are broadcast by printed media, television, and radio and by whatever other form of public instruments that use or invoke Christmas and everything that is related to the date of the birth of Christ in order to encourage the sale of good or services, are prohibited."

Vices that previously were fomented in Patron Festivals by Somoza and his followers, like prostitution, gambling, and drinking, have been prohibited. As a result, the festivals have been made saner, more pleasurable, furthermore more Christian, and fit better with the more genuine cultural efforts of our nation. At our festivals one can sample the many native dishes. The festivals also provide the opportunity to tighten our bonds with each other, to reaffirm the importance of community, as incarnated in a patron saint. The festival is like a real utopia where all the needs of the community and of those who pull it together seem for once to be fulfilled.

To us, culture does not occupy a separate sphere from social development. Furthermore, it is inconceivable in Nicaragua to have economic development without cultural development.

In Solentiname, a group of peasants gathered together with me once a week, bringing their poems. It was a poetry workshop. Children came also. One time a ten-year-old boy brought this brief poem:

> I saw a turtle in the lake.
> It was swimming
> and I was in a sailboat.

It seems to me to illustrate nicely that definition of culture proposed by UNESCO: that it is everything that man adds to nature. Apollinaire said: When man wanted to move more quickly, he did not create a third foot, he invented the wheel. The boy here had a cultural consciousness: The turtle and I swim in Nicaragua Lake, it swims with its flippers, and I go in a boat. I am like the turtle, but I am different from the turtle.

But we must develop the concept of culture more. I think of another poem from the workshop, this written by a peasant of Solentiname:

> I go away to the dark green guabo tree,
> that is at the beach,
> to wash the corn for tortillas.
>
> I take off my clothes to feel more comfortable
> and have remained only in my red pants.
>
> I scrub the corn until it is white.
> I finish, I wash my pink cotona, I bathe,
> and I come back.

A reflection about everyday peasant life, a great harmony with nature, a consciousness of the self and of the language, a desire for communication. Those elements, which involve a development defended against exploitation, ignorance, and alienation, made it possible for that peasant girl, after she was a guerrilla, to write a poem so classical and so free.

CULTURE: THE RIGHT OF THE MASSES

Culture within any given society depends on the capacity of the members of that society to develop their potential. If the members of a society are not given this opportunity, there can be no democratization of culture. There can be no culture, nor democracy.

Not too long ago, an article in The *Wall Street Journal* denounced the fact that in the U.S. works of art and literature have become mere decorative pieces to be preserved as bonds or fiduciary funds. Society does not expect a Secretary of State to have any deeper knowledge of history than that required for a sixth-grade exam. The article added: "The U.S. has made a business of its culture and a culture of its business."

In Nicaragua, on the other hand, we now have a new understanding of culture. The Nicaraguan writer, Sergio Ramírez, who is a member of the Government Junta, has said: "If culture was formerly the exclusive domain of a minority, now it will be the privilege of the masses, the right of the masses."

We also have a new understanding of the intellectual. Colonel Santos López, who fought alongside Sandino and later became one of the founders of the Sandinista Front in a jungle region, did not know how to read. Yet one of the Commanders of our Revolution, Victor Tirado López, has called him an intellectual. He considers that not having known how to read was one of this man's highest virtues because, as he once told him, you had to have a clean mind and a sensitive heart in order to understand what was happening in Nicaragua as a result of U.S. intervention. Commander Tirado then added, "The reason for his great success lies precisely in the fact that he did not go to school to learn to read his first words." This reminds me of what Gramsci once said, that culture is the critique of exploitation. This is the same as Socrates' famous maxim "know thyself," which means that the plebeians should know that they have the same human nature as the nobles who exploit them.

So for this very reason all of the Nicaraguan people were taught to read immediately after the triumph of the Revolution. The literacy campaign was started with the aim of producing liberated citizens. It was like a second liberation war against *Somocismo*, i.e. against the ignorance left behind by *Somocismo* (what Julio Cortázar called "the strategy of ignorance"). More than half of the high school students in the country became literacy teachers. This was voluntary and without pay. They were divided into brigades, columns and squadrons. The country itself was divided into various war fronts, the same ones that had existed in the liberation struggle: the Northern Front, Southern Front, Western Front, etc.... Each place in which the battle was won was declared "Victorious over Illiteracy." As in the other war, there was also a Final Offensive. And thousands of victorious youths entered Managua in endless lines of trucks, just as the Sandinistas had entered Managua triumphantly, acclaimed by all the people.

With our democratization of the alphabet, the *campesinos* not only learned the alphabet, but they learned about their reality and themselves as well. Edmundo, a sixteen-year-old literacy teacher says that "they learned quickly because we spoke of their reality, of exploitation, of the Revolution, and not about topics that were irrelevant to them."

To these young literacy teachers, the experience was also a school for learning about the Revolution. Oscar, a sixteen-year-old, said, "For me it was the best school, the best workshop, the best study session we've ever had, because we weren't just told about the life of the *campesino,* we actually went to see and experience the conditions in which *campesinos* live. We understood the moral obligation we had, as young people, to help remedy all the harm done by previous governments. Since then I have been committed to trying to consolidate the Revolution."

These young literacy teachers also had the experience of peasant work. Ligia, seventeen years old, said, "It was very beautiful because I did not know how to do farmwork." Another young woman recounts that she returned with the desire to study medicine immediately, and that this time would pass quickly, because those peasants needed her. A young sixteen-year-old said, "After the Crusade the collective spirit has impregnated many of us students." And a fifteen-year-old from a rich family says: "After the Crusade I found in my parents my political friends."

A REVOLUTIONARY EDUCATION

Teachers of literacy have continued receiving education. There has been a great growth in the quantity of scholars and universities. The University costs six dollars per semester, practically free. Also there has been a qualitative change in education; now Nicaragua is the subject of education and research.

As an example I will speak of the new kind of museums that we are creating with the help of UNESCO and the Organization of American States. Museums always have been elitist in the eyes of the people. The French Revolution opened the Louvre to the people, so that they could appreciate the works of art that previously were restricted only to the aristocracy. And this was an advance. But the people have always seen in the museums a mummified culture. And they have been passive spectators there. During Somoza's reign, our National Museum was not even this way; it was totally abandoned. A woman had been volunteer director of it all her life without salary. A little while before she died, we took her there in her wheelchair so that she could see the remodeling that we had done, and she was surprised to see how the Pharomachus moccino or the Momotus moto, which she herself had dissected, now were exhibited, and she said, "It seems to me that I am in another country." They have created more museums and remodeled others. But the new type of museums of which I speak will be like cultural centers; they will be created with the participation of the entire community and will be cared for by it; they will offer courses, will gain an audience for art. They will be a medium for popular culture for all ages and cultural levels. The museums will be like schools for the whole community. To make up for our insufficient schools, the museums will be a true medium for cultural socialization—an informal education, not academic, perhaps unconscious. The subjects addressed by the museums will be: health, agricultural technology, ecology, crafts, education, archaeology—whatever the community wants. The museums will not only be there to portray records of the past, but the needs of the present and the dreams of the future. In this way, the people will get their culture from the museums. The man in the community will have a consciousness of himself as a cultured being and a social being. We believe that if a village was capable of making a Revolution, it is capable of making its own museums. Theodore Law said, speaking of the museums, "Democracy and popular culture are synonyms." We have already inaugurated the first of these museums in a small village, and a group of the more important Latin American writers and artists who were at a gathering in Managua traveled a long and dusty road to the inauguration of that humble museum. We can perhaps say that this is a type of museum that contradicts the traditional concept of museums.

PART THREE

The Poetry Workshops have been created in crowded inner-city neighborhoods, in humble populations, in the indigenous communities of Monimbo and Subtiava, in the Armed Forces. Here, workers, peasants, police, soldiers learn to write poetry, and very fine poetry. Before I spoke of the Poetry of the Armed Forces. At Harvard, where I gave the closing address at a convention about Peace and Disarmament, I said that our army would be able to give technical advice to other armies about poetry. The Venezuelan writer Joaquin Marta Sosa has written of these workshops, "We can say that the

Sandinista Revolution, for the first time, has socialized the means of poetic production." He explained it further, adding, "The people have begun to become masters of poetry in Nicaragua: not because they read more and from expensive editions, but because they produce it."

I read last week in *Time* magazine that poetry books in the United States "do not usually pile up next to the cash register." In Nicaragua, poetry publications printed by the Ministry of Culture disappear rapidly; our magazine *Poesía Libre*, which is made up exclusively of poetry and is published on kraft paper, sells widely at the popular level. We have reissued the first editions because they continue to be in demand.

Our music has been able to have a social use along with its aesthetic value. UNICEF's indices for measuring the health of a village (number of doctors, paramedics, etc.) reveal that Nicaragua is faulty in this area. As in the literacy crusade, the entire population is mobilized in a health campaign to eradicate malaria or vaccinate all the children in the country. And music has been a part of that. During the war, our great composer Carlos Mejia Godoy wrote lyrics to go with the mazurka, teaching to arm and disarm a FAL and a Galil. The same thing happens with popular theater. Without worrying about action, time, or space, which play a great part in contemporary theater, our peasants, workers, and students use scenes to dramatize their daily life or their social or psychological conflicts. Nicaraguan cinema had its birth during the war, when battlefields were filmed. Now films portray all the aspects of the new society that is being created, basically like a documentary.

Sports are part of the Ministry of Culture, and the Revolution has a sports policy: it looks toward total participation by the masses in sports; sports as a part of daily village life; people as not simply spectators (as they were under Somoza), but as participants—sports for the whole society, all classes, without distinction by age or sex.

We desire mass participation in sports, not for the sake of sport itself, but for a strategic objective: what sport produces— improvement, emulation, collective work, brotherhood, health. Mass participation in sports strengthens competence, and this leads to selection with an eye towards excellence. The goal of excellence is common to all spheres of the Revolution. We cannot settle for less; we can have a gradual process, but the ultimate goal, in all things, is excellence. And the athlete who reaches the ranks of excellence is living proof of what the Revolution can and must achieve, and is an example for others. And the best will be able to compete in international events.

THE PEOPLE'S ANSWER

Due to problems with foreign currency and the difficulty of importing many articles, we produced a fair, "La Piñata," which was a huge national exposition and sale of Nicaraguan goods—crafts and products of small industry. By the thousands, people attended this large sale of toys, clothing, furniture, books, records, nutritious products and ornamental plants. Children came to break the many piñatas. Along with the fair there was a circus. There were booths with typical foods. There was music and singing.

The purpose of this fair was to create a consciousness of the value of native products; before it was believed that only the foreign was worthwhile. The purpose of this fair was not to promote a consumer society in the sense of useless consumption or waste. Yes, we want good consumption for our people. And this is also within the sphere of culture, not just of economics, in the sphere of a poor nation's culture. Our economic-cultural-political condition was defined very well by a toymaker crippled in the war in heroic Monimbo. He said when the fair occurred: "The question, comrades, is to each time make a toy more beautiful and durable because a wheelbarrow [with special features] is something with which the children can play for years." The great volume of vendors showed that this was a stimulus without precedent for Nicaraguan craft and small industry. And it was a political answer and an alternative by which to break dependence on other countries.

In Nicaragua, the bourgeoisie dressed itself in the stores of Miami. Bridal furnishings were bought in Miami (earlier, in Paris). The Revolution has revived the popular Nicaraguan dress. It is not merely for its colorfulness; it is for its beauty and furthermore for its usefulness in this climate. The cotona, this white shirt that I wear, has been the traditional shirt of the Nicaraguan peasant; at one time it had practically disappeared; now it is the most popular shirt in Nicaragua. As a peasant shirt, it is a symbol of work, of struggle, of freedom, of the Revolution. The cotona was the uniform of the literacy teachers. When thousands of those young people triumphantly entered Managua, they had the commanders of the Revolution put on those cotonas—the commanders who presided over the great public event were scarcely older than those young people.

Nicaragua is also beginning to change relations between men and women. But this is a long-term cultural transformation. "Before, I was an insupportable machista," says a sixteen-year-old youth, "and the Sandinista Youth movement has made me radically change my position with respect to women. Now I treat them differently." This indicates to us that the change we begin now will principally involve the future generations. There is now a law of publicity, prohibiting the use of commercial ads presenting women as sexual objects.

Our relationship with nature is also beginning to change. The contraband of wild animals and indiscriminate deforestation have been stopped. We begin to learn a new harmony with nature.

Since the deaths of Roque Dalton, Otto Rene Castillo and Pablo Neruda, no poet in the Spanish-speaking Americas has been as revolutionary, accessible and important as the comrade-padre of Nicaragua's Sandinista movement, ERNESTO CARDENAL. His stand against catholic orthodoxy represents a great resistance in the name of the poor people of the world, and his understanding of culture in its collective manifestations is nonpareil.

ROXANNE DUNBAR-ORTIZ
Surviving America

On New Year's Day, 1994, I was driving the fifty miles of Interstate 280 from the Silicon Valley to San Francisco, where I live. I had spent that holiday weekend with my older brother who lives in Cupertino, and my older sister who had driven up from Fresno, where she lives. Although my brother and sister are college teachers like me, they have never been involved in any kind of politics, and we agree about almost nothing, especially not about Rush Limbaugh and his views, which appeal to them. I was thinking about the phenomenon of Rush Limbaugh as I drove I-280 and reached that part that parallels the lovely lakes of rain water that nestle in the creases of the San Andreas fault. I turned on the radio to distract myself from the swelling anger rising in me as I thought of Limbaugh and hated the United States of America. It so happened that I switched on the radio to the top of the news on the hour.

"Armed Tzeltal Mayan Indians have seized and are holding dozens of towns in the state of Chiapas in southern Mexico. They are well-armed and appear well-organized. They are apparently protesting the NAFTA agreement. Many, perhaps a majority of them, are women. No further details are known."

But that's all I needed to know, to know that a dream of mine had come true. At one time I had named that dream a historical inevitability, but events since the 1980s steered me away from my certainty of revolution. For me the dream began almost exactly thirty years earlier when—coincidentally(?) my entire thinking had been changed a few months earlier while reading Simone de Beauvoir's *The Second Sex*—I traveled on decrepit buses deep into the Mayan country of southern Mexico. (I had never traveled east of the Mississippi, much less to another country, only to Oklahoma where I'd grown up, and to California, and the Southwest in between.) In Mexico, there were Indians everywhere, living Indians, desperately poor and oppressed, nevertheless surrounded by ample evidence of their ancient and glorious past. Where I grew up, in what once was designated "Indian Territory," Indians had been reduced to near

238

invisibility. I thought it was the same everywhere, but here was a whole, huge country of Indians.

Women's liberation and the uprising of the native peoples to retake the Americas formed the kernel of my revolutionary dream, born there in Mexico. I did not know how to become a revolutionary, and although my paternal grandfather had been an Oklahoma Wobbly/Socialist, probably I did not even know the word. What I decided to be was a writer and teacher, and what I wanted to write and teach was history, to find out the truth and to tell it, to unlock secrets of the past and free them. Right then and there in that Mayan jungle, I made the decision to spend the rest of my life trying to figure out and change the world, and never once afterwards have I questioned that fate. I was free. Before that, before Mexico, I nearly became reconciled to another fate, that of the poor and working class in the United States. Charles Bukowski expressed my sentiments in his poem "Spark.":

> I always resented all the years, the hours, the
> minutes I gave them as a working stiff, it
> actually hurt my head, my insides, it made me
> dizzy and a bit crazy—I couldn't understand the
> murdering of my years
> yet my fellow workers gave no signs of
> agony, many of them even seemed satisfied, and
> seeing them that way drove me almost as crazy as
> the dull and senseless work…
>
> I knew that I was dying.
> something in me said, go ahead, die, sleep, become as
> them, accept.
>
> then something else in me said, no, save the tiniest
> bit.
> it needn't be much, just a spark.
> a spark can set a whole forest on
> fire.
> just a spark.
> save it.
> I think I did

> I'm glad I did
> what a lucky god damned
> thing.
> —From *The Last Night of the Earth Poems*,
> Black Sparrow, 1993

Not a day goes by, no matter how miserable I might be, that I do not think those very words, "what a lucky god damned thing." Because not a day goes by that I do not remember that hopeless, desperate look in my mother's and my father's eyes, that I do not remember those hours and days and two years running that IBM proof machine in Liberty National Bank in Oklahoma City, those hours and days and two more years in the Oklahoma Natural Gas meter factory. By the time I worked on assembly lines at Fairchild and Siliconix in Silicon Valley, I was free. I was a revolutionary and it did not feel oppressive but defiant. I could never regress, once liberated, to that desperate mentality. I could work now forever in a factory and not mind, just as I suppose Bukowski did all those years in the post office after he started writing.

Finding a way to be a revolutionary was not easy and I am not even sure I ever did. I don't think I could have survived in my quest, not at this time of the proclaimed "end of history," without Mexico on my mind, the "Achilles heel of U.S. imperialism," as I called Mexico. During those thirty years, I escaped to Mexico to breathe the air of endurance and resistance as often as I could. In February 1991, in the midst of the bombing of Baghdad, I was driving across country on I-10 along the Mexican border and turned off when I saw a sign indicating a port of entry at Columbus, New Mexico, and took it, just to be outside the U.S. for an hour. The last time I was in Mexico City, during the independence anniversary in September 1993, I had a hard time detecting resistance in the air, although the Zócalo was crammed with peasants from all over the country who had been tossed off their communal lands to make way for free trade. I wrote in my note book:

> Mexico City, 14 September 1993:
> It happens more than once
> more than twice
> walking down the
> Paseo de la Reforma,

> In front of me strides a tall, broad, tanned, blond
> "Norteamericano,"
> as he is politely called now instead of "gringo,"
> a cellular telephone
> pressed to his ear.
> That is NAFTA to me.
> And in the Zócalo, landless Indians dressed in white,
> dusty feet in crude sandals,
> observe the dismemberment of the last vestiges
> of Revolution.

All those years it was easy, or so it now seems, to feel useful and to feel good about choosing the vocation of revolutionary, until that world came crashing down around us in the 1980s. Peeled like an onion of my outer skins, I was left questioning who I was and where I was going. That was not something a revolutionary was supposed to do. I began trying to figure it out by remembering and writing. I had always remembered only part of who I was, the oppressed female, the child of rural poverty, working class, child of a mother who was a part-Indian abandoned child.

I was born in San Antonio, Texas, almost in the shadow of the Alamo. Before I was a year old, my family moved back to my father's hometown in Canadian County, western Oklahoma, a stone's throw from the Old Chisholm Trail.

Canadian County, Oklahoma, part of the old Southern Cheyenne/Arapaho treaty territory, partitioned for homesteading in the late nineteenth century, was the northernmost point of my family's many treks.

San Antonio was dead center.

The southern point was The Valley—McAllen, Texas—where my grandfather had taken my father's family in the early 1920's, from Canadian County, Oklahoma, where he had farmed.

My grandparents on both sides had been born on the eastern periphery—Joplin, Missouri; Mena, Arkansas.

Three out of four of us children of that edge of the frontier moved west, as far as possible, to California.

In the middle of that territory lay New Mexico, a kind of mystical throbbing heart, for me anyway.

Aztlán.

I found a name for my homeland, that territory that expanded from the Pacific Ocean to the Mississippi River, from the Rockies to the Rio Grande, when I met Chicanos, who had just begun to call themselves Chicanos, at UCLA during the late Sixties.

Aztlán. The North.

And living in San Francisco, I found that mid-California was called Big Sur, the South, south of Monterey, south of the Presidio at San Francisco.

This was the geography of my upbringing and remains the geography of my mind, the center from which I relate to the rest of the world: that ancient territory of the Aztecs, north of Spanish conquest, that was finally liberated as a part of the Republic of Mexico, and was annexed by the United States in 1848.

When I decided to write my doctoral dissertation in Latin American History at UCLA on one part of that territory—New Mexico—during the precolonial and Spanish period, I was forced to transfer from Latin American to United States History, since this region was called the "Borderlands" of the U.S. West. So much for academic objectivity.

Borderlands. When I first heard that term, it rang a bell. I knew it meant me. Borderline, marginal, on the edge, neither this nor that, identity not certain.

In fact, the ancestors on my father's side were Scots-Irish (descendants of Scots colonial settlers in Northern Ireland), poor white farmers moving across a frontier forged by United States expansion into indigenous America; farmers, peasants; fenced out, starved out, seeking cheap land, ending up sharecroppers, farm workers, drifters, ranchhands ("cowboys"), the foot soldiers of the U.S. empire, not that different from the South African Boer voortrekkers, Calvinist and deeply white-supremacist.

But there were others—the mysterious maternal grandmother whose family name was unknown and who died when my mother was a toddler—an Indian, they said, actually they said a "squaw," married to or living with my drunken Irish itinerant grandfather, a "squawman," they called him. Then there was my father's paternal grandmother, Mexican, family name Angel. A few years ago, when my father was under sodium pentothal in surgery, he spoke for two hours in fluent Spanish (his surgeon was a native Spanish-speaker). For the first time in my life he informed me that his grandmother

242

had been Mexican and always spoke to him in Spanish when he was little, calling him "my little Angel" because he was dark like her.

During the valiant Sandinista decade, I spent a lot of time in Nicaragua and found another borderland, the Mosquitia, the eastern region of Nicaragua and Honduras, filled with marginal peoples—the Miskitos (mixed Indian, Black, White, who speak Miskito, an Indian language); the Creoles (same mixture but English-speaking); and the Garifunos (same mixture speaking a patois). It was there I finally comprehended my own historical/political theory of two decades—the power of resistance, the importance of borderlands, the ultimate Achilles heel of colonialism and imperialism. Although the term may seem quaint today, "class" best captures the unity of such disparate peoples and cultures, those dispossessed by capitalism.

Chicanos yes, and those Genízaros of New Mexico and Métis of Canada, the Cajuns, the Appalachians. And then there are the Panamanian Cholos; the Paraguayans, the majority of whom speak the Guaraní Indian language as their mother tongue; and those Morocucho in the Cangallo pampas and the poor whites of Pillpinto in the Andean province of Acomayo who speak only Quechua, the ancient Inca tongue.

And who knows what aspects of the cultures of the Seminole, the Choctaw, the Cuban and the Brazilian cultures are African or Indian or Portuguese or Spanish or Irish?

And all the others. Mestizos. The Cosmic People. The future of the world.

I do not like the concept of Mestizo or Métis or half-breed, in the sense that they refer to race. I prefer "new peoples." The less academic metaphor I prefer is "coyote," that wily, tough hybrid of the new world born somehow in the ashes of conquest and genocide.

Out of the wreckage of genocide and colonization that followed in the wake of that fateful voyage a half millennium ago, were born new peoples, new cultures, new art and music. Millions of Africans were hauled over to labor for the rich. Millions of native Americans—the whole of the Natchez Nation of the Mississippi Valley, the indigenous farmers of western Nicaragua, most of the Cree of the north, and millions of others—were forcibly transported to labor in mines and fields and woods. The destitute of Europe were also forced by a push-pull factor to emigrate, and they indeed make up the majority of the poor in many parts of the hemisphere today.

The descendants of the ancient Inca civilization speak of "rescuing the Mestizo." They have developed a kind of indigenous version of Bolívar's and Jefferson's ruling-class dreams of one borderless America, but with a difference, the difference being the recognition of the roots of "our America." I believe the "Mestizo," or "new peoples/coyotes," have a special role to play in the future of our America and the world. In a way, I see that role as a heavy responsibility. Many who fall within that massive and disparate category may be able to choose sides; "Which side are you on?" Fidel Castro, speaking in 1986, to the issue of commemorating the Quincentenary of Columbus' voyage, said that all Americans must choose to identify with the conqueror or the conquered, and that he chose to identify with the conquered.

The vast majority of the new peoples, from the Métis and Quebecers of Canada to the Chicanos, Cajuns and borderlanders of the United States, to the Mestizos of Latin America and the African-Americans of the entire hemisphere, and this century's immigrants from southern and eastern Europe, or from Asia, fall within the working class, employed or unemployed, and if they happen to slip out it may be temporary and limited.

It is there, at that cross-section of working for the man (or unemployed), that we coyotes have a responsibility. It is there that we artists/revolutionaries have a responsibility. For there are hundreds of indigenous nations throughout the hemisphere fighting for their survival, for their languages (another dies each year), for their dignity, their territories. The tough coyotes of the frontier should be in the front line in defense of the indigenous peoples, for it is those surviving cultures that have allowed the new peoples to be born and to persist, that keep the heart of America beating. Just think how you felt when you heard about the Tzeltal Maya uprising on New Year's Day, and you will realize that your very survival, the survival of life, depends on the survival and rebirth of native America.

More than anything, it is culture that will vindicate the conquest and fuel our resistance: Language—English, Spanish, French, Portuguese, Dutch, and indigenous languages, too, in all their variations—but resistance language transformed to literature that transcends conquest; music: that ubiquitous guitar, the flute, the human voice and the lyrics, language again, resistance, universal;

drawing, painting, murals, sculpture. Communicating through the senses is what the coyote can do best; and confounding, confusing, messing up every theory and straitjacket, and fighting to survive.

Resistance, that's the legacy, that's the heritage of those cruel five hundred years, and that is the hope, the future.

That is the proud and honorable legacy of surviving the invasion—resistance and continuance—and therein lies our responsibility.

ROXANNE DUNBAR-ORTIZ grew up in rural Western Oklahoma and became an activist in the Sixties, while studying at UCLA. She helped start the Women's Liberation Movement and was editor of its premier journal, *No More Fun and Games.* She has also worked with the Native American movement, has authored books on the Pueblo, the Sioux, and the Miskito Indians of Nicaragua. She is one of the founders of the Ethnic and Women's Studies Dept. at California State University at Hayward, where she is an activist professor. Her memoir, *Red Dirt: Growing Up Okie,* was published by Verso, and her Sixties memoir, *Outlaw Women,* was published in 2002 by City Lights Books.

ELIZAM ESCOBAR
Art of Liberation: A Vision of Freedom

The *political* is found in the least likely places, covered by multiple layers of ideological counterfeiting and acculturation. Our daily lives, our dreams, love, death, and even our bodies are all spheres of "invisible" yet intense political and human dramas that take place behind the "visible" political struggle. This inner struggle is more painful and more real than the outer one. For it is from *inside* that we must decide our real needs, both material and spiritual. Art of liberation springs from this perspective, recognizing the power of the imagination's struggle. Throughout history, the imagination's struggle against prohibitions based on fear and ignorance has been one of the leading political processes that push forward the liberation of the human spirit by rescuing and creating new territories of freedom.

I have been active in the struggle for Puerto Rican national liberation since the Sixties. From the socialist-Marxist perspective, I have simultaneously engaged in political-direct[1] as well as art/cultural work in support of this struggle, but not always with the same intensity or understanding.

In my "first period," I separated "personal" work—my paintings—from more "public" works—political illustrations, propaganda, caricatures, etc. Both activities were done under the dictates of my ideological assumptions. Nevertheless, there were always elements that would completely or relatively escape the dictates of my "ideology." Thematic elements drawn from my particular experiences exposed me to conflicts between what was supposed to be and what actually was, creating tensions that were contained by oneiric images (political monsters, doubts repressed by ideology, etc.). Formal elements, devalued by socialist realism and other "realist" aesthetics, also escaped.

The "second period" began when I moved from Puerto Rico to New York, and was defined by an almost total cessation of painting due to the demands of my job (schoolteacher), my political-direct work, and my mixed feelings about art. I was under the influence of a politics of "art is useless unless it is for direct propaganda purposes."

My work was limited almost exclusively to political caricatures for party publications. (Not a bad thing.)

In my "third period," I made an almost about-face toward the "personal." I was seriously dealing with the fundamental question of the relative autonomy and specificity of the theory and praxis of art (i.e., that art has its own "rules" with a space that is its own but always in relation to all other levels or spheres of "reality," so to speak), not out of an academic or abstract drive but as a result of an accumulation of experiences. Both my political and artistic commitment were more intense than ever.

In 1980, I was arrested, together with ten other Puerto Rican *independentistas*, accused of seditious conspiracy and participation in the Puerto Rican clandestine movement for national liberation. Since then I have been in prison. Here, my "fourth period" is taking place, and it is from the perspective of these experiences that I consider the visionary role of the artist.

THE STRUCTURES OF SIMULATION

We live in societies divided into social classes, where there is no true consensus, only the fictitious and spurious consensus determined by the ruling classes. Electoral processes are national epics manipulated in the name of the people to legitimize social control and coercion. To resolve these contradictions we must assume the class struggle in all its diverse forms and confront the questions of Power. Only then will the immense majority of excluded, oppressed, and exploited obtain the real power.

But we cannot wait for the day when the majority will rule in order to bring forward the structures needed for building a free, just, egalitarian, and nonclassist society. We must build within the ruins and the hostilities of present conditions by creating transitional alternatives now. We must build socio-economic, political, and cultural structures that are controlled by those struggling for change and the communities they serve. These structures, "schools" for discussing all these problems, will put into practice the notion that only by confronting the reality of subjection can we begin to be free and to create an art of liberation that frees people from the illusions perpetrated by the dominant culture.

The contemporary State creates structures of simulation. These are indispensable both to cover the real nature of the system and to show tolerance and acceptance of dissidents. Furthermore, they not only create their own structures, but they obligate us to create our own.

For example, the ruling classes create the simulation of cultural democracy (the illusion of real political power, equal opportunity and the freedom of difference, in order to make others believe that they have a real participation in the cultural space) through the mass culture and the media. They need "false enemies" to wage relatively inoffensive and limited "cultural wars" that end up strengthening the social body's health.[2] One example is what happened to the spontaneous street graffiti expression: from symbolic exchange it became another commodity with status-exchange value. In Puerto Rico under colonialism, popular art is institutionalized and becomes a folkloric domestication of the people's unconscious. Some of the left's culture of resistance has been depoliticized by obliging artists to make false choices between a sort of one-dimensional domesticated "nationalist art" and mass culture. This way, artists either turn their "criticism" against an abstract enemy or they wear themselves out by contributing an "original" aesthetic to the status quo (but always in the name of "Puerto Ricanness") because they fear the worse evil, that of U.S. statehood—to the benefit of the colonial bourgeois lackeys. Part of the Puerto Rican independence movement reproduces itself as a simulation model through this "cultural nationalism." At the same time, artists are domesticated by continuous government subsidies, status, fame, wealth, and by aspiring to national titles, while those who persist to the contrary, whose politics are to unveil the whole system of simulation, are censored even by some orthodox leftist publications, which want to reduce the debate to their own political good, that is—they won't allow dissent within the dissent.

Paradoxically, art (as the power of imagination), the only "true" simulation, is the one thing that can lead us to the *understanding* (not necessarily to the resolution) of that other "false" simulation.

THE CULTURE OF FEAR

But in order to liberate art from the nets of political power, we, the artists, must first liberate ourselves from the nets of the *culture of fear,* and the inferiority/superiority complex we have in our dealings at the political-direct level. If art is to become a force for social change, it must take its strength from the *politics of art,* art's own way of affecting both the world and the political-direct. It must take strength from that specific manner in which our praxis expresses the aspirations of the people, the political collective unconscious, the contradictions, etc., through a symbolic language. But the *politics of art* will happen only if the power of the imagination is able to create a symbolic relationship between those who participate, the artwork, and the concrete world, always understanding the work of art's sovereignty (or relative autonomy) in relation to concrete reality.

What is important is not the didactic pretension that we possess the solutions, but the idiosyncratic ways in which works of art can bring out the real aspects of the human condition in particular and specific contexts or experiences. Art is, from this perspective, an encounter where we have the possibility of a symbolic, political, and real exchange.

Since our forms are also used to deliberately appeal to people for political-direct goals, it is logical that at some point these strategies become dominant and conflict with the internal problems (the how) of art. If we can understand how the political affects and shapes everything else, and the difference between the specific practices of art and the practices of the political-direct, then the artist will be clearer about how to decide his/her strategies, sources, themes, aesthetics, etc. When it comes to the theory and praxis of art, the *political* is beyond any "political (direct) issues."

Most U.S. "Political Art," as I have come to understand it, wants to present political-direct issues through images, in a clear and communicative form, irrespective of the medium, the style, or the aesthetic selection. It presupposes that one can predict the kind of political effect a work of art is going to have. Thus the important thing is the message. This emphasis on the message is akin to Marshall McLuhan's naive optimism—"the medium is the message"—and finds its extreme in the inversion of McLuhan's dictum: "The message is the message." Both are founded in the arbitrariness of the sign, which artificially separates and reunites everything in terms of a signifier (in this case, the medium) and a signified (here, the message). The political and the symbolic are depoliticized by the imposition of a code that comes directly from ideology, since, as Jean Baudrillard argues, "every attempt to surpass the political economy of the sign that takes its support from one of its constituent elements is condemned to reproduce its arbitrary character."[3]

In this way the participants are excluded from creating meanings other than those already transmitted by the message since, once the signal is sent, you either accept it or reject it. There is no need to search for more. In this respect the *art of the message* shares common ground with the *formal theory of communication*,[4] which goes like this: transmitter (encoder)—message—receiver (decoder). One speaks, the other doesn't. The message is assumed to contain information that is legible and univocal, based on a pre-established and rationalized code composed of signs. Two terms are artificially reunited by an objectified content called message. The formula has a formal coherence that assures it as the only *possible* schema for communication, since a code names everything in terms of itself and anything else that is not "designed" or "adapted" to the agency of the code cannot be utilized since it won't work in this schema. The problem then is that this structure denies the ambivalence of exchange, the reciprocity or antagonism between two distinct interlocutors. As soon as ambivalence shows up, the structure collapses, since there is no code for ambivalence, and without a code no more encoder, no more decoder.

I am not saying that U.S. "Political Art" is equal to this obsession with "communication," but that it is constricted to the code if its intentions are mainly to present a message. Thus, anything that is not in the sign form is ambivalent, and it is from ambivalence (i.e. the impossibility of distinguishing respective separated terms and positivizing them as such)[5] that any symbolic exchange (allusions through images, discourse, objects, etc.) can emerge. On the other hand, this impasse is, of course, disturbing, since we cannot absolutely do away with the signific code.

The ironic dilemma is that we have to make use of this code though we realize that it reduces and abstracts the irreducible experience of that which we call "liberation" (or "freedom," "desires," "needs," etc.). It is the all-too-familiar situation where words (like "liberation," "political", " "freedom of expression") take command over the real concrete experience and are used to legitimize and justify a practice or a state of things. There is a brutal difference between "freedom" as exchange-sign-value or slogan of ideologies and abstractions, and the real freedom of experience—one that is as necessary as it is terrible. Even under extreme repression, individual freedom is unavoidable as we must keep on exercising our decisions and responsibilities. Here again art comes to the rescue, because it

250

has the inventive power and wit to deride, deceive, and betray censorship as well as self-censorship.

But how one is going to affect others is another matter, since it is almost impossible to know how an artwork will be taken. The effect is always diverse, contingent, and unpredictable. Whether this ambivalence is richer than a clear-cut message is for others to decide. But the important thing is that an artist must re-establish an element of confidence through his/her intentions of being as honest as possible and as consistent in his/her views as convictions allow. In this sense, a "solitary voice" is as strong as a collective one.

Works of art are provocations, but in order for an artist to be provocative she/he first has to have a true vocation, that is, true dedication to her/his art and to those who have been reduced to invisibility. It is from there that art can not only obtain relevancy but can also transcend its immediate references.

The political aspect of art thus is to confront all of reality, without ideological permission and through its own means. In order to discover our real needs we must be wary of what we are told and why we believe it. We must re-find the internal relationship between human desires and aspirations and human necessity, but in a new way. We must put into question any philosophical system or form of knowledge that claims to be the only and absolute truth. To that Marxist conception of freedom—"freedom is the knowledge (or recognition) of necessity"—I add a conception of art: *art is the necessity of freedom.*

ART, PRISON, AND LIBERATION

Twenty-five centuries ago, when Socrates was incarcerated, he wrote his first and only poems. Ever after, the experience has been repeated. In prison, many nonartists, men and women of action and thought who never saw art or poetry as important or "useful," have engaged in some sort of creative expression. Art has come through prison. But also, through art, prison has come to the outside; many poets, writers, and painters have had some essential experiences in prisons or other places of internment, and many others have become writers or artists in prison. Certainly, art usually comes to the rescue of those who have to confront these conditions at one point in their lives, people who otherwise might never have done much, if anything, for the defense or estimation of art. Art demands a certain introspection,

251

solitude, and abandonment, and a certain confrontation with the self and death—that is, themes that are usually repugnant to "revolutionaries" and "practical" people unless they have to do with heroism or the glorification of a personality. Therefore, it is no surprise that adversity and forced solitude are able to liberate that "obscure" region of the imagination.

In prison life, there is—consciously or not—a constant and extreme interaction between the pleasure principle and the reality principle (for example, the realization that in politics as in love one must learn how to wait), much sublimination/desublimination, daydreaming, hope/cynicism, disillusionment, anger, unreality, skepticism, repression, censorship, and hypocrisy. All this shapes one's life and art. We are penetrated as much by the means of communication as people on the outside—sometimes more, because of our encloistering and lack of direct outside contact. This combination of suppression and diversion keeps prisoners as apathetic consumers and participants in a vicious circle. The human condition, in a state of extreme control and intensity, is distorted to the most complete absurdity: either life is only a simulacrum (the art of the living death) or only through simulation are you able to survive.

There are exceptions, but the final balance is dehumanization, a waste of human lives. Cheap slave labor, and the continuation of criminal activity through other means and under different circumstances, are what characterize the "rehabilitation shop" of a society that is itself in need of radical transformation. The decadence of this society is displayed in its prisons through a spectacle of extreme collective madness. To "liberate" this experience through art is a responsibility to others.

Prison has reconfirmed to me the great importance of art in our lives because the deep reflection and the intense involvement that art requires help us to better understand the real necessities and the true meanings of freedom, for the individual as well as the collective. And to fight for that truth, to defend that truth, art also becomes a weapon—a weapon not only because one can create meaning for one's own existence or inspire others to continue the struggle, but simply because one can understand better the intrinsic relationship between the visions coming through the praxis of art and those unveiled aspects of the too-much-rationalized and arbitrary aspects of our ideologies, as well as our daily mechanical rituals and common nonsense. My own experience of repression expressed through art can relate to other general human experiences of repression and exclusion better than, let's say, if I start to think through my "ideological eyes." Art must spring from real life.

If art becomes theoretical discourse, *that* is also a necessary weapon. To theorize art directly from the praxis of art is a necessity opposed by those who would like to keep art as inoffensive "aesthetics" or as mere echoes of the political-direct. And since some people would like to reduce art to a slogan of metaphysical proportions, one must always make the distinction between the art of propaganda, publicity, or design, and art as an act of liberation. The fundamental distinction is that an art of liberation can neither be a model nor a specific aesthetic or style. It is a concept and an attitude with no specific formulations other than that it must be open to any strategy that can help liberate art (and through art, people) from the dictatorship of the logic, politics, and metaphysics of the sign.

ART OF LIBERATION

To me, art is the best argument for talking about freedom and necessity when one does not separate the body from the spirit. In my experience I have learned more about politics through art than through politics. And by *art* here I mean all the arts and their discourses—and all the ways in which the symbolic and the power of the imagination influence the political-direct and help us to better understand social reality.

I do not express this with blind enthusiasm. I have come to suspect all those who depend on and are moved only by enthusiasm. So when I say that I believe in the fundamental role of art in life—to provoke, to provide a critical outlook, a paradoxical reassurance of our common humanity—I am not implying that this is a universal, shared judgment. Nor am I saying that art should conquer the world. It is enough for me to be conquered by art and to be able to let it go wherever it must go. So my bet on art is my bet on life. It is my bet on the possibility of linkage between the political struggle and the struggle for survival in a hostile environment. I am not referring merely to prison, but to all those environments created by the prison of social systems, in the name of the people and freedom, as well as by the prison of "communication." Political awareness makes us confront all that reality. It makes us both assault the status quo and critically inspect ourselves.

Art is an extension of life, and if you have artists whose politics are insubordinate, committed, and uncompromised, then they become as strengthening and inspiring to others, artists and non-artists, as art is to life.

ELIZAM ESCOBAR, painter, poet, and intellectual, was born in Puerto Rico in 1948. He attended the Art Students League, City College and the Museo del Barrio workshops in New York City. During the Seventies he taught in high schools and art schools. He has contributed essays on culture to many of the country's leading journals, and his exhibitions of paintings have been accorded the highest public enthusiasm in New York, Chicago, San Francisco and most recently in San Juan, Puerto Rico. After 28 years of incarceration Elizam Escobar was released in an act of amnesty by the U.S. government in 1998. He lives in Puerto Rico.

This essay is reprinted from *Reimagining America*, edited by Mark O'Brien and Craig Little, published by New Society Publications.

Notes:
1. The *political* is ubiquitous in today's world, but its purer form is manifested by engaging *directly* in the struggles for change and power. Tactics and strategies involve who does or does not exert power, who has the right to decide for society: to lead, prescribe, normalize, control, and manage the social reality. So for the purpose of making a differentiation between this more specific aspect, I would call this one the political-direct.
2. See Roger Bartra, *Las redes imaginarias del poder político* (México, D.F.: Ediciones Era, 1981).
3. Jean Baudrillard, *For a Critique of the Political Economy of the Sign* (St. Louis, MO: Telos Press, 1981), 160.
4. Based on Roman Jakobsen and criticized by Baudrillard.
5. Example: "The Sun: The vacation sun no longer retains anything of the collective symbolic function it had among the Aztecs, the Egyptians, etc. It no longer has that ambivalence of a natural force—life and death, beneficent and murderous—which it had in primitive cults or still has in peasant labor. The vacation sun is a completely positive sign, the absolute source of happiness and euphoria, and as such it is significantly opposed to non-sun (rain, cold, bad weather)." Baudrillard, 98.

AMIRI BARAKA

The American Popular Song
"The Great American Songbook"

American culture is still unbelievably "abstract" to Americans themselves; at the same time, it can not possibly be, since it is their day-to-day lives and expression. It is "abstract" only in the sense that Americans do not really understand their culture.

For one thing, American culture is much broader, much deeper, much darker, than official commentators of the social status quo allow. For another, when these same unworthies talk about Western Culture, relating it principally to Europe, they infer the lie that makes for the abstraction, since the "Western Culture" is the Americas. America is the west, the Pan-American experience is the American Experience, El Mundo Nuevo, The New World.

If we look a little deeper we will quickly understand that behind all this "Western World equals Europe" misgeographic claptrap is simply colonialism and white supremacy, with an overlay of Eurocentricity.

In a recent poem of mine I say of this phenomenon, "Leave England headed West/ you arrive/in Newark." The whole of the Pan-American hemisphere and experience constitutes "Western Culture." Eurocentric worship, which identifies the essence of official American Culture, guarantees that the European powers can step off at the top of the standard of living, while most of the Pan-American countries are in a state of neo, or some in straight-out, colonialism.

Say all that to say, that in a concept of something like "the American Popular Song," we will see that, historically, the peoples that "discovered and settled" (a dubious labeling of colonialism) the Americas from Europe brought with them their own culture—i.e., their history and experience, their art and philosophy—but this culture underwent continuous change under the whole weight of the new culture they entered into and helped shape in many ways. But we know that native peoples existed in this hemisphere by the millions before the Europeans arrived, (Lief Ericson notwithstanding), and that the Africans—witness the Afro cultures ubiquitous throughout the whole of Pan-America, such as the striking heads on the west coast of Mexico near Acapulco—were familiar with the Pan-American world centuries before.

But the English (and Irish, Welsh, Scotch & Co.), French, Spanish, Portuguese did bring both living culture and artifacts and machines to this side; the Dutch, Germans, and even the Danes, all came this way. In the U.S. we can see historical evidence of English, French and Spanish in the main as the primary European settlers, before the doors of the 19th century really swung the New World open to the German, Italian and Irish masses. And with them came the working-class and small-and-middle peasant culture as well: their folk and traditional songs and dances, the history of experience and manners through which a people express their consciousness.

But from the Native American cultures that greeted the Europeans when they arrived, there had already been a particularity of "Americanness," what existed as history and artifact, institution and culture; but the English hymns and plainsongs, the chansons and arias and jigs and lieder came with the whole of the European migration.

Slavery and the Indian wars, the wars of conquest between the various European conquerors, served to keep the new world a spread—and multiple dotting—of "subcultures" held in the contrasting quilt of what had already existed in these lands previous to the conquest. The formation of the nation-state at the end of the 18th century made the nation a Eurocentric political construct sewn out of diverse cultural fragments, the most numerous always the non-European, native American and African pieces.

Part of the antidemocratic corruption at the core of the U.S. nation-state has always been the political betrayal of the American revolution and its continuing colonial epoch connection to Europe as "a white child." This is done, at base, for purposes of exploitation and superprofit, in whatever their forms. But it has also served to make the general citizenry of the place less intelligent than necessary.

The apparent separateness, yet confluence, of diverse sources that make up modern American culture, in this case North American, U.S., culture, are brought together, ironically, by the underpinning, the slave (and colonial) base of the society. As a fixed social base for a society stridently calling for social development, it meant that there was a cultural reference as well, a "bottom" like a bass line to the whole.

It is here important to make a distinction between the *popular* and the *commercial*. Sidney Finklestein in *Jazz, A People's Music*

(Citadel), says, much to the point, "Commercialism should be restricted, as a term, to what is really destructive in culture; the taking over of an art, in this case popular music, by business, and the rise of business to so powerful a force in the making of the music that there was no longer a free market for musicians. Instead of distribution serving the musician, distribution, where the money was invested, became the dominating force, dictating both the form and content of the music."

This period did not happen in the U.S. until the 20th century, and it was probably the late 19th century before there was even any sign that such a phenomenon could occur. The end of slavery, which signifies the end of competitive capitalism and the beginning of monopoly capitalism/imperialism, is what ushers in this ongoing period of commercial control of the arts.

But popular music arises as the confirmation of the living culture of the people. The African culture transformed by chattel slavery and the totality of the Pan-American cultural experience have been, since its introduction in the West, a binding and all-pervading influence on the whole of the American culture, not only in most of the Americas where the colonizers were always a minority, but even in the U.S., where the African and Afro-American slaves were a minority.

You can hear the influence of the Spirituals on the so-called Barbershop quartets and vocal music of the U.S. 19th century. In the south, that influence, particularly in the church music and the plantation and slave labor system, was almost immediately reflected.

White southern religious music and country and western music are deeply and very clearly influenced by Afro-American musical culture, in every venue where black labor was utilized; sailor songs, cowpoke songs, soldier songs, miner songs, lumber-camp songs, jailhouse songs, broadening as slavery first put slaves even into work alongside "free" white workers; and then, when it was overthrown, an even broader and deeper influence resulted. But even in the 1880s and 90s, Ragtime and what was called "Barrel House" and "Honkey Tonk" had already brought black influence into the mainstream culture. The field shouts and work songs and even the street cries go back to the 17th century. By the 18th century, there had already developed a tradition of Afro-American whistling (like the chilly homeboy with the boom box) evidenced in the American colonies.

The ending of chattel slavery, and the gradual releasing of Afro-

Americans from slavery's extreme restrictions, was, of course, the stream of cultural renewal that ultimately transformed the whole of U.S. culture, so that now it has a clearly Afro-American aspect.

The biggest impact on U.S. musical culture in the 20th century was the urban coalescence and explosion that marked New Orleans. The entrance of the black rural and slave elements into the urban and highly sophisticated context of New Orleans produced an urbane, though seemingly ingenuous, expression that summed up the post-slavery U.S.

The creation of New Orleans Jazz, and the urbanized blues it came out of, were developments of world-shaking immensity. European observers and critics, as early as Brahms and later Ernest Ansermet, attest to the impact of this music as a musical culture upon world culture.

On the one hand, anyone who has ever seriously contemplated the longevity of the African culture will understand the profound reach the continuing elements of that culture have. Certainly, there has been quite a bit written about the musical and graphic aspects of it. But the New Orleans development showed that the ancient aspect could be carried (e.g., voice-oriented, call & response, percussive & polyrhythmic, polyphonic, importance of improvisation, "possession" by the music, i.e., what DuBois called the "Frenzy"), could be raised again within the new impressions of the chattel, and could be raised yet again in the still newer context of the post-slave southern city to express a staggeringly precise aspect of a U.S. multicultural experience.

Certainly, Afro-American culture is "open," by history and social circumstance, to the broadest array of influences. Black people have never hesitated to borrow and add to their own stash of expression whatever interested them, no matter what the source.

New Orleans was truly a gathering focus of African and Afro-American, Caribbean, Latin-American, French, Spanish, English, and Native-American, and the so-called "Creoles" or Afro-Whatever cultural elements through a historical process that crystallized in that 19th century urbane venue to produce a high and sophisticated artistic culture.

There was minstrelsy and blackface in the 19th century, largely coming out of the south. But by the end of the century, the black minstrel circuits would begin to follow the rush of black people out of the south, as an addition to that circuit. (Though, even with all the out-migration, there were still more Afro-Americans in the Black Belt south than anywhere else in the country, and by the 1970s the largest migration of blacks was back into the south!)

Jazz and blues were coming out of the south even ahead of the masses of black people, to the extent that there were several white bands who had picked up the music, white singers who had even earlier picked up on the blues or some other variant of Afro-American musical culture and who were carrying them, at first as novelties, to broader venues.

But the emergence of Jazz and "Classical" Blues coincides with and gives substance to the early part of the 20th century in the U.S., called "The Jazz Age". And it is the spread of thousands of black people out of the south into the northern and midwestern cities that brings the heart of the black southern culture across the U.S.

This large migration out of the south helped transform the Afro-American people from largely southern, rural and agricultural to a people located in large numbers in the north and midwest, mainly urban and industrial workers.

One measure of the impact of black culture on the U.S. and the world during this period is what we have called "The Harlem Renaissance" (though the U.S. and Harlem are simply the most visible expressions of what is actually a worldwide anti-imperialist movement, the 1917 Russian Revolution being one indication). *Négritude* from African and West Indian students in Europe touched Africa and the West Indies; *Négrissmo* in Latin America; *Indigisme* in Haiti, are similar cultural expressions of what is essentially an international "Black Consciousness Movement."

The title "The Jazz Age" certainly sums up the great impact Afro-American culture had on the U.S. and the world. It is now necessary to use Jazz as the musical background for anything focusing on the early 20th century U.S., "The Roaring 20s."

When Mamie Smith (one of the famous and unrelated "Smith Sisters," with Trixie and the great Bessie) replaced Sophie Tucker and sang "Crazy Blues" (1920), it became a national hit, selling 8,000 records a week for a year. It meant that Afro-American popular music could be widely distributed throughout the U.S. Sophie Tucker was herself a "cover" for Black female blues singers, just as the Original Dixieland Jazz Band, New Orleans Rhythm Kings and later Paul Whiteman and Bix Beiderbecke were used to cover Louis Armstrong, Oliver, Morton, Bechet and the rest of the early Jazz giants. But the "covers" themselves were conduits disseminating the music even deeper into the mainstream U.S. culture, even though created as an expression of political and socio-economic domination.

The historic basis and continuing reference of African and Afro-American music is the voice. And always, not just the sound of the voice but the *spoken* word is the communicating expression. Even in the drum, the percussive form was a mouth, which *talked*. Blues, Jazz maintain the word as, Pres said, "a story" being told.

Louis Armstrong and Bessie Smith were the most influential singers in U.S. popular culture of the early part of the 20th century. (Just as Michael Jackson and Whitney Houston are today, though now these two are even more dominating because they are probably freer socially.) Of course, Louis Armstrong was also the greatest instrumental influence the music has seen.

Both Bessie and Louis are classic Blues artists and setters of the standard of how the Blues voice, now multi-instrumentalized, is drawn into the Jazz expression. They are the double barrels of Afro-American musical culture blasting across the early U.S. (and international) Twenties.

Naming black artists and white artists shaped by these two, singularly or together, is itself the subject of yet another long essay, though there have been hundreds already.

The fact of U.S. segregation and discrimination, the national oppression that followed slavery, meant that one of the most definitive and shaping aspects of U.S. culture, Afro-American culture, would be a ubiquitous emotional and stylish model or mode of American cultural expression; but the social repression of the Afro-American people, ironically, *limited* the extent to which the whole essence and body of that culture could be stunted (as *expression*) by U.S. commercialism.

As Finklestein states, commercialism "tended to force the musician into the status of a hired craftsman whose work was not supposed to bear his own individuality, free thought and exploitation of the art, but was made to order, to a standardized pattern" (Op. cit, p.158).

The irony is that the post-slavery Afro-American people were excluded from the mainstream of U.S. socio-economic organization. The marginalized existence of a people segregated from that mainstream, socio-economically discriminated against, as aspects of national oppression, was made more blatant because of its distinct racial character.

Afro-American music, because of its exclusion as a social product yet ultimate exploitation as a commercial object, could influence the whole of the musical (and social and aesthetic) culture of the U.S. and even be subjected to mind-boggling dilutions and obscene distortions; yet the source, the Afro-American people, was spared the full "embrace" of commercial American absorption because of their marginalized existence as Americans. This is reflected, as well, *in* the music, which is an expression of Afro-American life, hence a register itself of the pain and struggle that it exists as the expression of, as that beauty continuing to exist and be seen even more stunningly because of the ugliness which surrounds and limits it.

Armstrong influenced trumpet players, singers, drummers, saxophone players, &c. &c. Bing Crosby spoke often of his debt to Armstrong! (see the film *New Orleans,* where Bing plays the leader of "the best hot white band in New Orleans.") Billie Holiday tells us she was shaped by Bessie and Louis, listening to their records in a Ho Ho Ho house.

Frank Sinatra sings a song, *Lady Day*, and has often spoken of his debt to Billie Holiday. The whole panorama of U.S. musical culture, if we look at each of its "white stars" of popular music, shows that the general or even specific personal impetus is Afro-American music.

In the Twenties, Finklestein says, "The beloved American popular music of song and dance is a certain first of the Negro people, and then of the Jewish, Irish, Italian and other minority peoples."

The history of American popular music since the 19th century has moved on the impact and influence of Afro-American music and its songs and singers. Increasingly, into the 20th century, as imperialism and monopoly control of the music business intensified, many of the newer immigrants, the Jews, Italians and Irish, who, as Finklestein says, were stalwart contributors to American popular music, which increasingly carried a blues and jazz sound, were nevertheless pulled further into American commercialism at the expense of their art.

It was the price for assimilation into America, to give up that part of you that was "UnAmerican," especially that part that included the dissent of the first generations of struggling Jewish, Italian and Irish immigrants.

Just as James Weldon Johnson's hero in *Autobiography of an Ex-Colored Man* says at the tragic denouement of the novel, in which he is "passing" for white, "I have given up my heritage for a mess of pottage."

From the Jazz Age onward, and certainly today, there has been a significant change from what had been before, in minstrelsy and the caricatures of Chandler Harris and the like, primarily a ridicule of the Afro-American people and culture. For instance, there are thousands of artifacts, teapots, salt and pepper shakers, flour labels, all kinds of products, Uncle This, Aunt That, that still bear this legacy of racist ridicule of black people as their forms. This kind of poison continues as D. W. Griffith or Eddie Cantor and Al Jolson.

But then Jolson becomes not just a black-face mammy yodeler but "The Jazz Singer"; Benny Goodman "King of Swing"; Elvis Presley, "The King"; Bruce Springsteen, "The Boss"; and The Rolling Stones, "The Best Rock & Roll Band In The World!"

The 20th century saw minstrelsy "change into" a white style! Afro-American culture was now sufficiently accessible "within" the mainstream (or visible at its margins because it had so long been pimped and caricatured and imitated). From NORK and ODJB through Beiderbecke and the so-called "Chicago Style," "Dixieland," there arose a "white style." Actually, it was a reAmericanization of Afro-American musical culture that usually diluted and distorted it, depending on the performers.

By the late Thirties there were white swing bands to cover the Ellingtons, Basies, Hendersons, Luncefords, as a "white style" of jazz, &c., no longer minstrelsy. Except that the racial exclusion and repression of the black originals made the white styles bloodless replicas, because there is no sharp dialectical flow of equally responding registration, only drop and cop.

But by the same token there was still a genuinely engaging and meaningful cultural product created by the "ReAmericanization" process. Certainly the most interesting handling of Blues and Jazz by other than the original creators can be seen in American popular music.

We cannot be speaking of the present 1990s' plundering of the Sixties Motown treasure chest to plagiarize real lives in order to justify the nothingness of racist intellectual pretension and falsity. This is no better than open pimping by the corporations, using everything from The Supremes to Smoky Robinson to sell their soap.

But the Irving Berlins, Johnny Mercers, George Gershwins, Harold Arlens, Leonard Bernsteins, &c. &c., and Jerome Kerns, Cole

Porters, &c., &c., have created a creditable body of Blues and Jazz-derived American popular music which, especially when rekindled by the Blues and Jazz players themselves, becomes pure gold. A Classical American Music. Just think of the American popular song in the hands of the historical Blues and Jazz players, from Louis Armstrong to Duke Ellington to Billie Holiday to Charlie Parker to John Coltrane. (Dig, for instance, the trip Trane takes "My Favorite Things" on. Miles Davis would take it right to the fringes of sanity with stuff like "Surrey With The Fringe On The Top"!)

So that American popular music exemplified by its obvious popularity (discounting the commercialism which seeks to reduce any art to a packaged predictability of painless profit), from the Twenties white Jazz popularizers to the white pop composers of the Thirties and Forties until the second explosion in "white" American culture of the Fifties, Rock & Roll and the coronation of the new white "King" Elvis Presley; not only had minstrelsy become a white style, but now whites could pretend to be the original creators. (But even in the Fifties, Metronome's All Stars were almost all white!)

And today "Hip Hop," with its Vanilla Ices, Young Black Teenagers (Yes, Virginia, they're all white too!) &c., or the Madonnas and Michael Boltons (but only a little more so than the Beatles, Stones, Osmonds, Chet Bakers, or Barbara Streisands, or Aretha, oh yeh!) shows how the same trend goes on.

The musical culture of the whole American people becomes by open affirmation (exploitation, imitation, deception aside) at base, in large part, the creation of the Afro-American people. Like chocolate in a bottle of milk. Yeh, it is still milk, but why is it that color?

AMIRI BARAKA is an African-American poet, playwright and essayist who has evolved over the past two decades as a leading Marxist-Leninist-Maoist cultural spokesman. His many volumes of poetry, including *Selected Poems* (Morrow), as well as his essays and plays, are internationally known. He writes for *Unity & Struggle*, lives in Newark, N.J., and teaches at SUNY.

This essay first appeared in *DuMagazine*, Switzerland.

MARGARET RANDALL

Notes on the New Female Voice*

In 1981 June Jordan opened her essay, "Many Rivers to Cross," with
this sentence: "When my mother killed herself I was looking for a
job."[1] Quickly she sets a picture of a young African-American mother,
jobless, and recently abandoned by a husband she has seen through
school. Then she zeroes in on the events surrounding her mother's
suicide and her father's inability even to determine whether or not
his wife is dead: his fear, ineptitude, and vindictive rage. This
extraordinary piece concludes:

> And really it was to honor my mother that I did
> fight with my father, that man who could not tell the
> living from the dead. And really it is to honor...all the
> women I love, including myself, that I am working for
> the courage to admit the truth that Bertolt Brecht has
> written..."It takes courage to say that the good were
> defeated not because they were good, but because they
> were weak." I cherish the mercy and the grace of women's
> work. But I know there is new work that we must
> undertake as well: that new work will make defeat
> detestable to us. That new women's work will mean we
> will not die trying to stand up: we will live that way:
> standing up.[2]

Central to this new[3] women's work is—I will argue—a new
writing, a female voice. A body of U.S. literature which is *qualitatively*
different, as well as (obviously) written and published in
quantitatively greater volume than writing by women has ever been
written or published before.

This question of whether or not there is a woman's—or female—
voice is not a new one; nonetheless, against growing evidence that
there is, it continues to be asked. As with related questions (is there a
woman's eye, a woman's musical score or symphony conducting, a
woman's art in general?) we have on the one hand an increasing body

*This piece has been changed since its original publication—editor

264

of first-rate work to which we may go for the answer. On the other hand, mainstream high school and university literature courses, and the traditional anthologies and literary reviews, are as one-sidedly male (and white and heterosexist and elite) as they ever were.[4] One must necessarily conclude that those who continue to turn their backs on this work are doing so, intentionally or not, out of a prejudice that has nothing to do with literature.

The Jordan quote exemplifies something important about the new female voice, about the work of such women as June Jordan and Meridel LeSueur, Jane Cooper, Maxine Hong Kingston, Toni Morrison, Adrienne Rich, Audre Lorde, Alice Walker, Marge Piercy, Leslie Marmon Silko, Joy Harjo, Sonia Sanchez, Judy Grahn, Sandra Cisneros, Judith McDaniel. (How absurd to make lists that will forever be partial at best, at worst insulting in their omissions.) What this writing offers is centuries of silent honing powerfully articulated at last, a courageous externalization of the inner map *truly connected to the world out there.* Among its many characteristics are its discussion of body parts and functions far less encoded than in the past, its unselfconscious risk-taking, and a craft by any standard as good as the best. A retrieval of our history has made it possible for us to tap into a great communal re-memory, and there is a dialectical bonding: of women back through time, across the current man-made barriers, and out into a future we envision in our work. Additionally, because of the challenges within the feminist movement, many women writers have been abler than their male counterparts to speak from a history that recognizes difference, that crosses barriers of class, race, ethnicity, age, sexual identity, and physical ability.

For all these reasons, strong women (women who are not victims but who succeed in living) are finally solidly represented among our literary protagonists. Young women, those just beginning to read, may now select their literary role models from a much healthier canon. This hasn't always been the case. I think it's important to stop and ask what it meant for women writing (and for people reading) that *The Girl* by Meridel LeSueur remained unpublishable for twenty years because, as one editor after another told its author, "A book about a woman who is not a victim just won't sell."[5]

LeSueur, who was born with the century and died at the end of 1996, speaks with authority about a woman's creativity in the context of aging:

> [N]ow in the experience of ripening and even decaying
> and dropping the seed, it seems to me more
> inflammatory to have had communication of a superior
> intensity and frankness. It would be great if there could
> be creative hospices, not for the dying but for the
> ripening. I read somewhere that after seventy you no
> longer pass through the astrological houses but are freed
> from them and enter the galactic imagery which is
> planetary in nature and very strong. Some people die of
> its intensity, unable to entertain it (possibly alone). We
> need some kind of monasteries of being together, not to
> miss this extraordinary crop of the last season or the
> culminating protein memory.[6]

She often referred to growing old as a process of decay, in which the cells in decomposition give off a phosphorescence, light.

Through its body of work, the new female voice addresses the larger social issues with a power only the most intimate vision can bring (showing how a coherent movement from the general to the particular reflects the fact that, truly, the personal is political and the political personal). Standard textbooks to the contrary, women writers (working women) have rarely lived in ivory towers, and so we reject ivory-tower notions of art. Our writing involves the breakdown of formal genre divisions through the offering up of the ordinary female voice. We claim this voice as literature by mixing, or choosing to disregard, the traditionally male-imposed categorizations of essay, criticism, novel, and perhaps even poetry (the genres where men are said to excel), and private journals and letters (long thought to be the domain of women). Our voice is a revelation of our female self, calling forth a profound degree of risk (lesbian narrative, work by women with disabilities, incest and abuse stories). This work teaches a willingness, indeed a need, in our commodity-oriented society, to place process over product.

This new chorus of female voices has also opened doors for male writers, some of whom, finding their own traditions uncomfortable or alienating, have explored new territories influenced by women's vision. As certain women's work has broken with stereotypical ideas about the "female domain" in literature, a number of men have been freed to write out of the so-called female modes: emotion, sensitivity, re-memory, concern with process.

I prefer "female voice" to "women's writing." On philosophical principle I do not believe these new frontiers can be explored only by women, just as I do not believe only women can be feminists (or that all women are feminists simply by virtue of gender). Necessarily, however, women are the ground-breakers here; men fear they have too much to lose, and in the short term indeed they do. We of course vastly outnumber men in our explorations of the territory. Many so-called minority writers or writers of color (both labels suffer from the erroneous vision that views only white men as central, everyone else as *other*) express themselves out of an allied, if not always identical, consciousness. Clearly feminism, as philosophy and experience, has signaled the particular literary renovation that I call the female voice.

As school children, most of us—girls and boys—were urged to "write about what you know." But the male province was the standard against which all else was judged. We were already being taught to see ourselves as *other*, long before we were conscious of the imposed condition. As we grew, it was easy to see whose work was noticed, encouraged, published, reviewed. And so (prefeminist consciousness particularly), we emulated the men, glowed at the "praise" *you write like a man* or *you write as well as a man.*

For the past two decades, with notable forerunners, women writers have come into our own, writing about what we know, and—slowly, painfully—writing ourselves into the center. We have very literally had to make a place for our words on the pages of a literature that judged us trivial, overly emotional, gossipy, infantile, minor.

> Rainer had written my requiem—
> a long, beautiful poem, and calling me his friend.
> I was *your* friend but in the dream you didn't say a word.
> In the dream his poem was like a letter
> to someone who has no right
> to be there but must be treated gently, like a guest
> who comes on the wrong day.
> Clara, why don't I dream of you?...

This is from Adrienne Rich's compelling "Paula Becker to Clara Westhoff."[7] The passage speaks eloquently about how our history has been distorted. What has come down to us are the words of the great male poet (Rainer Maria Rilke). But Rich, speaking in Becker's voice, tells us where the friendship really was. She mourns her friend's voicelessness even as she reveals the relationships that engendered such silencing. A skewed history erases even dreams.

Many of the most powerful U.S. women writers look to our foremothers for sustenance and voice; poets like Muriel Rukeyser, Jane Cooper, Audre Lorde, Adrienne Rich, Paula Gunn Allen, and others have researched the histories of those women who have gone before us (Mmanthatisi, Rosa Luxemburg, Molly Brant, Sojourner Truth, Paula Modersohn-Becker, Willa Cather, Ethel Rosenberg). We have retrieved role models. And we have insisted on speaking in overlay; with their voices stopped in time and with our own, historically erased because they were silenced, sharpened today because they lived. Some of the best among us assume those women's voices, giving them back in rich and varied ways.[8] This actual taking on of another's history/memory, speaking in it, breathing it filtered through a fierce redemption enraged by centuries of denial, is undoubtedly one important component of the new female literature.

Important moments in this ongoing process have been Magda Bogin's discovery that the female troubadours did in fact write differently from their better-known male counterparts:[9] Linda Brent's autobiography;[10] Blanche Cook's gift of Crystal Eastman[11] and her biography of Eleanor Roosevelt;[12] Barbara Sicherman's use of Alice Hamilton's letters to weave a plausible and highly readable correspondence-biography of the latter's life;[13] Georgia O'Keeffe's letters;[14] Diane Arbus's personal journals;[15] Evelyn Fox Keller on Barbara McClintock,[16] and teacher/writers like Audre Lorde writing about themselves.[17]

Among the writers inviting us to look into their own lives, an autobiographical work, *Assata,* by Assata Shakur, is not only wrenchingly and beautifully written, but speaks from an experience shared by many, though too rarely translated into literature.[18] It is a particular class, race, and gender experience, that of an African-American woman in prison for a crime she has not committed, who preserves herself against terrifying odds, escapes, and makes a gift of the telling. This woman is at once unique and representative of all women of color. This prisoner is at once herself and the inhabitant of a hideously extreme, profoundly compressed version of the prison that has been the female condition for centuries. I want to quote at length from this book. In the opening paragraph:

"There were lights and sirens. Zayd was dead. My mind knew that Zayd was dead. The air was like cold glass. Huge bubbles rose and burst. Each one felt like an explosion in my chest. My mouth tasted like blood and dirt. The car spun around me and then something like sleep overtook me. In the background i could hear what sounded like gunfire. But i was fading and dreaming. Suddenly, the door flew open and i felt myself being dragged out onto the pavement. Pushed and punched, a foot upside my head, a kick in the stomach. Police were everywhere. One had a gun to my head. "Which way did they go?" he was shouting. "Bitch, you'd better open your goddamn mouth or i'll blow your goddamn head off!"[19]

We are on the scene of a capture, a contemporary version of the capture of Africans for the slave trade almost two centuries ago. As the book unfolds, we understand that the brutality of this initial scene perfectly reflects the fact that these officers of the "law" are guardians of a racist system attacking a vulnerable African-American woman, a woman whose history has taught her that there will be neither hope of, nor recourse to, justice. Shakur's consistent naming of the state and its representatives with lower case letters, while reserving upper case for those who struggle (except, interestingly, when she speaks of herself), makes language responsible to choice. Near the end of the book she chooses to give us this climactic moment, very much a woman's moment, very much a mother's:

"My mother brings my daughter to see me at the clinton correctional facility for Women in new jersey, where i had been sent from alderson. I am delirious. She looks so tall. I run up to kiss her. She barely responds...I go over and try to hug her. In a hot second she is all over me. All i can feel are these little four-year-old fists banging away at me. Every bit of her force is in those punches, they really hurt. I let her hit me until she is tired. "It's all right," i tell her. "Let it all out." She is standing in front of me, her face contorted with anger, looking spent. She backs away and leans against the wall. "It's okay," i tell her. "Mommy understands." "You're not my mother," she screams.

"You're not my mother and I hate you." I feel like crying
too. I know she is confused…I try to pick her up. She
knocks my hand away. "You can get out of here if you
want to," she screams. "You just don't want to." "No i
can't," i say weakly…look helplessly at my mother. Her
face is choked with pain. "Tell her to try to open the bars."
My daughter goes over to the barred door that leads to
the visiting room. She pulls and she punches. She yanks
and she hits and she kicks the bars until she falls on the
floor, a heap of exhaustion. I go over and pick her up. I
hold and rock and kiss her. There is a look of resignation
on her face that i can't stand. We spend the rest of the
visit talking and playing quietly on the floor. When the
guard says the visit is over, i cling to her for dear life. She
holds her head high, and her back straight as she walks
out of the prison. She waves goodbye to me, her face
clouded and worried, looking like a little adult. I go back
to my cage and cry until i vomit. I decide that it's time to
leave.[20]

"It's time to leave." Yes it is. Shakur has written as gut-wrenching
an exposé of an attack on the mother/daughter relationship as I have
ever read. It is not lost on us that those responsible for this common
travesty are the same who loudly proclaim they protect the
sacredness of life. Witness this fragment very close to the book's final
lines:

"Freedom. I couldn't believe that it had really happened,
that the nightmare was over, that finally the dream had
come true. I was elated. Ecstatic. But I was completely
disoriented. Everything was the same, yet everything was
different. All of my actions were super intense. I
submerged myself in patterns and textures, sucking in
smells and sounds as if each day was my last. I felt like a
voyeur. I forced myself not to stare at the people whose
conversations i strained to overhear. Suddenly, i was
flooded with the horrors of prison and every disgusting
experience that somehow i had been able to minimize
while inside. I had developed the ability to be patient,
calculating, and completely self-controlled. For the most
part, i had been incapable of crying. I felt rigid, as though

chunks of steel and concrete had worked themselves into
my body. I was cold. I strained to touch my softness. I
was afraid that prison had made me ugly.[21]

Although the above is clearly about a particular instance—
Shakur's escape from brutal captivity and her arrival in a land of
freedom—it is also a powerful metaphor for many women's lives,
lives that would seem (from appearance) to be far less dramatic than
hers. I would ask, however, that the reader try the above lines out on
such common women's experience as incest, rape, battery, or even
the less crisis-oriented everyday female oppression. Lines like
"Suddenly I was flooded with the horrors of...every disgusting
experience that somehow i had been able to minimize while inside,"
"I had developed the ability to be patient, calculating, and completely
self-controlled," "i had been incapable of crying," "i felt rigid," "i was
cold," "[it] made me [feel] ugly."

Many new women writers have looked beyond the limits of the
North American and/or western literary scene in their exploration
of a whole new genre: testimony. As women listening to women, the
pioneering works of Latin Americans and others of the so-called
Third World have been important.[22] I'm talking about contemporary
classics like *Let Me Speak!* and *I, Rigoberta Menchú.*[23] More recently
we have read works by Filipina, African, Middle Eastern, Australian,
and New Zealand women. These moving books encourage us in the
art of listening. If we can do so, we will hear voices that have
previously been ignored, silenced, despised.

Some of us have also learned to listen in a particularly useful way
to the multiple parts of our own retrieved identity. Such is the case
for Gloria Anzaldúa, who explores her many-layered reality as a
Mexican/American/female/lesbian in an extraordinary rediscovery
of language and meaning called *Borderlands/La frontera.*[24]
Straightforward narrative, poetic prose, and poetry combine English,
Spanish, Spanglish, and Nahuatl words to reveal a new sense of self,
one which, because of the existence of this book, now belongs to us
all.

In this collective retrieval we have also repossessed pages of sheer
beauty, forgotten while lesser works by men written in the same
period and place continue to receive endless acclaim. I'm thinking
particularly of Hemingway's "great white hunter" vision of Africa, as
compared with Beryl Markham's *West With the Night.* Both

Hemingway and Markham were foreigners on African soil, although she lived and worked there for years while he made occasional visits. His books have become classics; it took the explosion propelled by the women's movement to bring hers to the surface:

"Did you read Beryl Markham's book, *West With the Night*? I knew her fairly well in Africa and never would have suspected that she could and would put pen to paper except to write in her flyer's log book [sic]. As it is, she has written so well, and marvelously well, that I was completely ashamed of myself as a writer..." This is Hemingway himself, describing the prose of a woman previously all but lost to literature![25]

I have held hands
with fear;

We have gone steady
together.

Sorrow has been
my mate;
We have been bed-
companions.

The days of my night
have been long.

They have stretched
to eternity.
Yet I have outlived
them. And so shall you.

"I Have Held Hands with Fear" is by Mitzi Kornetz. Out of a poetry anthology? No. I have taken this poem from the chapter called "Cancer" in *Ourselves, Growing Older*, the new self-help compendium from The Boston Women's Healthbook Collective.[26] Women have taken our literature out of the academic texts and coffee-table artifacts and used it as well in books on health, exercise, dealing with cancer, addictions, incest, dying, and other difficult areas of life. And it has not seemed important to us to limit our field to a chosen few. In our lives and in our publications we welcome the contributions of women who might not define themselves primarily as writers, but whose writing speaks to us:

> He lets up the pressure for a second. "Mommy!" I scream. The door opens. She is here. The light from the hallway is bright; I am safe. In one thousand seven hundred and fifty seven days I will be sixteen years old. "What did you do that for?" he shouts. "This has nothing to do with her." "Mommy," I cry. Her arms are folded across her chest. All I can ask is that she rescue me. I cannot ask her for comfort. "Kate," she says. "You shouldn't upset your father…"

These are a few lines from "Like the Hully-Gully But Not So Slow" by Anne Finger. It's only one of dozens of nearly uniformly excellent pieces of poetry and prose in *With the Power of Each Breath: A Disabled Women's Anthology.*[27] Testimonial writing by women with disabilities,[28] prostitutes,[29] addicts and codependents,[30] incest and abuse survivors,[31] lesbians and their mothers[32]—these comprise a body of literature, not simply a collection of first-person accounts, how-to manuals, or scientific theses. When works by prostitutes or writers with disabilities are legitimized as literature, readers (as well as the authors themselves) are empowered to push through heavy curtains of fear, self-doubt, and immobility.

The women's movement taught us how silenced and hidden from us our role models have been. We have founded and sustained women's presses and magazines[33] not simply to publish ourselves (an overriding concern of the largely male-dominated small press renaissance of the Fifties and Sixties), but to make available this heritage as well. And so we have retrieved our great classics, Zora Neale Hurston's *Their Eyes Were Watching God*[34] and Agnes Smedley's *Daughter of Earth,*[35] to mention only two of the most extraordinary. Classics by any standard, yet in most of our universities still not considered "great books," nor even a part of the standard curriculum, basic reading on a contemporary U.S. literature syllabus.

There is immense variety in this new women's literature. Fantasy is explored in titles like Sally Miller Gearheart's *Wanderground.*[36] Ursula K. LeGuin is only one of a host of women who write science fiction.[37] A feminist interpretation of the natural world can be found in work by writers like Susan Griffin.[38] Anne Cameron's books explore spirituality and traditional women's wisdom.[39] Spiritual and political connections are made in such classics as Marge Piercy's *Woman on the Edge of Time*.[40] Making class/race/gender connections is often, in fact, an essential quality (condition) of this new writing.

> "Why " is not "how"
> is not a recital of physical causes
> physical effects
> it is meaning
>
> The bullet pierced her flesh
> because a finger pressed a trigger
> & she was in the way is "how"
>
> Why that gun was there at all
> why she was in front of it
> why that policeman's finger pressed the trigger
>
> not muscles but years are behind the answer
> not reflexes
>
> people…

In this poem, called "Facts,"[41] Susan Sherman deals with the mesmerizing media hype lulling us daily in an attempt to make us think that things are not what they seem, so that *we will not believe we are who we are*. Sherman addresses the way in which *how* is passed off as *why*, even in this country's most interpretive journalism. As women we must do battle simply to reclaim our history, our memory, ourselves. The classist, racist, sexist, and heterosexist media message, in the United States in the Eighties, is technologically advanced to the point where our very identities are jeopardized. Women are creating a literature that attempts to center us in all our multiplicity of mirrors.

> Home once again, I walked out alone
> nearly every day that first week. Or:
> still floating just above my body,
> I watched me walking out alone. The eighth day
> I met my mother, dead eight years.

As she walked toward me I peered
into her face. She was crying and smiling
at the same time. I had questions
to ask her but we did not speak.
I wanted to know how I could go on
living with so much shame:

I mean
with the memory of the children sitting
at their desks in the school that was only
a roof. Those bright questioning eyes
welcomed me, tested the cut of my blouse
and hair, welcomed my foreignness. Last year
they huddled in ditches as mortars
shelled their village for twelve days.
Seven died. I helped buy the bullets...

Judith McDaniel is dealing here with her own roots, with her decision to take risks, and with what she perceives as her relationship to events in Central America. McDaniel has been speaking out of the new female voice for as long as she's been writing. Her novel, *Winter Passage*, is about relationships between women. *Metamorphosis* is a collection of poems written about the experience of recovering from alcoholism. The above fragment is from a poem called "Dangerous Memory," from her book, *Sanctuary, A Journey.*[42]

A finely woven tapestry of essay, interview, poetry, poetic prose, and journal-writing, *Sanctuary* crosses not only the boundaries of literary genre but those of "personal" and "political" concerns as well. A powerful message in this type of work is that the traditional genre divisions are arbitrary at best. The female voice has, I believe, spoken to the problem of form and content in particularly relevant ways. Tracing this to feminist explorations of emotion/reason (and other sexual stereotyping) isn't difficult.

So many of our writers are prolific and at ease in a variety of genres: we have an Alice Walker, whose novels, short stories, essays, and poems are equally powerful. We have a Marge Piercy, who is as fine a novelist as she is a poet; a June Jordan, whose political essays sing right along with her verse. But we do not define the new female voice through "stars" alone. Indeed, our refusal to do so is itself an important part of our commentary upon it.

Our work is peopled by bodies, not by fragmented pieces of ourselves rearranged by those who have crafted a male literature (often resembling the world of advertising). Our bodies age and come in different shapes. They have "unsightly" hair, odors, and sagging flesh. And they are learning, painfully, to feel. The ways in which women write about our bodies, reclaiming our total physical selves, inform the feminist voice more powerfully, perhaps, than any other single feature of our work.

More precise definitions include a repossession of history/ memory/self, an attention to and an honoring of process, a gender, race, and class-conscious ear. We are concerned with stories, the stories that have been told outside literature for years. We know how important it is to reclaim the ordinary voice. We make corrections and search for the multiple faces of a new creative vision: one that insists on a world with everyone in it. Women have also begun to produce knowledgeable compendiums of our own literature. A particularly fine anthology of new women's poetry is *Early Ripening: American Women's Poetry Now*, edited by Marge Piercy.[43] The following is from her introduction:

> Women are writing immensely exciting, approachable, rich, funny, and moving poetry that can speak to a wider readership than it usually gets. Women are writing much of the best poetry being written, way more than half of it I believe, but remain poorly represented in anthologies, textbooks, reading series, prize lists, awards and every other institution controlled by white men who like the way things are presently run just fine. Women are still mostly read by women; men remain under the delusion that the poetry women write will not speak to them. I think that means that many men miss out on poetry that could get them far more involved than what they're inclined to read, or more likely, inclined to bow the head at and pass by: that's high culture, may it rest in peace.[44]

While the proverbial male anthologies have almost always been homogeneous (read: white, male, middle-class, academic, heterosexist, safe), this volume of women's work is homogeneous only in its literary excellence (remember the plaintive cry, "We would have published more women if we could only have found any good enough…!") There are many African-American, Latina, Native-American, and Asian-American, as well as white, women poets represented in Piercy's volume. There are both previously unpublished and well-known authors. There are lesbian as well as heterosexual women; poets who write out of a feminist perspective and others who simply write as women: poets who are not afraid of anger, physicality, process. I would like to close by quoting in full one poem from this anthology. This one, like much of the new female writing anthologized by Piercy, is strong in the language of our image. It speaks of a woman in the singular, and in so doing speaks about us all. It has memory and vision, it takes risks. It is Joy Harjo's "The Woman Hanging from the Thirteenth Floor Window":

> She is the woman hanging from the 13th floor
> window. Her hands are pressed white against the
> concrete molding of the tenement building. She
> hangs from the 13th floor window in east Chicago,
> with a swirl of birds over her head. They could
> be a halo, or a storm of glass waiting to crush her.
>
> She thinks she will be set free.
>
> The woman hanging from the 13th floor window
> on the east side of Chicago is not alone.
> She is a woman of children, of the baby, Carlos,
> and of Margaret, and of Jimmy who is the oldest.
> She is her mother's daughter and her father's son.
> She is several pieces between the two husbands
> she has had. She is all the women of the apartment
> building who stand watching her, watching themselves.
>
> When she was young she ate wild rice on scraped down
> plates in warm wood rooms. It was in the farther
> north and she was the baby then. They rocked her.
> She sees Lake Michigan lapping at the shores of
> herself. It is a dizzy hole of water and the rich
> live in tall glass houses at the edge of it. In some
> places Lake Michigan speaks softly, here, it just sputters
> and butts itself against the asphalt. She sees
> other buildings just like hers. She sees other

women hanging from many-floored windows
counting their lives in the palms of their hands
and in the palms of their children's hands.

She is the woman hanging from the 13th floor window
on the Indian side of town. Her belly is soft from
her children's birth, her worn Levis swing down below
her waist, and then her feet, and then her heart.
She is dangling.

The woman hanging from the 13th floor window hears voices.
They come to her in the night when the lights have gone
dim. Sometimes they are little cats mewing and scratching
at the door, sometimes they are her grandmother's voice,
and sometimes they are gigantic men of light whispering
to her to get up, to get up, to get up. That's when she
wants to have another child to hold onto in the night, to
be able to fall back into dreams.
And the woman hanging from the 13th floor window
hears other voices. Some of them scream out from below
for her to jump, they would push her over. Others cry
softly from the sidewalks, pull their children up like
flowers and gather them into their arms. They would help
her, like themselves.

But she is the woman hanging from the 13th floor window,
and she knows she is hanging by her own fingers, her
own skin, her own thread of indecision.

She thinks of Carlos, of Margaret, of Jimmy.
She thinks of her father, and of her mother.
She thinks of all the women she has been, of all
the men. She thinks of the color of her skin, and
of Chicago streets, and of waterfalls and pines.
She thinks of moonlight nights, and of cool spring storms.
Her mind chatters like neon and northside bars.
She thinks of the 4 a.m. lonelinesses that have folded
her up like death, discordant, without logical and
beautiful conclusion. Her teeth break off at the edges.
She would speak.

The woman hangs from the 13th floor window crying for
the lost beauty of her own life. She sees the
sun falling west over the gray plane of Chicago.
She thinks she remembers listening to her own life
break loose, as she falls from the 13th floor
window on the east side of Chicago, or as she
climbs back up to claim herself again.

—Hartford, Connecticut
Winter 1988

MARGARET RANDALL is particularly interested in women and creativity,
and the ways they intersect. She lived for almost a quarter century in Latin
America and when she returned to her homeland in the mid eighties, the
U.S. government invoked the McCarran-Walter Immigration and
Nationality Act and ordered her deported because of the opinions expressed
in her books. Supported by writers, artists and others, she won her case in
1989. Among her most recent titles are: *This Is About Incest, Gathering Rage:
The Failure of Twentieth Century Revolutions to Develop a Feminist Agenda,
Sandino's Daughters Revisited, The Price You Pay: The Hidden Cost of
Women's Relationship to Money, Hunger's Table: Women, Food & Politics,
Coming Up for Air,* and *Where They Left You for Dead / Halfway Home.*
Forthcoming from Rutgers University Press is *When I Look Into the Window
I See You: Women, Terror and Resistance.* She lives outside Albuquerque, New
Mexico.

This essay is reprinted from *Walking to the Edge: Essays of Resistance*, edited
by Sheila Walsh, published by South End Press.

Notes:

1. "Many Rivers to Cross," in *On Call, Political Essays*, June Jordan (Boston: South End Press, 1985).

2. Ibid., p.26.

3. By "new" I mean women's literature written in the period roughly between 1970 and 1990.

4. A notable exception is *The Heath Anthology of American Literature*, Volumes I and II, edited by a group of scholars headed by Paul Lauter (Lexington, MA: D.C. Heath and Co., 1990). The first volume covers the colonial period and early nineteenth century; the second, the twentieth century.

5. *The Girl*, Meridel LeSueur, (Albuquerque, NM: West End Press, revised edition 1990). LeSueur's work was in fact silenced almost in its entirety when she was subpoenaed in the early Fifties by the House UnAmerican Activities Committee (HUAC). A byproduct of the McCarthy era, the activities of this congressional committee affected artistic freedom in this country in ways still being felt. Indeed, the censorship and self-censorship generated by that particularly dangerous phenomenon changed the course of U.S. artistic expression. LeSueur's work began to become available again when, in the early Seventies, she was rediscovered by the women's movement. West End Press published several of her books, and Feminist Press followed with what remains her most complete collection, *Ripening* (1982). LeSueur was born in 1900.

6. Meridel LeSueur, letter to author, dated "Last Sunday of March, 1990."

7. "Paula Becker to Clara Westhoff," in *The Fact of A Doorframe, Poems Selected and New, 1950-1984*, Adrienne Rich (New York: W.W. Norton and Co., 1981).

8. This assumption of women's voices from other historic moments has been a poetic practice exercised by North American poets Muriel Rukeyser, Jane Cooper, Adrienne Rich, Paula Gunn Allen, and others. It has also influenced the way women have approached the research and writing of the biographies of our foremothers. See especially *Voices of Women: 3 critics on 3 poets on 3 heroines*, by Martha Kearns, Diane Radycki, May Stevens, Muriel Rukeyser, Adrienne Rich, Jane Cooper, Kathe Kollwitz, Paula Modersohn-Becker, and Rosa Luxemburg, with an introductory essay by Lucy R. Lippard (New York: Midmarch Associates, 1980).

9. *The Women Troubadours*, Magda Bogin (New York: W.W. Norton and Co., 1980).

10. *Incidents in the Life of a Slave Girl*, by Linda Brent and edited by Lydia Maria Francis Child, was published during the author's life. A contemporary edition was made available by Harcourt Brace Jovanovich in 1973. More recently, a more complete edition, *Incidents in the Life of a Slave Girl Written by Herself*, was attributed to the real author, Harriet A. Jacobs (Cambridge, MA: Harvard University Press, 1987).

11. *Crystal Eastman on Women and Revolution*, ed. Blanche Wiesen Cook (New York: Oxford University Press, 1978).

12. Blanche Cook worked for a number of years on a biography of Eleanor Roosevelt. It combines Cook's meticulous historical research with her profoundly revealing feminist vision.

13. *Alice Hamilton, A Life in Letters*, Barbara Sicherman (Cambridge, MA: Harvard University Press, 1984).

14. Most recently in the catalog book for the traveling show, *Georgia O'Keefe, Art and Letters* (Washington, DC: National Gallery of Art, 1987).

15. In the 1972 *Aperture* collection of Diane Arbus's photographs, journal entries edited by Diane's daughter Doone. *Aperture* has recently reissued the collection.

16. *A Feeling for the Organism, The Life and Work of Barbara McClintock*, Evelyn Fox Keller (New York: W.H. Freeman, 1983).

17. See Audre Lorde's early biomythography *Zami, A new Spelling of My Name* (Freedom, CA: Crossing Press, 1982). More recent are *The Cancer Journals* and *A Burst of Light*. Among her books of poetry are *The Black Unicorn* and *Chosen Poems, Old and New. Sister Outsider* is an important book of essays.

18. *Assata, An Autobiography*, Assata Shakur (Westport, CT: Lawrence Hill & Co., 1987).

19. Ibid., p.3.

20. Ibid., pp.257-58.

21. Ibid., p.266.

22. Although I have sometimes continued to use the term Third World for more immediate reader comprehension, I would like to quote from a note with which June Jordan opens her book *On Call*: "Given that they were first to exist on the planet and currently make up the majority, the author will refer to that part of the population usually termed Third World as First World."

23. *Let Me Speak!* by Domitila Barrios de Chungara, as told to Moema Viezzer (New York: Monthly Review Books, 1978); and *I, Rigoberta Menchú, An Indian Woman in Guatemala*, ed. Elisabeth Burgos-Debray (London: Verso Editions, 1983). There have been a number of other such books of oral history of women in recent years, including: *Sandino's Daughters, Testimonies of Nicaraguan Women in Struggle*, Margaret Randall (Toronto; New Star Books, 1981); *Don't Be Afraid, Gringo—A Honduran Woman Speaks from the Heart*, ed. Medea Benjamin (San Francisco: Food First, 1987); and *Enough is Enough, Aboriginal Women Speak Out*, as told to Janet Silman (Toronto: The Women's Press, 1987).

24. *Borderlands/La Frontera*, Gloria Anzaldúa (San Francisco: Spinsters/Aunt Lute, 1987).

25. *West With the Night*, Beryl Markham (San Francisco: North Point Press, 1983).

26. *Ourselves, Growing Older*, ed. the Boston Women's Health Book Collective (New York: Simon & Schuster, 1987).

27. *With the Power of Each Breath*: *A Disabled Women's Anthology*, eds. Susan E. Browne, Debra Connors, and Nanci Stern (Pittsburgh, PA: Cleis Press, 1985).

28. I used *disabled* and then *differently abled* until I read E.J. Graff's letter in the January 1988 issue of *Sojourner*. She writes: "I prefer to think of myself as a woman with a disability, not a disabled woman. The former recognizes my handicap. The latter seems to define my entire being..." See also *With Wings: An Anthology of Literature by and about Women with Disabilities*, eds. Marsha Saxton and Florence Howe (New York: The Feminist Press at the City University of New York, 1986).

29. See *Sex Work, Writings by Women in the Sex Industry*, eds. Frederique Delacoste and Priscilla Alexander (Pittsburgh, PA: Cleis Press, 1987).

30. There are a great number of literary titles in this category, as well as many books by psychologists and others. A visit to a good women's bookstore or library should provide a wealth of material.

31. Among the titles in this category, I would recommend the novel *Searching for Spring*, Patricia Murphy (Tallahassee, FL: Naiad, 1987) and *This Is About Incest*, Margaret Randall (Ithaca, NY: Firebrand Books, 1987).

32. Lesbian literature—novels, short stories, poetry, essays—is much too broad a category to even begin a comprehensive listing here. A look in any good women's bookstore will reveal dozens of excellent titles.

33. Some of the important U.S. publishers of women's writing are Feminist Press, Firebrand, Naiad, Cleis, Spinsters/Aunt Lute, Seal, and Crossing. Although South End and West End are not women's presses, their feminist titles are worth noting. Among the feminist literary magazines are *Ikon, Sinister Wisdom, Heresies, Calyx, Conditions*, and *Thirteenth Moon*.

34. *Their Eyes Were Watching God*, Zora Neale Hurston (Urbana, IL: University of Illinois Press, 1978).

35. *Daughter of Earth*, Agnes Smedley (New York: The Feminist Press at the City University of New York, 1973).

36. *Wanderground*, Sally Miller Gearheart (Watertown, MA: Persephone Press, 1979).

37. Among Ursula K. LeGuin's many titles, the most important is *The Left Hand of Darkness* (New York: Ace Books, 1983).

38. Susan Griffin's *Woman and Nature: The Roaring Inside Her* (New York: Harper & Row) was ground-breaking. *Made from this Earth, An Anthology of Writings* (New York: Harper & Row, 1982) is a comprehensive introduction to her work; *Like the Iris of an Eye* is poetry.

39. Anne Cameron's books include *The Journey* (San Francisco: Spinsters/Aunt Lute), *Daughters of Copper Woman* (Vancouver, BC: Press Gang), *How Raven Freed the Moon* (Madeira Park, BC: Harbour Publishing), all prose; and *Earth Witch and the Annie Poems* (Harbour Publishing), poetry.

40. *Woman on the Edge of Time*, as well as most of Marge Piercy's other novels, is available from Ballantine/Fawcett (New York). *Circles on the Water* (New York: Knopf, 1982) is an anthology of her poetry books through *The Moon is Always Female*. Also see her new book of poems, *Available Light* (New York: Knopf, 1988).

41. "Facts," Susan Sherman, first published in *Ikon* Second Series 5/6, New York, 1986. It has been reprinted in *We Stand Our Ground*, Kimiko Hahn,

Gale Jackson, and Susan Sherman (New York: Ikon Books, 1988). This title is particularly interesting in that it presents the work of three women with a lengthy introductory conversation in which they speak of their origins, politics, feminism, literature, and writing.

42. See these books by Judith McDaniel: *Winter Passage* (San Francisco: Spinsters Ink, 1984), *November Woman* (Glen Falls, NY: Loft Press, 1983), *Metamorphosis: Reflections on Recovery* (Ithaca, NY: Firebrand Books, 1989), and *Sanctuary, A Journey* (Ithaca, NY: Firebrand, 1987).

43. *Early Ripening, American Women's Poetry Now*, ed. Marge Piercy (Methuen, 1988).

44. Ibid., p.2.

ARTURO ARIAS

The Meaning of Exile for the Contemporary Latin American Writer

In the United States, the concept of "exile," in that which concerns literature, has traditionally been associated with the notion of "spiritual exile." Such was the case with Hemingway's "Lost Generation" migrating to Paris, or Joyce's Stephen Dedalus, who needed to abandon the spiritual decay of Dublin in order to regenerate himself through his communion with continental Europe. Eliot's *Prufrock* and *The Waste Land* are also emblematic of this need to abandon philistine capitalism and seek a symbolic renewal, a contemporary "fisher-king" (Hitler and Mussolini, in Eliot's and Pound's cases, respectively).

However, for the Latin American writer, the issue has been a down-to-earth pragmatic one. If you stay in your own country and open your big mouth, your life is genuinely at risk. As such, it is simpler—and healthier—to give expression to one's grievances from the safe distance of another country.

In the United States, we have experienced symbolically the intolerance of monologism (prefigurer of totalitarianism) in catch-phrases such as "America, love it or leave it." However, their symbolic value has remained confined to the semantic level. Since McCarthyism, precious few people have been forced to actually "leave it."

The monological practice in everyday reality, however, has been all too real in most Latin American countries. There, a long list of dictators who make Saddam Hussein look gentle and meek have terrorized their citizens with the full blessing or indifference of the U.S. government and a large portion of its population.

Being fully aware that they can literally get away with murder, and that, until very recent times, most first-world nations would "look the other way" (and also knowing full well that the disappearance of a writer could only matter to other writers anyway, unless they succeed in becoming *causes célèbres,* as in Rushdie's or Solzhenitsyn's case), the local dictators have felt ample liberty to dispose of the voices that insist that the emperor has no clothes, to break the fingers of those who point the blame in the direction of the president-for-life.

A Latin American writer might be well known in his/her own country, and might even be a very good, sensitive writer. But if he/she is not published in English (or, second best-case scenario, in French and German), he/she still doesn't exist in the modern world. He/she is still an invisible man or an invisible woman as far as world opinion is concerned. It would even be so in Brazil, which takes its cues from New York or Paris and not its own neighboring countries.

Invisibility is highly perilous in authoritarian Latin American countries. It paves the way for what many feel are the inevitable options of a writer south of the border: death, prison or exile. A Latin American writer has the obligation to become famous (i.e. published in English, French or German) if he/she expects the death squads to think twice before striking.

However, given that breaking into the U.S. market in the Eighties and Nineties if your last name is not Márquez, Fuentes or Llosa is tantamount to hitting one's head continuously against a brick wall, the "fame option" is rather limited indeed. It has seldom been attained by a writer who did not begin publishing in the Sixties and who was not part of the so-called "boom" generation, which includes the authors previously mentioned (Isabel Allende might be the only significant exception; Manlio Argueta enjoyed immense popularity for a while, but his stock has gone down in recent years). Thus, exile becomes the least painful of the available alternatives. It certainly beats jail or death, and I would presuppose that it hurts less than betraying one's own principles and values and becoming the jester in the dictator's court, praising him (a dictator is always a "he") until you empty yourself of the minimum kindness and generosity necessary to transmute feelings into words that mean something to somebody else in a dialogic engagement.

Exile is painful. Still, it can be a very rewarding experience for a writer. On the one hand, one is forced—against one's will, most of the time—to separate oneself from the ambiance that nurtured one's own writing. One no longer sees, interacts on a daily basis with, the environment and the people whose everyday activities one needs to recreate in order to make sense of them for oneself. It becomes harder to affirm one's own existence by shoving people of color in the face of an indifferent planet that refuses systematically to acknowledge citizens south of the Tropic of Cancer as regular human beings.

One stops hearing the language that is sweet to the ear, the everyday enunciations, the very words, the very utterances that drip from the tip of the tongue and stain the empty page like a teardrop. One doesn't reproduce them on one's palate anymore. On the contrary. One is forced to enunciate strange sounds that regurgitate with consonants you had seldom pronounced together before. They constantly rebel and seek to come out from unexpected corners of the mouth. They betray your dignified need to fit into your new country. Your face turns purple as you read in your listener's eyes either the mockery at your pronunciation or the well-intentioned incomprehension that your utterances generate. How many times one wishes one could chop off one's tongue for disobeying one's intentions, like an old dog incapable of learning new tricks!

Books are made of words. Words are what marble is to the sculptors. To lack our words, the ones that conform to the edifice we need to build in order to live, is without a doubt the most painful experience of a writer in exile. Their loss is the most frightening threat outside of confronting death with one's eyes.

And then, you wander about the streets and discover all the other things which constitute your world, your cultural frame of reference. People eat strange foods, and at different hours from when your own people eat. They go to bed when your own people have finished a good digestion tempered by laughter and prepare themselves for a night on the town. They sit and talk, drink in hand, when your body demands the contortions of dance and music. They lucubrate rational, abstract thoughts in perfectly preordained logic when you desire the sensuality of poetry or simply to reach into your soul with the basic rhythms of your native music. They do not understand your jokes or allusions and you do not understand theirs, and you yearn to caress skin that doesn't have the color and consistency of skimmed milk.

If you did not know it before, you discover just how much all your world was pregnant with specific cultural referents, with specific symbolic connotations, and you discover just how much of all that has turned to ash, seeped through the cracks of the long voyage. You laugh about different things, cry about different things, are angered by different things, indifferent to indifferent things. You feel indeed like a stranger in a strange land, evoking echoes of lost voices to comfort your laughter in the dark before it turns to melancholic yearning for what never was, what never could be, because of the biological dictatorship that condemned you to be the citizen of a non-hegemonic country, of a nation that in the best-case scenario is a poor cousin in disrepute with the rich members of the global family.

Exile can spell loneliness, spiritual torment, guilt feelings, death wishes. It can point the way to self-destruction, and to the end of your creative life. And many an artist has ended his actively creative life by drowning his talent in alcoholic self-pity.

However, one can also look at it another way. Exile forces you to plunge into the unknown, to rise to its challenge, and to become a better person because you dared to break away from your self-induced comfortable habits and tackle the hurdles set before your feet.

Exile forces you into multilingualism, and multilingualism paves the way for multiculturalism. One becomes a global citizen to the degree that one can relate to and revel in at least two languages, at least two cultures. Multiculturalism opens the doors to tolerance, as the presence of "the other" becomes less threatening; and the relativism of the many who, while being culturally different, are all essentially human, tempers the passionate excesses which provincialize thought and sensibility.

Knowledge of another language illuminates the comprehension of your very own, gives it new layers of meaning, makes your own works infinitely more polysemic. Nabokovian trilingual puns become second nature.

But it's not only the language. It's also the distancing. By pulling away from the midst of your own society, you can understand it better. You are no longer immersed in its everyday battles, caught in the whirlwind of activities with no time to pause and think about what it all means, and whether it all makes sense or not. The pause you never made while living in the thick of it becomes a forceful meditation on the roads taken and not taken, and a more encompassing—perhaps more generous—synthesis of the reality of your own nation. This comprehension, facilitated by the perspective that only the luxury of distance offers, enables you to make, perhaps, a more lasting contribution to the attempt to cure the ills that afflict your nation. Probably this more sophisticated awareness makes a better writer out of you as well.

The fact that you are gone, that you cannot go back to visit, or can visit only very irregularly, also forces you to stretch your imagination to the limits. You have to remember how your native mountains look when the sun is shining on their sides; how the lakes glimmer on cloudy days; the rapid, short-paced walk of people carrying baskets full of fruits to market; the chattering of children playing soccer in the muddy streets. Your memory and your imagination are forced to cover that which you can no longer experience. You have to remember which stores line your favorite commercial street, and the terms people employ to signal endearment, distaste, or simply playful fun. It is an exercise for which a writer has to train as much as a long-distance runner, but one that can be as rewarding as winning the Olympic marathon. The stresses that imagination and memory are required to undergo, and the elasticity that ensues, give added depth to the writing, plunge you into depths you never dreamt you could withstand, enable you to sustain levels of coldness you never dreamt you could endure.

In other words, you become a better person and a better writer, a true spokesperson for your people in the world's arena and perhaps—though not necessarily—a decent human being as well.

The Nineties are very gradually lessening the direct threat that Latin American writers had to endure in the Seventies and Eighties in unforgiving regimes, such as those of Argentina, Chile, El Salvador or Guatemala. Nonetheless, given the economic and ecological crisis of the continent, there are no guarantees that the recent lessening of tension can be anything but an all-too-brief affair.

However, the world is beginning to operate in more planetary fashion, even if the balance is still unjustly tilted in favor of the First World, which now imposes its new global order without hindrance and without consulting those who have to endure it.

Nonetheless, the planetary tendencies are irreversible. In a world that will increasingly become multilingual, multicultural, in a world that might be peopled by a new cosmic race if human folly does not first eliminate life on the planet, the lessons learned—and transmitted through their works—by writers who have endured exile and survived it to become better people and better artists, might point the way for the future of all humanity. They might also point the way to the travails that will still have to be undergone in order to prevail in this universe.

ARTURO ARIAS is Director of Latin American Studies at the University of Redlands. Co-writer for the screenplay for the film *El Norte* (1984), his most recent novel in English is titled *After the Bombs* (Curbstone Press,1990). Author of five novels in Spanish—*Después de las bombas* (1979), *Itzam Na* (1981), *Jaguar en Llamas* (1989), *Los caminos de Paxil* (1991) and *Cascabel* (1998)—he is a winner of the Casa de las Americas Prize and the Anna Seghers Scholarship. In 1998 he published two books of criticism, one on Guatemalan 20thCentury fiction, *La identidad de la palabra*, (The Identity of the Word), and another on contemporary Central American fiction, *Gestos Ceremoniales* (Ceremonial Gestures). He is currently the President of the Latin American Studies Association (LASA).

This essay was first published in *San Francisco Review of Books.*

CSABA POLONY

A Conversation with Etel Adnan

Csaba Polony: Could you describe the general development of your life's work? What have been your most important concerns through the years?

Etel Adnan: Let me begin when I was 20 and went to college in Beirut. It was not a regular college but an Institute for Literature attached to Lyon University in Paris. We started with only 12 students. The founder of the school, Gabriel Bounoure, was a specialist in French poetry. He was a poetry critic for *Nouvelle Revue Française;* and, though he lived in Beirut, would send his papers and go to Paris every summer. I remember lectures on Baudelaire, Descartes, Gérard de Nerval. One class was called "Descartes and Pascal, readers of Montaigne." It was a very intense situation, to such an extent that we lost all interest in everything but poetry.

I then got a scholarship to study in Paris. This was difficult because I was my mother's only child and my father had died, so it was very difficult for me to leave home. My mother became very ill after I left. Partly this was because she was not really at home in Beirut. She was a Greek from Smyrna. My father had been a Syrian serving as an officer in the Ottoman Empire. He had met my mother in WWI. He was 20 years older than she. So, in a way both my parents were foreigners. My father less so because his hometown was only 60 miles away, but the Ottoman Empire was no more and Lebanon had become a French colony. But my mother was totally alien to Beirut. It was only later that I realized what a shock it had been for her.

My first major work, written when I was 24, is a long poem called, "The Book of the Sea." It is kind of a cosmic erotic poem on the marriage of the sun and the sea. It's written in French and has never been published. So I've always had these secret little books. Besides "The Book of the Sea," there is "The Book of the Night" *(Le Livre de Nuit),* "The Book of Death" *(Le Livre de la Morte).* Years later, after a friend had committed suicide, I realized that there is something beyond death, and it is what I called "The Book of the End." Death is still an active thing, it affects our lives, somebody's death. But worse than death is when you lose interest or forget. "The Book of Death" came out in a magazine in Beirut, in French. "The Book of Death" and "The Book of the End" came out in Arabic. They were translated by a well-known Arab poet, Adonis. The others have just stayed in my drawer and none have been translated into English.

CP: You've mentioned two different languages in your youth, Arabic and French. What languages did you speak while you were growing up?

EA: I grew up speaking Greek and Turkish. My father was educated in a military academy. He was a Moslem from Damascus. He was commander of Smyrna at the time he met my mother. It was his second marriage, and he had had three children by his first wife. My parents spoke Turkish to each other, but my mother talked to me in Greek. And when I went to school, we were taught in French. The kids talked in Arabic at home and in the streets, but were taught in French in the schools. Which, by the way, had disastrous effects politically. Much of the civil war can be traced to that. Most Phalangists are French-Jesuit-educated, so they are alienated from the Arab world and look down on it. They don't want to be Arabs but they're not French either, so they don't know what they are.

But as educators, the French priests and nuns were very efficient. They created a very educated people. We had exactly the same textbooks as they had in Paris, and could compete with French students on the same level. Educationally it was a bonus, but what it did to the native culture and to political tensions was disastrous.

Of course, as a child, I didn't know all this, but I always felt a bit distant. Maybe because here I was growing up in a family where the parents were a bit foreign, a bit like refugees. My father was very conscious of being in Beirut because he had lost the war. He was an Ottoman officer, not an Arab nationalist. He was from a military caste and he never questioned that order. He saw wars as clashes in history. He was not concerned with ethnicity or revolution. He had the code of honor of an officer. He never liked the French because they were the enemy he had fought, and the occupiers. So he had no connection to the glamorous new Beirut, the boomtown, that the French presence created. So we were marginal. That is why I very naturally understand marginal people. I didn't need a political education, I understand it just like I drink water, you see?

So anyway, in these early years my poetry was very personal. I read a lot of Baudelaire, Rimbaud, and Rilke. This was my first mental world and it was a very divided world. At home, I lived the Middle East writ large: the Greek Orthodox and the Islamic world. Then my mental world became French and more and more literary.

When I went to Paris as a student in 1949, it was still very much under the impact of the war and occupation. The atmosphere was bleak. As a scholarship student, I was able to get a room in the *Cité Universitaire*, which is like a huge dormitory city on the outskirts of Paris. Each nation had its own "house," with a required percentage of other nationals. I found a room in the American pavilion. That's where I met my first Americans. Of course I had grown up with American movies. One of the biggest influences on my life, on the dream side of my life, was the movies. The movies were shown in very dingy places, and very few bourgeois families would go to see them. But my mother would go and take me. The people who went to the movies were taxi drivers, shoeshine boys, street vendors—they were *popular*, extremely popular. The "movie" was as much in the theater as on the screen. They would shout, eat, *participate*. One thing that I am very grateful for in my life is that there was nothing bourgeois about my family. On the one hand there was my father who had a military code of honor, chivalrous but without a European aristocracy behind it. It was rather a moral aristocracy, as people from all walks of life could become officers. Then my mother came from a very different background. Her father was a wood carver, a carpenter. She was very proud of everything made by hand, even in the way she cleaned pots and pans: "Look," she would say, "they shine like the moon!" You know what I mean?

CP: What you really seem to be describing is a home environment devoid of capitalistic values, of values being determined by profit, "what's in it for me," money, commodities...

EA: Totally! Totally! We were not poor; my father had a military pension, and he worked as an engineer. But he was completely honest. For example, they would ask him to sign that he used more materials than he did. He would refuse and every time he did so he would lose his job. So he was a bit of a Don Quixote.

In part because of this, I went to work when I was 16. The war had started, inflation was very high, so l had to help out. l got a job at the Bureau of Radio and the Press. I saw the world there, news coming in from all over the world. I worked there for two years, and I also managed to finish high school (which was more like a junior college) while working. My whole life has really been like those early years: divided between the literary, academic world and the journalistic, political world.

CP: In an interview by Kathleen Weaver, published in *Poetry Flash* in May of '86, you said that "Every other person is somehow in exile. Either a refugee from a country or a refugee from an event." Could you go into this some more?

EA: Yes, you see when I was a student in Paris in 1949, I was exposed to all these people from different countries. There was a woman from Czechoslovakia. People would say that she was a little strange. She was a refugee, maybe from a concentration camp, I don't know. There was a Yugoslav girl. She said that she was too poor and left home for Paris to become a Doctor. There were Yugoslavs who had fought against Tito, right-wing Yugoslavs. So there was this fantastic atmosphere. There was a French family. There was something tragic about them. The mother was sick, strange, she had skin rashes on her arms, she refused to talk when people came to their home. She would hide. Then I found out that they were French Jews and that one day the Germans came and took the father away, just like that, and they never saw him again. So *I* saw all this. I saw so many things! Things constantly came as shocks.

Later, in 1955, I got a scholarship to study in Berkeley. I was in Paris and went home to Beirut, as my mother had had a stroke. I felt so guilty I couldn't face it. So I went to Berkeley until 1957. My mother died in 1957. Then I went to Harvard for one year, but after the year, I was broke and tired of going to school. So I gave up the Ph.D. and eventually got a job teaching at Dominican College in San Rafael, California in 1959.

In 1956 I met the first Arab students in my life. I never consciously identified with the Arab world until I came to this country. It started when I was sick with back trouble. A simple case of rheumatism was diagnosed as a disc problem. They operated and took out a healthy disc and left in some cartilage. The whole operation had to be done over. So while I was sick, I guess the Arab Student Association found out somehow about this young woman from Lebanon being sick, and one day a young Arab girl came to my room in the hospital. She introduced herself and asked how I was and if I needed anything. And I just started to cry. It so happened that she was a Palestinian studying mathematics. She came from a very well-known old Christian Palestinian family, the Hanania. Pottery in Jericho has been found with the family name on it. So she would take me to meetings, and there I found out about what went on in Palestine. It was only then that I learned about Deir Yaseen, about how the Jewish Underground, Shamir, Begin, had left messages after the massacre on the walls: if you don't leave, this is what will happen to you. They terrorized the population and so her family left. They had lived in West Jerusalem.

So I met all these Arab students and became very much involved emotionally. This was in 1956, when the French, English, and Israelis attacked Egypt. It was the time of Nassarism at its best, so I became a Nassarite. There was this general enthusiasm among many Arabs that Nassar would decolonize the Arab world for good. So when the Suez Canal was attacked, there was a lot of discussion among students, and I grew to realize Americans, and the American Press, were biased.

CP: You write in different languages—French, English—as well as having been part of different cultures. Could you say a few words about the multilingualism and multiculturalism that you've worked and lived with? What are the difficulties, the peculiarities, where or how do you find the common strain through these "differences?"

EA: It of course happens in my mind. I think you have to see the notion of language per se. There are "universes of meaning." A word always has particular connotations within each language. For example, in French and English we say "bread and butter." In Arabic there is no butter, so you say "green pastures" to convey a similar meaning. Or Turkish, for example, has a lot of words about facial expressions. You don't describe a facial expression, there are single words for them. For example, there is a word for "eyes," *mahmour*, which means, "eyes which are like in a fog," you know, a bit watery, dreamy, like before or after crying. When you use this word you are really writing a poem. They have all these expressions. So you see languages are specific creations with their own strengths and weaknesses in relation to other languages.

But there is never a single answer to a question: there is always a group, a cluster of answers. I like to write in English because I like the language—I like its nervousness, but also for political reasons that I discovered later. With French, I have a love-hate relationship because of the colonial situation. In fact, I even stopped writing in French during the Algerian war.

CP: I'd like to pursue a little further the question of the differences between languages and cultures—not just in the verbal sense of words meaning certain things. There's been a tendency recently in this culture to create these "Chinese walls" between groups of people—ethnicity, national background, sexuality, etc., each having its own place and so forth, almost to the point that communication between these different "ideologically" sanctioned groups is assumed not to be possible. Initially, this was supposedly a progressive move, particularly in this country because of the oppressive domination of WASP culture—the "melting pot" idea and all that—but it's gotten to the point now where it seems to have broken down communications in an authentic sense. People are automatically categorized and responded to according to the ideological presumptions of the particular category. These divisions then, in making true communication difficult, make it very difficult to build and maintain progressive coalitions. In other words, this fragmentation is very useful to the powers that be. Now in your case, where you've had to deal with this question of multicultural influences in a very concrete sense, I'm just curious to see where you see the communality…

EA: Yes, you know I am aware of what you say. Very often to correct something we do the same thing in reverse. Like you can fight one form of racism and be a racist in another way. For example, many people think they are leftist and progressive because they like one type of cause. Let's say, for example, they want to liberate Chile, but they don't care how many Afghans die. Or like Mrs. Dukakis said in the paper this morning, that she is especially interested in Cambodian refugees; fine, but what about Palestinian refugees, about which she knows much more? You see, people get away with that, and it is a very dangerous trend. In a way it's worse than being outright racist because you give a good image, you console yourself that you care, and yet go on being underneath a racist.

I think that in this day and age, there is no one who is "pure" culturally. This is an illusion. It's a dynamic situation between what you are and what you think you are, your family background, and the whole of the 20th century. We chose, we have our loyalties. But we should not make them into solid entities. For example, coming from the Middle East, having met so many Arabs, knowing many Palestinians, makes me very sensitive to the Palestinian issue. In that sense you could say that I am an Arab. And I am also very sensitive to Arabic culture, particularly because in a way I have been cheated out of it. I had to regain it, to give it to myself, and I find important values in it, values worth standing up for.

CP: Could you go into what those values are?

EA: First of all, Arabic is not a "nation," not even a "culture," it is a *world*. A world is always cosmopolitan, it is always rich, multiple, a synthesis of its own, a civilization. And Arab civilization carries so many values, even contradictory values, which have created some of the essential things in history. You can go back, for example, to the Babylonian. The *Enuma elish* ("When on high"—opening words of the Babylonian Poem of Creation, about 19-17th century B.C.—Ed. note) which precedes Genesis, and has this *directness*. Like *Gilgamesh*. Let's take *Gilgamesh*, it is that awakening of human culture. He was half-god, half-man, but he died; therefore the man's side took over: his humanity, his vulnerability; he discovered death through his friend's death. That epic has, aesthetically, an economy of means of expression which is a marvel for today's writing. It's not that they are myths; it's the *way* these myths are written. They are written as convincing experiences. In judging poetry you know when something is phony and when it is not—more or less. And this text gives the impact of a direct experience—so strong that it touches you today. So Arab civilization touches that, and much of what we call "western history" evolved in the Arab world: Babylonian, Egyptian, early Christianity evolved in Syria. Saint Matthew was from Antioch, for example. You have Byzantine art, which covers Syria, Egypt, and parts of Mesopotamia. Through Syrian Christian art you get the beginnings of Romanesque and European art. And even in the Arab people, although they have beastly governments, they have wonderful values. The hospitality is not a little thing, this openness.

CP: Would you say then that the values you find valuable in the Arab world are the same values that you liked in your home, that is, those non-capitalistic values that see the relationship of the human being to the world as a whole as important and not looking at everything individualistically, as inert objects from which profit can be squeezed for personal advancement?

EA: Yes! For example, according to Islamic Law, earning interest on money is wrong. Of course, many of these values are disappearing, or have disappeared, but the dream that maybe something could be salvaged remains. The capacity to sustain loss is still an Arab value. Take Lebanon: in spite of all the destruction, people have survived because these old values came back to the fore. For example, a guy emigrates, and he sends his money back to feed his relations: children, parents, nephews, aunts, uncles. I don't think that this is an American value. It is probably hard to find an American who will work to feed a dozen people without begrudging it. In the Arab world they still do this. Not just that they do it, but it is done without resentment. The responsibility is assumed without question.

Another thing, the Arabs like money and gadgets, almost too much; but they know they are toys, gadgets, and they can live with it or live without it. Americans, for example, who work in Saudi Arabia don't understand; they say, "These guys have Cadillacs and suddenly they go and sleep under tents." I'm not saying that they don't deserve criticism, but what bothers me is that they are often despised for what is best in them and admired for what is worst in them. If we don't know how to be poor and live simply without breaking down, we are in trouble. People need to be able to take disaster and survive.

Here's another example: in Arabic culture it used to be considered almost sinful to be sure of what you're going to do tomorrow. They would say, "I will do it, if God so wills." So there always was a window of uncertainty, leaving room for spontaneity, for other logic and happenings, for life.

CP: Your poem, *Jebu*, I think, deals with some of these issues. You write:

Jebu is the father of the Cyclops

shaman archetype son of the animal
bedu inhabitant of the tree crawl on

your belly come to the well drink
swim in the underground petroleum and emerge

BLACK

Jebu is the homecoming distributing
the land telling matter is for all
tying the knots reinventing the
Sun-God Ra to the universe

I read *Jebu* as a symbol for a pre-Judeo-Christian (or by extension
non-western) consciousness which isn't dominated by the rational
mind—by an attitude which dominates and subjugates nature and
human nature—repression as a means to survive. The poem *Jebu*,
when I first heard it, I saw as taking the current Mid-East conflict
and tracing its roots through an epic panoramic view of the whole
historical process; and the current Zionist expropriation and
subjugation of Palestine, and the struggle of the Palestinians for self
determination as being a kind of contemporary microcosm of this
process. It's one of the last gasps of a blatant colonialism. But now
the "natives" are no longer subdued and exterminated so easily, and
now

The ancestors will come out of their mirror

…and the double visage of Jehu
appeared: alone vulnerable obscure prophet
he is all of us since the prehistoric
cell and the rivers that followed

perpetual revolution is perpetual Prophecy

Am I reading this correctly? I'd like to hear your comments.

EA: Well, what you see in the poem is a large part of it, but I see
different aspects as well. *Jebu* was written after the 1967 war and the
annexation of Jerusalem by the Israelis and their claim that the city is
theirs and theirs only. And in the poem I said that they didn't even
found the city, besides the fact that, since Jerusalem is such an
important city to three religions, some solution must be found that

respects everyone's needs, not just one party's. So it has to be an open city.

So I said, let's go back and see where it started. And I took as a means Jebu, a mythical person I invented, but it does have an historical basis. Jerusalem was founded by the Canaanites. It is a pre-Judaic city and David conquered it. *Jebu* is a pre-monotheistic being. Monotheism is a double-edged thing. It is very monolithic, projects an image of authority, and so on. That's why I usually like the word "divine" better than the word "god." "God" personifies "divine," makes it an aspiration. I said that matter belongs to us all, I meant that we are the product of the soil and so matter is our common denominator. The rain forests, for example, don't belong to Brazil; the fact that the whole human race depends on them makes them the property of the whole human race. We are not free to destroy certain things by saying "it's mine." You can't claim jurisdiction over the air we breathe, the forests that we all need, the rivers, the oceans. The same is true about any major resource, even medicine. Nor should we have atomic weapons because, if they are used, not only the belligerents would be destroyed, but others who had nothing to do with the war would be, as well. There is such an interconnectedness today that, in a way, the world does belong to everybody.

CP: In your essay on Marguerite Yourcenar, published in *Poetry Flash* (Feb. '88), you wrote that "…she gave us not her whereabouts, whims, and experiences, but the *sound* of her inner soul, the tone of her books being the very temperature of her own heart; that *tone* is the second, crucial, and nonverbal message…" Could you elaborate on this?

EA: Well, this is integral to any writing. For example, some people tell me that political poetry is not poetry. They'd say that poetry has to be personal. Well, politics can move you as much as the death of a loved one; it certainly is personal. And poetry is political, because politics is not only about what you do but about what you don't do as well. We can go to Sartre who said that even if you are not working politically that's still a statement, you're still involved. But, it's more than that, you always speak about yourself. There is something in the music, this tone, like in body language. For example, let's say you describe a tree, you say something about yourself in the very way you attack the first sentence. Language poets, for example, think they're not talking about themselves, but if you're astute you know as much about the writers as if they wrote love poetry—by the tone of their sensitivity or lack of sensitivity. Not in small details, but *in what they are about*. I mean there is an acoustical element in people, you can *hear* people like you can hear music. You can see it in painting: you can draw an apple, you can draw an abstract shape, but there is a quality to your line that you cannot run away from. It is your *tone*. It is the same in writing. Like your handwriting. So I feel that there is an acoustical handwriting in people's texts, and I like to hear this tone. For me it is equally important to what they are literally saying.

CP: Isn't it true that good writing, or art, is what makes that communication easier? What would you say it is that makes this possible?

EA: We don't know. Maybe, philosophically, it is a passionate commitment to what you're saying. The passionate energy that's behind the writing. I find this in Darwin, in Hume, for example. Or Kant: it's as if he wrote a novel, it's practically a novel of his mind.

CP: Perhaps it's the closeness or unity of the intention and the expression.

EA: That's it. It's this merger of the clarity of thinking, and the clarity of what you want to say and the passionate honesty. Where you have that fusion is great writing—regardless of the subject matter. It doesn't have to be "literature." Darwin is the best example; there is an epic grandeur to Darwin. "*The Origin of Species*" is like the "*Iliad*," it is the "Iliad of Being."

CP: Are you saying that in essence there is no difference between poetic and rational or scientific processes?

EA: In a profound sense, no, there is no difference. You see these are really very Western 19th-century categories: this is thinking, this is the imagination. But these things are practically the same thing. We have destroyed the underlying unity of things. We took our categorizations for actual entities. But they really were ways to put order in your house. These are filing systems, but we shouldn't take every file as an absolute.

CP: In that same essay you write of Marguerite, "In her own work—and soul—she reconciled that mysterious duality of the masculine and feminine, as if they were not two parallels meant to never meet, but rather the two poles of a reality which is continuous, call it human nature, being, mind, or the universe." Could you elaborate on this, particularly in view of a common strain in contemporary feminism which, in effect, moralistically severs this creative dialectic by labeling the male as "bad" and the female as "good"?

EA: Let me start with a conclusion, if we keep in mind that it is a mystery. I like to keep that sense of mystery. Biologically, it is obvious that there are man and woman, throughout nature, in animals, in some plants. And we know what this generation has won: the stereotypes have just a bit disappeared. When I was growing up, man had this stereotypic image: he had to be strong physically, he had to be courageous, aggressive, and he had to have the upper hand in decision-making in regard to woman—regardless of the different religions or whatever they say in their books. By the 20th century there was a standard of behavior set up as a model. In movies, Hollywood movies, I was amazed to see how much glamorous stars like Humphrey Bogart would slap the woman, and this was considered glamorous aggression. So women did revolt against that, mostly in the West, because these were the countries where women started to work. And by working they already destroyed a myth, that jobs were biologically distributed, because biologically there is nothing a woman can't do jobwise that a man can do. So little by little woman conquered domains previously reserved to man. I don't think that it is challenged any longer in the western world or in the communist bloc—only in some parts of the third world is it not yet fully accepted. So on a mythical level it is accepted, but it is still not accepted fully in everyday life. It is still harder for a woman engineer to compete with a man, if she applies to Bechtel, for example.

Some women, in this fight, went over into the deep end, and this is where the problem starts. Instead of trying to be accepted as equal, instead of fighting for equality, they really fought, without even knowing it, to have the whole field to themselves. They turned the tables. They said, "For centuries you said that masculine is good and feminine is bad; well, the opposite is true." And this has become, in some small circles, a new dogma. And like every dogma, it has to be challenged. Because, in my opinion, you cannot replace one wrong with another.

Let's start from the beginning. We should deal with reality as it is; otherwise what are we doing? There simply are man and woman in this world and there are always going to be unless the world disappears. For me it is a relational problem, it is not an absolute problem. You cannot define man unless you define woman. What makes a man is that he is not a woman and what makes a woman is that she is not a man. You see, I think we got a very bad lesson from physics. When we say "positive" and "negative" poles, we use the word "negative" almost in a moral sense, and this is the mistake. Maybe it should be "A" and "Z," for example. If we see poles as "negative" or "positive" we will never get out of the problem. With electricity it doesn't matter, but it does in society, among people.

The two poles should be seen as complementary. And I would like the difference to persist, because it makes room for attraction, for dialogue, for life. But that difference is not an absolute, otherwise there wouldn't be a problem. There is a mysterious common denominator, we call it human nature for lack of better words. But in each of us we have the other, so it is a double dialogue. There is a man and woman in each of us, with one being dominant.

There are practical problems between man and woman, and they should remain practical. For example, if a husband is violent, it will do the wife no good just to say that he is violent because he is a man. This will lead nowhere. Solutions would come by society changing its values. Violence, for example, comes from adherence to values— as a society—which promote and create violence. It is something that children breathe in this society as a whole, added to which is technological violence. How can you not be violent when every tool you touch is violent? Everything is noisy; a car is a violent thing.

This is why, if you would just exchange power from man to woman without changing the system, the problem would not be solved. We have to change our mythologies, our models, our values.

We need to change our environment. Ecology would be the best way, because ecology is more than "be nice to plants"; it is really respect for all life. Once you respect your environment, be it plants, mountains, or streams, you already admit that there is a larger good than your own. What is necessary is to break our solitude. It's not how many people you see that will break your solitude. You may see nobody and not have this solitude if you feel this belonging to a larger universe. America, for example, has tried all the religions and none of them have helped much, so maybe what we should have is what the American Indians had: a broader sense of belonging to nature. Once you belong to nature you already belong to the other person, because you are already opened up. Some little change, a switch, should happen in our mental set-up.

You see, we live in a society where one ego is always pitted against another. You are brought up against others: the kid sitting next to you in school—you have to have better grades; the guy living next door—you must have a better house. Then you have the same battle among couples: "Why should I give in?" Why should you, in a society where nobody gives in? Cohabitation is always a compromise—a series of little give-ins, hopefully from each side. In this society, where competition is the highest value, a group as a group cannot function harmoniously, nor a marriage, because this competitiveness is so ingrained that we aren't even aware of it. People do not feel internally obliged to take into account anybody but themselves—not even their families. It gets reduced to each isolated individual.

So feminism cannot solve this problem if it does not see the situation more broadly. It is not just a man-woman problem. It is a metaphysical problem: we have no image of the universe; we need a nature, a universe, a cosmic-type imagination, and start from there. The world from the level of atoms to the universe is a series of balances. And I call a balance a compromise.

CP: The values that you were talking about that you find worth saving in the Arab world are essentially positive values of the old pre-capitalist, patriarchal, feudal (and earlier) world. The problem, it seems to me, is how can you—or can you?—resurrect, re-create, or create anew the positive kernel of those values which really do contain essential emancipatory needs, in a world that is truly egalitarian.

EA: That's what I meant in *Jebu* when I said that matter belonged to everybody. We need to create a society in which exists the basic awareness that we all have a moral right to everything—not that everything be shared equally, but the knowledge that we all belong to this earth equally. To me this is a fact of nature that we do not now translate politically.

CP: I would like to end by asking you about the future. What are your current concerns? Where are you going?

EA: In a sense what has happened to me is that I had gotten so involved with the political situation in the world that I became saturated. So I found a need to regain what I had been like in my "previous life": the innocence I had when I was 18 or 20. I've tried to get back in touch with that.

CP: Perhaps what you mean is similar to Hegel's saying that, "The harmoniousness of childhood is a gift from the hand of nature; the second harmony must spring from the labor and culture of the spirit." Have you had any success?

EA: Well, I don't know. Perhaps it comes through in my recent poetry, like in the "Lindell Tree" poems. But, it's been my love of nature, as the mother of us all, and by "nature" I mean the universe. That to me is a fact, it's what I call the divine. But by this I am not running away from politics; it's just that much more that I try to incorporate.

CP: I think that it's very important to keep an overall cosmic picture. Many political people, on the left anyway, forget that, or dismiss it as reactionary, and then end up becoming cold, calculating, manipulating people, out of touch with reality.

EA: Also, if we want to keep caring we have to be sane. It's like getting out of the fire to the next floor. After all, I come from a city, Beirut, which was destroyed. It's an apocalyptic event. It's not "objective," "intellectual" politics, it is in my flesh. And although I am more cosmopolitan than nationalistic, still Beirut was my beginnings, my frame of reference. All that has been shattered, all the hopes that I put into the Arab world and the liberation, and I just see it grow more reactionary. I became physically ill many times. But this love of nature is something that is very deep in me. Sometimes I think about it just to rebalance myself. I like to read Parmenides again, the pre-Socratics, because they have this sense of the *youth* of the universe.

It's eternal youth. I was close to that when I was 20, to the elements. The sea, I would sit for hours and watch the sea. So I am trying to rediscover that, not to the exclusion of the other, but to have both.

ETEL ADNAN is among those distinguished French-speaking poets of the Third World—Lebanon, Haiti, Algeria, Martinique, etc.—who have written some of the most significant poetry in that language but have been culturally marginalized or overlooked. Her *Jebu* and *The Arab Apocalypse* (the latter published by the Post-Apollo Press) are considered by many to be among the foremost poems in the French language since WW II. She lives in Sausalito, California, where she also writes poetry in American English, and paints as well.

CSABA POLONY is the editor of the noted journal, *Left Curve*. He recently edited and translated a collection of poetry, essays, and visual art on the Balkan Wars called *Balkan Autopsy*, the works in which were created by artists from the former Yugoslavia.

This interview is reprinted from *Left Curve #11*, 1988-89.

PAUL LARAQUE

Poetry:
Haiti, the Caribbean, and the World

[This essay was first delivered at the opening address of the 4th International Poetry Workshop at the Caribbean Culture Festival, the "Fiesta of Fire," in Santiago de Cuba, July 1994. It has been translated from the French by Rosemary Manno.]

Solidarity with the struggles of the Caribbean people, particularly in Cuba and Haiti, dates back to their early history. The native resistance was first symbolized by Caonaba and Anacaona the "samba" (poet), both victims of Spanish barbarism, then by the cacique Henry, who according to Haitian legend, went off to Cuba to continue their common struggle.

Boukman came from Jamaica and led the general slave uprising in 1791 in Santo Domingo. Following the traditional path of pan-American solidarity, launched with help from Dessalines to Miranda, from Pétion to Bolívar, always on the condition that slavery be abolished in the freed territories, José Martí and Máximo Gómez found refuge in Haiti in the course of the first struggle for Cuban independence. Gómez, a Dominican, is a Cuban hero; Jacques Viau, a Haitian, is a Dominican hero; and Che Guevara, an Argentinian, is a hero of the Americas. Antonio Maceo was the son of black Venezuelans transplanted to Cuba, and Jésus Cos Causse's grandfather was a comrade-in-arms with Charlemagne Peralte against the American military occupation of Haiti, which lasted from 1915 to 1934.

Due to an extraordinary history, the uniqueness of its culture, and the richness of its French and Creole literary tradition, Haiti has become the Black Mecca of the Caribbean. C.L.R. James discovered the "Black Jacobins" there; Aimé Césaire and Toussaint L'Ouverture discovered Négritude there; Vincent Placoly discovered "Dessaline, or the Passion for Independence"; Alejo Carpentier found there "the marvelous reality," which Jacques Stéphan-Alexis developed into a "marvelous realism." André Breton saw and confirmed there "a basic thesis" of Surrealism through the permanence of a "lyric element" in the very existence of its people. Wifredo Lam met Hector Hippolyte at Dewit Peters' "Art Center," and later André Malraux encountered the painters of Saint-Soleil. The towering giants all came in their turn—Langston Hughes and Nicolás Guillén, Jean-Paul Sartre and Michel Leiris, Léon Damas and Léopold Senghor. And they will keep coming. Haiti, for Alfred Metreaux, is "earth, men and gods"; for Paul Moral, it's "the Haitian peasant," and for G. Barthélemy it's "the countryside." From Graham Greene to Amy Wilentz, from the Bishop of Evreux to Randall Robinson, from Katherine Dunham to Ramsey Clark, from Jacques Barros to Jack Hirschman, from Susan Sarandon to Harry Belafonte, personalities from across the globe have shown their solidarity with the Haitian people's struggle for bread and dignity against terror and exploitation, against local oligarchies, against yesterday's thugs and the monstrous butcher of our time—imperialism—whose neocolonial instrument is the native army of occupation. As it is for freedom, the struggle to defeat these forces is one and indivisible.

The first time I witnessed poetry was from the lips of a poet who was my role-model, my cousin Fernand Martineau, whom I loved like a brother. Hearing him speak in verse, I understood, as I still understand today, that poetry is a matter of life or death. This feeling was reinforced by another god of my youth, Jean F. Brierre, whose voice became immortal as the very voice of Liberty at the height of the American occupation of Haiti. A bolt of lightning struck in the name of love and a phoenix was reborn from the ashes in the manner of a daily miracle. The principal meeting of my life was with the magus, as I've described in my testimony entitled "André Breton in Haiti," which appeared in *Nouvelle Optique* in May 1973. Before he was kicked out of Haiti, along with Wifredo Lam and Pierre Mabille, Breton wrote me a letter dated February 1946. That letter appears on the back cover of my first collection of poems, *That Which Remains,* written in 1945 but not published until 1973 in Montreal. Several of these poems had previously appeared in the magazine *Optique* (1954-56) in Port-au-Prince, under the pen name of Jacques Lenoir. Breton forever united for me the trinity of poetry, love and liberty.

Exiled in New York City and stripped of my nationality by the bloody dictatorship of François Duvalier (1957-71), I learned through another letter from Haydée Santamaría, comrade-in-arms with Fidel at Moncada and in the Sierra Maestra, founder and then President of Casa de las Americas, that I was to be the first-time French-language winner of the Casa's prize for my book *Les Armes Quotidiennes/Poesie Quotidienne* (1979). This work was translated into Spanish by the Cuban poet of international stature, Nancy Morejón, whom I met in Havana in 1981. Now here I am in Santiago de Cuba, birthplace of José Maria Heredia and home of the Cuban Revolution. I'm grateful to Jesús Cos Causse, the most Caribbean of Cuban poets, general coordinator of the International Poetry Workshop, for his having honored my country by choosing one of its poets to give the opening address for the 4th International Poetry Workshop, as part of the Festival of Caribbean Culture organized by the Casa del Caribe under the direction of Joel James Figarola. This is an opportunity to pay homage to the Caribbean people, those who have given us our history, our culture and our arts.

The product of social activity, culture, which among other elements understands oral and written literature, is dependent upon poetry, and poetry cannot be separated from history. From the Spanish conquest to the present, our hemisphere has been marked by native resistance to colonialism, to genocide, by Blacks rising up against slavery, by popular struggles against imperialism, by masses in revolt for economic freedom and for social, political and cultural liberty. This progress has been interrupted by the collapse of socialism in the Soviet Union and in Eastern Europe, and is all the more threatened by "the new world order" of the giant capitalist powers headed by the United States. Far from believing, with Kundera, in the end of all ideology, we affirm with Jacques Barros that Marxism is an "unovertakeable horizon."

Between the two world wars the important events in the literary world have been the Harlem Renaissance, Surrealism, Indigenism and Négritude. Langston Hughes transposed the rhythms of the Blues and of spirituals into African-American poetry, just as Nicholás Guillén did with the sounds of Cuban poetry. Seeking a Haitian identity in the form of cultural resistance during the American military occupation (1915-1934), after Charlemagne Peralte and Benoît Batraville were crushed with the peasant guerrilla "cacos," Indigenism found two venues—the *Revue Indigène* (1927) under the direction of poet Emil Roumer, which ushered in the era of modern poetry in Haiti; and *Thus Speaks Uncle* (1928), an essay by Jean Price-Mars that denounced the "bovaryism" of the Haitian elite; that is, "the power a society has to conceive of itself as different from what it is in reality."

In "Black Orpheus," the preface to the *Anthology of New Black Poetry*, edited by Léopold Sédar-Senghor, Sartre states that "Black poetry in the French language is the only great revolutionary poetry in the world today. Though it's been surpassed as a movement, Négritude, founded by Aimé Césaire, Léon Damas, and Senghor, presents—and this must be stressed—two contradictory aspects: a reactionary one fundamentally based upon race, and a revolutionary aspect based upon history—i.e., uprooting, slavery, and revolt. This is particularly shown by Jacques Roumain, who integrated the concept of Class in the Marxist sense without any distinction as to color, as did Frantz Fanon. Along with Roumain, one of the great Haitian voices of revolutionary Négritude belongs to Jean-Fernand Brierre. Among the poets who have survived them are two living legends: Césaire, who has submitted the French language to Caribbean rhythms and has brought these demands to delirious heights; and Félix Morisseau-Leroy who across the globe has given voice to our people, tying the Creole (Haitian) language to the struggle of the masses and to popular arts.

At the edges of Surrealism are two works that marked a decisive turning point in Haitian poetry—that of Magloire Saint-Aude and his search for "the philosopher's stone," according to Breton; and that of René Bélance, whose "violent fervor" Roumain had opposed, as he had the barren hopelessness of the former. It's also noteworthy to name the *Lucid Spurts* of Hamilton Garoute, for which I wrote the preface. My personal ideal is an explosive alloy of Surrealism, Négritude and Marxism.

As for René Depestre, I'll say that I continue to admire this child prodigy of Haitian poetry and pilgrim of communism, who dazzled our path, having reached the "age of reason"; but I'm sorry to say that this renegade has replaced love with sexual obsession and brotherhood with egocentricity.

With Anthony Phelps, Villard Denis a.k.a. Davertige, René Philocete, Roland Morisseau and Serge Legagneur, *Literary Haiti* was born in 1960. Among these fine poets, Phelps is the most well-known, twice the winner of the Casa de las Americas prize, and for whom—as for myself—the poet is "the conscience of the world;" Davertige whom Alain Bousquet has presented as "genius in the primitive state;" and Philoctete, poet of "wild grasses" and novelist of "the people of troubled lands," who founded Spiralism along with Jean-Claude Fignole and Frankétienne, the latter of whose work, the only one that reminds me of the *Chants of Maldoror,* projects both in French and in Creole an image of Haiti that is as hallucinatory as it is real. Regarding the work of Jean Métellus, discovered by Maurice Nadeau and sung by Claude Mouchard, it's essentially "the transposition into literature of the epic poem of our people and our race."

The two principle elements of Haitian culture are Creole and Voodoo. In the cultural realm, the connections Voodoo has with Cuban santería, and Brazilian macumba and condomblé—all of African origin—should be remembered. In the chapter entitled "Poetry in Haiti from 1950 to 1980" in the 1984 *Anthology of New Creole Poetry* (Editions Caraïbéennes), the professor and critic Maximilien Laroche looks at the three generations of poets—those from 1950, 1960 and 1970—indicating that the meaning of the word "generation" here is equivalent to a decade. I have the honor of belonging—along with Morisseau-Leroy, Roumer, Frank Fouché and Claude Innocent—to the first decade. Indeed, in 1951 Morisseau's *Diacoute* opened the era of Creole poetry on a national scale; and then, when his *Antigone in Creole* played in Paris at the Theater of Nations in 1959, the language of our people was given an international audience. I have followed the path thus opened with two collections of poetry, one of them translated from Creole into French by our national bard, Jean-Fernand Brierre, and the other into English by the North American communist poet, Jack Hirschman. The journal *Conjunctions* in Port-au-Prince in 1992 published "100 Creole poems" by 50 talented writers. Undoubtedly the most gifted among them is Georges Castera. Didier Dominique and Rachelle Beauvoir have been the first to win the Casa de las Americas prize in the Creole language, with their study of Voodoo. The best representatives of the present Haitian generation are Jan Mapou in Creole and Joël Des Rosiers in French. Among the Caribbean female writers, we must mention Marie (Chauvet) Vieux and Rose-Marie Desruisseau in Haiti, and Marise Condé and Simone Schwartz-Bart in Guadeloupe.

Surely Haiti comes first in my heart, just as for Cuban patriots and revolutionaries Cuba is dearest of all; but ideologically I am closer to the Cuban Revolution than to "Lavalas" (The Flood), which symbolizes the democratic Haitian movement, with its inherent weakness owing to its "non-violent" line. In my opinion, only a popular army is capable of guaranteeing the unconditional defense of the fundamental interests of the masses and the nation.

Confronted by poverty and satrapy, what can poetry do? What can words do front-up against weapons?…What can weapons do front-up against the spirit? My brother Guy F. Laraque has been assassinated—he who demanded for us "the right to hope"—but his work lives on. "Each collapse bears proof that the poet responds with a thrust to the future," wrote the poet René Char. At the cost of life, poetry is the endless search for the grail or for "another world" that, according to Paul Eluard, is "but another part of our own." Magus or militant, magus and militant in the flight against the shadow, the poet carries the torch of truth.

From St. John Perse to Derek Walcott, we celebrate, beyond those already mentioned, other great poets of the Caribbean: Roberto F. Retamar and Pedro Mir, Edouard Glissant and Ernest Pepin, Edward Kamau Brathwaite and Andrew Salkey.

Caliban has reversed the mirror: no longer looked at but to *look* where the Other, suddenly objectified, refuses to be recognized until the day when, beyond all differences, the unity of the human condition and nature will be realized as prophesied by the first inhabitants of a new continent.

Revitalizing Marx and Rimbaud in order to "transform the world" and "to change life," remembering Mayakovsky at the dawn of the Bolshevik Revolution, nourished and inspired along with Nazim Hikmet and the "stale bread of exile;" singing the Canto General of Neruda to the Black rhythms of Guillén; connected to our comrade Roumain's "fighting weapon," to the "miraculous weapons" of Césaire; having learned from José Martí and Roque Dalton that Art unites dream and action, poetry and revolution—each generation in the Caribbean breaks new ground in fresh earth so that it's always ready for an "Endless Threshold," as Jack Hirschman puts it, "a threshold without end, a threshold to infinity."

Poets and comrades, we pay homage to the eternal poetry of our Caribbean, "center of gravity of the unbelievable," as Gabriel García Márquez puts it: the creation of being and speaking made inseparable, with myth and history connected across sound, color and language barriers, and at the same time flesh and spirit.

One and many, poetry is at the heart of America, confronting and bringing together in deepest intimacy the two continents of Europe and Africa—the multiracial America of Walt Whitman and Toni Morrison, of Jorge Amado and Rigoberta Menchú; voice of men and women mixed, voice of people and gods, collective and singular voice, urgent call to the universal and to immortality.

In conclusion I leave you with the words of hope of Nicolás Guillén:

"The dawn is long but it's coming."

Reflections on Poetry and Revolution

"Reflections" are selections from: (1) Personal Notes by Paul Laraque; (2) "Preliminary Text" in his Everyday Poetry *(1979); (3) his essay, "André Breton in Haiti," in* Conjunction *(1992); (4) his preface to* On Poetry *by Guy F. Laraque (1992), and (5) his preface to* A Philosophy of Art *by Anthony Lespes (forthcoming). I made the selections and translated and edited the French texts sent to me by their author.—Jack Hirschman*

In the debates on a Haitian national poetry opened up by René Depestre—then in exile—to which Aimé Césaire responded with a poem in French and Félix Morisseau-Leroy with a poem in Creole, I also intervened in the magazine *Optique* (Port-au-Prince, 1954/56) under the pseudonym Jacques Lenoir; I pled for a poetry of both French and Creole expression, rooted in the popular culture, whose forms, dynamized by revolutionary content, would assert themselves through rhythm and images fitting to us with respect to community.

The poet is the organizer of dreams. Individual dreams and collective dreams. Poetry is revelation and metamorphosis: revelation in that it shows us what is hidden behind appearances, what takes place *on the other side of the mirror*; metamorphosis in that it changes reality into what will be. It "gives sight," Paul Eluard whispers to us. Through the power of the word—the only thing in the world, Ponge tells us, that is interior and exterior at the same time—it recreates the world. Not comprehending limits for itself, it integrates "the repellent worlds of politics" into its domain and transforms them into green fields of liberty. It carries its demands to the heights of ecstasy. At the same time, it is the "miraculous weapon" Césaire defines it as, and the "weapon of combat" according to the concept of Jacques Roumain, which united the call to arms of Marx with the delirious cry of Rimbaud. The transformation of the material conditions of existence must be realized in terms of a "new human understanding." After all, what good is it to "transform the world" if not in order to "change life"? It is therefore necessary to revolutionize the economy and the lyric, reality and the imagination, form and substance, art and life. In this way we'll succeed at creating the new man and woman that Che dreamed of. Poetry is liberty. When there remains for us nothing more to conquer, that "nothing," André Breton suggests, will be the very object of poetry and of liberty. Then poetry will be made by all, according to the prophecy of Lautréamont.

The Haitian poet Franketienne utilizes French when he interprets intimate feelings, and Creole when his people speak through him. As for me, I try to transcribe the interior murmur in language itself, as it assumes...the personal adventure of the poet fused with the epic of his people.

Poetry is consciousness of self and others, consciousness of the world not through the intellect but through sensations, emotions and feelings. In order to know myself, I have to discover myself, have to plunge into the dizzying depths of my very being and at the same time situate myself in the context of my environment, in relation to other human beings and all the things that make up the universe.

At first, I discovered myself as a Black in a world dominated by Whites and so-called "Western Civilization." Then, racial solidarity, without my denying it, was changed into social solidarity in the struggle of oppressed people throughout the world, in the daily struggle for bread and dignity, for love and liberty. "On A Roof of Wind" reveals a different experience. This time it was as if the words were dictated directly to my hand...The voice that speaks here is entirely independent of my reason. It is only through accepting the poem, in taking upon myself what it has to say, that I become responsible. The title itself is an example of surrealist metaphor in which two elements which differ, (as "roof" which suggests stability, protection and security; and "wind" which, on the other hand, evokes instability, adventure, and danger) are suddenly reconciled and create, in an unexpected manner, what Breton called "the light of the image" or "convulsive beauty…"

Poetry is first of all given to us. Afterward, it's necessary to deserve it.

One day the idea came to me to write a poem, at the very least a line each day written at dawn between sleep and waking. At such a privileged moment images offer themselves abundantly and likewise lose themselves for want of being caught in the net of memory. So it's a question of gathering them at the source; but this isn't a pure and simple return to automatic writing.

What dream furnishes here is the raw stuff of poetry and like the African goldsmith in *The Black Child,* the poet has to transform the work with the gold into a magic operation. It's with this perspective that this book is written. It is new evidence that inspiration doesn't dry up if one but lends an ear to what Césaire calls "the interior murmur" and, in particular, to those phrases which, as Breton says, "knock against the windowpane."

However, after the amazement of the first few times, such activity tends to become a routine rather than a surprise, a discipline rather than a desire, an exercise of mind rather than an exercise of liberty. The magic is changed into art instead of the art being changed into magic and, finally, it's the art itself which risks taking place merely as craft.

You have to stop experience and, watching over the power to awaken, allow poetry every license to manifest itself in its own good time. Words then "would make love" when it suits them.

In the final analysis, that voice which comes from the depth of ourselves reveals only ourselves and the external world so that it reflects itself and is transformed in us: the world of the child, lost paradise which is able to recreate itself only in our work and the world of human beings: world of the present and the future, world of struggle and of hope, world where exploitation and oppression will have been abolished, world where "the leap from the realm of necessity to the realm of liberty" will have been accomplished, world of love and poetry—in a word, the promised land that only revolution will carry from dream to life.

Poetry is dialectical. Contradiction itself, it aims at the resolution of all contradictions. When history poses the question of life or death to a people, it's only natural that poetry should have become a daily weapon; the miracle is for life itself to become everyday poetry.

What Surrealism represented for us (Haitians), before anything else, was that leap into the unknown. In a world which, in the name of logic and reason, condemned us to choose between the lie and despair; in a world which allowed to those who "said No to the shadow" no other outlet but madness or suicide, the surrealists opted for a plundering of traditional values. Beginning with total negation, it was no longer a question of creating or inventing but rather of discovering. Man had presented himself to himself under one of his faces which, without any justification, he not only granted primacy to the other, but the exclusivity of his regard as well. It seemed that there had existed in him a shameful area about which he wouldn't speak. The virtue of the surrealist grouping, engaged in the open road through Freud, is to have relentlessly pursued the prospects lying in the subsoil of man. The hold surrealist consciousness has for us corresponded to the *revelation* of the personality of Breton, spiritually through the mediation of his works, but above all, in an uncontrollable way, through a completely physical attraction. As for me, where I am most indebted to Breton is in his having brought me lucidity. The more I perceive myself inwardly, the more the columns of shadow give way to clarity. I don't deny that at a certain level everything risks confusion but, without doubt, there is a spear that transfixes. Little by little, I decoded myself, the world grew clearer. In that sense, Breton is truly a visionary of life.

It's not my purpose here to study the influence of surrealism on Haitian literature, but to illustrate the perspectives it opened. Perhaps a single example will suffice to clarify, that of René Bélance, whose work marks a decisive turn in modern poetry written in French in Haiti. Constantly advancing on itself, it is a work of both the synthesis and the surpassing—through surrealism—of the other principle tendencies in Haitian poetry: Indigenism, Négritude and revolutionary humanism. Surpassing the folkloric level where, as Anthony Lespes notes, the drum very often conceals the man; surpassing the exclusively racial sway of consciousness which, in the political domain, results in a new racism and in the exploitation of Blacks by Blacks; surpassing the purely demanding stage where revolutionary slogans, necessary in the field of action, don't count for anything in the field of art—but surpassing without disavowal, since there had been integration or rather interiorization of different tendencies—from Jacques Roumain to Magloire Saint-Aude—to the degree that they were now part of the substance of being. With

Bélance, man is always front-up, whether he descends into his own darkness in order to perceive more, or rises to the light in order to better apprehend the universe. Even though desperate, he never renounces the struggle against despair and the causes of despair. What characterizes him is the power of negation. Automatic writing reveals the profound self of the poet, his subconscious, and this subconscious is that of a man who is grappling with the conditions of existence—that is, in the Haitian context—of the Black race vis-á-vis colonialism and imperialism, and of the organization of society on a world scale, having developed a position in favor of the total liberation of mankind on a material as well as spiritual plane…it is an explosive poetry made of hallucinatory images and following a dizzy rhythm without coherence or regard for formal logic. From then on, his interest is centered on language, language freed from the tutelage of Cartesian reason and all formal constraints; language, the liberator of unappreciated or unknown forces; language, the revealer of "the other side of the mirror" where what's unusual in reality borders on the wonders of dream; language, the creator of another world, the supreme quest of poetry which is…according to Paul Eluard, whose word is like cut-glass evidence…nowhere else but in our own world.

The new generation follows, with its own means, the roads opened by Surrealism as much in the domain of the imagination and sensibility as in the domain of language. As for myself, the values that reside essentially in my life are not exclusively surrealist but only Surrealism has been able to gather in such a shower of lightning flashes:

> poetry, which "breathes on the wings of the doors" and realizes the voyage through the mirror;
> love, "so that between two beings the invulnerable is raised up"; and
> liberty, "the color of mankind."

Without doubt it isn't a question of making Surrealism a point of arrival, but one can make it a point of departure, at the very least in poetry. On the plane of action, we've seen and recognized, once and for all, its limits. The more important movement which followed it—existentialism, structuralism—was manifested outside the poetic domain. The only poetic movement of the century situated historically between the two World Wars and two aborted attempts at verbal destruction (Dada and Lettrism), Surrealism was extended and renewed in Négritude, which is like a Black child in it. Certainly the ivory tower was finished—and so was the notion of a utilitarian art. The problem of the writer, that is of writing, is to speak, through which he reveals himself and the world as well, so that in himself he changes it. Thus he does not reflect reality; he transposes it, contests it, discovers what is hidden behind it or what can be born from it; he metamorphoses it; finally he creates it anew. The work is an end in itself and in any case will not know how to be a means without disavowing itself. The prophecy of the poet-seers is fulfilled. As high as genius is elevated, the summit from which the Verb thunders remains accessible to the slow and violent ascent of man.

Explosive alloy of Surrealism (the dream and the present that it supplies), of Négritude (race and the fabulous past that our people reinvent), and of Marxism (the struggle of the classes and the classless society of the future)—my own ideal is that poetry be revolutionary in form and substance, and that the poet himself live it not only in art but in life.

Poetry can not be insulated from mankind.

Nature doesn't mean God. It isn't any longer a substitute for Him in exhibiting its attributes. It has its laws which science has discovered and continues to discover, reducing more and more the space of the "mystery," which is to say what men don't succeed in showing any more, but which poetry sometimes reveals.

Capitalism would like to escape the laws of nature and human society, but as with slavery and feudalism it is condemned to die. In its very own womb has been born the economic system that must replace it: Socialism, in order that material and cultural riches, products *by all*, be *for all* as well. Socialism and democracy are, moreover, as compatible as are revolution and culture.

In Haiti, following Morisseau-Leroy and Frank Fouché, poets writing in Creole at first followed French etymology because they were addressing the francophonic readers of their class in reclaiming however from them an attempt to learn to read their maternal language. On the other hand, when they began to write for the people with the intention of being understood even by those who didn't know how to read, once having been read by the majority, there was a great need for them to adopt the popular pronunciation and orthography, what they had left in the care of experts, linguists and educators.

Transforming destiny into liberty, the poet recreates the world in the image of his love.

Poetry is response to the enigma of the sphinx, without its ever ceasing to be an enigma itself.

Science deciphers nature. It opens for us the big book of the world that has to be read page by page, line by line.

In a picture, a look, a flash, art delivers the universe to us.

Science is inquiry, reflection, the supremacy of reason, even if intuition is not averted.

Art is revelation, illumination, creation commencing from intuition even if technique is not denied.

"There's never been art without a dialogue with divinity." That is to say, what the human being has of the eternal or, at the very least, aspirations to the eternal divinity by which, dialectically, art creates man.

Between Marx and Rimbaud—the dialectic of reason and intuition—the communist poet discovers unity.

The frontier between art and science is abolished.

PAUL LARAQUE is one of Haiti's leading poetic voices. He is respected as a poet in both Haitian Creole and French, and as a Marxist analyst of the cultural and political dimensions of life both in exile in the U.S. and in Haiti itself. In the 1980s he headed the Association of Haitian Writers Abroad. Curbstone Press has published his French poems, translated by Rosemary Manno, under the title *Camourade*. The original volume of *Camourade* was the first French volume to win the Casa de las Americas for poetry in Cuba, in 1979. His Creole poems, *Fistibal/Slingshot,* translated by Jack Hirschman, have been published by Seaworthy Press (San Francisco) in conjunction with Samba Editions (Port-au-Prince). He coedited the first major anthology of Creole poetry, *Open Gate,* translated by Hirschman and the Haitian poet Boadiba, published by Curbstone Press in 2001.

Three Voices / Together:
A Collage

[The following excerpts were edited from a series of letters, discussions and taped conversations that took place from July through October, 1987.]

"MY WORK IS INFORMED BY WHERE I AM FROM..."

Kimiko Hahn: Some of my earliest memories rise from my family's visit to Maui to see my (maternal) grandparents. I was four and very confused about nationality, about being "American." (I'm half Japanese-American, my mother's from Hawaii; and half German-American, my dad's from Milwaukee.) Children called me Chinese or Japanese—physically, I look Asian. Could I be Japanese and American? Part Japanese?

I remember asking my grandmother if she were Japanese. She laughed and said, "Yes." Then she asked me. I replied, "A little bit." I remember being confused and being asked a lot: "What are you?" (Now people ask, "Where are you from?")

When I was nine, we lived in Japan while my father studied art. The children in my Japanese school called me "amerikajin" or "gaijin" (literally, "outsider"). I felt I never fit in. I never felt fully "at home." My poems address this ambiguity.

Growing up in a white middle-class suburb in effect polarized my identity. I grew away from the Western tradition in a sense (except for poetry and rock-and-roll). I was raised with a lot of Japanese culture mainly because of my father's deep interest and my mother's heritage; my sister and I studied flower arrangement, classical and folk dance, calligraphy, tea ceremony. In college, then graduate school, I went on to study Japanese literature, seeking both the familiar and the new. Something that felt comfortable. In my poem, "Revolutions," I open with the little known fact that the "golden age of literature" was dominated by women in Japan. This influence of theirs happened for social reasons because the men were writing in

319

Chinese (the same way people wrote in Latin instead of in the vernacular), whereas the women were writing in the vernacular in Japanese. So the women's writing was an explosion; it was a release of material and feelings—so much so that men would write in the female persona. The "female sensibility" was that dominant. To me this is a very important piece of history and part of myself. It inspires and informs much of my own art.

Parallel to this was my political "awakening," beginning with a feminist orientation. I sold copies of the original newsprint booklet of *Our Bodies, Our Selves* in high school. When "caught," I retreated to a nearby parking lot where the girls picked up their orders. My own sexuality became a territory for me: my body is mine, my responsibility. This "territory" also gave me an increasing awareness that women's bodies historically have not always belonged to them: for instance, fathers using their daughters as marital pawns or husbands using wives to produce sons.

It is strange that while I do not consider my ideology "Feminist" (capital F) in the sense of men, or patriarchy being the enemy, all my work is deeply committed to women's relationships (with one another, with men, with society). I view revolution not as a "midwife" but as birth itself. My poem "Revolutions," is more or less about a female culture or aesthetic, while another poem, "Seams," was commissioned by Bill Brand for his experimental film (*Coalfields*) on Black Lung advocate Fred Carter; my particular subjective contribution (I was also interviewed and helped edit) takes a "feminist position" envisioning the strip-mined land as "female" and reaching for the kind of power (sexual and social) the word "virile" engenders. Other poems further explore a female subculture: through metaphors of weaving (traditional women's work); through the metaphor of closure/divorce. It may be simplistic to say, but because women have been unencouraged and unpublished for centuries, what we say today is new and exhilarating. Our work and concerns are very different from men's and it has something to do with biology (the powerful, mysterious and vulnerable uterus) and a lot to do with history. I'm not knocking male writers, rather expressing my particular need for other women's voices.

Gale Jackson: I am a Black woman. An African-American woman. My mother's first child. My grandmother's fourth, but first

American-born. Older sibling. The one who writes. My great aunt's special. And sometimes "patti g."

On my mother's side my people are African Caribbeans from Jamaica, the West Indies. Their continuous immigrations (I've never thought of my people's immigration as a static concept) allowed me to understand internationalism at an early age. I heard I took my first plane ride at age six months with my great-grandmother. She was a great traveler—up through the island nations, through South and Central America, as one did working in the colonized world of that day. My father's side of the family are African-Americans who have been in this country longer, I suspect. The truth is that I don't really know.

I grew up in a very large household (very African I've learned, very West Indian also) with several generations and family groups and special names and relationships to everyone. I have always lived with older people and new-born babies, belonging to a community with a measure of security and a measure of rule. We were not particularly rich or poor but I am, have always been, clear that our well-being as individuals was absolutely tied into our helping each other along. This is the axis of my politics. This is what we were told and what we saw done. I grew up with cousins and lived in the same household as great-grandmother, grandmother, uncles and aunts. My mother always worked. The older women, at different times, kept house. We were taught (maybe the saving naïveté of immigrant children) that we could create the life that we would.

I grew up in a home of women who were smart, independent and self-sufficient. These are the things you learn by osmosis. I am sure that I am among many writers of similar background who attribute their love of stories to their early delight in listening to the women talk. The women in my house gossiped, talked music. Talked politics. Talked sports. They spoke several languages. They have, as Jamaicans, a dual concept of home. (They don't pronounce the "h" but they say home and mean Jamaica, even here, while they live in the psychic space that they've created in this country which they also call, in a way, home.) To imitate not only their storytelling but also the language of their stories was always a special game for me as a child. I remember longing to be grown so I would have stories to tell and a language of my own.

I come from a place where there is a lot of love and respect. I feel gifted and responsible. Having been socialized to share and to see myself as a part of a community—my family and by extension my people and then by extension our world—leaves you with tremendous strength and the real responsibility to carry on. To take it further. To put something back. Like a new place. New words. New possibilities for home.

My work is informed by where I am from; my Africas in America, my Caribbean journeys, loving myself, women, children, (smile) even how I love the men. I want the work to be loving portraits, reminders to people of their strength, stories to extend the imagination about where we can go. Like in my poem "the untitled" which begins with my friend's grandmother, Mrs. King, a woman who is an emotional and physical axis for her family. The poem begins with this real Black woman at its heart, then takes you to Central America and her women, to South Africa and the real women there, back to Brooklyn, back and forth until it is one place, a place where we can begin to imagine what will happen when she has had enough and decides to "soar," change the world, take it out. Possibilities. The language to tell. The language to see with and be empowered by enough to reach on out and connect. In a language that is our own.

Susan Sherman: I like the word "origins" because to me it means not only your childhood or your roots (your starting point in time) but what continues, what makes your work, your daily life possible. In my prose poem "Ten Years After" there's a line, "...what we move toward is what moves us most." My origin: what moves me, touches me; what moves me, activates me, defines me, most.

I was born in Philadelphia, Pennsylvania, in 1939, grew up in Los Angeles during the Forties and Fifties. My memories of my family are attached to those years. When I finished college in 1961, I came to New York and didn't return to California for over seventeen years.

Berkeley in the late Fifties and early Sixties—the Beat Generation, the San Francisco Renaissance, North Beach, poetry, the "sexual revolution" and my first real experiences with sex and love (unfortunately then not the same) my first relationship with a woman, the House Un-American Activities Committee, "police riots"; the first time I saw a real alternative to the life I had known or the lives I knew about, an alternative I wanted to embrace.

New York, 1961, '62, '63, poetry readings at the Deux Magots, Le Métro, writing and directing plays at the Hardware Poets Theatre, working for $28 a week, apartments on Delancey and Suffolk, on 9th St. between B & C, the riots in '63, '64, the episodes of disassociation, panic, not seeing my family for years. The struggle to survive. The mid-Sixties—Angry Arts Against the War, the Free University, the Alternate University, the founding of the first series of *IKON* magazine, "coming out" in 1961 and then slowly retreating in and then "coming out" again. The trips to Cuba in 1967 and '68 and consciousness of a reality totally separate from any I had recognized before—loss of job, ulcer, loss of magazine, turning that loss into intense political involvement and commitment and creativity not born from, but energized by, anger—as my poetry had been, from personal anger, from a consciousness of my parents' brutality years before.

The Seventies—Chile, breakup of first long relationship, the Fifth Street Women's Building, the Lesbian/feminist movement, the stillness of years that were a pulling together as well as a breaking apart; *Sagaris*, a bad automobile accident. The Eighties—Nicaragua, the new *IKON*, a new relationship. All that I remember, all I have forgotten. My origins, what made me, make me what I am.

To talk about all this with any completeness would take a book in itself—being close to fifty, almost a half century now, I'm actually in the process of writing that book. More than anything else to try to get some of the feeling of those years down, not "my" years, the years themselves. So much of them, as so much of our own individual histories, forgotten or distorted.

My childhood was characterized by a lack of roots, of specific place. I never knew exactly where my grandparents were from, my parents never spoke of it, if they knew themselves. Partly from fear, partly because they wanted desperately to forget those years, to fit in. I am Jewish, and that was thought of then in racial, not religious, terms. I wasn't brought up in the Jewish religion, I went to a Christian Science school—I left Christian Science when I was fifteen— although we celebrated most of the important Jewish holidays at home, and I was often the only one who went to synagogue with my father on high holidays. I was always very aware of being Jewish and of a proud and troubled heritage.

It was only long afterwards, when I learned about words like "background" and "class," that I realized how important my parents' immigrant experience was in explaining a lot of what happened to me in my early life, and the importance of understanding that experience now. The multiplicity of cultures and the constant pitting of those cultures against each other. The multiplicity of centuries in a place like New York, in the space of a few square blocks. And the incredible problems and the incredible energy and creativity which that produces.

Our class definitions were confused—my mother was the only child in her family born in this country; my stepfather (who raised me) came here from Russia at the age of five—he never went past grammar school. My mother hated poverty; I think there was a certain grayness attached to her childhood memories, to being poor, that became a kind of metaphor for her. It wasn't until I got much older that I realized how many of her choices were conditioned by that hatred. She moved as far away from her family as she could get, so I never had "family" around when I was growing up. I remember only once visiting my grandparents when I was quite young. I remember them being nice to me—they didn't speak English so I couldn't understand what they said—and that their apartment smelled of crackers and warm milk.

As I get older, it seems the hardest part is being able to continue defining myself in terms of my hopes, my dreams, my vision—to keep identifying and re-identifying myself with what I believe, what I think is human and just.

And, perhaps most important, to allow myself to risk being wrong. In my writing as well as in my life.

"BREAKING THROUGH TOWARDS EXPRESSION..."

Gale: I write because I am compelled to, by circumstance, by desire. I write like I could scream sometimes. Or sing. Compelled by love to mark the moment. Compelled by pain.

Writing is like living. It is absolutely intimate and absolutely social. It is something that is personally felt even while it is resonant with many voices. Conscience. Haunting. It's that close. The world around you is insistent and specific and real and you have to put it down. You have to say something about how we are living. About life. To say. To shape. To explore. With words. With voice. To celebrate. To mourn. To recreate.

The kids out in the street can be so shouting, so wildly alive. While in our silences we are dying a little each day with AIDS, famine, the death squads who invade. You write to tell the stories that need telling. Of course that is political. Our culture is our social heart. Our histories. Our possibilities. Our names. How we survive whole. This is about how a woman moves through the world alone. This is about Nicaragua's sovereignty. About Palestine's homeland. About South Africa's freedom. About hunger. About home. You write to tell the stories that need telling. You hear it and it matters. You nurture the imagination of voice as it rises up...a scream, a note, a song, a shout, a silence, a cry...making way in the world.

Kimiko: It was a real need for other voices, like yours and Susan's, that thrust me into poetry. Writing for me is the process of breaking through towards expression, and finding time to write is important to my well-being.

When I look back at my childhood, although we were a family of artists and were close in mutual activities, we did not express our emotions to each other. I vividly recall my mother and father telling me to put on a cheerful face in spite of whatever I was feeling, then turning to my friends and encouraging them to express themselves. In high school it became heightened when my father would tell me my "bad moods" ruined his day. My parents assumed my sullenness was an adolescent stage.

Susan: It wasn't an easy thing to speak in my family either. Often when really emotional about something, I would start to stutter— not a noticeable stutter to anyone, more like a hesitation, an inability to force the words out, to find the right ones. I feel my writing expresses that deep part of me. It takes the language of the poem, the images of the poem—reaching beyond words—to do it.

From the time I was very young reading was my refuge, but I never read poetry. The poems I had contact with were typical grade school and high school poems, written in another century, in another language, having nothing to do with me. The poems I wrote when I was a teenager were about my own life, my own dreams, written in my own language, unsure and poor as it was.

It was when I was in Berkeley in 1958 and met Diane Wakoski and all the poets there that poetry came alive for me. It was about me, my generation, my hopes, and in my language. As I read those poems, and often mimicked their gestures, my own language in writing changed, and my own voice began, slowly, to emerge.

Gale: Someone once said "Art is like a lover" because it is the job of art to show you, like a lover can show you, the things that you can't see. The things that are there that are not yet seen. There are ways of sharing vision. Art. Of caring. I remember once finding my mother's drawings in a sewing stool, in those years when I was very young and making books and selling them to her for nickels and encouragement. She is a very fine artist. Realistic. Drawing portraits. Concerned with the lines. The feelings in the human face. Though she no longer draws, she has created that kind of a household. Around her. So full. And the cozy and wide-angled world-view which begins with the intense importance of each individual face.

Kimiko: I was just thinking about what it means to be an artist right now in this environment. I was thinking that it's so much like working a second shift—second shift, third shift, whatever. You work, you come home, and the day begins again doing your true work; it's a continual tradeoff and compromise.

My life works best when everything is integrated—making money, politics, my art, my relationships. Everything is really intertwined. But when did that ever happen! I can only think of one time—when I worked on *Coalfields*. I traveled with Bill Brand in West Virginia, conducted, then excerpted, interviews. I didn't promise him poems because I usually don't write on assignment like that, but I said I'd write some text and I wrote two poems I really like—I think they're probably my best. They're political, they're sexy, they're forceful.

For ten days we did nothing but talk to active miners, retired miners, their wives, their kids in some cases, and heard extraordinary stories. I'd return to my motel room exhausted, but type away, and that's where those poems originated. The whole experience integrated what I love, what I feel passionate about—that is so rare and it just needn't be. Why should we always think of ourselves as having to scrape around for moments to do our artwork! (And being a mother now means even less time.)

Susan: We're trying to do our art now as women who have to work to survive. As women who can't depend on anyone else to support us. Who are self-supporting. Well, this is obviously nothing new. This is the reason women, people of color, working people, have always been so under-represented in the art world, not because of a lack of talent, because they have lacked both the time to do the work and the places to publish or show their work.

Gale: There are a lot of myths about what and where art is. On this side of the "arts" spectrum there are women, people, the majority of the world who, it's true, have not had the establishment forums, but who have always had art in their own lives and their own (even when it has been very confined) spheres. For most of us, maintaining our cultural identity has been a crucial, political act. There has always been a people's art. It may have been quilt-making to tell the story of family generations, jewelry, craft that identified a particular people, or pictures cut from magazines and pasted up to give color to a wall. At our best we create a living art. Today we are, again, saying that we want to take the best of that tradition and imagination, particularly as women, and exercise it in the widest international spheres. We are saying we want to take the art, the beauty, the understanding and the values that have informed our lives and insured our survival, what we've used to make a home, to make a just and better society.

I feel very utilitarian about art. I look at what the traditional functions of art have been—they've been about education and comfort, about being in harmony with the world and getting dreams out. Art is a vehicle not just for beauty, but for all the possibilities of things people have inside. Folk tales, for example, teach people, remind them of the rules of their society, kindle their imaginations, their concept of possibility and of reach. Storytelling, like quilt-making, brings people together with a vehicle of expression within the context of what they must do. Within the context of their society and its work. It is at best an interaction, a progress in the world that is interactive, not self-destructive.

I always think of the Inuit people and the storytelling they do through the dark days, because it's freezing cold and this is a part of the tradition they have created to sustain themselves and be in harmony with their environment. Well, in this country, in this city, the question is, how do you bring that here, to this wild urban place?

Connections are very important for me. I feel that my strength as a writer grows with my ability to tap into my cultural traditions. From knowing who I am. Being an African-American woman, for instance, in this time, is an extraordinary moment in history that I am a part of. Understanding that allows me to move in and out in powerful ways. It allows me to connect with other women from a very strong place. It allows me a very international understanding of myself in my time. My political work is for me the logical extension of my understanding and my concern, in the same way that my writing combines caring and craft to move towards broader understandings, visions.

From the time I was thirteen, I knew that I lived in an absolutely interdependent world economy. This is a real challenge to the human imagination. My mother couldn't say that, my mother didn't wear socks from Afghanistan or have an idea of what was happening in Afghanistan and see it on television. There is a balance, a tension, a consciousness between the particular (the one loved one, the family, the self) and the international (the universal, the world). Within that tension somewhere is where I live and write.

Kimiko: I write from a very unconscious place. When I write I sit down with a blank piece of paper and I just scribble. Whatever comes up, that's what I shape and rewrite and work over. Vision and revision! There are occasions when I have something I have to write about, but what I do is store the idea until it becomes part of that place I write from. We all self-censor to a greater or lesser degree, but my most successful poems are the ones that spring from that un-selfconscious place.

Susan: In every poem I have ever written I am looking for meaning. Not "How?"—which is a series of physical causes, but "Why?" We have been taught not to ask, "Why?"—with the result that we wind up unable to understand even the most obvious truth, what's right in front of us.

I find my inspiration, as far as form is concerned, first of all in music—which is one of the things I love most. It is the rhythm of the poem, the music of the voice that captures me. And then with imagery—to make the statement precise and unusual. And simple. The complexity of the simple, of the simple statement. I'm not telling stories in most of my poems; I'm not describing events. If anything, I'm painting states of mind, composing themes, trying to come up with new perceptions, new ways of relating what I observe around me—like the old way philosophy was written, in poetry—but adding our new consciousness, our personal and social life, and the events that take place around us.

I understand how philosophy got and continues to get "bad

press," but I'm not talking about a kind of intellectualism that plays with language or abstract concepts and refuses to be grounded in any kind of real social context. Behind everything we do and say is an assumption, and one of the things philosophy is about to me is understanding and questioning those assumptions.

With Anger/With Love was an appropriate name for my first full book. Love is an obvious connection, but the anger is not anger that ties you to the hated object; it is anger that energizes you to change that condition.

"POLITICAL INVOLVEMENT IS NOT AN ABSTRACT THING..."

Kimiko: While no one escaped the influence of the Vietnam War, I was not a conscious voice in the Movement (say in the Sixties to early Seventies). When I did venture towards Asian-American organizations (which is to say an organized struggle) there was a little animosity: being part white translated to part enemy. Back then.

Not until I lived in New York and began to feel oppressed by the economic and social environment did I begin to understand my own personal dilemma: female, nonwhite, artist, member of the working class. My boyfriend said to me, "Well, what are you going to do about it (your anxiety and anger)?" As a step toward comprehension and vision, I began to study Marxism-Leninism. For the first time I cared about the study of history and political economy and through those studies I began to think in an analytical manner quite different from what I had encountered in college. A scientific manner. I began to appreciate science and to learn I could use my mind to understand current world events. However, this was the early Seventies, a time when sectarianism was rampant, and the left was isolated from "the working class."

But my real cultural and political work did not take off until October '81 at the American Writers Congress, a gathering of over 3,000 writers in New York. I found myself in the midst of political people who had trained in every place you find writers: trade union newsletter editors from steel and auto plants to university professors to street poets. We were there to talk politics. Dissent. Make resolutions. (The most concrete product, or byproduct, was the National Writers Union.) I was in my element, though still young in the sense of being politically "fresh." At this time I met more Asian-

329

American writers and, having completed a stint in graduate school, I was aching to quit the libraries, to write and organize. My activity began with my editorship at *Bridge: Asian-American Perspectives* (now defunct).

After a few years of projects, projections and a couple of trips to Nicaragua (where I met Susan), I was invited to help form the Poets and Writers Committee of Artists' Call Against U.S. Intervention in Central America. This would be my next "leap forward." I met other writers/political activists and began to hone my organizing skills. Being on the Steering Committee gave me a chance to exercise my political views, which were to keep Artists' Call on track as an organization against intervention (and undeniably pro-Sandinista). The organization faded away after a couple of years for a variety of reasons, both personal (many original organizers started families) and political. Political? In my opinion we should have linked the issue of intervention (the bloated military budget, for example) with our real needs here. Artists' needs are not separate: we need food, housing, medical care, schools for our children. Part of the reason we (and most of society) don't have adequate social services is because so much is taken up by the military. I consider illiteracy, unemployment and homelessness our real national security risks. I wish we could have made these links, brought the issue of intervention closer to our own needs, rather than conveniently keeping it one of "the poor Central Americans." We cannot afford to be sectarian any longer: our allies, (say in shelters for the homeless here) may not even know what socialism is. They may never have heard the word "proletariat," but if they are struggling against this economic system, we must become allies.

Gale: One favorite writer friend says, "Be subversive." Subversive be much of the crux of it. Inadvertently. At first. I found that this imagination would be the only way for me to make a living and write and care.

When I began my work with Art Against Apartheid, I was working as a Black Heritage librarian. Doing a lot of cultural programming. Telling stories. Helping to build the collection in a very special community-run space—the Langston Hughes Community Library and Cultural Center. He had always been my first poet. A working artist.

Five years before that I had been standing at Grand Army Plaza in Brooklyn trying to figure out what I could do here where I lived. It was the museum. The park. Or the library. So library it turned out. I had, still have, these biographies for children I wanted to do. I been in and out. Doing some freelance research. Uncovering. Discovering. In Black women's history. In myself. The concept of the book arts, story arts, and the politics of information.

Much before that were lots of beginnings. Some anti-nuclear work in college, some coming together with other Black students. In a women's space. Around then was when I began to do research and writing for community-based organizations. I worked with the War Resisters League. Some extraordinary people who had been around, militantly for peace, more than twice the time of my life. Learning about finding and disseminating information in organized "alternative" structures. The educational work for justice. Had many important apprenticeships. In writing. In organizing as well. I grew up to be a librarian through alternating between these special works and some of the regular jobs women find themselves doing at one time or another. All these things forced my eye. The political work. The craft. The shit work. I went naturally into the work with children and it has stretched me out in all possible directions. To teach. To perform. To program and organize in the arts. To be faster and more smart.

I keep being a librarian in different settings. Now at Medgar Evers College, a predominately Black women's college in Brooklyn, pushing the status quo out—I feel like I'm still building. Being a juggler. But no more than the women before me who got me to this spot. To that multi-generational coalition I must attribute (smile) the strength of imagination for survival.

Susan: It has always seemed to me that the greatest weapon that can be and is used against us is isolation. Separating us from one another. What depresses me most, inactivates me most, is when I feel that I'm totally and completely alone, in my work as well as in my relationships. That I have no community.

I'm not talking about the physical event of being a single entity in a room. You can be in a room with a thousand people and still feel alone. I first heard this conceptualized in the Sixties when I was teaching at the Free University—or School, as it came later to be known because of legal restrictions—a place where I felt I was really able to share what I knew and at the same time learn from people

331

who were gathered together there to learn and teach for the purpose of directly influencing and changing the world they lived in. Or rather the worlds, since we came from many different places. Where information was used instead of stored, where, at its best, there really was dialogue, a willingness, an eagerness to participate, to talk and to listen. To break down the artificial and imposed separation between words and action, poetry and real people's lives.

At many crucial points in my life, from childhood on, I have seen and experienced forcefully and often quite painfully the results of isolation and lack of community, not only on myself but on people around me. That's why it's been so important to me to make connections. To edit a magazine that makes connections. To speak with you.

Kimiko: My political involvement has profoundly influenced my writing. In the same way relationships (romantic relationships, my relationship with my mother, my father, my sister) influence my writing. I think it's given it a totally new dimension and I don't feel at all "agitpropy," like I'm writing something that's for a placard, or that, in fact, I can only write one way. I feel very much that there's a new dimension added to my writing that makes it much more powerful. And yes, it means not being separated.

Gale: Your politics really mean the configurations of your relationships. We live in a world together, and that is a political construct. How we choose to live, our collective imagination about how we can live and what we can do, is so tied to our culture. Our culture is after all our eyes. My eyes allow me to see, to have relationships with folks close and far, all my relationships, with my family, my love, my friends, with even the women far away. All that feeds into who I am, my political being. I am in Brooklyn, I can imagine what it must be like to live in a house where soldiers are standing on the roof, with guns. This is all my world. I write from here about that voice, about the place where it joins my own. The world is very much with me. Sometimes so much it is difficult to write. But always so important, so urgent, that it brings me back to a place where I have to. You care. You want. A safe place. It is a politic of the deepest desire. We are always saying something about the connections that we forge with one another. We are at best saying something about human possibility for humanity, for a particular articulated beauty, for change. Politically, culturally, it is my job to provide the information about that, how much life means.

Susan: Political involvement is not an abstract thing. You write about it the way you'd write about anything else you have a deep commitment to. It's very fashionable now to argue that American writers are free of the necessity to include political or social issues in our work because those necessities don't impinge on our very existence the way they might in another country like, for example, El Salvador. The implication, of course, being that not only are political issues not an "authentic" part of our existence, they shouldn't be central in "real" art, and that, in this country, one must finally chose between being an artist or an activist. That being a "true" artist automatically means putting issues of "language" first and "society" second. Being a "professional" is a full-time job.

Of course, this conveniently excuses from responsibility the very group of people who are directly or indirectly the source of the problems that necessitate activism to begin with. My question, and I think it's crucial, to these writers, artists, intellectuals, would have to be this: even if your own individual life isn't threatened at this particular instant, at what point do you decide what's being done to other people is worth involving in your writing, your world; at what point do you take responsibility for it; at what point do you suddenly discover that it is your world, your responsibility, your work?

The real danger, it seems to me, when you become politically involved, is not in your choice of subject matter, but how to keep from being overly self-censoring. Maybe it's partly generational, but when I first became involved politically in the middle Sixties, I started asking myself questions like, "Should I write about this subject?" "Should I change these words?" I went back through my essays and changed all the masculine pronouns that referred to humanity as "man." And I think that was absolutely right. But it can be carried too far. There was an internalized part of me constantly saying: Is this revolutionary? Is this correct?

And it did affect my work and did inhibit me for awhile. I'm trying to write about my family now, and I feel a lot of conflict and a lot of difficulty trying to be careful, trying to be fair, trying to be political, in the face of an anti-Semitism I acknowledge I cannot possibly understand. After all, I was a child raised in the Forties when the fear of what was happening in Europe and the prejudice and danger that engendered here was an undercurrent that ran through my parents' everyday existence. Fears that were passed on to me in much more subtle ways: the obsession with, whenever possible, passing, assimilating; the contradiction of, at the same time, building a wall around you of your own people, your own customs, traditions, of excluding the life-threatening "other;" the fear that falling out of line, being pointed out, being too obvious, would affect not only you, but your family, your whole people; that an individual act could be lethal to the community as a whole.

Gale: How do you be all the things that you are? How can we all be? How can a commitment to humanity be maintained? As we struggle to survive, as we fight wars between and among ourselves, there are a lot of things we have yet to learn. But there has to be something in the deepest voice that you trust and that is the place where you write from. There is something in there that as a cultural worker you are constantly in the process of teaching and learning. We live in a very complicated time. And this is one of the big challenges before us— teaching ourselves to re-listen, to be human, to liberate our hearts. I have to believe that is possible. That we have whatever tools we need in our histories. In our stories. There are some very harsh realities. Believing doesn't make me anguish-free. But it makes that contradiction, that anguish, that isolation a little different, a little less.

I was talking to somebody about relationships and they were saying, you know, look at the world we live in. We live in a fucking insane world. You want to read the paper, you know what I mean. How do you think that you make it through loving someone else, anybody, how do you think that you get through that scot-free and perfectly and you're always a good person. That none of your society gets into you. But, of course, it does. Into all of us. Women. Men. The children.

Susan: A child has no alternatives. A child's world is prescribed by the adults in it. They define that world. I once wrote, that the most important thing you can discover is that there is an alternative. And later I learned that if there isn't one, you have to fight to create one. Because that's what being an adult, being in control, means. We are kept in the position of children by being deprived of choice.

My trip to the Cuban Cultural conference in 1968 taught me

about the history of my own country, because it placed me in a context outside myself, separate from me or the interests of people around me. Because it taught me about revolution, about change and about how art, how culture was part of that process. Because I met writers from Argentina and Chile and Mexico and Colombia and the rest of Latin America, many of whom I had seen in *El Corno Emplumado* (the bilingual magazine co-edited by Margaret Randall in Mexico in the Sixties), possibly the only place in this country those works were available then, but had never really understood as part of my own culture, my own hemisphere.

In the Fifties, with the Beat Movement, poetry really moved out "into the streets" and became a dialogue you spoke out loud, that people listened to and responded to—the readings in the North Beach bars in the Fifties and the open readings in the early Sixties in cafés and bars in New York.

The Black civil rights movement and liberation movements, the women's movement, Lesbian and gay struggle, Chicano, Puerto-Rican, Native American, Asian-American movements, produced the energy that has motivated and empowered all people to creatively express themselves, to demand their work be recognized and that those artists and activists and thinkers and human beings that form their culture, their "origins," be published, be heard. As progressive Jewish groups had done earlier and now again, and the Irish, Italian, and all the other groups that came before and will come after, carrying on in a long tradition of struggle and change.

And the base of American culture has changed, because the way was opened for a new underpinning of culture that was truly representative of the United States as it is today, for all of us, a United States no longer grounded exclusively in European art and criticism.

I'm not talking about stealing someone else's ideas or work, as so often happens in popular music. I'm talking about the fact that we now have so much access to what is truly ours. All the wonderful work that is now available from our America, as well as writers like Gabriel García Márquez and Luisa Valenzula and Isabel Allende and Pablo Neruda from Latin America and Sembene Ousmane from Senegal and Fumiko Enchi from Japan. They are there for us to absorb the way I read Rainer Maria Rilke and García Lorca in college until they became part of me, part of my history, my own voice, and they were important, but it was a limited history, a European history, and a limited voice, and now it's not, it's an "American" heritage which is all of us in close contact with our own hemisphere, with Central America and the Caribbean and South America and Mexico and Canada too.

I think making a dichotomy between art and politics is part of that whole process of continuing to separate us, of silencing us.

I think that it's very important and that people who are involved politically keep saying it, that what we're fighting for is not a world that's smaller than the world we live in. If it gets any smaller, none of us are going to be able to breathe at all. What we're fighting for is a world that's larger, where all people can express themselves, where they can express their differences. Where we can express our differences.

"I SAY 'POET' NOW..."

Kimiko: I think when one talks about politics and art, history and memory are essential elements. One is not entirely subjective, the other objective. I think women's history in general is most important to me. I identify with the collective difficulty to express and/or publish that expression. (In fact, this discussion is one avenue against that historical silence.) Of course, the stereotypical Japanese woman is a passive, silent one. I defy that. I use history and memory to defy it.

The history of the artist in general is one of margins. We are part of the intelligentsia, and therefore, in times of social turmoil, we can throw our lot in any direction. We don't have set allies. The social margin we occupy is one that denies us full participation as citizens (especially in being able to make a living) and does not take our occupation seriously. I used to be hesitant to tell people I was a poet. I'd say "writer" or "student." That sounds legitimate. But to admit to being an artist (even though I grew up in a family of artists!) was somehow saying I was not to be taken seriously. I say "poet" now.

Politically I do my organizing with artists because I don't think real social change is possible without cultural change—that's where artists come in—yes, even poets! Who reads and listens to poetry? I read in a variety of places and that's where people mainly hear me. And a great many people write all over this land—I mean there are a lot of poets out there. Nicaragua is called "A Land of Poets" because you can go anywhere and find them. Well, I think that is true here though our society doesn't value poets/artists as highly. Just look at the proliferation of journals, newsletters and workshops. What I'd like to do politically is say to these writers—your lot is really cast with all working people; therefore, everyone, from meat packers in Minnesota to welfare mothers in Atlanta, is our social ally.

What is really the opposite of repression? Usually we think of the opposite of repression as being liberation, but a major part of liberation is expression. Expression empowers people towards liberation, or within a liberation movement, or the liberation of one's heart, or whatever. I was thinking of expression as being perhaps the true opposite of repression. I was thinking of it in a social way.

I grew up in a very white suburb where my sister and I and my mother were the minority. And later on, when I started getting involved with people who were in the Asian-American struggles, some people would look at me as being part white and they somewhat rejected me. Later on it was okay—never mind that in the detention camps during World War II, if you were some fraction Japanese you were in the camps. I consider my daughter Japanese-American, because if it came to having to go into the camps, that's where she would be. I don't know what she'll consider herself; that is for her to decide and for her to live out. But I consider her Japanese-American.

My husband's mother, when we announced our engagement, turned to him right at the dinner table and said, "Why don't you marry an American?" What she meant was white, but what she said was American. American means white, Anglo-Saxon, Protestant. Probably not even Catholic or Jewish. If I'd been Jewish, she would have said something somewhat different, but with the same meaning.

Susan: The truth is, when it comes to the bottom line, the society you live in always tries to enforce its definitions of who you are on you. And, even more important, what you mean and what value you have. Sometimes fatally. Which is why it's so essential to make our own definitions and to struggle to change social definitions.

Gale: We're talking about human education here. That's when you talk about seizing traditional forms, the arts, traditional forms of reaching people, and turning them modern and figuring out how to teach these lessons again because somehow people have watched too many commercials not realizing that culturally, or through the lack thereof, we've been pushed to the brink of survival, against the wall, literally to the edge of the fatal possibilities of the world we're living in. Somehow you have to reach people and bring them back, mindful that peace will only come with justice. That eye for eye for eye could go on and on. Somehow you have to reach people 'cause we have to talk. There are a lot of things that, for starters, we need to learn and remember. A lot of history has been taken away from people and one of the first restitutions would be to begin to restore. People's very stories have been taken away, made inaccessible, till we don't all know who we are. Culturally. Till we don't have no home. Real or metaphoric. Then there is all that is going on that is not being told. The news. Our country's not-so-covert wars. In my work as a writer, as a librarian, I be finding that people don't know. This tragedy of repetition. When it becomes clear that culture, art information, is first and foremost political, it is clear that people need to use that to reach and teach. To explore. People need to know. To imagine. To know.

Kimiko: You've touched on something really important. I keep speaking as if the artists are over here and the oppressed people are over there, and we're going to meet, but in fact the majority of artists are part of the survival movement. I can find the time to write because I'm fortunate enough to have a rent-stabilized apartment. But that's part luck and part living in a place for ten years through drug wars and everything else—sticking it out. But the fact is there are people out there who may not consider themselves "poets" but actually are. There are groupings of homeless poets' workshops. Several groupings. So they're already out there working together. It's a matter of seeing our interests as one and the same.

Susan: When I was in Berkeley in 1959, there were the "artists" and there were the "political" people. I was an artist and I didn't consider myself one of the "politicos," although I fancied myself terribly anti-establishment. We slept together, we ate together, we went to parties together, but there was a very distinct separation.

When I went to the demonstration against HUAC (the House Un-American Activities Committee) after the demonstrators had been washed down a flight of marble stairs in San Francisco in 1960, when I went to anti-war demonstrations after coming to New York, I still considered myself an "artist"—period. I was just protesting certain unjust actions. It was really after my trip to Cuba in 1968, along with the repercussions from that trip (loss of job, the magazine, friends, my health), that I became much more conscious politically, that I began to make connections—to connect the poverty that I suddenly "saw," the racism, the commercialism, and recognize their interrelations, to examine their cause.

At the same time I started to identify myself as an artist who was also a political person, and recognize where those two things came together. It was a huge change for me, as big as the one I went through when I first went to Berkeley. And that I would go through later as a result of feminism.

My recognition of myself consciously as a "woman," rather than a being who somehow magically transcended such mundane categories as gender, came through the "Fifth Street Women's Building Action," which took place in coalition with the squatters' movement in the early Seventies. I'll never forget that night—standing precisely at midnight in the middle of a snow storm on New Year's Eve, on the corner of First Avenue and Fifth Street, guarding a van full of provisions as women crawled, one by one, each holding a flashlight, into a broken window on the first floor of this huge abandoned building almost directly across from the 9th Precinct. We intended the building to be used by community women—for daycare, for the homeless, for community activities. And it was. At least until we were busted by the Tactical Police Force and it was demolished to make way for a parking lot. It was always my feeling, with the level of energy we women showed, they didn't dare leave that building standing.

One of the main organizers of that action was June Arnold, the head of the Literature Committee of the Women's Center, a feminist author who started one of the first women's presses—in fact, it might have been the first—Daughters Inc. Our slogan was "Our hands, our minds, our feet, our bodies are tools of change."

My poem "Lilith" was a direct result of that Fifth Street action and the months of organizing and "consciousness-raising" that went along with it. I call it my "coming-out" poem—that expression to be taken on a number of levels. It is also a strong statement of support for the many brave woman who had put themselves on the line in the Sixties for what they believed in, some of whom were in prison or underground at the time, and, additionally, a connection with the late Fifties and early Sixties, living as a poet on the periphery of society.

Kimiko: What we're talking about really is culture. You can change laws and you can change institutions but culture is something that continues from one state to the next and you can't say "Smash it" like you can a building or an institution or a structure. It is, like history, something that continues.

My feeling is that there are social motions right now that are not your conventional political motions; for example, it may be more like homelessness, undocumented workers. We have to look at things that are happening and not expect to see the same things. Again, that's where the artist as a visionary and as a creative person really plays an important role, because we don't always look for things as they're supposed to appear.

Gale: I think of a lot of the stories of Black women writers, and myself included, who really trace the beginning of their writing to people telling stories, to women telling stories, or the kitchen you know. But that's a reality for so many people. That's an underground culture. A subversive survival culture. The same kind of thing that was somehow able to happen in Japan, that certainly nurtured the story-telling instinct of so many writers today. So many Black women writers now. From a place that people understand. The trickle-down theory clearly doesn't work in economics, in politics, or culture, or anything else. You have to figure out how much is here from a language that people all speak, from a language that gets defined as you speak it. This movement—for life, for peace and social justice— must tap into creating a way for people to be empowered. To write the scenario for their own lives. We want to claim the power for people to really name themselves and to make some decisions about how to live.

You know, there's some kind of meeting in between people who have learned to move people, and work with people, i.e. political people, and people who have learned to move people, and work with people, i.e. artist people—there's some meeting of their knowledge that's absolutely necessary, that's an even exchange here. And that needs to be recognized, you know? And both sides suffer from that lack of recognition.

If you don't liberate people's hearts, you pass the civil rights bill one more time. And again and again and again. The problems we face demand the fullest of our capabilities. Our imagination. Anger. For example, picture yourself in this city, how do people find new structures for dealing with what our lives are? Once you get to the core—somebody doesn't have a home, what do people do then? That takes incredible imagination. These are the places that organizing and imagination absolutely must meet.

Kimiko: This doesn't mean that we have to write only about those issues in order to ally ourselves with them. I read at a demonstration put on by the National Union of the Homeless—homeless people who organized themselves—and I read mainly love poems. The context was like this: if a husband or wife or whoever are in a shelter, now how are they ever going to have any intimacy? You know, if you don't have a home, you don't have a home life. I wanted to read love poems in that context.

People of color, poor people, are being blamed for pulling down the standard of living and for the violence in our society, when in fact it's the fault of the system itself that creates those conditions, exploits people and victimizes them. There's a different way to lynch people these days. You just let them be homeless, or you shoot them in the back and get away with it. I think the way artists can work against this is through political clarity, through understanding what's going on and trying to use their voices, because artists have a platform that other people don't have. Again, not that we have to write poems about any particular subject—if people want to that's fine—but you can also get up and say a word on your platform and then do what you gotta do, sing a song, or play a flute, or whatever. But I think clarity is what's important.

Gale: Which happens within groups of people, groups of people learning about themselves in the way you learn about yourself from the inside out, and at the same time between people looking at each other and learning something else about themselves by learning something else about somebody else. And that kind of process being able to happen, which assumes the absence of fear. And in this society that's a big assumption.

Susan: You know, that really brings up our relationship to each other. This kind of discussion that we're doing doesn't come out of nowhere. It's the continuation of a process rather than the beginning of one. And part of it is that I felt that I could sit down with you and not be afraid to talk about anything. That we trust each other because we've known each other for a long time—we've worked together and respect each other.

Kimiko and I met at the Conference on Central America in Managua, Nicaragua in 1983; we worked together on the original organization of Ventana—a cultural support group for the ASTC (Sandinista Cultural Workers Association), and in connection with Artist's Call. Although I published a poem of Gale's in the second issue of *IKON*, we didn't actually get to know each other until *IKON* organized a benefit poetry reading for Art Against Apartheid, a coalition of artists and arts organizations.

Gale: That was in 1984 when we were initiating a major drive to inform and agitate people on the anti-apartheid front as well as drawing the domestic issues connections. Then *AAA* and *IKON*, Susan and I came together again to edit an anthology, *Works for Freedom*, of anti-apartheid work; a collection of over one hundred artists' work...Now me and Kimiko, we met in Blue Mountain doing some strategic planning (smile) for artist response and networking in urgent political times....

I like the concept of collaboration and what it can be when it's good. I think that it's like what musicians do when they jam and create a new moment in music. The trick is to understand the differences in each voice. The different needs. The different tones. And roads that bring us here. Each player brings her own music. One comes for the challenge. One comes to hear the sounds. Another comes out of the need to move with others. You kinda cup your ear. Like a good singer. Pick up your beat. Your key. Your notes. Then I guess it's like jump rope: there's a moment, then the downbeat opens up and you can slide in stride. One voice after another gets in there. Best if they all be distinct. But you get a new music. Familiar and different in the end.

SUSAN SHERMAN is a poet, playwright, essayist, and editor of *IKON Magazine*, has had twelve plays produced off-off Broadway, and has published four collections of poetry. Her most recent awards include a 1997 New York Foundation for the Arts Fellowship and a Puffin Foundation Grant to help her complete her personal chronicle of the Fifties and Sixties. In October, 1992, two of her plays were produced at La MaMa, E.T.C. and her English adaptation of *Shango de Ima*, a Cuban play by Pepe Carril, was performed at the Nuyorican Poets' Cafe during the summer of 1994. Her collected essays and poems, *The Color of The Heart: Writing from Struggle and Change 1959-1990* was published by Curbstone Press in 1990.

KIMIKO HAHN was born in 1955 just outside New York City to a Japanese-American mother and German-American father. Her influences primarily come from her Asian background, including the study of classical Japanese literature, as well as American poetry, rock 'n' roll, political work and feminism. Her most recent poetry collections are *The Unbearable Heart* (Kaya Press, 1994), and *Mosquito and Ant* (W.W. Norton, 1999). She has received fellowships from the National Endowment for the Arts and the New York Foundation for the Arts. She teaches at Queens College (CUNY).

GALE JACKSON is a librarian, storyteller, and historian who received a National Endowment for the Humanities grant for her work in African-American history and the Griot tradition. She is on the faculties of Sarah Lawrence College, Elliot Lang College, and The Hayground School. Her publications include: *Khoisan Tale* and *Bridge Suite: Narrative Poems Based On the Lives of African and African-American Women in the Early History of These Black Nations* (Storm Imprints, 1998); and *Art Against Apartheid: Works For Freedom* which she co-edited (NY: IKON Press, 1986).

This piece is reprinted from *We Stand Our Ground*, published by IKON.

RICHARD EDMONDSON

The Thriving of Tyranny in Darkness... Taking Back the Airwaves: Electronic Civil Disobedience

"It is my wish at this time to remind you that I have always believed, and still believe, that artists who live and work with spiritual values cannot and should not remain indifferent to a conflict in which the highest values of humanity and civilization are at stake."—Pablo Picasso

We are out there. Capitalism, though a system abounding in much human waste and misery (four million homeless people in the U.S., and growing, is a statistic which speaks loudly and clearly), has throughout time asserted, with a proud, rather proprietary air, a certain credo as one of its most basic tenets: that where there is a niche, it will be filled. Such, so the theory goes, is the law of the marketplace. It is not my purpose here to attempt to answer whether capitalism fills all of its niches. But if truth is a commodity, its absence in the "market place" is a niche that certainly yearns to be poured into. Thus: we are out there.

I remember in the Sixties when TV journalists like Dan Rather, decked out in spiffy white safari jackets probably purchased at Bloomingdale's, stood in front of TV cameras on Vietnamese soil and brought us news of the war. I'm not sure when my view of Dan Rather changed from Master Journalist to that of Master Propagandist, although the line separating the two is anything but fine. It didn't happen overnight. Professional Journalism in the Sixties, for all its failings, at least had the integrity to point out the absurdity of the statement, "We're bombing the country in order to save it." Today the public official who uttered that egregious comment would be quoted verbatim, his statement going unquestioned, and he would be presented to the American public as a sane, rational speaker of truth. Thus we are out there.

They call us pirates. I for one have never owned an eyepatch. But this is what we're reduced to in this age of mass media doublespeak and Orwell's nightmare come true: concealed in dark spaces, huddled over cheap homemade electronic equipment whose reliability is not the greatest, even under the most propitious of conditions, fearful of discovery. Fearful of fear. The fear takes twin forms. One is that of the official knock on the door: "Hi. We're from the FCC. We tracked down your signal. You're under arrest." Then you think of the gunshots fired randomly into the home of Mbanna Kantako in Springfield, Illinois. Which brings you to fear number two: that of the unofficial knock on the door. A hand encased in a black leather glove holding a revolver with a silencer: "Let's shut these people up before they cause too much unrest in the society we control." And they really do such an amazingly good job of controlling it, all things considered. A CIA hit. A death squad from the SFPD. I imagine even Dan Rather would have to admit he's come a long way from the day—in 1974 was it?—when he stood up to Richard Nixon, saying, "No, Mr. President. Are you?" A long way, yes, from then, to the evening in 1993 when the reversed anchorman sat on a panel and allowed Henry Kissinger's statement—"You can't believe anything an Arab says"—to go unchallenged.

You think of a new category for the Guinness Book of World Records (more niche-filling): "The most mentally ill person to ever pass as sane in an insane society." And you think of a logical choice to fill it: Henry Kissinger.

You console yourself with the thought that an assassination with witnesses would be harder (though not impossible) for them to carry out than an assassination without witnesses, so you start looking for broadcast locations that are both "concealed" and yet "public." A hard bill to fill. But if enough of us get into the bloodstream, perhaps, we can waylay the assassin before his bullets fly, force him to take to his bed in a state of severe illness.

Could an "infection" of citizen micropower broadcasters subdue a state which makes vigorous, robust use of terror and oppression, much in the same way that an introduction of diseased micro-organisms might lay low a healthy body? "What is the state of our union? It is growing stronger," Bill Clinton said in his '94 State of the Union address. This is of course more nonsense going unchallenged by Professional Journalists, who shed their integrity at some distant, amorphous point back in the late Seventies or early Eighties. The country is ripped asunder by greed and the looting of its institutions, and by leaders who have no intention of stopping them. Politicians (the word never forms on an American's lips unaccompanied by cynical disdain) have lost virtually all esteem, respect and credibility in the public eye. If the climate were more favorable to honesty and less addicted to the narcotic of euphemism, campaign contributions would be called what they are—bribes. But to answer the aforementioned question takes more prophetic skills than I possess. There are too many incalculables. We can only try—try to bring about the changes in society necessary to bring us out of the death spiral, out of the assassin's gun sights. As a friend (and fellow broadcaster) says, "It's the only game in town." So we try. The future of humanity (can I actually say this without sounding trite or pretentious?) depends on it.

IT IS NOT ENOUGH

Let's say for instance that, despite the risks, you're interested in becoming a micropower broadcaster. Once your transmitter is operational you might be tempted to think: Ah-hah! Now all I have to do is go on the air and start telling the truth—people will eventually respond accordingly, society will correct its ills, and the planet will be a much safer and better place to live. For it to be that simple, people would have to have not been brainwashed for as long as the corporations have been in control of the media, and that is a lot of years. What is meant by "brainwashing?" It can be a lot of things. For instance, TV commercials on cars, clothes, cosmetics and everything else imaginable. Brainwashing, sure. But this is a more "overt" brainwashing, and most people, especially those who regard themselves as "sophisticated," are aware of the advertiser's unabashed attempt to influence their buying habits and pride themselves on not succumbing (even though in reality they do) to such transparent efforts to manipulate them.

Then there are the less obvious ways of controlling the public mind, such as selective coverage, and the insertion of subtle inflections into that which *is* covered and labeled as "news" and masqueraded about as "neutral." Hardly anything is neutral. All "statements of fact" are grounded in a premise from which they originate and take form, a perceived reality—a reality, it might be added, that is not shared universally. Be that as it may, there are certain issues dealt with by the media/government juggernaut that are irrefutably molded by the putty of doublespeak. The Middle East is one of the most egregious examples, although there are many. Palestinians who kill Israelis are "knife-wielding" and usually dubbed simply "Palestinians," which, thanks to years of conditioning by the same media/government juggernaut, is a term which connotes "terrorists." But Israelis who kill Palestinians are "settlers." The mainstream news media's long-time bias in favor of Israel has been exhaustively documented by Solomon, Said, Chomsky and others, so there's no need to go into it in great detail here. Suffice it to say, however, it is not enough simply to "get on the air." What you say once you are there is the all-important key; and it is here that FCC-licensed institutions, such as Pacifica Radio, that deem themselves "progressive" or "alternative," have dropped the ball, failing (after 40 years of broadcasting) to force the government to accept political change.[1]

TACTICS OF THE ENEMY

In the vocabulary of capitalism, if truth is a "commodity," then it must be "presented," "packaged" and "sold" as such. Only thus can you penetrate the consciousness of a populace humidified by the strobe light of constantly flashing commercial messages and the stock discourses of juggernaut-sanctioned pundits. Suppose during the Persian Gulf War Madison Avenue had launched an ad campaign designed to sell the idea that Iraqi women and children were dying in large numbers. There would have been far fewer parades welcoming the troops home. If the adage that fire must be fought with fire is true (as it in reality is, successfully), then micropower broadcasters must learn to emulate the tactics of our enemies.

To that extent, the juggernaut has two big advantages over us, the first and most obvious being size. ABC (as only one case in point), controlled by Capital Cities Corp., owns eight TV stations and 21 radio stations; possesses 2100 radio affiliates, 227 TV affiliates; owns 7 daily newspapers and 7 weekly newspapers.[2] And ABC is only one of a handful of large communications conglomerates. A few micropower radio stations in isolated pockets of the country cannot hope to overcome such thunder.

A second advantage retained is that of sheer experience. They have been doing this longer, have refined the art of propaganda to a level that would have made Goebbels envious. But micropower broadcasting by private citizens is not wholly without some built-in advantages of its own, and it's here that the FCC becomes a double-edged sword. Being unlicensed by the FCC , we are hence unfettered by FCC regulations over what we can say. "Shock" radio has, over the past decade, transcended from the avant-garde to the mainstream, its ability to "shock" fading, as inevitably it must, as the Howard Sterns of the genre, in their eternal quest for maximum "allowable" taboo-breaking (mostly in the area of sex), must search ever wider and deeper for material to evoke public response at an octane level necessary to fuel the ratings engine. Even so, there are waters with which they have yet to wet their feet. In a sea of propagandistic distortions, truth and reality have a certain shock value of their own. By treading these virgin waters and employing creativity in our programming—"packaging," as it were, "dangerous ideas" in a colorful container—micropower broadcasters have the potential to make anything put on the air by the corporate media look stale and sterile by comparison.

At San Francisco Liberation Radio we took a tape recorder and listened to the words of numerous victims of police brutality. We found them at demonstrations, at organizational meetings, at community speakouts (in San Francisco, unfortunately, it is not hard to find people who have been beaten by police). Then we went back to the studio. We edited and spliced. The resulting sixty-second "commercial" (if we're employing juggernaut vocabulary it would actually be called "public service announcement") was reminiscent of the Pepsi Taste Challenge. Music—we chose Peter Gabriel's deeply ominous "Fourteen Black Paintings"—provided the backdrop for the message. Then we let the people we had interviewed do the work for us. One told of being beaten so hard that the baton cracked. Another, a young woman, had watched her boyfriend's head rammed repeatedly against the side of a police van. A Latina woman who had witnessed, as a girl, her father being beaten and kicked "just like Rodney King was," told us of presently seeing the police "looking the same kind of way at my little grandchild." All of these were spliced together with the Peter Gabriel music running underneath, closing with a female announcer's voice: "This is San Francisco Liberation Radio reminding you that Mayor Frank Jordan and the Board of Supervisors have repeatedly failed to address the problem of police brutality in our community, and that as a result *YOU* could be the next victim." The shock value of the spot was unquestionable, but in putting such a piece on the air we had successfully emulated a tactic employed by countless corporations in commercial advertising: that of the public testimonial. We had done the equivalent of going into shopping centers and having housewives tell us why Tide is their favorite detergent.

Another tactic employed by the corporations is that of the celebrity endorsement. We put Vietnam veteran Ron Kovic, author of *Born on the Fourth of July*, on the air condemning San Francisco's genocidal homeless policy, known as the Matrix Program. Kovic had been moved to join the homeless rights movement after a homeless man asleep in a doorway had been doused with gasoline and set on fire. Even in the anti-homeless hysteria of San Francisco, fueled by the rhetoric of the mayor, something about the burn victim's fate and the way it was perceived through the fickle corporate media's coverage of the incident touched the public's collective heartstrings. It was in this climate that we found Kovic at a demonstration in support of the homeless. We put our microphone in front of him and found him very willing to speak.

Bleak and dark as things may be, it is important to remember that humor is a powerful force. Political satire, when used skillfully by the micropower broadcaster, can be a deadly weapon. "You know what they do on Saturday Night Live," says Napoleon Williams, who runs Black Liberation Radio out of his home in Decatur, Illinois. "Well, we'll take statements some of these people (local politicians) make and reveal them for the fools and hypocrites that they are." Since going on the air in 1990, Williams' broadcasts have so angered Decatur officials that police and a local prosecutor have waged a seemingly interminable war against him, which has included numerous arrests, a para-military style raid upon his home, and the taking of one of his children. While these things have been difficult and painful for Williams and his family, each incident has been a further measure of the success of his radio station—which remains on the air!

At San Francisco Liberation Radio we took our cue from Williams and wrote a series of humorous skits. I should mention here the invaluable asset a CD full of sound effects can be. (A simple recording of pigs grunting has its obvious political uses, but if you let your imagination wander, the vistas can be endless.) One of the people with San Francisco Liberation Radio is also involved with theater and drama. We got her and several members of her cast together one afternoon to "act" out the skits we had written. That small group of people became known as the Jolly Roger Comedy Troupe, solely a creation of San Francisco Liberation Radio. One of the skits involved the mayor of San Francisco and one of his top advisors, dressed as hunters, standing on the balcony at City Hall taking pot shots at the homeless people on the streets below. ("Now don't hit the children," cautions the advisor. "Why?" queries the genuinely puzzled mayor. "Because it wouldn't be sportin' like. We have to give them a few years to grow up—and *then* shoot 'em!") That one ten-minute skit was a more potent criticism of the Matrix Program than endless hours of editorials. There were other skits as well, including one about Santa Claus's elves losing their jobs due to NAFTA; and about this time there had come to light a story in the local press about night-shift officers on the University of California police force being caught by video camera watching movies all night long in the school's film library. What a grand opportunity for us! Needless to say we capitalized on it quickly, coming up with a skit entitled, "At the Movies with the UC Police," featuring two police officers of questionable literacy, "Officer Petroni and Officer Wood," "reviewing" various movies à la Siskel and Ebert.

One shorter skit we designed to be used repeatedly as a station i.d. opens with the words, "Ladies and gentlemen, we take you now to San Quentin Prison where an execution is about to take place," which is followed a series of sound effects; cell doors opening and banging shut; a guard telling a prisoner to "come on, it's time;" and finally the warden's officious utterance: "Your crimes have been horrendous. You have shown no remorse for your deeds nor any inclination for being a useful citizen in the world corporate state. Do you have any last words?" The condemned prisoner replies quietly, "Yeah, I got just one thing I'd like to say," then thunders defiantly: "Fuck the State! Viva San Francisco Liberation Radiooooooooooooo!!!" The actor's voices were given just a touch of reverb, adding to the sense of being inside a prison. In employing the spot, we would always have it precede a well-known musical selection with a hard, fast, rousing beat.

Revolutionary poetry and book readings, news off the Internet, communiqués from guerrilla forces such as the Zapatistas in southern Mexico—all of these round out our programming, interspersed with a wide variety of music, including rock, punk and hip-hop. We also came up with a "Fascist-of-the-Week Award," bestowed usually upon some local politician or judge particularly deserving of the title. We live in an insane society, but I firmly believe the mental illness starts at the top and works its way down. Those who run our society thrive on, and profit from, war—on Viet Nam, Iraq, Somalia, Panama, maybe soon on North Korea. Those same people are now telling us we need 100,000 new cops to fight a "war on crime," the famous "war on drugs" perhaps having become a bit passé. But people sense, on some level (perhaps pausing for a moment's thought as they sneer at the word "politician,") that the insanity began at the top and, unlike that which ever came to pass in economic prosperity, "trickled downward." That's why at San Francisco Liberation Radio our guns are always on the leaders.

THE PEOPLE'S TECHNOLOGY

Through the auspices of Free Radio Berkeley, our sister micropower station across the bay, transmitter kits (present law prohibits the sale of fully assembled transmitters) are now available by mail order to the general public.[3] This in itself is a striking accomplishment. In achieving it, the challenge that had to be met by the engineers was not merely coming up with a working transmitter—such would have been simple enough—but designing one which could be 1) afforded, and 2) assembled by almost anyone. The basic mono 5 watt FM transmitter which, depending upon terrain, gives its user a broadcast radius of 3-6 miles, can be purchased for around $50. This can be coupled additionally with a 30 watt amplifier for extended range. (The basic rule of thumb is that to double your range you must quadruple your power output.) The two kits together can be purchased for around $100 and come complete with instructions and parts. Stereo kits are also available. A filter kit which, once assembled and put on line with your transmitter, prevents "harmonics" or "bleed," causing interference with your neighbors' reception,[4] can be purchased for seven dollars.

Computer bulletin boards, such as the Internet, have become a key means for disseminating information and are becoming a powerful weapon in the arsenal of the micropower broadcaster as well. The Internet is rapidly evolving to the point where, with proper usage by micropower broadcasters, it could usurp wire services such as AP and UPI. In doing so, its potential for circumventing the corporate-controlled news media is clear. The Internet in essence is becoming a "people's wire service," and much of our news at San Francisco Liberation Radio comes "hot off the Internet." It was our source for Zapatista communiqués and was also the means through which we learned of right-wing Christian attacks against the Sister Spirit Camp in Mississippi. (So rapid was the Internet in getting the latter story out that, to my knowledge, we were the first Bay Area radio station to broadcast news of the Sister Spirit attacks.)

With computers now capable, as they are, of making audio transmissions, a whole new interesting set of possibilities develops. In 1992 the Food Not Bombs Radio Network was born. The network's programs are in the format of a high-quality news magazine with a focus on people organizing to resist the new world order. The programs have been perceived as "too radical" by the corporate-owned media and are currently carried on only ten FCC-licensed stations in the U.S. But micropower broadcasters have greeted them with an astounding enthusiasm! The Food Not Bombs Radio Network will soon be transmitted by modem; with that opening, plans are underway at the network for production of a nightly newscast and, sometime in the future, conceivably an hourly one. Meanwhile the mail-order clearinghouse at Free Radio Berkeley is exploring the possibility of making the computer, the modem, and the transmitter kit all available to the would-be micropower broadcaster in one package. For one price—let's say in the neighborhood of $1500—you could get a fully appointed, people's-technology-equipped radio station, complete with a network affiliation! Contrast that amount with the hundreds of thousands of dollars it now takes to start an FCC-licensed commercial broadcast operation using corporation-designed technology. Right now this is only a vision for the future. But such a network of citizen-owned radio stations, linked by computer, could begin to change the media landscape of America.

Audio transmissions via computer may enable the micropower broadcaster to simply bypass satellite technology, making a "people's radio network" feasible within the near future. Two other projects, that have graduated from the drawing-board phase and definitely will be on line and available through Free Radio Berkeley are AM radio transmitters and TV transmitters compatible to home VCR's. A word about AM, because it can have certain advantages: FM, being "line of sight" (if you can see it you can broadcast to it), is extremely dependent upon height, i.e. for maximum signal range your antenna must be placed at the strategically highest possible locations above all other closely located objects, such as buildings or hillsides, which may interfere with it. One of the properties of AM signals however is their increased versatility; they have more ability to travel above, around, or through obstacles. You can observe this phenomenon at work by listening to your car radio as you drive through a tunnel, where AM stations can be far more readily tuned in than those on the FM band. At San Francisco Liberation Radio we will soon be making the jump to AM. Why? Because of our de-emphasis on music (relative, at least, to other FM stations) and because of the topography of San Francisco—lots of hills—capable of killing a signal that, left unblocked, might otherwise have traveled for miles. We have decided to go to AM because it is right for us in San Francisco; but such a decision must be made individually by each micropower broadcaster based upon his or her own singular terrain, desires and goals.

TO BE OR NOT TO BE LICENSED

We are presently fighting the FCC on two fronts: in the legal arena, through the courts, on the one hand; and in the court of public opinion, on the other. I have discussed this with other micro-broadcasters and there seems to be a feeling, pretty much unanimously shared, that presently the FCC literally doesn't know what to do about us. True, they have levied fines ($10,000 in my own case), few of which have been paid. This places them in the quandary of determining how much repression they are willing to risk. They must weigh their desire to shut us down against the possible consequences in terms of public reaction.[5]

In handing out fliers advertising our station, I have encountered many people who are perfectly conscious of the fact that they are being lied to by the media/government juggernaut, and that what they are told about such things as Iran/Contra or civilian casualties in the many foreign wars has little to do with the reality. For all their skills in doublespeak and artful propaganda, the mainstream media seem to suffer from extraordinarily low public opinion. The facade is crumbling. Ironically, however, the same media have focused some considerable publicity on the micropower broadcast movement, Free Radio Berkeley at one point making it onto the front page of the *New York Times*. We have been treated sympathetically by the reporters who have written about us, many of whom wish they were doing the same thing. At any rate, the public is aware of us now, and I've yet to hear of anyone who disagrees with what we are doing The only negative comments so far, in fact, have come from the FCC itself. On the contrary, the concept of "pirate" media has ignited the public imagination. People are excited about us. They genuinely want us to succeed. Any attempt to shut us down right now, regardless of any judicial system rationalizing, would be viewed by the public as a clear violation of the first amendment.

Does this mean that if offered a license by the FCC we would even accept one? The FCC's argument, that the available broadcast frequencies are limited in number and must therefore be regulated, is specious and misleading. Even in a media market the size of the Bay Area, there are many "holes" in both the AM and FM bands, holes that are not being filled presently by any FCC-licensed stations (or even by unlicensed micropower stations). These "holes" may not be apparent, especially if you live in a big city, as you go up and down your radio dial; but keep in mind that the AM/FM tuners on the market today are far more precise than anything that was available when the FCC's guidelines were drawn up. "To enforce (its) absolute prohibition (against micropower broadcasters) the FCC is relying upon regulations...which were promulgated long before the advent of the technology that makes possible microradio; indeed even before the advent of FM broadcasting."[6] As one judge on the U.S. 9th Circuit Court of Appeals noted[7], the "holes" in the broadcast bands become ever more noticeable the further one drives from the major media market areas, while in some rural areas of the country it may be possible to find only one or two stations on an entire band.

Why do such holes exist if, as the FCC argues, broadcast frequencies are "limited"? One reason is the astronomical cost involved in putting a 100-watt station (the FCC currently refuses to license anything under 100 watts) on the air. To merely apply for the license requires a filing fee of $2,300. So far the FCC has shown no inclination to relax any of its dictatorial regulations and, until it does, the question of "to be or not to be licensed" is moot. But suppose the regulatory scheme did undergo a change and San Francisco Liberation Radio were offered a license "with conditions"? Would we accept it? It would depend.

Mbanna Kantako, who runs a black liberation FM station out of his housing project home in Springfield, Illinois, has no use for any license the FCC might offer. Kantako is African-American. He is also blind. In the words of one attorney, "He's the perfect defendant." Kantako's position is that he can broadcast if he wants to. The FCC has nothing to say about it. Period. End of story. Kantako recognizes no authority over him held by the FCC. And the reality is that Springfield's black liberation station, like Napoleon Williams' in Decatur, 35 miles away, is still on the air after more than five years. Considering the abuses inflicted upon the airwaves by the corporate media and by the FCC, a classic example of another government agency controlled by the industry it's supposed to regulate, we have nothing but the utmost respect for Kantako's position. But this begs the question: should the FCC have any powers to regulate at all? Would San Francisco Liberation Radio accept, say, a frequency assignment? Only if it came with no restrictions on the content of our programming. None. Zero. But what about profanity? you ask. We can't have people on the air just mouthing obscenities right and left, can we? Yes, we can, and we must. At San Francisco Liberation Radio we have imposed only one standard of "self-censorship" upon ourselves: we don't advocate violence against any human being. But what about those with no such scruples? you ask again. Should white Aryan groups, for instance, be allowed to operate micropower radio stations? Again the answer is yes. Besides we already have right wing Christian stations on the air (FCC licensed to boot!) whose hatred for gays is legion. Would I restrict their right to broadcast? No. If we are going to have free speech in this country—and it has been argued that micropower radio is indeed the modern equivalent of the soap box—then we must have it with no qualifications. Society must not be afraid to look in the mirror and see its own blemishes. Once you start imposing restrictions on what may and may not be said over the air, or commence "filtering" out undesirable viewpoints by making the licensing process so costly that only the megawealthy can afford it, then you end up with the system we have now.

RICHARD EDMONDSON was born in Nashville, Tennesee, in 1953 and, after college, worked as a journalist thereabouts. He joined Food Not Bombs in San Francisco and was jailed with them in 1990. He has published one volume of poetry, *American Bus Stop*. In May 1993, he began broadcasting San Francisco Liberation Radio on airwaves "taken back" for the People. He has continued such broadcasts despite the FCC's having targeted him with a $10,000 fine and possible arrest.

Notes:
1. On the contrary, in the back yard of Pacifica's premier station, KPFA in Berkeley, California, police have used rubber and wooden bullets on demonstrators; and brutality against private citizens, particularly the homeless in People's Park, is rampant; much of which KPFA, for political reasons or not, has turned a blind eye to, preferring instead the "safety" of a more "national" or "international" focus. This, of course, overlooks the most fundamental reason for a radio station to exist: to serve the people in its own community.
2. Drew, Jesse (ed.), *Paper Tiger Guide to TV Repair*, 1992, San Francisco Art Institute and the Paper Tiger Television/West Collective.
3. Free Radio Berkeley, 1442-A Walnut St., #406, Berkeley, Ca. 94709. Ph. 510-464-3041.
4. One of the FCC's favorite arguments against "pirate" radio stations is that many don't filter out their harmonics, causing interference with other people's radio reception. With a seven-dollar piece of equipment, we have solved that problem and thereby neutralized the FCC's strongest argument against citizen access to the airwaves.
5. Contrary to the media hype, the "Los Angeles Rebellion" of 1992 was in no way limited to the city of Los Angeles. The not-guilty verdicts of the four cops triggered numerous urban demonstrations in virtually every sector of the country, with martial law declarations in both San Francisco and Berkeley.
6. Hiken, Louis, written response to FCC notice of apparent liability in the case of Free Radio Berkeley.
7. In the case of the FCC vs. William Dougan.

San Francisco Liberation Radio can be reached at:
350 7th Ave. #35, San Francisco CA 94118
Ph. 415-487-6308

"Mural, Mural on the Wall"

"...On a couple of tables the American women
set out their paints condemning the birds of prey,
a motor deafening those who would rape and loot
and they mixed their colors as peoples mix their deepest love."
—Omar Jota Lazo Barberena
Nicaragua, December, 1983

FEBRUARY, 1994:

I decide to go over my old writings and journal entries to try to coalesce ideas about why I chose muralism as a way to express revolutionary activism through art. Sorting through the yellowing papers, some of the manual typewriter pages look like antiques in this computer age. I read them, thinking about how much has changed over the last twenty years. How many of the old thoughts were rhetoric or idealism—what still holds true? What have we learned, what have we lost, and how do we carry it on?

CULTURE NOTES, AMERIKKA 1973:

First we have to ask, what is culture? Culture is how people live their lives and what they create to reflect and express that experience. Culture develops over thousands of years of a people's relationship with their land, such as in Vietnam. Many rich cultures exist throughout the world, but when we look at the world today we see there is a global struggle in progress. There is another form of culture besides the natural interaction of the world's peoples with their planet. That is the culture that has been created by a profit-motive imperialist society. This culture, sometimes termed "death-culture" in current slang, is imposed on people throughout the world through corporate control. It drains them of their natural resources and exploits their labor in order to create great material "wealth" for a small group and a mass culture here in the U.S. with the aim of keeping people divided, unsatisfied, manic consumers, wage slaves, out of touch with their bodies, and uninformed on all levels. How does this culture of control manifest itself? A few examples are: the smashing of creativity and imagination in most of the society's educational institutions, the tracking by class in the school system, the deeply penetrating and pervasive racism and white supremacy, the contempt for women, the rampant sexism and heterosexism. From every side, in every orifice, we are flooded and pounded with images and limericks to force us to adopt the cultural ideology of the ruling classes—where everything has a price tag and money is God. They use TV to indoctrinate whole generations, grinding in racist cowboy and Indian myths, rhyming advertisements, and patriarchal roles. The films portray stereotypes and raw violence and enforce surface beauty standards. Ads from all sides try to convince us we can't be happy unless we buy this or that, with women's bodies being one of the heaviest sales pushers, capitalizing on the deep sexual frustration and confusion this society has created. A Victorian strain of shame for bodies is coupled with an anti-touch, anti-intimacy that tries to teach touch=sex=dirty, twisting and debasing natural human interaction, a beautiful source of joy, into something oppressive, scary, and decadent. Songs blare out over the radio enforcing concepts such as man is strong and violent, woman is weak and passive, or enforcing the concept of other people as private property. An incredible arrogance of "white is right" is bred deep into this nation's dominant culture, fueling fear, ignorance, and violence. Doublethink and doubletalk set up strange and frightening concepts, such as it's all right to napalm Third-World babies but it's not all right to physically love someone of your own sex. People are brainwashed to always try to look young (for which of course they need to buy many products), while the young are discriminated against and chauvinized. People are flooded with misinformation—LIES—about many, many things—from the situation in the world to the situation in their own bodies and how to keep them healthy.

This society creates millions of alienated, frustrated people, cut off from their connections to one another and the universe. A system of empire has many sophisticated levels of control. And when the soft ways don't work, there are the occupying forces of the police, the prisons, and out-and-out genocide. The imperialists have proven themselves to be beyond any scruples in the lengths of atrocity they will go to protect their interests. But the active resistance, rhythm, collectivism and love that blossom among the world's peoples is like a strong green shoot pushing through the earth, beyond the Coca-Cola factories, CIA torture squads, and tiger cages.

So what is the role of artists here in the U.S. today? We must always learn from and study the example of other peoples throughout the world, but we do have to analyze our own conditions here in the belly of the beast. We, as conscious artists, must combat the torrent of mind-control with a real alternative—murals, songs, dance, poetry that contain different values and have educational content as well as beauty. As Mao Tse Tung said, besides a military army, a revolutionary struggle needs a *cultural army, which is absolutely indispensable for uniting our own ranks and defeating the enemy.*" If we want the planet to exist, for nature to flower, and for people to know harmony and economic security, we know that our life is one of real struggle.

How do we combat the culture of exploitation and overpower the vampires of greed? It will grow from how we treat each other, live, struggle and work together. It will grow from how we respect our diversity. Our poems, plays, songs, and paintings will reflect this respect for people and life. How we teach and learn from our children creates the future. There is a war for people's minds going on, and art and culture are a vital element in that struggle. As Haydeé Santamaría, Cuban revolutionary, expressed it:

"I might say that everything is political, and not just that which seems so on the surface. Even that which seems least directly connected with immediate action...Haven't you seen the Revolution's enemies spend all their time talking about how we revolutionaries disregard beauty, how we do everything in a sad, ugly way? When the truth is, only the Revolution makes beauty available to everyone instead of it being a privilege for a few, and we struggle so that life itself will be more beautiful!"

JOURNAL ENTRY, 1969: SANTA FE, NEW MEXICO. AMAZING!

A group of Chicano artists calling themselves "Muralistas Guadalupaños de Aztlan" are transforming space around here. Old adobe buildings becoming canvases of history unfolding, bursting with vision, pride and color. I want to do this. What a way to combine politics and art!

JOURNAL ENTRY, 1970: BACK IN SAN FRANCISCO.

Haight Street "riot," and uprisings in inner cities throughout the country. Storefronts smashed. Windows covered with plywood. We're going to paint murals on those boards! And when the next big demonstration comes down this street they will witness images supporting their efforts!

1972: People's art is a powerful weapon in revolutionary struggle. Murals are an art form that is out in the street for everyone, where people can watch and participate in the process of art being made, talk to the artists, share their ideas, opinions, and criticisms. There is a mystique built up around art in a bourgeois society: only the gifted few, with God-given "talent," can be artists. How art gets created and how to develop these skills are kept from everyday people: mystified. Murals break down that mystery because everyone around can see the whole process, from the preparation of the blank wall to the first sketch, the layers of paint, the changes, the mistakes. The finished painting emerges through a process visible to all. Neighbors participate in the ideas included in the design, and often in the actual painting. This public and open process strengthens and encourages the creativity in people, and gives ideas for new possibilities and projects in their lives.

Art reflects social conditions, and we want our art to be where the poor and working people are, not in a private gallery for high prices. We want our art to be relevant and take a clear stand. Murals can be effective inside buildings as well as outside on the street. Wherever they are, murals are never a commodity, they can't be bought and sold.

The monumental size of murals helps encourage the development of collective forms of creating art. The problems of content and composition can be worked out in a group. Many artists have a lot to learn about working together, and murals are a good practical form in which to learn to utilize each other's strengths, assist each other's weaknesses, sharing resources and knowledge. The results can be exciting for everyone and all the more powerful because many people have put their energy and skill together to create the mural. Some murals are painted alone, but the important principle in a revolutionary or community mural is that the theme of the mural is not developed in isolation from the people who live and work around the site of the mural. There are many methods of getting people's input on what they would like to see in the mural. A few are: holding community meetings, circulating questionnaires, and having a table on the street. During the painting of the mural, the artists should always be open to suggestions and changes from the people around. If the groundwork is done well with the community, a mural is respected, cared for, and loved.

Murals bring life and color to gray city walls—they educate about true history, express peoples' pride in cultural roots, and make visual their dreams and aspirations.

1976:

The "BUY-Centennial," as we're calling the celebration of 200 years of the United States, permeates the airwaves. In response, I've completed and dedicated two murals with the Haight-Ashbury Muralists,[1] "Our History Is No Mystery," and "200 Years of Resistance."

After a peak of muralism in the Thirties in the United States, there was a lull until the Sixties. Then William Walker and the group Obasi created the important work, "The Wall of Respect," on the south side of Chicago. It was designed to incorporate community participation, a collective celebration of outstanding contributors to Black history. Soon a large mural proclaimed "We Are Not A Minority" from the housing projects of the East Los Angeles barrio. Since then thousands of walls have captured the rage, pride, and vision of oppressed communities throughout the land, reflecting and contributing to struggles for self-determination, justice, and equality, with energy and color. There's really a mural movement happening here, inspired and nourished by roots in the revolutionary murals of Mexico. The walls are alive—Paint them!

There's a lot of anger in those streets right now, a lot of questions being asked, a need for and possibility of a new tidal wave of social action, in which muralists will play a part. Interacting with people, putting their hopes, dreams, ideas, struggles up there in beautiful form and color stimulates more creation, more action.

For the artist, the mural form fights the individualism and privateness that characterizes so much "art." We have a chance to work together, pooling our spirits to create something larger than any one of us, and joining with a worldwide movement of public art.

We build community ties, and the mural becomes part of the neighborhood's daily life. If the youth are talked to all through the process, and given a chance to participate, they will help to protect the mural.

But sometimes our work is attacked. Recently our mural "Our History Is No Mystery" was seriously vandalized with silver paint proclaiming "Fuck Commies" and "Kill Commies." In addition, all of the portraits of African-American leaders, including Malcolm X, Paul Robeson, Mary Ellen Pleasant, and George Jackson were painted over with white paint. An out-and-out right-wing attack. But the community came to our aid in great numbers, helping us with the painstaking work of removing the defacement and repairing the painting. The support was heartwarming.

This has made me think about who attacks murals and why. Of all painted art in history, murals suffer the most political repression. Even way back to Michaelangelo, the genitals on his beautiful nudes were covered as the Church tightened its control.

1980: "THE ARTIST MUST ELECT TO FIGHT FOR EITHER FREEDOM OR SLAVERY. I HAVE MADE MY CHOICE."
                                      —PAUL ROBESON

In these times when we are virtually held hostage by our government's ruthless drive towards war, intervention, and nuclear madness, it is crucial that we do everything we can to affect peoples' consciousness, and create in the environment the vision of a different reality.

The painting of murals in any community in the world is an empowering process. It breaks down apathy, low self-esteem, and hopelessness, while transforming a space. Here in the United States murals create images that challenge the advertising and distortions of the "Big Lie." International mural exchanges promote understanding and communication—the cornerstones of peace.

So much of traditional political theory is about integrating theory and practice, and bringing the word "to the masses." The community mural process is so grounded in the daily life of a community, it's a fertile environment for the joining of political theory and its embodiment in practice. Murals provide an outlet for much discussion of ideas and venting of frustrations. This discussion of themes and concepts becomes translated into concrete images and works, synthesized into a collective vision. We need to create images of what we're fighting for, not only what we're up against.

The murals in our communities help us work through the contradictions that keep us divided. They also simply create beauty and pride and show the possibility of unity. Our children need something real to compare with the bombardment of advertising— a vision of peace helps make it real. But there can be no real peace without justice, and all over the world, murals are part of peoples' struggles for dignity. In some countries, artists are killed if they are caught painting murals, yet the walls still flower. Murals are messengers. They remain long after the artists have left the wall. Murals are like jazz; they sing of improvisation, survival, and resistance. Their forms and colors hold our hopes and our dreams.

1983: "*LA SOLIDARIDAD ES LA TERNURA DE LOS PUEBLOS*" "*SOLIDARITY IS THE TENDERNESS OF THE PEOPLES*"

I'm honored to accept an invitation from the Association of Sandinista Children to paint a mural on the front of the first children's library in Managua, Nicaragua. I assemble a team of Odilia Rodriguez, Marilyn Lindstrom, and myself. We raise funds here, purchase all needed supplies and go to Nicaragua. A children's library like this would have been unheard of in the Somoza years, but now, with the Government of National Reconstruction, many new programs of education, health and art are being promoted. Before the Sandinistas, only very privileged children had access to books and good education. Now there is a nationwide literacy campaign, raising the level of literacy among all levels of society, young and old. The mural is painted in the year of "Paz y Soberanía" (peace and sovereignty) and will reflect the benefits of this campaign, the restructuring of community values, and the preciousness of the young. Its title is "Los Niños Son el Jardín de la Revolución." ("The Children Are the Garden of the Revolution.")

The poorest part of Managua was chosen as the site for the library, in a new park, Parque Luis Alfonso Velásquez, named after a young Sandinista activist murdered by the Somocistas. Now the park bustles with life. Lighted basketball courts, food stands, play structures, and children streaming in and out of the library. What a dream project!

Working with Nicaraguans every step of the way, we are often visited by musicians and poets who play and write while we paint. Art forms nourishing each other. We're told how important to the morale of the people in Nicaragua it is to see people from the U.S. who do not support our government's interventionist policies. We're wearing silk-screened shirts that read "North American Artists in Solidarity with the People of Nicaragua." People from all over the world will see this mural and know it is a gift from the North American people.

As muralists from the U.S., we're accustomed to a lot of difficulty, disrespect for our craft, and red tape. It's a welcome contrast to be somewhere where muralism is respected as an important art form and is supported and facilitated at the highest levels of government. There is even a new mural school, offering all types of instruction, including fresco, mosaic, and structural techniques.

We've learned so much from the immense love and determination of the Nicaraguan people. As the Contra war heats up, the losses touch more and more families. The mural remains here as a symbol of our solidarity with the Nicaraguan people and their revolution. As soon as we return to the U.S., we will produce color postcards to send back to Nicaragua to be sold for material aid.

1985: BACK IN THE U.S.

We need to continue our work for Central America here, where it is so important to reach people so they can pressure our government. We form a group named PLACA, and write this statement:

PLACA: to make a mark, to leave a sign, to speak out, to have image call for a response. PLACA: a group of artists who are determined to speak out against U.S. Intervention in Central America through imagery on the walls of the city of San Francisco. As artists and muralists, PLACA members aim to call attention to the situation that exists today in Central America as a result of the current administration's policies. The situation in El Salvador, the situation in Nicaragua, the situation in Guatemala, the situation in Honduras. PLACA members do not ally themselves with this administration's policy, which has created death and war and despair and threatens more lives daily. We aim to demonstrate, in visual/environmental terms, our solidarity with and respect for the people of Central America.

We pick a site in the heart of the Mission District of San

Francisco, Balmy Alley, where the first local Chicano murals were painted in the early Sixties. The whole alley will be painted by over 25 artists who can interpret the theme of peace and non-intervention in Central America any way they want to. These murals bring home these issues to the people of the neighborhood, many of whom had to flee repression in Guatemala and El Salvador.

Mural environments totally transform a space, a metaphor for our ability to transform the world. What was a neglected barrio alley has become an incredible outdoor art gallery, regularly visited and photographed by people from all over the globe.

1985: "AN INJURY TO ONE IS AN INJURY TO ALL"

50 years have passed since the 1934 General Strike in San Francisco. Many gains were won in that strike, including the eight-hour day and the right of the unions to have hiring halls. We're commemorating the strike and the ongoing workers' struggles by erecting a sculptural mural of 14 tons of shaped cold rolled steel, painted on all surfaces, standing right on the site where the strikers were killed by the police.

An experienced team of 10 artists make up M.E.T.A.L.: Mural Environmentalists Together in Art Labor. It's been a long process working with the I.L.W.U. and developing the theme. It feels good to try a new form of muralism.[2]

SEPTEMBER, 1986: "A TEACHER...MUST BE A FOUNTAIN OF LOVE, A DEFENDER AND PRACTITIONER OF JUSTICE, A MILITANT OF BEAUTY:"—COMANDANTE TOMÁS BORGE

Myself and other members of PLACA—Juana Alicia, Arch Williams, and Ariella Seidenberg—are invited to Nicaragua by the Ministry of Culture and the Nicaraguan Teacher's Union (ANDEN). We stay only three weeks, but working closely with ANDEN, the National School of Plastic Arts, the National School of Muralism, and many Nicaraguan painters, we design and paint a large mural in that time!

"El Amanecer" (The Dawn) tells of the militant history of the teachers' organization in the insurrection that led to the triumph of the revolution in 1979. It also shows the role of the teacher in present-day Nicaragua—not only teaching students, but also participating in all aspects of Nicaraguan life, including coffee and cotton harvests, cultural activities, and defense. The center of the mural shows a group of people teaching and learning from each other, a basic concept of modern Nicaraguan education. The large chilamate trees in the mural reflect those in the surrounding park, Parque de Las Madres, full of these beautiful strong trees. The spreading roots represent the deep roots of the Nicaraguan people, and their branches dance in the dawn of new hope.

The experience of painting and sharing ideas, art, and laughter was inspiring and intense. We come back with new bonds of friendship and determination to work for peace. Over and over again we were struck by what a colossal lie is being told to the people of the United States about the nature of the government of Nicaragua and the Sandinistas. If everyone could experience for themselves the reality of Nicaragua Libre, as we did, it would be impossible for these lies to be successful. There is so much potential between our peoples for creativity and joy...little by little, through our art and our lives, we will build that bridge of friendship and solidarity. We will be "militants of beauty," as are the dedicated teachers of Nicaragua.

1987: "IF WE ARE TO SURVIVE AS A SPECIES, IT IS NECESSARY FOR WOMEN TO COME INTO POWER AND FOR FEMINIST PRINCIPLES TO REBUILD THE FOUNDATIONS OF WORLD CULTURE."

As time goes on and I reach the close of the fourth decade of my life, more and more I feel the historic destiny of women's growing role in helping to lead the world in a new direction. We must move away from our present reality of "the arrogance of hierarchy and the celebration of violence that have reached a point of destructiveness almost out of control,"[3] and move into a new age of knowledge of and respect for the interconnectedness and value of all life, where decisions are made from that understanding.

In many ways we are at an historical crossroads. The time is critical—either we find the way to bring our earth into harmony and justice, or we will destroy the possibility of life. I believe we have the potential to positively transform the Earth, using the lessons of the past and the visionary creativity of our present to light the way for our children and all future generations.

Women, who are socially and biologically more in touch with the cycles of nature, and who are reclaiming their true histories and learning to know and love themselves, are healers for everyone in these troubled times. We are a growing circle, allying with women and men who share and work for a vision of peace and justice for all peoples, free from the threat of nuclear annihilation, based on respect and reverence for the natural world and all people's cultures and their right to self-determination. There is enough for all on this Earth.

Within this immense time of turmoil and contradiction in which we live is the blossoming of some incredible dreams...from Nicaragua to South Africa, from Chile to the Philippines, from Chicago to Mexico, etc.—ALL OVER people are creatively seeking solutions and building unity. Artists are able to contribute tremendously to this process. I believe women artists have a unique and crucial role to play, through the integrity and power of our creativity and wisdom, embracing the wholeness of life.

In order to find our creative voice, we need to respect and believe in ourselves and our art. This is often particularly hard for women. Until recently, in any art history class one would get the impression that all great artists have been men. As we reclaim the legacy of our grandmothers and great-great-great-grandmothers, we are more capable of gaining the self-confidence and respect for our own expression of creativity that is absolutely necessary for the development of ourselves as artists.

I learned mural painting through painting murals. It was the beginning of a love affair with muralism that has deepened and grown more passionate over time.

As women muralists, out there on those walls, up on those scaffolds, publicly creating—we are an example of women as capable and brilliant contributors to their communities. As we work together to create monumental art, attitudes begin to change as to the roles and potential of women, and of men—creating new paths for the children to walk on. Murals are wonderful tools to unlock the creative potential in everyone, to inspire pride and critical thinking, to expose and illuminate history, and to prophesy visions of our future.

There is a lot of amazing art work being created by women. Let's fertilize our collective genius by supporting each other, encouraging skill development and experimentation, soothing each other's pains, and sharing responsibilities. Let's struggle with and advise each other, inspiring one another to evolve our powers of creative expression to dynamically and decisively contribute to the positive transformation of our Mother Earth and her sacred web of life.

1988: "TO BE WITNESS TO INJUSTICE AND DO NOTHING IS TO BE ACCOMPLICE TO THE CRIME."—THE TALMUD

Driving across the bridge today I confronted myself. I have done political and artistic work around many issues. Solidarity in Central America, anti-racist struggles here at home, etc. Many years ago I participated in a study group about the Middle East, and have long supported the concept of Palestinian rights, but have I done anything? No.

My parents weren't religious, but they taught us to be proud of the fact that Jews had a tradition of standing against injustice, had experienced oppression and resistance. Songs from the Warsaw Ghetto lived on through our childhood, along with a love of poetry, art, and learning. Meetings, marches, discussions, and organizing campaigns were a part of our daily life. We were short on money, but long on love.

I realize I am choking on my own silence, anger, and shame about the situation in the Middle East, and my silence is strengthening a betrayal of the best of our traditions, the love of justice—the very legacy my parents had left me. As long as I am silent, those who claim that Zionism and Israeli expansionism is the ideology of all Jews in a way do speak for me. I can't allow that. I want to do something to challenge that assumption, loud and clear.

The National Council of the Palestine Liberation Organization just voted to create an independent Palestinian State in the West Bank, Gaza and East Jerusalem. The Intifada is transforming Palestinian society in the territories. Now is a good time to do something. But what?

JULY, 1989: "THE ARTIST MUST BECOME VOICE, MESSENGER, ORGANIZER, AWAKENER, SPARKING THE INFLAMMABLE SILENCE."—MERIDEL LESUEUR

I form the "Break The Silence Mural Project" and gather three other Jewish women artists to form a team.[4] We want to join with the women in occupied Palestine, who are a backbone of the struggle against the occupation, and women of the peace movement inside Israel. We all share the conviction that Palestinians deserve the power to control their own resources and the freedom to live in peace in their own sovereign State.

We arrive in the West Bank in the middle of the historic uprising, the Intifada: a coordinated combination of civil disobedience, education and economic self-sufficiency projects, mass street resistance, regular communiqués from a coordinated underground leadership, and diplomatic initiatives. The Intifada is very much a living process, and the progress is uneven. What is so impressive is the Palestinian people's commitment to finding the way through generations of a dehumanizing occupation, to admitting mistakes and trying again, finding the paths to self-determination and a restructuring of their lives. The Intifada has replaced denial and dispossession with a renewal of national consciousness, creative problem-solving, self-discipline, and hopefulness in all stratas, classes, and ages of Palestinian society. "Intifada" in Arabic means "awakening," or "to change something from the roots."

The Palestinian community is welcoming us so warmly. We are living with a family in a refugee camp, experiencing firsthand both the constant threat and terror of living under a violent occupation, and the joy, dignity and hope of a people caring for each other and creating a future.

We see new examples of the collective process in the work of the Palestinian Women's Committees, the Popular Committees, and the cohesiveness of the community in the face of occupation.

Cooperatives provide people with ways to participate actively in economic self-sufficiency projects while creating new social relationships and organizations that contribute to the infrastructure of a new state. The daily afternoon general strikes, and the frequent all-day strikes memorializing community members killed, project unity of action and strengthen the boycott of Israeli goods.

We haven't had the opportunity in the U.S. to experience such community cohesiveness. Were aspects of the Montgomery bus boycott something like this? A united people taking a stand.

Issues focus with a new clarity. Our work becomes concrete, serious, and part of an allied effort with our Palestinian hosts. Because we are living under a military occupation, we need to develop our ability to be flexible, to shift our thinking and adjust our goals as the conditions change, sometimes quite abruptly.

AUGUST 9, 1989:

It's funny the way things happen sometimes. While I've been drawing the first sketches for the international solidarity section of the mural, we've been trying to think how to represent ourselves as Jewish women. It's always a challenge in a mural to decide what goes in, what stays out, and how to represent things that have to be simplified and symbolic without stereotyping. We have sketched in people of the world playing "London Bridge," the arms of the adults building bridges for the children to run through. A Palestinian woman and Katherine Smith from the Navajo nation at Big Mountain form the first arch. But it just hasn't been coming to us how to include ourselves. We don't want to paint self-portraits, we want one figure than can stand for all of us.

During a break I was thumbing through a book of poster art belonging to one of the Palestinian artists who is taking our graphic design class; as I turned a page, a striking poster about Ethel and Julius Rosenberg jumped out at me. Yes! As I looked at the image of Ethel's strong featured face, with the dark serious eyes looking out across the years and the barbed wire, memories flooded me of family stories of my mother getting more signatures than anyone else in the U.S. on petitions to stop the execution of the Rosenbergs. And yet they were killed. I want to paint that face, a Jewish woman who held to her beliefs, however unpopular, even when that meant her death.

AUGUST 10, 1989:

We are living with a leader of the Women's Committees and her family in a Kadura refugee camp in Ramallah. Her parents, who want us to call them "Mama" and "Papa", say they are our Palestinian parents. Papa is 95 and has seen four occupations. Mama is so strong and wonderfully warm. She is the epitome of so many of the older women here; dignified, hard working, very traditional, but right there in the daily demonstrations. Today she hid the banned Palestinian flag down the middle of her embroidered dress and carried it through the streets so that it could be put over the coffin of a boy that the occupying army killed this morning.

AUGUST 15, 1989:

In the midst of constant shootings, house demolitions, arrests, and torture, we work with the Center for Popular Culture to hold children's art classes. The Israelis have shut down all the schools, and many teachers are imprisoned. Clandestine classrooms try to fill the gap. We want to help too.

We brought paint, paper, brushes, clay, crayons, and assorted art supplies. We wait for our first class to arrive. We expect around thirty. Fifty or sixty show up! A few speak fluent English and they help us translate. The kids are polite and patient with our attempts at Arabic. We learn the essentials: the names of colors, paper, words of encouragement.

After a few days, we notice on our walks home more people coming out of their homes to greet us, inviting us to tea, giving us little drawings they have made. We are doing something good for their children, the heart of the nation. The grapevine has spread this message, and the hospitality warms our hearts and strengthens our determination. "Tell your people," they say, "we want peace!"

The kids are all ages, many shades of beige and brown, wearing hip-hop shorts or worn jeans or skirts and sneakers, always very neat. They arrive in bursts. Some are always early and help us set up. They make images of the banned flag on paper, on plates, on their hands. They draw street scenes, rocks, burning tires, olive trees, soldiers, and more flags, always more flags. They use up the paint as soon as we mix it. The level of cooperation and conscientiousness is so high we discuss it with the parents. They tell us that it wasn't always like this, but that the society-wide cooperation that is the core of the Intifada has affected the children too.

LETTER EXCERPT, AUGUST 20, 1989:

I can't tell you how much it moves me to see, in such a collective and concrete way, women moving a nation forward. I had some worries that it might be difficult to get to know women because of isolation in homes or other factors, but any concerns about not being able to connect and work with women were unfounded. Women are everywhere, and more and more they are the ones who have to do many things because of the mass arrests of the men.

The woman we live with is really becoming a friend and an

inspiration in her activism, humor, and leadership. She's so full of nitty-gritty, fight and brains. She just came home, laughing through the door, filling us in on the day's events. Just a few days ago, she was uncontrollably sobbing on the couch. A friend and co-organizer of many years had just been murdered, shot in the back a few blocks from our home by the army. Our friend will help to fill his shoes. The Intifada has changed many things for women, who are a crucial element in the resistance.

JOURNAL ENTRY, SEPTEMBER 1, 1989:

Stones. Stones everywhere. *"Silence is intensified into a stone: broken circles are closed: the trembling world, wars, birds, houses, cities, trains, woods, the wave that greets the sea's questions, the unending passage of dawn, all arrive at stone, sky nut: a substantial witness."* Favorite words of Pablo Neruda sing in my mind. Bearing witness, to the stones in the hands, the stone homes emerging from the stone hills, the ancient stone terrace walls everywhere solidly balancing, affirming a long history. The rock-hard determination of the people here, echoing the poem about South African women: *"Now you have struck a rock, hit a boulder..."* We are painting many stones into our murals here.

1990: AUSTIN, TEXAS.

Resistencia Bookstore and LUChA (The League of United Chicano Artists) commission Raúl Valdez, Ambray González, and me to paint a portable mural combining local and international issues. The day before I arrive, a 14-year-old kid is killed by the police. The Gulf War is beginning, "No Blood For Oil" is echoing in the streets. Political prisoners sit in jail. We connect these issues, contrasting them with images of the youth of the world reviving the uprooted tree of humanity, setting free birds of all types, flying towards a brighter day. The mural will stay in Austin for awhile and then travel to San Francisco and hopefully other sites.

1991:

We want to make visible here in San Francisco the lessons of the Break the Silence trip to the Middle East. We find a wall on a building owned by a Palestinian family. We go through a process with them and local organizations to develop the design for "Our Roots Are Still Alive," the first public mural about Palestinian Statehood in the U.S. The street corner becomes a hotbed of discussion and education. The mural emerges. When we write in English and Spanish the subtitle: "Todos tenemos derecho a una patria libre—Everyone has a Right to a Homeland," many conversations occur in Spanish with exiles from Central and Latin America, and many parallels are drawn.

This mural is a tribute to the irrepressibility of Palestinian culture throughout all the attempts to silence it. The portraits reflect the continuation of the rich heritage and the vibrancy with which the Palestinian people embrace life—their determination to keep their roots alive.

We celebrate the mural's completion with an all-day street fair with music, education, fun. Muralism can bring a community together. We're glad to get this issue out of the closet and into the streets, and to welcome visually the thousands of Palestinians who live here in San Francisco and are part of our cultural life.

1991:

Demonstrations on campuses across the country for educational equity. At the University of California at Davis, a united group of students of color hold a hunger strike and campaign for a cross-cultural center, tenured positions in Ethnic Studies, and...a mural! The theme will challenge the dominance of Eurocentric education and make visible the beauty and contributions of cultures worldwide. It will take an activist stance—a society of equality in diversity doesn't happen automatically, but through people standing up against white supremacy, bigotry, and ignorance of all kinds. Kim Anno and I have been chosen to design and paint the mural. Sometimes muralists function as cultural mediators in charged atmospheres. I am honored to have this opportunity to commemorate this struggle and solidify the students' demands.

1992:

Within a few weeks, two of my murals are destroyed or vandalized. In Nicaragua I learn that thousands of gallons of gray paint, donated to the Chamorro government by Fuller O'Brien Paint Co. in the U.S., have been used to paint out many murals and any visual images of the Sandinista years. The children's library mural has been totally annihilated. It hurts. The murals may be temporarily painted out, but, hopefully, the sentiment and power that went into them will persevere and re-emerge.

And here in the U.S., the Palestine mural, "Our Roots Are Still Alive," is attacked for the second time. Someone down the street saw the car stop at 3:00 a.m. and two adult men run out with premade paint balloons filled with a tar-paint mixture, throw them at the mural, and speed away. The attacks coincide with events in the Middle East. The damage is major, but of course we will repair it. We refuse to keep this statement invisible.

SEPTEMBER, 1993: "IT'S NOT JUST BREAD WE FIGHT FOR; WE FIGHT FOR ROSES TOO."

Finally getting going on the Women's Building mural. It's a monumental work, covering most of two sides of the four-story building. After a year of planning meetings and the circulation of thousands of questionnaires for input from the community, a team was selected and the theme decided.

The Women's Building houses many women's organizations and provides numerous services to the community at large. The fifteen-year process to pay off the mortgage is almost complete. The mural will be a brilliant testimony to celebrate the survival and growth of this important institution.

The mural has several main messages: the historical contributions of women worldwide and throughout time, and the healing power of women's wisdom for the entire community.

We are combining portraits of famous and unknown women, fabric patterns from around the world, cultural icons, references to specific historic occurrences. Woven throughout the fabrics are hundreds of names of women throughout time, collected during the outreach period, painted in gold calligraphy.

The team is myself, Juana Alicia, Edythe Boone, Susan Cervantes, Meera Desai, Yvonne Littleton, and Irene Pérez. Collectively we have over 100 years of mural experience. What a collaboration this one is!

Shortly after we erected the scaffolding, we were ordered to stop, and had to have a long struggle with several official agencies. The Women's Building is registered as an historical landmark because of the year it was built and its background. Murals on Landmark buildings are opposed by the Council on Historical Preservation. They could block our funding, and we couldn't do without it. We lost a few months, and had to jump through a lot of hoops, but we persevered and won a "Memorandum of Agreement," which is mostly an agreement to disagree, but we can continue the project. We'll do one wall this year, and one wall in the Spring of 1994, with a big celebration in the Fall. It's been stressful. Dealing with stalling bureaucracies wielding power, trying to stop us from creating beauty, made me scream and eroded momentum. Here is a building with the mortgage being paid off this year by an organization of women, and they are told they cannot put their history on it, that the architecture (and the settler colonialist history it represents) had to remain untouched. Of course, the real opposition to this mural, and most opposition to murals in general, has a racist core. To fill the streets with color, and people of color, touches the cultivated fears of "the natives are coming" (and they are, thank goodness!) and threatens the dominant culture's control of reality through the environment.

It's been an interesting and complex process. The core group of seven artists has an age range from the twenties through the fifties, diverse in many ways. The collective process of creating a sketch with a team that has never worked together before, has different histories, styles, national origins, cultural roots, and sexual preferences is challenging. But the spirit among us has been wonderful. We face the inevitable struggles and contradictions among us fueled with our commitment to the magnitude of the mural and its theme. Trying to pull a cohesive design out of literally hundreds of suggested approaches was mind-boggling. You can't say it all. How to get to the essence, and yet satisfy the requests. It's been tough, but very rewarding.

The cooperation and harmony displayed by the team members affect the public in positive ways. A model is provided for overcoming the divisions in the population. The respect shown to the community by the mural team, and the great support and appreciation given back to them, heals some of the wounds of alienation and despair.

Any fears we had about an all-women's team (all the volunteers are women, too) touching off hostility in neighborhood males have proved unneccesary. In fact, it's been interesting how supportive a broad spectrum of men have been. "Hey, you women sure can paint!" "Thank you!" "Brightest thing in the neighborhood!" "Talk of the town!" I think the awe of seeing women climbing up and down eleven levels of scaffolding and putting this complexity on the wall tempers any resentment. Maybe the message we hoped to spread—that the rising of the women means the rising of us all—is getting through a bit. And the effect the mural has on women is mind-blowing! So many feel very affirmed by it and are practically ecstatic.

One of the great things about murals is that, as the muralist, you always get strokes of appreciation from neighbors and passersby. But this time it's incredible, the amount of gratitude and praise we are receiving. Maybe it's partly because some people became aware through newspaper articles about our struggles with the Landmarks Board. In the midst of desperation and scarcity, I also think this support stems from a community sense that this mural is a gift of beauty and care, free for everyone, the nourishment we hoped it would be.

A woman wrote this for us as the mural began to reveal itself:

> "She is alive. The building shouts and dances, rising out of the earth, celebrating the cityscape context in the heart of the Mission District. As a community cultural center, the San Francisco Women's Building is home and catalyst to a variety of projects. It is a new social form: a sanctuary, a greenhouse, an antidote. The mural project displays an architectural testimony to international women's leadership and the liberation forces which inform and guide its activities."—Margaret Pavel

DECEMBER 1993:

This mural on the Women's Building is a labor of love. It's tough times, mean times...times of homeless, exhausted men sleeping in the doorway when the building is closed. Times of social services being cut. Frustration raging and tearing at the fabrics of our communities. Ugly rifts split our potential unities; frustration gives way to isolation.

With every brushstroke we put forth hope, strength, the spirit of resistance to oppression, and healing love. For ourselves, for everyone. Look at the colors, the symbols, the faces. Take a deep breath. Take it in. Here is some beauty for you—some inspiration for your best self.

JANUARY 15TH, 1994:

Martin Luther King's birthday. Got me thinking about the relationship between spirituality and justice. This Women's Building mural feels like some kind of prayer, pulling the best of the team's skills and spirits out, spreading it to all the volunteers and onlookers. We hope the vibrations we're putting into these brushstokes reach out and are understood at their deepest levels. We're casting a spell here—we're seriously concentrating the energy we put into this.

Many of these images are not obviously militant, although some are. But there's a very subversive revolutionary wish in the message of this mural. The overthrow of ignorance, of male supremacy and patriarchal structures, the rebalancing of forces. This is not a passive effort. We offer a beautiful alternative, and we are trying to open the hearts of people, inspire their pride, help them drop their fear of empowered women. The planet needs us desperately.

The huge portrait of Rigoberta Menchu with a Pre-Columbian speech glyph emerging from her mouth will be seen for blocks. She symbolizes women speaking to the world. We hope the world listens.

FEBRUARY 1, 1994:

Many things have changed over the last twenty years of muralism, and the last twenty years of political movements. Major disappointments, cruelties, massacres, injustices, setbacks, defeats. The grinding violence of poverty. Schisms in isms. Closing schools and building prisons. Things are grim and looking grimmer.

But our mission has not dampened. It still calls out urgently. We learn to let go, we learn to re-create. We learn to go deeper, face our errors and internal contradictions.

"Culture contains the seed of resistance that blossoms into the flower of liberation," Amilcar Cabral wrote, and murals can nourish that seedling. All over new forms of mural art appear. Memorial walls for Yusuf Hawkins, and hundreds of others keep memory alive in urban neighborhoods. Inner-city youth develop spray can art to new heights. The creative human spirit has been painting on caves, on walls, throughout all of history... and it ain't stopping now! It is the passion we put into our art and the passion we put into our resistance that will birth our new possibilities. The ancestors sing in our bones, pushing us on.

FEBRUARY 1994: "WHEN SPIDER WEBS UNITE, THEY CAN TIE UP A LION." [ETHIOPIA]

Silken threads from Northern Ireland; silken threads from the Hawaiian sovereignty movement and the ancient turtles still swimming free at Punaluu. Silken threads from the Zapatistas of Chiapas, from Managua, from Cuba, Puerto Rico, the Philippines. Silken threads from the highlands of Guatemala, from the liberated zones and negotiation tables of El Salvador. Silken threads from the survival of indigenous wisdom worldwide, from the elders passing it on. Silken threads from the territories of occupied Palestine, from the Lebanese refugee camps. Silken threads from the people of Africa, from the shantytowns of Haiti and Panama. Silken threads from the factories shut down by NAFTA; from the battered women's shelters; from recovering addicts. Silken threads from the people inside the prisons dotting our landscape, from Pelican Bay, San Quentin, and Lexington Federal Penitentiary. Silken threads from the Lesbian and gay movement claiming space for love, from people living with AIDS, from everyone who is "acting up and fighting back." Silken threads from wheelchair dancers. Silken threads from those young rappers who defy misogyny, cut through the hype and keep poetry in the streets. Silken threads from the jazz masters, carrying it on. Silken threads from sisters doin' it for themselves, from the endless creativity of young people finding new languages to express themselves. Silken threads from the children's laughter filling the air, from the flight of wild birds. Silken threads from those living outdoors, the so-called "homeless," urging us all to struggle for a true home on our Earth. Silken threads from a thousand directions, invisible, waiting, weaving, resisting.

MARCH, 1994: "NOTHING IS PERMANENT BUT CHANGE."
—KARL MARX

This truth is echoed in the natural world. The volcanoes erupt and the hot lava forms the foundation for new earth.

Murals emerge through the interplay of light and dark, line and solid. Their process emanates from creative thought to concrete manifestation.

Political movements emerge through the interplay of oppression and resistance, old traditions and fresh approaches, individual and group processes.

The movements will change, and the murals will change. But the walls will keep blooming—carefully tended gardens of color, strength, and hope.

MIRANDA BERGMAN was born in St. Paul, Minnesota in 1947 and moved at the age of four to the inner-city of San Francisco—then the Western Addition—with her parents, who were victims of the McCarthyite scourge in the Midwest. She grew up on the streets and in the schools of San Francisco.

Notes:
1. Jane Norling, Arch Williams, Vicky Hamlin.
2. Nicole Emanuel, Tim Drescher, Lari Kilolani, Ray Patlan, Eduardo Pineda, Jaime Morgan, James Prigoff, O'Brien Thiele, Horace Washington.
3. Adrienne Rich, "Resisting Amnesia, History and Personal Life."
4. Susan Greene, Marlene Tobias, Dina Redman.

FERRUCCIO BRUGNARO
In Order to Affirm

At this dangerous moment in history, it seems to me that the world and humanity have a strong need for poetry, but I sincerely have some difficulty speaking communally and traditionally about poetry or giving an expert discourse on poetry.

Nevertheless, I don't believe writing is above taking sides, or above anything.

I don't believe in gimmicks, in dirty linguistic tricks of technique that make the result so lofty or so profound no one can succeed in attaining it.

The grand illuminated mind, the great soul that sees and understands and feels everything from its window, is a hoax that ought to be unmasked once and for all. It's a poisonous, terrible lie that's created so many victims; it cannot and should not be told to anyone anymore.

I'll say right off that I'm a guy who takes sides. Yes, a man of partialities, from a section of the working-class, from the workers; from the section of the exploited and marginalized. Yes, I'm a man on the side of the Palestinian people, the Kurdish people, on the side of poor African, American, and Asian proletarians.

I'm a guy against any war. No discussions about making war; wars have got to be rejected. Period.

Consequently my feelings and words are born from within human social and material conditions and convictions; they're born from a thousand anxieties, oppressions, rough situations, tough and lonely ghetto-izations hidden ever more subtly by hollow affirmations of democracy, liberty and participation.

My language is born from the suffering and privation of people the world over who want to rebel against the unjust and unacceptable social and economic conditions of life.

While the story of the people and the world these days seems to be going decidedly backward, it's difficult to affirm such things; it puts one in a cold sweat.

While it seems that the future of those who won't accept, who protest, is forever being entrapped and led to resolution inside hellish prisons and with great suffering, it's not easy to support one's own convictions and one's own deep choices.

In these dark and cannibalizing times, it's tragic to express oneself with courage in order to affirm the hope that one day the exploited throughout the world, rejecting the blackmail of atomic missiles, will reclaim the necessary life that struggles for a world that won't exclude anyone and won't condemn any human being to pain and death.

So I don't believe in the birth of a language separate from the daily facts of pain, exploitation, racism and intolerable violence. What very often is passed off as engaged experimentalism and linguistic questing is nothing but free-rein personalism and individualism, desired alienation, a conscious/guilty absence of arena or field of conflict.

Language doesn't exist for me outside of the human and social history we're living.

The true word for me is formed only with difficulty, in the great labors the blood encounters as it circulates within us and the world. In struggle, in the limitless search for love, for peace to be born, the word also suddenly appears as the form of feeling, the new thing in life, language—a concrete instrument of existence, a reaffirmation of human existence.

In such a way, the journal of working writers, *clothes-work,* has emerged in these years. A lot of silence has resulted, and continues to—with respect to this work—and the hostility of various groups and literary and non-literary Mafia, belonging to every faith and ideology, has been, and continues today to be, ratty.

But the experience of publishing these journals is ever more revealing of (through a lot of material coming from factories, from disparate places of work, from the most marginal and humble zones of society) the discourse on the poets and artists as human beings and on humanity as a whole.

But what do *poet* and *artist* mean?

I've never understood. I've never succeeded in understanding what a poet, musician, or painter, separated from the complexity of mankind, means. I've said it many times and stirred up criticism, but have never tired of repeating that, for me, there are essentially human beings, woman and man, and in them there is also the capacity to write, to make music, and paint pictures as they might every day make houses, chairs, freeways.

I don't believe in innate capacities, in gifts from heaven, in inspirations, and even less in things said to be genius. There are histories—goddamned lies that the ruling classes have thrust into our hearts and brains for centuries. It's necessary instead to speak of expropriations, of marginalization, of violence used against all the people, on the weakest from the origins of human history, in order to understand the mystifications that they pass off in their conversation under the category defined as *artistic*.

It's exhausting to declare at this historical moment of fratricidal war, of individualistic and privatized flights, that real writing has been and continues to be a writing essentially of revolt against all the social injustices, the atrocious inequalities and humiliations. It's exhausting, but it's right-on and so I feel no shame in continuing to affirm it.

My stubborn words are intentionally expressed in order to change (make that "overthrow") the aberrant conceptions of life and death, of pain and love, that the ruling classes continue absurdly to spread among all the people of the earth.

Translated by Jack Hirschman

FERUCCIO BRUGNARO was born in Italy in 1936 and lives near Venice. He is a well-known worker-poet who for years distributed his poems at the factory he worked at, as well as at schools, in memo form—poems that now are widely published. His poetry is written along a spine of fiery discourse. Curbstone Press published his poetry under the title *Fist of Sun* in 1998. He toured the U.S. with his translator, Jack Hirschman, upon the book's publication.

CAROL TARLEN

The Making of a Working-Class Intellectual

Recently, I was asked to write an essay on my experiences as a working-class intellectual. This request caused me much anguish. First of all, I don't feel particularly intellectual. Most of the time I have difficulty just waking up in the morning and dragging myself to work. Who has time to think when you have to transcribe other people's words, stand at the Xerox machine endlessly copying medical journals, stuff paper into a thousand files? Moreover, I'm suspicious of people who claim membership in the intelligentsia, because so many are sycophants of the ruling class. Finally, I work in a university and have firsthand experience of intellectuals, even self-described Marxists, who fire workers on a whim if it suits them.

Although I have a Master of Arts degree (I earned both my college degrees by working full-time and going to night classes), I am now and always have been a member of the working class. Not only did I grow up poor, with a father who was a (frequently out-of-work) truck driver, I earn my living not as an academic with secretarial support, but as secretarial support for academics. I do not hire, fire or review others' work performances—my work is evaluated, and if I do not live up to the expectations of my superiors, I'm canned. My labor is not prized for its intellectual content, but for its lack of typos. I may not get my clothes dirty (unless I am called upon to fix a jammed Xerox machine or change the ink cartridge in my laser printer), but I work with my hands—and I have scars from surgery to correct carpal tunnel injury to prove it. I get as much respect for the way I earn my living as my father did earning his. I know what it is like to be sneered at because of your class. I also know how ignorant and insensitive middle and upper-class people can be, and how they can ignore your feelings, no matter how loudly or frequently you articulate them.

My class background has deprived me of subtlety and nuance. When people use truck drivers as examples of ignorance and prejudice, or when they say that I am too intelligent to be a clerical worker, I tell them that they are bigots, and that my job is hard and

I'm not ashamed of it. For some reason, these people continue to make offensive remarks, and then are surprised at my anger and bitterness.

I use my class and my education in both my political and artistic work. I have rage, and I use it, in my poetry, in public speaking, in political actions. I am not afraid to take over the street, get arrested, or walk a picket line any more than I am afraid to face an audience at a poetry reading. My poetry expresses the hurt and anger, as well as preference of community over individuality, that come from my present and my past experiences.

The motivation for my writing is very simple, and it's not nice. I write to get even with everyone who was mean to me in high school. I am motivated by revenge and the pain and anger that comes from being rejected because of my class background. I want to prove to all those girls whose parents had "professional" jobs and lived in Glenmore Gardens—the ones whose hair neatly curled into pageboys; who wore plaid knee-length pleated skirts and lamb's wool sweaters; the ones who quit associating with me when I said I lived in Stanley Davis, the housing tract notorious for its Latino and Okie inhabitants; and especially the ones who assumed that having an old mattress on your front lawn was a sign of intellectual inferiority and moral degeneration—I want to prove to that clique of middle class "nice" girls that the tough girls from the other side of the highway can't be shoved to the back of the classroom anymore, that we have lives filled with love, honor, imagination, risk. See me, I want to say, acknowledge my talent and intelligence. You may have become a matron with a wealthy husband, an executive with an M.B.A. degree, or Chairwoman of the Hillsborough Republican Party, but I am an in-your-face, unrepentant, working-class writer.

When I was in high school, Diane, my best friend, called these girls "society." Diane was French-Canadian and Indian, but because she was dark-skinned, she was assumed to be "Mexican," and being "Mexican" meant that you went to boring classes taught by bored teachers who didn't bother to remember your name, that the "white" guys made nasty remarks as they passed you in the hallway and assumed that you were a "whore," someone the Glenmore Girls didn't speak to but were afraid of. That is, unless you were really Mexican, like our shy friend Dolores, a recent immigrant with a scar on her chest from a heart operation. Some of the Glenmore clique caught her alone in the bathroom, called her names like dirty spic, and roughed her up. When Diane heard, she went after those Glenmore girls. Diane had a reputation, and they got scared, started to cry. Diane didn't hurt them, just laughed, called them chicken-shit and walked away.

I feel privileged that my lowly address and my lack of middle-class finesse kept me out of the Glenmore Girls Clique. My experiences of racism and sexism have formed my politics and my writing. But I am more than just working-class. Although my father was a truck driver who never finished high school, my mother has a B.A. degree in English literature. She comes from a long line of teachers and farmers. Although she embraced downward mobility, she couldn't erase all traces of her class. She wrote poetry and told us great, original stories. She gave my brother, sister and me a love and respect for books, ideas, and the imagination. Because of my family's poverty—and because no one informed me, a buxom blonde from the wrong part of town, of available scholarships—I couldn't go to a prestigious university, but I was motivated to enter junior college and eventually a state university, where I earned both a B.A. degree and a Masters in Creative Writing. My literacy and white skin not only enabled me to complete my education, but also to write about my working-class background.

My volunteer work with San Francisco's Food Not Bombs, an organization that provides free food for the homeless community, made me face these contradictions. My personal values and my expectations were sometimes in conflict with those of homeless people. Having college degrees, even from publicly funded institutions, and particularly having white skin, are conditions that separate me from people forced onto the streets or into the jails of this nation.

The night I spent in jail because I defied the law and fed homeless people without a permit illuminated my own class privileges. My cellmates didn't have to worry about supervisors spying on them or faculty members evaluating their job performance. They had guards with keys who could take away simple privileges like television. There was no sense of real time in San Francisco's women's jail because there were no windows to look out of to see if it was day or night. The lights were continuously on—darkness was a forbidden luxury, as was privacy. A shower was a privilege doled out by the guards. I learned something that night without having to write an NIH grant to fund a demographic study. The vast majority of women in prison are African-American, although Latinas, Native Americans, and white working-class women without college degrees and jobs also make up the population.

My education and class were apparent the moment I stepped into the cell, dragging my mattress behind me. I was treated very nicely by the other incarcerated women, I think because my crime was feeding people like themselves. They did not have much respect for most forms of civil disobedience, and made disparaging remarks about arrestees from recent actions against U.S. intervention in Central America. "They should care about Americans" was the standard remark. I didn't mention that I had also been arrested for those issues. Food Not Bombs is a popular organization in the city's prison, but the majority of us who are jailed are white and considered middle-class, no matter what our backgrounds may be.

Despite the class contradictions that I have to face in both my political and "intellectual" work, my creative writing does not contain nostalgia or guilt. Having never left the working-class, I do not feel a necessity to sentimentalize it. The vast majority of the poets published in a recent anthology of poetry about factory workers, are university professors whose educations were paid for by the broken bodies and spirits of blue-collar parents. The poems are often tinged with guilt and relief at having escaped the fate of their fathers by entering academia. While wanting to flee the assembly line is understandable, it isn't necessarily heroic, and the poets sense this. I find this emotional ambiguity problematic. The writers seem to feel that they have failed their parents, and that nobility is reserved for those who stay and suffer. Well, my heroines are those who stay and try to change the working conditions at their jobs.

I understand that people have limited choices. We all do what we have to do to personally survive. What is surprising is how many working-class people have escaped into academia and the rather constricted arms of the intelligentsia. Holocaust survivors say they feel alienated from those who didn't experience their horror. I think working-class refugees also feel alienated. And lonely. The slights I receive because of my parents' or my work aren't imagined, and I am sure that professors, journalists, and editors with my background also are insulted. The difference is that I have nothing to lose, so I fight back.

If intellectualism means critical thinking, skepticism, and risk-taking, then I qualify as an intellectual. However, I doubt that many so-called academics are worthy of the term intellectual. I share Gramsci's suspicion of the intelligentsia. I have read polls demonstrating that a majority of college graduates support Republican presidents and their policies (including financial and military aid to the Contras in Nicaragua), while the majority of high-school dropouts support the Democratic presidential candidates (and were against support for the Contras). I think the intelligentsia realize that their economic interests lie with conservatives, and high-school dropouts would like U.S. tax dollars spent at home on their needs. Most of the neo-conservative intellectuals I read in the *New York Review of Books* or the *New York Times* are self-serving and use isolated facts to justify preconceived ideology. Furthermore, they frequently indulge in purple-prose smear tactics. Then there are left-wing intellectuals who have graduate degrees in Semiotics or Deconstructionism, and who do the above, but instead of using purple prose they bore you to death with obscure language that bears no relationship to people's actual experiences with the written word, advertising, or just living in a modern city. I get a real kick out of reading "culture studies" about who "owns" Madonna or rap. These academicians are engaging in an economic battle about who gets tenured faculty positions in universities or employment in "think tanks" funded by corporations, who gets published in academic reviews, who gets grants—or, in the case of Camille Paglia, who gets on T.V. talk shows.

Recently I had to make an emergency visit to my parents, who live in a suburb of Denver. My mother, who is recovering from a mastectomy, had discovered a lump in her remaining healthy breast, and needed a biopsy. The message she left on my answering machine sounded scared, and I was worried that if the lump was malignant, it would mean that the medication she is presently taking isn't working and she would have to undergo chemotherapy. At age 75, I didn't think that she would be able to handle that ordeal. Although I was broke, my husband out of work, and my credit cards bulging, I decided to charge the airfare and see my parents for what might be the last time. That trip brought me closer to my class origins than all the political and artistic work I have done over the last ten years.

It was my father who seemed hungriest for conversation, particularly political talk. For decades, he had complained about foreign aid, and his reasons were similar to my cellmates' in the San Francisco jail. The United States should take care of its own. But now he has a sophisticated, leftist analysis, one I wholeheartedly agree with. Our tax dollars are spent to keep corrupt dictators in power, and many individuals from this country, as well as private relief agencies, also profit. He had read *America, What Went Wrong* by Donald Barlett and James Steele, and the book had convinced him that the United States needs a Labor Party. "The Democrats are elitist and are run by and for corporations just like the Republicans. We need a party run by workers," he said over and over.

Finally my mother, the loyal Democratic party worker, got upset. "Are you finished, Bob? I can't get a word in edgewise."

If one believes the media, these aren't the opinions of working-class white men, especially one who was raised on a farm in Kentucky during the Depression and who has a ninth-grade education. He's not supposed to look toward women like Pat Schroeder, or African-Americans like Jesse Jackson, for leadership, which he does. My mother was always the liberal of the family, but my father has become a radical.

I learned more about my parents than just politics. My father, the proud owner of several rifles and handguns, told me stories about hunting raccoons when he was young. "Coon skins were valuable then," he said. "I only killed animals for food or money, though. I always hated to hunt. How can anyone call that a sport? I could never shoot an animal now."

Religion has been a source of trouble between us since my parents became born-again Christians twenty years ago. This time we didn't argue. I refrained from loudly announcing my atheism, and they entertained me with stories about the church they belong to. The pastor and his followers have embraced the religious right, and my parents are outcasts because of their political opinions. Once Pastor Bob stood in front of the congregation and refused to offer them a blessing. The other Democrat in the church, Assistant Pastor Ed, was driven out, forced to preach to a congregation so poor it met in the living rooms of members' homes. Finally, in order to support himself, Pastor Ed began sticking up banks, and now he is a successful preacher with a large congregation made up of his fellow prison inmates. Daddy corresponds with Pastor Ed, who writes that he will be released soon. The thought of all these working people becoming Republicans just so they could be respectable Christians made me laugh, and my parents thought it was funny, too.

My parents have spent years trying to survive recessions, layoffs, strikes. They are now struggling with illness and its financial burden. Most of my father's Teamsters pension is spent on hospital and doctor bills, and medication. Medicare pays for little, and staying alive in a country with a for-profit health-care system is exorbitant. But they survive together. Mother gives Daddy his insulin shots; Daddy bathes her three times a week because her cancer surgery has inhibited the use of her arms. I imagine him lifting the wash cloth out of the water and slowly, gently scrubbing her naked back.

The morning that I left, Mother and I dressed together. She told me that she was embarrassed to be so vain at her age, but she missed her breast. I looked at the large, s-shaped scar, the nipple-less, puckered skin, the arm made frail from the stripping of muscle during surgery. I thought of how she had helped neighbors whose husbands were laid off or in jail, how sometimes they would have to borrow our bathroom because their water was turned off, how she taught me never to cross a picket line, and to respect the weak, the poor, the imprisoned, the uneducated. And especially, I remembered how my mother and daddy taught me to believe that if people struggled together, they could win not only better working conditions and higher wages, but justice. I learned that solidarity is more than just an ideology or a tactic, it is an everyday action. I am a product of my parents' long, hard lives, and their working-class ideals.

The working-class is stereotyped by the middle-class white Protestant ideology of this country. I have attempted to use my writing to break down bigotry and stereotyping. I don't like to be dismissed because of my job or background, and I don't like it when my family, neighbors and co-workers are sneered at either. But what I have learned through many years of poetry readings and publications in small literary journals is that my audience isn't those Glenmore Girls now grown into yuppies, but intellectuals like myself, especially working-class intellectuals and, surprisingly, my co-workers and union brothers and sisters, who are very receptive to poetry that portrays and celebrates their lives.

Looking at what remained of my mother's breast, I realized why I am an artist. Like the poets in the anthology about factory work, I write because I love my parents. It's that simple.

CAROL TARLEN was born in San Diego, California in 1943. Her poems and other writings have appeared in such journals as *Compages* and *Real Fiction*, the latter of which she edited. She has also been anthologized in *Calling Home—The Writing of Working-Class Women*, published by the Rutgers University Press. She lives in San Francisco's North Beach district.

This essay is reprinted from *Liberating Memory: Our Work and Our Working-Class Consciousness*, published by Rutgers University Press.

LUIS J. RODRÍGUEZ
Poetry and the Politics of Difference

Do we know our country? Clarence Thomas is accepted as a Supreme Court Justice despite damning testimony of sexual harassment and a record against equality and justice for all. The Los Angeles County Sheriff's Department has shot 57 people this year—80 percent of them from communities of color, all of them unarmed or shot in the back. A new statistic states that if the current rate of incarceration continues in the United States, by the year 2053 half of the adult population will be in prison.

The "New World Order" is coming into focus.

What has this to do with poetry? Why not everything? When the official news sources are openly censoring and distorting the truth, then the truth must be told through other means. Why not poetry?

A consideration of this today is the issue of cultural diversity. In American arts and letters, there seems to be an opening up of the gates once used to keep out, silence, or marginalize a significant section of the population. Perhaps I'm talking multiculturalism, the prevailing term. But I'm really talking about equality in the arts— and this has more to do with politics than culture, which has more to do with history.

In October, 1991, I went on a reading tour of the West Coast. In Albuquerque, I spoke in five high schools and an elementary school. In cities like Los Angeles, San Jose, San Francisco and Berkeley, my readings involved college students, bookstore audiences, the homeless, poetry centers and living rooms. Poetry alone was not the draw.

What kind of an impact must a poet have in a place like Rio Grande High School in Albuquerque, which has a wall of 19 plaques with the names of students who were killed, had car-crashed or had committed suicide since the beginning of the school year?

Or Mountainair High School in one of the poorest rural regions, near the Chilili land grant area, where Mexican, Indian and rancher white kids sold tacos, baked goods and other food items to pay the small fee that would bring me there to read?

Or the El Paso Club on Main Street in Los Angeles, on Skid Row, one of the largest single homeless enclaves, where the locals come to read their verse, play music, and listen to me perform? Or in an art gallery and alley in San Francisco's Tenderloin? Or across from the People's Park Annex, an "unlawful" gathering of the street people who police pushed out of Berkeley's 1960s battleground of free speech?

The poems better connect. They better have meaning. They better reveal.

I saw much about the United States on this trip—catching glimpses of Anita Hill's testimony on every TV screen—and much about what's really going on, about the thousand points of blight, and how integral the struggle for daily survival is to equality and inclusion in the arts.

In an interview with Bill Moyers, Richard Rodríguez, author of *Hunger of Memory,* says he "lost his Mexican soul" in America, seduced by Lucille Ball, Walt Disney and Technicolor. I don't agree with most of his conclusions (he's against bilingual education. He says "if I can make it, anyone can"—an "Hispanic" version of Clarence Thomas). But I agree when he says, "There is no one in America who does not speak Black English, there is no one in America who does not speak Yiddish. There is no one in America who does not sigh with the sigh of Mexican grandmothers."

American English is an immigrant language. A world language. A transfigured tongue that draws from its European roots, its Africanness, its Native songs, its migrant spirit, to make the language sprout in branches and veins and leaves.

Yet there's a dominant character in American culture and language. Some call it Eurocentrism. This goes against the broader anthropological concept of culture as the summation of human achievement. All culture changes, evolves and belongs to the whole of society. The British sonnets, the Spanish décimas, the haiku— they're all ours. But a ruling class which holds the power, which owns the principle means of production, the mass outlets of creativity and the institutions of public maintenance, imposes its own standards and limitations on the culture at large.

Dominance comes from this class rule. In this country it's expressed as national, racial and gender superiority. This dominance is against all culture because it tries to destroy or distort aspects not deemed "worthy" of existence. Whenever there's such a lie, a part of the world is murdered.

Does being equal mean being the same? Of course not. It's not about melting pots or "losing your soul." Equality is the recognition of differences. It means the celebration of various voices and histories while insuring the collective well-being and nurturing of all.

Does this imply, however, that we should destroy or belittle the forms of cultural expression which are European-rooted? I have been on a few panels on poetry, politics and multiculturalism this past year. They have been powerful discussions, but there seems to be a tinge of blaming Western Civilization for all the evils we face in the hemisphere, that it's inherently against all peoples, etc. "Ho, Ho, Western Culture's Got To Go," say student chanters on a few campuses.

But I want to take as much from European cultural expression as from those that are indigenous to this soil, or rooted in Africa, Asia, or in Islam.

Let me say it again: culture is the summation of human achievement—transcending classes, epochs and politics. The problem is not European culture, or "white" people, but a capitalist ruling power that reigned in Europe, and subsequently in most of the world. The problem is the exploitation of culture for their narrow class aims. Ruling classes are the ultimate gatekeepers. They may make a feint for democracy and seem to allow anything—except a challenge to their power. Full and complete culture, encompassing all of humanity, is such a challenge because it predates classes, because it can profess a world free of exploitation and privilege.

Another point: The politics of difference are not the same as the politics of "the other." It's not a matter of adding a "multicultural" component to all the history, art and literature classes or programs, of tacking on our stories, our histories, our very lives, to the existing canon. As Sansei poet David Mura says, the center is shifting.

We need to challenge the current canon—and not so much from outside the existing cultural arenas, and not so much just the forms. Again, the resources and wealth are controlled by a small group of capital-owning elites. And while they may manipulate form— witness the systematic destruction of Native, African or Latino cultural forms, or the Nazi upholding of "Aryan" forms over others deemed inferior—the principal field of battle for them is the content of culture. This should be the battlefield for artists as well.

Is an opera inherently evil? Is a rapper's chant inherently good? Why can't progressive, revolutionary and vital ideas be expressed through both? Through all forms?

Nor can we abandon the so-called legitimate areas by declaring off-limits the arenas funded by government or foundation money under the guise that it's "bourgeois" (and we can still explore new forms—most everything receives no funding).

The content of any art form can be enslaving or empowering. It can be about race superiority, patriarchal and sexual politics, the continual exploitation of the laboring masses, violence and fascism. Or it can be founded in classes or peoples who have been exploited and oppressed, be against economic expediency, and thereby be against inequity.

It's not so much a matter of the "third world" versus the West, minorities against majorities, the colored against the non-colored, to be for or against Columbus. (I'm descended from Columbus. I don't have to reject him. What we need is a historical corrective that recognizes that there were people rich with value and great accomplishment here on this continent before the Europeans conquered it. I'm against the genocide and the enslavement that Columbus' voyage brought to these shores. But there's a transfiguration that inevitably resulted—and I'm a product of it.)

It's in the content of art or poetry that the ideas of an advancing, revolutionary society and that of a retreating, stagnant one are fought out. This is a process, not a category. Aware, we can be with it or against it, but not long outside of it.

This is why there's censorship—to cut off the platforms that allow new ideas, based on objective material conditions of life, to play themselves out. To be against censorship in the abstract is not my interest. I'm against censorship, either political or economic, that shuts down the platforms, closes the gallery doors, marginalizes the creativity—in other words, keeps me out of the battlefield.

I refuse to be on the outside, heard by a few, among the malcontents. I need to be in the heart of things, with everyone else, and this requires a high level of craft, a high level of commitment to the forms, if you will, so that the content is clear and accessible to all.

The censors who wield moral authority today are the most immoral people on earth. They never worked a day in their lives, they never fought in a war—it's time we took that authority back!

As artists, poets, musicians and journalists, we have the ear of the people. At various times and through various means, we can dissuade, persuade and invade. It's not a time for doubt. It's not a time for vagueness.

We have reached the end of 500 years of European dominance on the continent. The center is shifting. We had better have learned something, better be prepared to remake our continent with the full and equal participation of all—prepared to assist the end of a social system based on scarcity and want. If we are to survive the next 500, we had better know our country, the real country, that has claimed us.

THE FOLLOWING ESSAY WAS PRESENTED AT THE UNIVERSITY OF PARIS CONFERENCE, READING IN AMERICA, DECEMBER 1991.

> "Being a Chicano writer is like being in a constant state of pregnancy."—Abelardo "Lalo" Delgado

As a published and award-winning poet, journalist and critic, language is my life. The conveying of ideas, sentiments, expressions—of values and curiosities—to the degree I've achieved, requires a strong commitment to words, their meaning and significance. This was not always so. And the power of words continues to elude millions of minority and working-class members of American society.

Illiteracy in the most powerful and resource-rich country in the world is a complex and persistent problem. As we enter the electronic age, where information—its gathering and dissemination—has become an industry, no one can afford to be left out of the process. Yet little is being done to expand and extend the promise of the new technology. Instead, more young people are coming out of high schools and some colleges ill-prepared for the future. We are seeing the marginalization of a growing section of the next generation.

The fact is, all of us—whether of African, Puerto Rican, Mexican, Asian, Native, or European descent—have possession of some form of language as children: either that of our parents, our community, or what is conveyed to us through the major means of communication (often aspects of all). But something happens in the process of "homogenization," of equalizing the tongues. Those from communities outside the so-called norm (based on Anglo-derived roots and branches) fail miserably in reading and writing.

A child can come into a school system speaking Black English, Polish, Spanish, Vietnamese, or any number of American dialects. Instead of being bridges to universal literacy, they become hurdles that set back the learning process years. Once a child is defeated so early at something so basic as language, a lifetime is often not long enough to overcome the damage.

As a writer of Mexican descent, I have been through a particular experience that I believe to be endemic to the problem.

I entered the Los Angeles school system at the age of six with a relative command of one language, Spanish. But in those days, the early 1960s, there was no way to accommodate a child like myself. I spent the first year building blocks in a corner, ignored. My brother, who is three years older than me, was placed with retarded children. Teachers and school officials punished anyone caught speaking Spanish in the classroom or on the playground. No wonder almost 50 percent of the Mexican children where I attended school dropped out before high school. And those who did make it not only stopped knowing how to speak Spanish, they were unable to speak or read in English very well either.

In effect, we were being rendered incommunicable. This does not imply we couldn't talk. We spoke in mixed terms—code switching from Spanish and English in something called Spanglish— or used new words created to replace those not learned. The *pachuco* dialect is an example of this. Words like *lisa, jaina, tramaos, tando, calcos, thrucha, escamo, aquite,* and others have no equivalent in Spanish or English (the above words roughly mean *shirt, girl, trousers, hat, shoes, watch out, scared,* and *boring*). Puerto Ricans had a similar transfiguration of language. Even the argot of the South Bronx, which gave us terms like *hip-hop, word, def, chillin, crimey, fly,* were created through the cracks between languages or forms of expression.

Despite the obstacles, we continued to create, to speak, to reform words and concepts. This was fine at the level at which we were forced to maintain ourselves—at the level of the street, our community or on the job. But what if somebody wanted to advance the level of language development?

If you were me then, at 25 years old, hardly literate, you had to go back to school, sacrifice work and being able to fully provide for a family, in order to make up for the years in school when the language limitations were first imposed.

This takes a certain drive, an inner dynamic, that compels one to go beyond the boundaries. For me, it was the need for creative expression—through poetry, fiction, and creative journalism—and the need to impact society politically. Being "incommunicable" became a hindrance to my full and complete participation in society at any level I chose, what I call complete literacy.

Literacy then is more than learning letters and phonetics. It's about having the wherewithal to function at the highest levels of society. It's about participating in and knowing how to use the institutions governing our lives. It's about asserting one's rights so that one isn't left to exist only on a subsistence level—to understand the objective economic and political laws at play so that we have the freedom to obtain the full and decent life society as a whole can offer.

Illiteracy is an issue for democracy. You can't have true democratic participation without an informed, educated and literate community. Only those educated and thus informed will take part, make the laws, run for office and have an impact on the decisions that affect all our lives. Only a minority can have a say-so.

This is of course as insidious a censorship as any imposed by a governmental or moral authority. One is silencing the voice, the other is making sure it has no tongue.

CREATIVITY FINDS A WAY

But creative expression has to sprout, busting through the concrete walls of dominant culture, race and national superiority, and class rule. In the 1960s for example, in the Watts and East Los Angeles communities where I grew up, there was an explosion of art, literature and song. The Watts Writers' Workshops, Mechicano, and Goez Art Studios, Self-Help Graphics, Barrio Writers' Workshop—muralists such as Gronk, Willie Herron, Barbara Carrasco, Judith Baca, Los Streetscapers, writers from Quincy Troupe to Helena Viramontes.

Bilingual education programs began to address the problems people like my family and I had in school. Institutions of higher learning began to open their gates to people of color.

This was a time in which the first major Chicano literary writers emerged. Tomas Rivera, Rudolfo Anaya, José Montoya, Ricardo Sánchez, Sandra Cisneros, Ana Castillo, Cherrie Moraga—on down to the present. Some have accused this literature of being sloppy, badly written, immature. But although the forms were still finding shape, they were highly significant and necessary. They had for the most part a content of liberation through culture, and highly penetrating expressive powers. Most of these writers were published in small, non-commercial publishing ventures. A few were picked up—and then quickly dropped—by the major publishers. Yet a generation of Chicano youth now have a body of literature to relate to. They have something to identify with and which serves as a foundation for future literary outpourings. It was crucial that this literature saw the light of day, despite many fanciful critiques of sloppy verse and bad prose.

Today many of these writers have matured in skills as well. Sandra Cisneros is now with Random House with a book (*Woman Hollering Creek*) that can stand up with any contemporary literature. Poets of power and vision, such as Jimmy Santiago Baca, Martín Espada and Benjamin Saenz, are receiving long-due acknowledgments. Victor Villaseñor, in fact one of the veterans of the Chicano novel, now has a new book, *Rain of God*, which is fast becoming a bestseller and is slated to be made into a TV mini-series, although it has not been published by a major publishing house (it was taken up by Arte Publico, the country's leading publisher of Latino literature). And of course there is Oscar Hijuelos, the Cuban-American novelist who recently won a Pulitzer Prize in literature—the first American-born Latino to do so.

But something fundamental has transpired. Today the very programs that assisted this opening are gone or cut to shreds. All major school districts are in crisis, including those in white communities. Where will the future carriers of the word come from without the proper nurturing and incentives? When even the basic necessities of life—such as food, clothing and shelter—are provided only with a harder-to-obtain price, what chance do the literary traditions have of surviving?

And just as people of color are beginning to master the language and take it to new heights, just as multiculturalism is beginning to find its proper place in the canon, here comes an economic crisis whose proportions are challenging the existence of a broad literate and active population.

There is an increasing polarity between wealth and poverty. It's not a matter of skin color anymore: white workers are being driven to the brink of survival. The strategic consideration here is that we are seeing an economic equality between those traditionally left out of the mainstream—workers of color—and a section of the working class which is white. On this common ground is being laid the future of power politics in America, and I believe the future of reading and writing.

Multiculturalism, literacy, the nurturing of the writers' and artists' spirit, are issues of power. Just as are homelessness, unemployment and equality. Equal access is not enough. "I could speak fluently, but I could not reveal," says Jamaican-born writer Michelle Cliff.

Those who have developed the necessary language and communication skills carry an extra burden of writing well, of reaching broad audiences, of mastering the forms, if you will, to be able to reveal, to be moral beacons in these trying times, to heroically and dramatically point the way out of social crisis.

Chicano poet Abelardo Delgado once said being a Chicano writer was like being in a constant state of pregnancy. This is the case for writers of color in general and for those who have an ideal of the world, unrealized because of the present capitalist relations of production. Such a writer is always full, always in labor—but no baby.

Now is the time to be a midwife to the baby. Language then is a field of battle in the war America has been waging against meaning. Again, literacy is more than a practical matter (only to read bus schedules or job applications); it's also a cry from the heart. Poems now lose their decorative value. In some cases they become the place to get the real news of what's going on when the regular news outlets espouse outright lies (witness the Persian Gulf War débacle).

But they're still poems. They're still about the words—only now situated and informed by the burning issues and revolutionary content of our time. That, my friends, makes for powerful poems. That, my friends, is where we've come after all these years—not just to speak fluently, but to reveal.

LUIS J. RODRÍGUEZ has become a leading spokesman for the growing poor-people's movement in the United States. Poet-author of *The Concrete River* and the widely hailed account of L.A. gang life, *Always Running: La Vida Loca* (both published by Curbstone Press), as well as two children's books *América is Her Name* (Curbstone Press) and *It Doesn't Have To Be This Way: A Barrio Story* (Children's Book Press). Rodríguez has been a steel-worker, a radio journalist, and a teacher of poetry workshops for homeless people. He is the winner of numerous awards both for his literary acheivments and his human rights work, including the 2001 "Unsung Heroes of Compassion" Award presented by His Holiness the Dalai Lama, and the National Hispanic Heritage Award. He has appeared on *The Oprah Winfrey Show*, *Good Morning America*, and CNN, and radio programs such as NPR's *All Things Considered*, *Fresh Air*, and *Morning Edition*. He is a cultural worker totally accessible to the poorest strata of the society.

This essay first appeared in *Letter eX: the Chicago Poetry Magazine.*

MARTÍN ESPADA

Multiculturalism in the Year of Columbus and Rodney King

[This essay was originally presented at a public forum sponsored by the Loft, University of Minnesota-East Bank, Minneapolis, Minnesota, September 26, 1992.]

Few words of recent coinage in our contemporary vocabulary are so praised and damned, so powerful yet misunderstood, as "multiculturalism." In 1992, this perspective challenged one event—the celebration of Columbus and the 500th anniversary of his encounter with the New World—and faced a challenge from another—the Los Angeles riots that followed the acquittal of the police officers who brutalized African-American Rodney King. In the whirlpool of these struggles, we must stop swirling about long enough to question, comprehend and commit. The principle of multiculturalism becomes essential.

Multiculturalism is an *approach,* but it is also a *movement,* with an impact on many realms of life: literature, the arts, social science, education, politics. The multicultural viewpoint recognizes that this society is not monocultural, that we cannot all be measured by the same narrowly elite experience, a yardstick that would have a few of us sharply dressed and most of us wearing suits with sleeves that slap us and cuffs that trip us.

Multiculturalism rejects the assimilationist model for society, one that insists on unity through the surrender of identity, that perpetuates the romantic fiction of a past when the nation was one with itself. A multicultural perspective transcends mere "tolerance" of diversity—an odd choice of words, given that "tolerance" implies a barely repressed repugnance—and instead revels in that diversity.

Multiculturalism as a way of seeing explodes the myth of meritocracy, focusing on the reality that no institution, no matter how intellectually or artistically endowed, is immune from the social forces that surround it, and that therefore the liberal arts colleges, as well as the erudite literary magazines, may have to confront their own bigotries.

Multiculturalism expresses the potential for solidarity between very different groups of people who share both their marginality and their need to move from the margin to the rest of the page. Multiculturalism is thus driven by a democratizing impulse, one which is by nature inclusive, embracing not only people of color, but broadening to include a spectrum of cultures: other ethnic groups, gays and lesbians, the working class, people in prison. The literatures of these diverse people then cross-pollinate: Sheila Packa, a poet I read with in St. Paul, was inspired to use the Finnish language of her ancestors in her poems, after reading the bilingual (Spanish-English) poetry of Puerto Rican Victor Hernández Cruz.

Multiculturalism is ultimately about change, as Eduardo Galeano writes, for "those who have been standing in line for centuries to get into history." Viewed from the perspective of centuries, the demands of multiculturalism are reasonable indeed. But demands they remain: for new pedagogy, new books, new analysis of racial dynamics, new cultural values, new history, and new opportunity. And demands they must be: Frederick Douglass understood this when he said: "Power yields nothing without a demand. It never has and it never will." If words and ideas matter—and those in power are well aware that words and ideas matter—then multiculturalism matters, profoundly, which serves to explain in part the backlash against the movement.

Multicultural perspectives have been slandered as "political correctness," either trivialized as a new set of manners and mores designed not to offend, or demonized as the new McCarthyism, a wave of censorship soaking the nation's campuses in silence. This is the stuff of *Time* magazine, making its millions by scaring the middle class, which is cowed into believing that the tuition paid on behalf of their sons and daughters is diverted to courses on Swahili rather than Shakespeare, or worse, Shakespeare *in* Swahili. A false dichotomy is thus created between diversity and quality.

Dealing with the avalanche of criticism becomes overwhelming for the advocates of multiculturalism. People who have never read a book arising from this movement have heard of multiculturalism and its evil twin, political correctness, and have been led to believe that this is indeed the new McCarthyism, perhaps the most insidious charge of all. As education attorney Camilo Pérez-Bustillo puts it:

"Name one person whose life was ruined by multiculturalism. Name one person who has gone to jail. Name one person put on a blacklist, who had to write under a pseudonym. Name one person who could not leave the country, or who could not return, because of multiculturalism." Even the term "political correctness" is a misnomer, for what could be more politically correct than holding political power, or identifying with those who do?

The criticism of the multicultural movement takes on an almost hallucinatory quality. The marrow of multiculturalism is dissent, and yet this dissent supposedly stifles dissent. The call for debate is heard as a cry for censorship. An institution or individual confronted with a charge of racism is smothered in sympathy. Hang a Confederate flag from a Harvard dorm window, as one student did, to become a courageous defender of the First Amendment (which never applied to the slaves laboring beneath the Stars and Bars). The racist substance of what is said is never examined in the rush to defend the right to say it. The assumption here: it is worse to be called a racist than to actually be one.

Certain writers of color have calculated the profit of being right-wing in a right-wing age, and have peeled off their skin in a striptease for the applause of white politicians and academics who two centuries ago would have rationalized their enslavement. Thus, these sages condemn bilingual education, reject affirmative action, or rail against multiculturalism on campus, all apparently indifferent to being manipulated as weapons against their own communities.

In one extreme incarnation, the reaction to multiculturalism becomes the English Only movement. This movement, the most xenophobic in years, is a bigotry-driven campaign to make English the official language by law, spearheaded by a group called U.S. English, founded in 1983, which five years later had 7 million dollars with a membership of 350,000 (according to the book *Hold Your Tongue*, by James Crawford). According to Crawford, the organization, which once included such luminaries as Walter Cronkite and Saul Bellow, has devoted its energies to opposing bilingual education, ballots, government services, street signs, 911 operators, foreign language broadcasting, the Yellow Pages in Spanish, and even a Spanish language menu at McDonald's. Its founder, John Tanton, was forced to resign after the leak of a blatantly racist anti-Latino memorandum where he warned that the Latino birthrate would consume Anglo America: "Perhaps this is the first instance in which those with their pants up are going to get caught by those with their pants down."

The zealots of English Only believe that the English language is being corrupted from the bottom up: by "Spanglish," by "Black English," by all non-standard English as spoken by poor and working-class people. If anything, the English language is being eroded from the top down, by the deliberately obscure dialects of the powerful: legalese, medicalese, bureaucratese. These dialects conceal meaning; their intent is not to communicate, but to control.

Still, the stereotype persists: the lazy immigrants who do not want to learn English. According to Camilo Pérez-Bustillo, "In fifteen years of working with bilingual education programs, parents, and students, I have never met a single person who didn't want to learn English. What they want to do is also retain their own language, culture and identity." This is pluralism, the essence of a democratic and multicultural society.

The hostility against people who do not speak English is, of course, not new. Theodore Roosevelt recommended early in this century that any immigrant who did not learn English within five years should be deported. That means that many of us would not be here. This hostile climate breeds absurdity. I was involved in a case at English High School in Lynn, Massachusetts, where the Spanish language had been banned at lunchtime. And tragedy: in Lowell, Massachusetts, in 1987, a Cambodian schoolboy was drowned by his white counterpart during a citywide battle over desegregation and bilingual education. The mystery remains: if someone goes to school and learns two languages, that person is considered a genius; if the same someone is born and raised with two languages, that person is considered an idiot.

The backlash exists for a multiplicity of reasons. The paranoia of the powerful is a factor. In a right-wing age, multiculturalism is a rare progressive movement that appears all the more threatening due to the vacuum that surrounds it. Although in absolute terms its impact is still modest—hardly in control of the cafeteria, much less the campus—there is more multicultural activity, involving a broader spectrum of people, on campuses and elsewhere, than ever before, scaring the guardians of the status quo. This increased presence also means a new accountability: people of color, for example, are less likely to countenance blatant prejudice or discrimination than before.

There is also the deniability factor: the U.S. educational and political system has always denied the history and literature of those outside the narrow mainstream, especially with respect to race, the way a family might deny its own darkest sibling. In general, there is the usual headbanging struggle against change: Johnnetta Cole, an African-American administrator charged with curriculum reform at the University of Massachusetts, and now the head of Spelman College, commented that, "To ask a faculty to change its curriculum is like asking someone to move a graveyard."

Yet the movement for multiculturalism launched a serious challenge to a historical icon in 1992: Christopher Columbus. Even those defenders of the Admiral who shake with indignation at the egging of their hero must admit that the vandals with the eggs *are* at the gates, smacking luckless Columbus with the occasional egg fastball. This admission is itself a victory of sorts; the multicultural perspective is irrevocably part of the debate. Consider this: the left has had a far greater impact on the Columbus debate than the debate over the war with Iraq.

The salvo against Columbus is multiculturalism at its source. How can we respect African-American and Native American people without recognizing their history of slavery and genocide in the Americas, as it began five hundred years ago? We cannot respect that history, and kowtow to Columbus too. The defenders of Columbus must argue that the benefits of the conquest outweigh the costs. But slavery and genocide cannot be so weighed. The scale breaks.

Others argue that Columbus must be separated from the historical consequences of his actions, which were unintended and unforeseeable, a chain reaction over which he had no control. This argument is demolished by books such as *The Conquest of Paradise*, by Kirkpatrick Sale; here we find Columbus the slaver, who first ordered "seven head" of indigenous people kidnapped and brought to his ship, then enslaved thousands of others. This argument also ignores Columbus the plunderer, so obsessed with gold that he referred to it more than 180 times in the journal for the first voyage; and it ignores, too, Columbus the tyrant, who, as governor of Española in 1495, initiated a tribute system whereby "Indians" brought gold dust to the Spanish or had their hands cut off. During his administration, indigenous people were hanged by the Spanish in groups of thirteen, in honor of Christ and the Twelve Apostles.

If the movement for multiculturalism often finds itself doing battle over curriculum, even at the grade-school level, then the battle over Columbus is no different. I recently found a book about Columbus at a local daycare center, with a cover depicting the Admiral trading beads for parrots with the "Indians," leaving the impression that the conquest was a combination craft fair and exotic bird show. Left unsaid: that the indigenous population of Española evaporated in the steam of its own blood, *from eight million to twenty-eight thousand in just over twenty years*," according to Sale.

The only inheritance of the conquest worth saving is multicultural. Hans Köning points out the creation of a new people in Latin America: "That race, as it now exists, of mixed Spanish and Indian and African stock…these children of conquerors and slaves are the only achievement of the conquest, the only wealth it produced."

And Columbus? He will continue to be lauded as what Nancy Murray calls "the first European immigrant," the first pioneer, the first entrepreneur, confirming "self-celebratory myths" about this America. Thus the Knights of Columbus, defending the icon, have condemned all criticism of the Admiral as "neo-Marxist." But the Knights are too late. Eduardo Galeano sees the anniversary as an opportunity: "Not to confirm the world…but to denounce and change it. For that we shall have to celebrate the vanquished, not the victors." The advocates of multiculturalism have seized this very opportunity, organizing events ranging from a huge gathering of Native American writers in Norman, Oklahoma, to a camp of Latino poets, artists and musicians assembled at Columbus, New Mexico (the site of Pancho Villa's famous raid), to a small cultural event in Worcester, Massachusetts, where I read African-American, Lebanese, and Abenaki Indian poets, all against Columbus.

The racism espoused by Columbus to justify conquest, slavery, and plunder is still with us. The swords used to slash Taínos, who had never seen steel, have become billy clubs. Those billy clubs battered Rodney King relentlessly after the African-American motorist was stopped by police in Los Angeles for a traffic violation. The notorious videotape was not enough for a jury that believed in the gospel of racism with more fervor than they believed in their own sense of sight. This was too much for the *olvidados*, the forgotten ones of that city, and their combustible rage exploded. Even the victims of the legal system must believe that the courtroom is just. When that illusion disappears, then only the stink of gasoline is left in the air.

If the struggle over Columbus represents progress for the forces of multiculturalism, then the Rodney King affair and the L.A. riots constitute a major challenge. How relevant is a multicultural curriculum at the moment when Rodney King bleeds on asphalt, symbolizing the power of the state to enforce racism through legalized violence? What impact could multiculturalism possibly have on the rioters, who had nothing then and now have less? Does multiculturalism have any chance whatsoever of converting the white suburbanites who glared at the television during the days of the riot, as all their stereotypes of the Dark Other were confirmed, or who bought handguns anticipating that the Dark Other would charge through the patio door?

These questions are perhaps unanswerable, but having asked, I must answer. We must begin by acknowledging the limits of multiculturalism. This is not a panacea. We will not find salvation. We must not exchange one religion for another. Neither can we afford to sanitize multiculturalism, satisfied with the Latin American Market on Diversity Day at the local high school (I actually gave a reading at a high school on "Diversity Day" and was interrupted at noon by the official loudspeaker announcement that "Diversity Day is now over!"). There are always the perils of hand-holding sentimentality or sniffing condescension. Tokenism is tokenism.

And yet, the answer is more multiculturalism, not less. More multiculturalism can eventually generate more respect among people, whether in the classroom or on television, the bookstore or the movie theater, the community center or a street festival. Multicultural history is vital here: children who learn the history of lynching in this country could point to the videotape of the Rodney King beating and say, "I read about this in school." The presence of multiculturalism in our lives as a real, tangible force would mean that Rodney King could no longer be regarded as a mere abstraction. He is a human being, so reminiscent of other African-American human beings we know and cherish that his humiliation becomes their humiliation, and ours.

True, the movement for multiculturalism may be too late for the most desperate, those who must riot, who must speak what Martin

Luther King called "the language of the unheard." Neither will multiculturalism reach those in love with their own racism. But multiculturalism may well reach the children of the rioters and the racists.

In times of crisis, the state and its corporate media will endeavor to divide us. A multicultural analysis will resist the urge to divide, that aggravation of genuine or invented tensions. During the riots in Los Angeles, African-Americans were portrayed as the aggressors. Nothing was said about African-American victims of the riots. Koreans protecting their businesses with guns were paraded by the media as evidence of African-American racism. Nothing was said about Asian rioters. A white truck driver was beaten by African-Americans, again on videotape, which served to portray whites solely as victims of violence. Nothing was said about white rioters, or the lethal retaliation of white police. Latinos were rendered invisible, despite the fact that nearly half the businesses destroyed and nearly half the people arrested were Latino. The media message: The races are hopelessly polarized. Lock your doors.

Thus divided from one another, people were less likely to notice reports of more than fifty dead in Los Angeles, many—no one knows how many—killed by the same police force whose brutality has been documented by Amnesty International. Thus divided, people were unlikely to notice the mass deportation of Latinos back to México and Central America following their arrest for anything from petty theft to a curfew violation. Thus divided, people might forget the name of Lawrence Powell, the police officer who led the beating of Rodney King, "the killer who kills today for five million killers who wish a killing," in the words of Carl Sandburg. Thus divided, people were more likely to accept the bizarre explanation of the riots offered by the Bush administration: that the Great Society social programs of the 1960s were to blame. Multicultural solidarity—slowly taught, slowly learned—strikes at the heart of that imperial dictum: divide and rule.

Ultimately, the advocates for multiculturalism must organize themselves. There must be national organizations, able to coordinate national action. There must be not one magazine or newsletter, but many. There must be more multicultural daycare centers and art centers and community centers. There must be more truly multicultural literary programs. There must be more multicultural anthologies, but we must write them; there must be more multicultural art exhibits, but we must create them; there must be more courses with a multicultural perspective, but we must teach them. The poet June Jordan said it: "We are the ones we have been waiting for."

I do not see multiculturalism as simply a campus phenomenon. To confine multiculturalism to college campuses only would be to cultivate a monastery garden, and no more. If we remember the poets of the monastery, let us not forget the poets of the kitchen. Let multiculturalism be the language of adult education programs and prison writing workshops, barrio teen centers and inner-city preschools, wherever people gather to teach and be taught.

I return to a broad definition of multiculturalism: not only an approach but a movement. As such, we can learn from the history of other movements, whether for civil rights or for women's suffrage or for the rights of labor: the strike, the boycott, the coalition, the raising of consciousness. Or, as Frederick Douglass advised: "Agitate, agitate."

MARTÍN ESPADA was born in Brooklyn, New York in 1957. He is the author of numerous books of poetry, including; *Rebellion is the Circle of a Lover's Hands* (Curbstone Press), *Imagine the Angels of Bread* (W.W. Norton), *A Mayan Astronomer in Hell's Kitchen* (W.W. Norton) and a book of essays, *Zapata's Disciple*, (South End Press). He is also the editor of *Poetry Like Bread: Poets of the Political Imagination from Curbstone Press*, and *El Coro: A Chorus of Latino and Latina Poetry* (University of Massachusetts Press). He has won numerous awards, including the PEN-Revson Award for Poetry, a Before Columbus Foundation's American Book Award, the Paterson Poetry Prize, and the Gustavus Myers Center Outstanding Book Award, and is the recipient of fellowships from the NEA and the Massachusetts Cultural Council. Espada is a professor of English at the University of Massachusetts. He has been called "*the* Latino poet of his generation" and was recently named the first Poet Laureate of Northampton, Massachusetts.

JACK HIRSCHMAN
Culture and Struggle

Dumpsters, alleys littered with what's been discarded, including human crumples, panhandlers at corners or along walls scribbled with graffiti, hungry men and women on foodlines, public suffering misery waste shame dregs garbage of porn and drugs and drink, the lost job, broken home,

can't sell soul, one big hole, feel like a mole, down in the depths or on the lam standing still in the Tenderloin of an inner-city everywhere now.

Such images increasing in replication represent the fate of more and more people in this land, in a time when technological advancement on a global scale is creating merciless conditions wherein millions and millions of people will be, if they are not already, economically and then physically holocausted,

while the profound truth uttered by the Native American Wassaja—"We are hoodwinked, duped more and more each year; we are made to feel that we are free and we are not"—throbs in our being.

Everything's being driven backwards to the wrong Right, not to right the wrongs but deeper into a corporate state whose media-evil snares and traps are thick with decay, info-terrorism, more doubletalk than hands could shake ten fingers at; and bodies and souls everywhere are lowered into vats of diminishing wages, all watched over by massively growing police-brutal state apparatuses.

It's a system of corporate profiteers, haywire stock market-mongers and thugs of all sorts feeding on us poor people, and we want that system brought down once and for all.

We know it's in the deep shit of its own decay and has been rotting amid its desperate half-assed triumphs for more than two generations. We want to help, as cultural consciences, finish off its carcass, which has been stinking up humanity for as long as most of us remember.

And transform it into something authentically new and young and fresh and appealing:

we want the way money is amassed and distributed and thought about changed, and the way the poor, the homeless and immigrants are dealt with changed,

and we want rule by private property and the lie of "free enterprise" changed.

The "We" I've been talking from is really These States, composed of all those who daily feel the bite and bark of a dogging capitalist/imperialist system, including those who are not only aware that genocide, economic or otherwise, is at its core, but who are actively engaged in the fight against that genocide

who either must fight or physically die; that is,

must break into buildings or die in the cold,

must answer every charge of welfare fraud with a rally for people's justice,

must straighten the twisted information that immigrants are the enemies of workers here, or that the young rather than the banks and the corporations are the thieves and addicted monsters,

must broadcast over airwaves liberated by takeovers (just as with abandoned buildings) because only corporate wealth has claim to widespread kilowatt power,

must graffiti because there's no unbought place where writing, drawing and the protest-cry weigh the same and, by their very existence, attack private property.

And underlying all these "musts" are the will and desire to change history, and the belief that the people of this new class can do precisely that.

We don't see a difference between poetry, prose, graphic arts, song, music etc., on this terrain horizoning with the construction of tomorrows. Separating these genres is another kind of division the ruling-class enslavers have washed many a brain with.

We know their intelligentsia is all bullshit fake aesthetic segregations.

We know because, at the heart of this seminal and budding poor-people's struggle, is a propagandance inclusive of all the arts.

Moreover, and despite the attempts on the part of the cowardly ruling-class intelligentsia to palm off the revolutionary story as nothing but a "humanistic" one accommodatable by the corporate academy,

we know that we are all in possession of a modern classical tradition, including everything from the Internationale to Native chants, as well as union and slave songs en route to collective affirmations and liberation, respectively;

a revolutionary tradition including the poems of Blake, Whitman's great majesties, abolitionist narratives and the writings of Frederick Douglass, the poems of Hopkins ("I look forward to nothing more than the communist revolution," 1871), the great active meditations and strategies on the end of war and hunger that are the center of the writings of Marx and Engels;

and then, in our own century, the works of Mayakovsky, London, Lorca, Brecht, Sinclair, Neruda, Hill, Vallejo, Roumain, Hughes, Parker, Dalton, Monk, Castillo, Pasolini, Eluard, Hikmet, Aragon, Laraque, Darwish, Baraka, Adnan, Gramschi, Benet, Scotellaro, Heartfield;

and Robeson, Luxemburg, Rivera, Lenin, Siquieros, Orozco, Pollack, Lowenfels, Benjamin, Lourde, Ho Chi Minh, Rugama, Quemain, Stephan-Alexis;

and the hundreds, no, thousands of poets—man, woman and child—as well as artists, musicians, dancers, in collectives or theater companies or struggling forward in their creative solitudes, believing in and fighting for the total liberation of humanity from its chains, over and above the walls of the narrow one-celled alienation, isolation and imprisonment which the capitalist world visits upon us all.

It's to this revolutionary and progressive cultural tradition, which all poets and artists intuitively recognize as related to the working class, the working poor, and the new class of the permanently unemployed, the homeless, the criminalized, and those economically abused by the whiplash of electronic means of production in the hands of the capitalists,

that my own work has specifically united itself with for more than twenty years. It's a tradition that's engaged the energies of my poems (because in fact it *creates* the energies of my poems), as well as of my translations of revolutionaries from other lands; my verbo-visual "talking leaves;" my painted books and larger paintings; agitprop journalistic articles; the editing of different anthologies relative to the struggle; the "printing" of poems "in the journal between the ears" on the streets, in the name of revolutionary communication; and the works done for cultural brigades like the Roque Dalton Cultural Brigade, the Jacques Roumain Cultural Brigade; in addition to the Union of Left Writers, the Coalition of

Writer's organizations, the Communist Labor Party and the League of Revolutionaries For a New America.

This revolutionary tradition, which came into existence about 150 years ago—a young tradition! a vibrant tradition!—continues to expose the rats of capitalism for the garbage they are, and the system itself for the null and void it is, while affirming, re-affirming and ever-affirming the struggles and victories (however small, however large) of the poor and exploited.

And it's because we especially defend and affirm the poorest sectors of society, those who are most vulnerable, the good and beautiful Truth of revolutionary potential cuts through the current habits and trends of intellectual adherences to Nothingness.

We are never decorators of Nothing. Nor do we pretend we are the avant-garde while actually engaging in backbiting competition— a mirror of capitalist relations—for what comes down to : Bux.

Our rage, a rage for change, is, in part, yes, because we are poor; but it mainly is because others are, and in misery and oppression.

At the heart of it all, why else does a poet write?

We furthermore say that we *know* the enemy and it is not ourselves. It is rather a system of daily and grinding economic and social squalors, commodifications, degradations, and losses of dignity.

That's why poem, painting, music, etc. all are so very necessary. And why we remember, in the immediate now and for the future, the resonating affirmations of, say, Whitman, those expanses of generosity and mimpathy which he dreamed for us and which we know the system we live in the trap of has fogged and trashed, via the profit-murder it executes us with, every living moment;

but whose expanses of inner feeling and whose vision of These States not as a corporate monstrosity and prison of prisons, but as a mass process of compassion collectively unfolding as a people of diverse ingenuities and loves

we continue to recognize and reverence

because in fact it's in its budding form, that revolutionary flowering, even amid the general and specific rots of the day,

and we aim to help it blossom forth.

Our society is already luminously informed by a diversity of expressions come from Native, African-American, Latino, Caribbean, Asian, Middle-Eastern, African, Pacific Island and European cultures all comprising the multinational working class.

Many of these cultural expressions emerged in the wake of the important Civil Rights movement, which spread nationally from the South during the Sixties. Because the African-American struggle for freedom from slavery is so important, African-American liberty—its ironies, bitternesses and failures in the midst of achievements—is very fresh, very raw with them, one of the reasons why their musics (from slave-song to gospel to scat; from jazz to bop to R&B to rock and roll, and progressive and experimental music extending from jazz, and rap), because they arise out of the direct struggles for survival and "dreams deferred," are the sounds and melodies of a living and continually oppressed and vulnerable people, the measures of *all* the people; because African-Americans are the ones the system of capitalism most derogates and uses to terrorize and control the rest of the population.

And it's precisely because the other poor peoples know—even if unconsciously—that the Black struggles have been able to galvanize struggles for cultural autonomy on the part of others within the "Rainbow" of the States.

And also because, long before the fight against slavery in the South (go back to the riots in New York City in 1642), Blacks refused to accept the system—in essence, capitalism—knowing its roots lay in human slavery and the turning of people into things, we have been witnesses to an ever-manifesting resistance that has inspired cultural and social motions throughout our century.

For example, jazz has been a popular expression on an international level since WWI—this nation's most distinctive and enduring popular art form. Its influence, say, on the Beat movement (see the works of Kerouac, the poems of Bob Kaufman, the opening lines of both "Howl" and "Kaddish" by Ginsberg) has been central. And in response to a question relating to his important "Projective Verse" essay, Charles Olson remarked that the new experimental field-prosody he was espousing was "all Charley Parker." Such words actually mimicked those of Robert Creeley, who had written them in a letter to Olson years earlier; but, in fact, Parker, and especially Thelonius Monk, *did* relate to Olson's "Projective" suggestion to poets to use a typewriter as a piano (Monk is perhaps the most literary and dialectical of modern jazz composers.) And it is a fact that the "opening of the field" of the page of poetry, which came to full fruition in the Fifties and Sixties and continues today as among the most exciting aspects of poetic composition, is rooted in jazz experiments emerging from the Harlem Renaissance as *they* merged with other cultural forms—abstract expressionist painting, for example—that served as explosive preludes to the monumental composition that was the Civil Rights movement itself.

And today, spoken writing like gangsta and other Rap, manifesting out of authentic situations of poverty, exclusion and institutionalized racism, presents the protest of a constructive nihilism, and beats on the drum of and for YouthYouthYouth, as if a rhythmic, oral, African or Haitian voodoo communications system were passing important signals through the computerized night.

In the United States of poetry today, certain Rap lyrics contain the most vivid attacks on the private-property system by revealing and satirizing the nihilism inherent in the money-madness and the hatred of everything—self, other, and world—that is the plight of so many young people in this land.

In Rap, moreover, such an intricate rhyming—often spontaneously composed—has not appeared in serious poetry since the Russian poems of Vladimir Mayakovsky, the great poet of the Bolshevik Revolution and the first street poet of the Twentieth Century.

And don't think the powers-that-be want Mayakovsky's lyrics out there any more than they do those of Rap. In fact, in the recent Penguin edition of 20th Century Russian literature, get this— Mayakovsky is excluded, as if the greatest poet of the Soviet period simply no longer existed (indeed, to date, only about half of his collected works have been translated into American English)!

And it's precisely that kind of annihilating exclusion—meant to deny the very existence of an important historical phenomenon— that Rap artists are experiencing as well, not simply as a censorship, but as an as/if Rap didn't really exist at all (a condition African-Americans well know on the ontological plane);

and that would be an incredible loss because, if really seen and understood in motion on the streets and in the parks of this land (not simply as something "star-studded" in a one- or two-man teevee gig), Rap represents a genuine breakthrough in oral co-operation and collectivity,

one rapper "passing" meaning and rhythm to another; the other, to another, with variations in lyric and rhythm both; until the dovetailing and ricocheting raps and the built-up strophes of meaning given out by each rapper after a while assume the anonymity of real process, genuine social statement and authentic communal participation.

Precisely, of course, what the system has to control or destroy, lest it grow as a model of organized culture in action, that is Revolutionary Culture.

Graffiti (which the system also detests and outlaws, just as it detests and outlaws any cultural form whose social rage and ingenuity are difficult to commodify completely), like Rap, also has its toilet-door, obscene and scatalogical dimension,

but also and likewise: revolutionary slogans; sheer energetic ecstasies of code-tagging and letter shape; and, above and within all, a dynamic "possessing" (in the sense of taking over) of private property and making it public through an act of alphabetic or logographic affirmative/defacement.

Something of the same elements go on in Rap, which gives the illusion—if it doesn't present itself as the fact—that it is "written" spontaneously and off the top of one's head, with a drummy, possessive and grabbing beat, and a social message included within it.

Both Rap and Graffiti are part of the contemporary Projective arts involving youthful participation in a growing—sporadically and seminally but very definitely—new-class consciousness.

Both are victims of censorship and whitewash. Both are textured as outlaw and guerrilla art forms. And both are cultural weapons in the development of the poor-people's movement.

A third important and courageous weapon is exercised by a small but growing brigade of airwave liberators, those who set up microtransmitters and fight the corporate state and its FCC apparatus by freeing airwaves for the people. They might be broadcasting about police terror and brutality from and to a poor housing project in Springfield, Illinois; reading an attack on San Francisco's Mayor for his Matrix program's criminalizing of the poor; reading a communiqué from the Mayan guerrillas fighting the NAFTA governments of Mexico and Washington, D.C.; or they might be calling for—and not simply announcing the results of—a demonstration or protest march.

These techno-guerrillas are on the cutting edge of the cultural front at a time when there's been a deepening of police-state tactics with respect to the poor; when the ruling class and its media jackals are everywhere broadcasting crime-terror-mayhem-rape in order to keep sowing divisiveness and terror among the people.

As such, the radio liberators are taking back technological space/time, the relativity robbed by the capitalists, and putting it back into the hands and ears of those to whom it really belongs.

I've mentioned the importance of the poor people's struggles as they extend from the Civil Rights Movement. But there is an equally important resistance that the poor can always make contact with in this land, and that is the resistance of the Native peoples.

We know the names, like Geronimo and Crazy Horse, Wounded Knee, Sequoyah, and Sarah Winnemucca. We know likewise of a continuous colonization that has been staked out by the imperialists across the Native territories.

But what is most important, culturally, as far as the Native dimension is concerned, is that the revolutionary future we foresee when the poor and exploited and oppressed peoples of this land come together and organize to finally have done with the thieving system that is currently and viciously in place—that revolutionary future will be one in which the new means of production, the computers and media and other technological advancements, will not serve as profit-Frankensteins but as instruments to further a non-mercenary progress for all the people so that they no longer are hungry or homeless or divided one from another.

It will be a co-operative society, with authentic sharing and reciprocity, reverberant to the historically recent and still existing peoples of this continent, who exploited neither each other nor the living creatures around them.

Toward that future, our responsibility as poets and painters and musicians and dancers, all interfacing and opening out, ought to be to "present the present" as irrefutably a part of the revolutionary process, and beacon toward that time—with new poems, songs, dreams, yearning and inspirations—when all our individual selves are massed to finally spring humanity from its prison.

JACK HIRSCHMAN has been putting poetry, graphics and agitprop polemics in the service of the communist movement for more than two decades. He has published more than ninety books and chapbooks of poems and translations from eight languages, and is a correspondent for *The People's Tribune,* the newspaper of the League of Revolutionaries for a New America.

CURBSTONE PRESS, INC.

is a non-profit publishing house dedicated to literature that reflects a commitment to social change, with an emphasis on contemporary writing from Latino, Latin American and Vietnamese cultures. Curbstone presents writers who give voice to the unheard in a language that goes beyond denunciation to celebrate, honor and teach. Curbstone builds bridges between its writers and the public – from inner-city to rural areas, colleges to community centers, children to adults. Curbstone seeks out the highest aesthetic expression of the dedication to human rights and intercultural understanding: poetry, testimonies, novels, stories, and children's books.

This mission requires more than just producing books. It requires ensuring that as many people as possible learn about these books and read them. To achieve this, a large portion of Curbstone's schedule is dedicated to arranging tours and programs for its authors, working with public school and university teachers to enrich curricula, reaching out to underserved audiences by donating books and conducting readings and community programs, and promoting discussion in the media. It is only through these combined efforts that literature can truly make a difference.

Curbstone Press, like all non-profit presses, depends on the support of individuals, foundations, and government agencies to bring you, the reader, works of literary merit and social significance which might not find a place in profit-driven publishing channels, and to bring the authors and their books into communities across the country. Our sincere thanks to the many individuals, foundations, and government agencies who support this endeavor: J. Walton Bissell Foundation, Connecticut Commission on the Arts, Connecticut Humanities Council, Daphne Seybolt Culpeper Foundation, Fisher Foundation, Greater Hartford Arts Council, Hartford Courant Foundation, J. M. Kaplan Fund, Eric Mathieu King Fund, John D. and Catherine T. MacArthur Foundation, National Endowment for the Arts, Open Society Institute, Puffin Foundation, and the Woodrow Wilson National Fellowship Foundation.

Please help to support Curbstone's efforts to present the diverse voices and views that make our culture richer. Tax-deductible donations can be made by check or credit card to:
Curbstone Press, 321 Jackson Street, Willimantic, CT 06226
phone: (860) 423-5110   fax: (860) 423-9242
www.curbstone.org

IF YOU WOULD LIKE TO BE A MAJOR SPONSOR OF A
CURBSTONE BOOK, PLEASE CONTACT US.